THE CAMBRIDGE
COMPANION TO
HERMAN MELVILLE

The Cambridge Companion to Herman Melville is intended to provide a critical introduction to Melville's work. The essays have been specially commissioned for this volume and provide a comprehensive overview of Melville's career. All of Melville's novels are discussed, as well as most of his poetry and short fiction. Written at a level both challenging and accessible, the volume provides fresh perspectives on an American author whose work continues to fascinate readers and stimulate new study.

Robert S. Levine is Professor of English at the University of Maryland, College Park. He is the author of *Conspiracy and Romance: Studies in Brockden Brown, Cooper, Hawthorne, and Melville* (1989) and *Martin Delany, Frederick Douglass, and the Politics of Representative Identity* (1997).

Cambridge Companions to Literature

The Cambridge Companion to Henry James
edited by Jonathan Freedman

The Cambridge Companion to Faulkner
edited by Philip Weinstein

The Cambridge Companion to Hemingway
edited by Scott Donaldson

The Cambridge Companion to Wharton
edited by Millicent Bell

The Cambridge Companion to American Realism and Naturalism
edited by Don Pizer

The Cambridge Companion to Twain
edited by Forrest Robinson

The Cambridge Companion to Thoreau
edited by Joel Myerson

The Cambridge Companion to Whitman
edited by Ezra Greenspan

The Cambridge Companion to T. S. Eliot
edited by A. David Moody

The Cambridge Companion to James Joyce
edited by Derek Attridge

The Cambridge Companion to Ibsen
edited by James McFarlane

The Cambridge Companion to Beckett
edited by John Pilling

The Cambridge Companion to Brecht
edited by Peter Thomson and Glendyr Sacks

The Cambridge Companion to British Romanticism
edited by Stuart Curran

The Cambridge Companion to English Poetry, Donne to Marvell
edited by Thomas N. Corns

The Cambridge Companion to Shakespeare Studies
edited by Stanley Wells

Continued on page following Index

THE CAMBRIDGE
COMPANION TO
HERMAN MELVILLE

EDITED BY
ROBERT S. LEVINE

CAMBRIDGE
UNIVERSITY PRESS

CAMBRIDGE UNIVERSITY PRESS
Cambridge, New York, Melbourne, Madrid, Cape Town, Singapore, São Paulo

Cambridge University Press
The Edinburgh Building, Cambridge CB2 2RU, UK

Published in the United States of America by Cambridge University Press, New York

www.cambridge.org
Information on this title: www.cambridge.org/9780521554770

First published 1998
Reprinted 1999

A catalogue record for this publication is available from the British Library

ISBN-13 978-0-521-55477-0 hardback
ISBN-10 0-521-55477-2 hardback

ISBN-13 978-0-521-55571-5 paperback
ISBN-10 0-521-55571-X paperback

Transferred to digital printing 2006

CONTENTS

CONTENTS

CONTRIBUTORS

JOHN BRYANT is Associate Professor of English at Hofstra University. He is the author of *Melville and Repose: The Rhetoric of Humor in the American Renaissance* (1993) and of many essays on Melville. He has also edited *A Companion to Melville Studies* (1986) and (with Robert Milder) *Melville's Evermoving Dawn* (1997), and he is the current editor of *Melville Society Extracts*.

LAWRENCE BUELL, John P. Marquand Professor of English at Harvard University, is the author of numerous books and articles on nineteenth-century American literature, including *New England Literary Culture: From Revolution through Renaissance* (1986) and *The Environmental Imagination: Thoreau, Nature, Writing, and the Formation of American Culture* (1995).

ANDREW DELBANCO is Julian Clarence Levi Professor in the Humanities at Columbia University. Among his books are *The Puritan Ordeal* (1989), *The Death of Satan: How Americans Have Lost the Sense of Evil* (1995), and *Required Reading: Why Our American Classics Matter Now* (1997).

JENNY FRANCHOT is Associate Professor of English at the University of California, Berkeley. She is the author of *Roads to Rome: The Antebellum Protestant Encounter with Catholicism* (1994).

PAUL GILES is Lecturer in American Studies at the University of Nottingham. He is the author of *Hart Crane: The Contexts of the Bridge* (1986) and *American Catholic Arts and Fictions: Culture, Ideology, Aesthetics* (1992).

WYN KELLEY is Lecturer in the Literature Department at MIT. She is the author of *Melville's City: Literary and Urban Form in Nineteenth-Century*

New York (1996). Her essays have appeared in a number of books and journals, including *Melville's Evermoving Dawn* (1997), *American Literature, Partisan Review,* and *Melville Society Extracts,* of which she is Assistant Editor.

ROBERT S. LEVINE is Professor of English at the University of Maryland, College Park. He is the author of *Conspiracy and Romance: Studies in Brockden Brown, Cooper, Hawthorne, and Melville* (1989) and *Martin Delany, Frederick Douglass, and the Politics of Representative Identity* (1997).

ROBERT K. MARTIN is Professor of English at the University of Montreal. He is the author of *The Homosexual Tradition in American Poetry* (1979), *Hero, Captain, and Stranger: Male Friendship, Social Critique, and Literary Form in the Sea Novels of Herman Melville* (1986), and numerous essays on British and American literature. He is also the editor of *E. M. Forster: Centenary Revaluations* (1982) and *The Continuing Presence of Walt Whitman* (1992).

ROBERT MILDER is Professor of English at Washington University. He is the author of *Reimagining Thoreau* (1995) and editor of *Critical Essays on Melville's "Billy Budd, Sailor"* (1989), *"Billy Budd, Sailor" and Selected Tales* (1997) and (with John Bryant) *Melville's Evermoving Dawn* (1997). His essays on Melville have appeared in a number of books and journals, including *The Columbia Literary History of the United States* (1988), *American Literature, Prospects, Approaches to Teaching Melville's "Moby-Dick"* (1985), and *Melville Society Extracts.*

SAMUEL OTTER is Associate Professor of English at the University of California, Berkeley. He is the author of *Melville's Anatomies: Bodies, Discourse, and Ideology in Antebellum America* (1998).

ELIZABETH RENKER is Associate Professor of English at The Ohio State University. She is the author of *Strike through the Mask: Herman Melville and the Scene of Writing* (1996).

STERLING STUCKEY is Presidential Chair and Professor of History and Religious Studies at the University of California, Riverside. Among his many published works are *Slave Culture: Nationalist Theory and the Foundations of Black America* (1987) and *Going through the Storm: The Influence of African American Art in History* (1994).

CINDY WEINSTEIN is Associate Professor of English at the California Institute of Technology. She is the author of *The Literature of Labor and the Labors of Literature: Allegory in Nineteenth-Century American Fiction* (1995).

ACKNOWLEDGMENTS

It's been a pleasure and an honor to edit this collection. My thanks to T. Susan Chang for the invitation and for her invaluable assistance at the planning stages. Anne Sanow at Cambridge University Press has been wonderfully skillful in helping me to bring things to completion; I am especially grateful for her enthusiastic support of a volume she inherited. My thanks as well to the indefatigable Louise Calabro and Helen Greenberg for their expert work in production and copyediting.

The contributors performed their parts in this joint effort with professionalism, intelligence, good humor, and grace. One of the sad results of actually completing this volume will be the loss of their regular e-mail companionship. For their help along the way, I'm particularly indebted to Jonathan Auerbach, John Bryant, Leonard Cassuto, Ivy Goodman, and Wyn Kelley. Finally, I wish to thank Stephen Donadio for introducing me to the endless fascinations of Herman Melville.

1819   Born New York City, August 1, third child of Allan Melvill, merchant and importer, and Maria Gansevoort Melvill, daughter of American Revolutionary hero General Peter Gansevoort. Brothers and sisters: Gansevoort (1815–46), Helen Maria (1817–88), Augusta (1821–76), Allan (1823–72), Catherine (1825–1905), Frances Priscilla (1827–85), Thomas (1830–84).

1825   With Gansevoort, enters New-York Male High School.

1828   Named best speaker in the high school's Introductory department.

1829   Enters the grammar school of Columbia College, joining Gansevoort.

1830   After Allan Melvill liquidates his failing business, the Melvills move to Albany. With Gansevoort, Herman enrolls at the Albany Academy. Lemuel Shaw, Allan's friend and Herman's future father-in-law, named Chief Justice of the Supreme Judicial Court of Massachusetts.

1831–2   For financial reasons, Herman is withdrawn from the Albany Academy in October 1831. Allan journeys to New York in late November 1831 to take care of business matters. On his return to Albany, on December 10, he's forced to cross the frozen Hudson River on foot. Feverish, delirious, and in debt, he dies on January 28, 1832. Herman begins clerking at the New York State Bank. Sometime between 1832 and 1834, perhaps to dissociate the family from the father's failures, Maria adds the "e" to "Melvill."

1833–7   Continues with his bank job until spring 1834, when he begins working at Gansevoort's cap and fur store. Attends the Albany Classical School in 1835 and then the Albany Academy (1836–7). Continues working for his brother until the business fails in 1837. In the fall of that year he teaches at the Sikes District school near Pittsfield.

1838 Publishes in the March 24 issue of the *Albany Microscope* satirical remarks on the area's young men's debating clubs. In November, after the family's diminished finances force a relocation to Albany, Melville enrolls at Lansingburgh Academy, where he studies surveying and engineering.

1839 Under the pseudonym "L.A.V.," publishes two sketches, "Fragments from a Writing Desk," in the May *Democratic Press and Lansingburgh Advertiser.* On June 4 he signs on as a "boy" with the merchant ship *St. Lawrence.* Sails from New York to Liverpool and back from June 5 to October 1. Shortly after his return, he begins teaching at the Greenbush and Schodack Academy in Greenbush, New York.

1840 Leaves his position at Greenbush because of the school's inability to pay him. Teaches in the spring in Brunswick, New York, and then, accompanied by his friend Eli James Murdock Fly, visits his uncle Thomas Melvill in Galena, Illinois, to explore vocational possibilities in the West. Returning East, he signs on with the whaling ship *Acushnet* in New Bedford after failing to find a job in New York.

1841–4 Departs for the South Seas on the *Acushnet* on January 3, 1841. On July 9, 1842, he jumps ship with Richard Tobias Greene at Nukahiva Bay in the Marquesas Islands, remaining among the islanders of Taipi Valley for four weeks before signing on with the Australian whaler *Lucy Ann.* At Tahiti, he is sent ashore and nominally imprisoned as a mutineer, only to escape in October with John Troy. He then signs on with the Nantucket whaling ship *Charles and Henry* in November 1842. (At around the same time, his first cousin Guert Gansevoort is involved in putting down the "mutiny" on the U.S. brig *Somers.*) Discharged in May 1843 in the Hawaiian Islands, Meville works at various jobs – pin setter in a bowling alley, clerk in a store – until enlisting in the United States Navy in Honolulu and sailing as an ordinary seaman aboard the frigate *United States* on August 20, 1843. He returns to Boston on October 3, 1844, and soon after his discharge rejoins his family in Lansingburgh.

1845–6 Writes a narrative of his adventures among the Typee islanders, which is rejected by New York's Harper & Brothers in May or June 1845. Gansevoort, after stumping for Polk in 1844, is rewarded in spring 1845 with the position of Secretary of the American Legation in London. Once there, he helps to place his brother's *Typee* manuscript with John Murray, who publishes it in his prestigious "Colonial and Home Library" in late February 1846 under the title *Narrative of a Four Months' Residence Among the Natives of a Valley of the Marquesas Islands*. On March 17 the book, now titled *Typee*, is published by New York's Wiley & Putnam. After meeting Toby Greene in Rochester, who "authenticates" the facts of *Typee*, Melville prepares a "Revised Edition" with an appended "The Story of Toby," which is published later that year. Gansevoort dies in London on May 12, 1846.

1847   Attempts to find a government job in Washington, D.C. *Omoo* published by Murray in London (March) and by Harper & Brothers in New York (May). On August 4, Melville marries Elizabeth Shaw, daughter of Chief Justice Lemuel Shaw. After honeymooning in New Hampshire and Canada, they move into a large row house in Manhattan purchased with the help of Lemuel Shaw. Living with Herman and Elizabeth are Allan Melville and his wife, the four unmarried Melville sisters, mother Maria Melville, and (on occasion) brother Tom Melville. Writes for the *Literary World*, edited by Evert A. Duyckinck, and for *Yankee Doodle*, edited by Cornelius Mathews.

1849   Rejected by Murray, *Mardi* is published by Richard Bentley in London (March) and by Harper in New York (April). *Redburn* is published by Bentley (October) and Harper (November). Birth of son, Malcolm, on February 16. In October, Melville departs for a trip to London and the Continent, returning January 31, 1850.

1850   *White-Jacket* published by Bentley in London (January) and by Harper in New York (March). On August 5, Melville, while vacationing in Pittsfield, meets Hawthorne and they quickly become friends; later that month he publishes "Hawthorne and His Mosses" in the *Literary World*. In September, with money borrowed from his father-in-law, Melville purchases a 160 acre farm in Pittsfield, which he names "Arrowhead," and moves there with his family.

1851   Dedicated to the "Genius" of Nathaniel Hawthorne, *The Whale* published by Bentley in London (October) and, with the title changed to *Moby-Dick*, by Harper in New York (November). Birth of second son, Stanwix, on October 22. In a famous test of the Fugitive Slave Law, Chief Justice Shaw, in April, orders Thomas Sims returned to his southern owner (in 1854, in another famous case, he orders the fugitive slave Anthony Burns returned to his owner).

1852   Rejected by Bentley, *Pierre* published by Harper in New York (August) and by Sampson Low in London (November).

1853   Between 1853 and 1856, Melville publishes fourteen tales and sketches in *Putnam's Monthly Magazine* and *Harper's New Monthly Magazine*. Birth of daughter, Elizabeth, on May 22. Melville's family makes an unsuccessful effort to secure him a consulship. Evidence suggests that he completes a book manuscript, *The Isle of the Cross*, which the Harpers choose not to publish.

1855   Serialized in *Putnam's*, *Israel Potter* published by Putnam in New York (March) and by George Routledge in London (May). Birth of second daughter, Frances, on March 2.

1856   *The Piazza Tales*, which collects five of the pieces in *Putnam's*, including "Bartleby, The Scrivener" (1853) and "Benito Cereno" (1855), published by Dix & Edwards in New York (1856) and distributed in England by Sampson Low. Concerned about his son-in-law's health, Shaw finances Melville's travels to Europe and the Holy Land (October 11, 1856, to May 20, 1857). Melville visits Hawthorne in Liverpool in November 1856.

1857–60   *The Confidence-Man* published by Dix & Edwards in New York (April 1857) and by Longman in London (April 1857). Between late 1857 and 1860 Melville undertakes three lecture tours, speaking first on "Statues in Rome" (1857–8), next on "The South Seas" (1858–9), and finally on "Traveling" (1859–60). In 1860 he fails in his efforts to publish a poetry manuscript. With his brother Thomas at the helm, he embarks for California on May 30, 1860, aboard the clipper ship *Meteor*. Shaken by their perilous journey around Cape Horn, Melville in November returns via Panama to New York without his brother.

1861   Journeys to Washington, D.C., in another failed quest to obtain a consulship. Lemuel Shaw dies in Boston on March 30.

1862   After returning to Pittsfield, Melville is severely injured when thrown from a wagon.

1863	Purchases his brother Allan's home at 104 East Twenty-Sixth Street and moves to New York. Allan purchases Arrowhead.
1864	Visits Civil War battlefields on the Virginia front with Allan. Hawthorne dies May 19.
1866	Publishes four Civil War poems in *Harper's*. *Battle-Pieces and Aspects of the War*, a collection of Melville's war poetry, published by Harper in New York (August). On December 5, he assumes the duties of District Inspector of the United States Customs Service at the port of New York.
1867	Unhappy in her marriage and evidently fearful of her husband, Elizabeth Melville discusses with her minister, Henry Bellows, the possibility of a legal separation. In May, Bellows proposes a kind of kidnapping scheme to help Elizabeth obtain sanctuary with her Boston relatives, a scheme which she and her family eventually reject. On September 11, the Melvilles' son Malcolm dies from a self-inflicted gunshot to the head.
1872	Maria Gansevoort Melville dies April 1 at the age of eighty-two.
1876	*Clarel* published in New York by Putnam (June). Melville's uncle Peter Gansevoort pays for the publishing expenses.
1885	Resigns from his position as District Inspector of Customs (December 31).
1886	The Melvilles' son Stanwix dies in San Francisco on February 23.
1888	Privately publishes *John Marr and Other Sailors* in an edition of twenty-five copies after receiving a bequest of $3,000 from his sister Frances Priscilla.
1891	Privately publishes *Timoleon* in an edition of twenty-five copies. Dies September 28. An unpublished volume of poems, titled "Weeds and Wildings Chiefly," the sketch "Daniel Orme," and *Billy Budd* are left in manuscript. The first published version of *Billy Budd* appears in 1924.

ROBERT S. LEVINE

INTRODUCTION

> But I dont know but a book in a man's brain is better off than a book
> bound in calf – at any rate it is safer from criticism.
>
> Melville to Evert A. Duyckinck, letter of 16 August 1850

This collection is both a handbook to Melville and a provocation. As expected of a Cambridge *Companion*, it provides readers with comprehensive analyses of the major writings and motifs of a canonized master of world literature. At the same time, this volume has been conceived in a Melvillean spirit of suspicion and revision. Accordingly, it is animated by a dialectical interplay between traditional and newer approaches to Melville. This is a particularly opportune time for such a volume. Over the past two decades or so, the "American Renaissance" has been dramatically reconceived by feminist, African-American, new historical, and other critical approaches. Such key works as Michael Rogin's *Subversive Genealogy* (1983), Wai-chee Dimock's *Empire for Liberty* (1989), and Eric Sundquist's *To Wake the Nations* (1993) are but three of the many books that have offered new ways of thinking about the ideological and political implications of Melville's art. There have also been major developments in more traditional, archivally based Melville scholarship. Recent discoveries of Melville family papers (now at the New York Public Library), the publication of such important works as John Bryant's *Melville and Repose* (1993), Stanton Garner's *The Civil War World of Herman Melville* (1993), several volumes in the nearly completed Northwestern–Newberry edition of Herman Melville, and biographies by Laurie Robertson-Laurant (1996) and Hershel Parker (1996) have helped us to make better sense of Melville's compositional practices, aesthetics, sources, biography, and relation to contemporaneous literary debates. The renewed attention to Melville hasn't been confined to the scholarly world. As the contributors to this *Companion* were completing their essays, Hershel Parker's reworking of *Pierre*, replete with illustrations by Maurice Sendak, was published to considerable fanfare by a commercial press; the Robertson-Laurant and Parker biographies appeared one after the other (also to widespread public notice); Melville scholars were featured in a television special, "Great Books: *Moby-Dick*," on the Learning Channel; and a debate in Melville studies between "traditional" and "revisionary" scholars on the subject of Melville's possible misogyny (and wife beating) was the subject of a feature article in a December 1996 issue of the *New York Times Magazine*.[1]

Discovered – or rediscovered – in the early decades of the twentieth century, Melville now more than ever seems *the* monumental writer of nineteenth-century America whose presence on the literary and cultural landscape is all but inescapable. And yet with the monumentalizing of Melville comes the risk that his texts will lose their ability to speak to readers in fresh and provocative ways. Emerson's warning about the pitfalls of canonization seems particularly apt today. As he writes in "The American Scholar" (1837), there is the danger that the "love of the hero" will become corrupted into the "worship of his statue." When such hero worshiping occurs, acolytes tend to perform the "grave mischief" of making the celebrated author's genius a matter of "the record" and "accepted dogmas." Tendencies toward cultural monumentalization may suit the annotating needs of the "bookworm" but, Emerson continues, they risk doing infinite damage to the possibilities of what he calls "creative reading," the sort of reading that encourages dynamic interactions between reader and text.[2]

Melville was acutely aware of the harm the canonizing practices of his own literary times could do to readers and writers (see especially Book XVII of *Pierre*). In remarks perhaps antithetical to the very title *Cambridge Companion to Herman Melville*, the narrator of *White-Jacket*, in the course of discussing his seemingly undisciplined reading practices on the *Neversink*, refers to the "companionable" text: "My book experiences on board of the frigate proved an example of a fact which every book-lover must have experienced before me, namely, that though public libraries have an imposing air, and doubtless contain invaluable volumes, yet, somehow, the books that prove most agreeable, grateful, and companionable, are those we pick up by chance here and there; those which seem put into our hands by Providence; those which pretend to little, but abound in much." Though it's difficult to imagine a reader who could pick up a Melville volume these days without sensing its "imposing air," I think we should take the sentiments of this passage seriously as a statement of Melville's desire to engage readers outside the imposing networks of institutional and cultural authority. For the reader willing to "*dive*," the act of adventurous, unmediated reading, a kind of taking to sea, could provide an enviable education, what Ishmael, with reference to whaling, calls "my Yale College and my Harvard."[3]

I would suggest that Melville could write so buoyantly in *White-Jacket* of the excitement and value of extra-institutional reading because his narrative strategies really do make him the best sort of guide to his works. Throughout his career, even in the seemingly elusive *The Confidence-Man*, Melville has regularly assumed a metacritical role of guiding and challenging readers' responses to his works by foregrounding issues of interpretation. Consider, for example, the ways in which Melville in *Typee* links tattooing with writing (and reading); the ways in which he develops connections between reading *White-Jacket* and reading White-Jacket's white jacket; the numerous moments in *Moby-Dick* when he elaborates analogies between reading whales and reading his complex novel about whales. Melville hardly provides interpretive answers or reassurances, but, even if one grants that the motif of con artistry is central to his writings, his numerous efforts to complicate the reading process are mostly done with the intention of helping readers to become better readers of his texts. As he suggests in *The Confidence-Man*, reworking *Redburn*'s notion of the novel as a kind of guidebook, "true" novels offer something like a map to the reader: "the streets may be very crooked, he may often pause; but, thanks to his true map, he does not hopelessly lose his way."[4]

Convinced of Melville's status as "companion" to his texts, I should confess that before I took on the job of editing this volume I had to question its need, even with the upsurge of critical and popular interest in Melville. I also recalled my own experience of beginning to learn how to read Melville. In the 1970s, when I was an undergraduate, I talked myself into a graduate lecture class on Melville, where I expected to be immersed in the latest structuralist, poststructuralist, and historicist approaches to an author I had always found to be imposing and distant. Instead, much to my surprise (and retrospective delight), the professor simply had us read most of everything Melville wrote, in the order in which he wrote it, starting with *Typee* and concluding with *Billy Budd*. (At least I thought he had had us read everything Melville wrote until I learned several years later that Melville was also a poet of the first rank.) The professor's method of regularly calling our attention to those moments in Melville's texts when the narratives reflect critically on the interrelated dynamics of writing, reading, and interpretation – and demanding that we come to terms with those moments as central, defining occasions in Melville – quickly helped me (and my classmates) to feel a more intimate connection to Melville's art. And so we spent a good deal of time discussing analogies between the

.ered interpreters of *Typee*, "Bartleby," and "Benito Cereno" and read-
.f those works; the connections between fashion and interpretation that
ᵢₙₜₒrm *White-Jacket*; the similarities between heroic voyaging and intrepid
reading developed in *Mardi* and *Moby-Dick*; the dualistic rendering of trust
and con artistry that animates *Redburn*, *Pierre*, and *The Confidence-Man*.
Alternately presenting himself as guide and con artist, his texts as scriptures
of the age and testaments to blindness and silence, Melville insistently calls
attention to the risks, stakes, limits, and joys of interpretation. Attempting
to rise to the interpretive challenge, while at the same time remaining aware
of the inevitability of a certain sort of enlightening failure, would seem to
be the fate of his most sympathetic readers.

All of which may not make Melville sound like the best of companions,
except that he is usually never more companionable than when he is the-
orizing on the complex interpretive challenges of his texts. In fact, Melville
has proved eerily prescient on many of the critical concerns that would
come to engage twentieth-century theorists. Consider just a few of the theoretical dimensions and implications of *Moby-Dick*. Representations of Ishmael's various interactions with Queequeq anticipate twentieth-century
interrogations of gender, sexuality, race, and nation; "Cetology" points in
Thomas Kuhnian and Foucauldian ways to the relation of interpretive paradigms to cultural meanings; the chapters describing whaling practices in
the larger context of capitalist enterprise anticipate materialist criticism; the
numerous chapters on the whale's body are at the cutting edge of body
criticism; "Fast Fish and Loose Fish" raises the kinds of questions about
the politics of reading that would come to inform twentieth-century reader-
response criticism; and "The Whiteness of the Whale" and "The Doubloon" chapters anticipate Derridean deconstruction and developments in
neopragmatism. And more: "Does the Whale's Magnitude Diminish? – Will
He Perish?," with its musings on the possible disappearance of whales,
anticipates ecocriticism; "The Carpenter," with its vision of the mechanical
constructedness of humankind, cybercriticism; and the novel's grand conception of a global chase on a ship manned by an international crew, current debates on nationalism and transnationalism.

Given Melville's own theoretical predispositions, I would suggest (to return to my role as guide to this *Companion*) that doing theoretical work
as part of reading and interpreting Melville is hardly a violation but rather
of a piece with Melville's own authorial labors. Yet in Melville criticism a
divide has arisen between what Emerson might term the "bookworms" and
the "creative readers" – those critics who, on the one hand, practice an
accretionary, author-based approach committed to recovering Melville's intentions by paying close attention to what is known about his biography,

reading habits, compositional methods, and so on, and those critics, on the other hand, who pay a bit less heed to the ascertainable facts in order to explore from more theoretical and speculative perspectives the cultural discourses, logics, and concerns informing Melville's texts. In the Historical Note in the Northwestern–Newberry *Moby-Dick* (1988), the editors address the divide from the perspective of what one might, perhaps unfairly, call the bookworms. Reminding us of the initial critical fruits of the Melville revival, the editors celebrate "the great generation of Melville researchers of the 1930's and 1940's, whose labors first significantly coalesced in Willard Thorp's *Herman Melville: Representative Selections*, then culminated in 1951 in the first edition of Jay Leyda's *The Melville Log* and in Leon Howard's *Herman Melville: A Biography*. The debt to that generation of scholars remains deep, but this NOTE . . . also benefits from a new stage of scholarship on Melville – a stage arrived at, in part, from the accumulation of biographical and textual knowledge incorporated into the volumes of the Northwestern–Newberry edition published over two decades and still in preparation" (586). After pressing upon its readers the importance of attending to the forthcoming revised *Log* (edited by Northwestern–Newberry editor Hershel Parker), the forthcoming Northwestern–Newberry editions of Melville's letters and journals (since published), and Parker's forthcoming biography (the first volume of which has also since been published), they take aim at what could be called the creative readers, the "many professors [who] . . . have cast their harpoons at phantoms rather than the actual *The Whale* or *Moby-Dick*." Concerned about what they perceive to be the irresponsible (or parricidal) nature of such work, they assert that those more speculative critics have "trivialized . . . criticism or scholarship" and in doing so are "as solipsistic as Ahab" (756).

On the evidence of recent Melville scholarship, the divide between critical camps has only become wider since the Northwestern–Newberry editors made their pronouncement in 1988. For a quick impression of this divide, one can do little better than to look at recently published books by John Wenke and William V. Spanos. In *Melville's Muse: Literary Creation and the Forms of Philosophical Fiction* (1995), Wenke, drawing on important studies of Melville's reading by Merton M. Sealts, Jr., and Mary K. Bercaw, examines the ways in which "Melville's attraction to ancient and Renaissance writers became integral to his complex response to, and reformation of, Romanticism." For Wenke, Melville's engagement with Plato, Shakespeare, Montaigne, Emerson, Carlyle, and many others was part of a "deeply rooted process of creative rehabilitation" that constituted "a tour de force of intention." Diametrically opposed to Wenke's celebration of Melville's brilliant appropriations of canonical figures is Spanos's demonumentalizing *The Errant Art of Moby-Dick: The Canon, The Cold War, and the Struggle for American Studies* (1995). Whereas Wenke discusses Melville's reading and writing apart from the social and political debates of the nineteenth century, Spanos insists that Melville was a "writer whose *raison d'être* . . . was to interrogate the relationship between cultural monuments and sociopolitical power." And he maintains that critics (and readers) who fail to challenge Melville's monumental status are complicitous in "the dominant cultural and sociopolitical formation," racism, imperialism, and the like. Rather than working with known facts about Melville's possible political perspectives, Spanos develops a Heideggerian "destructive" reading of *Moby-Dick* as a form of cultural critique.[5]

This *Companion* has been conceived with the notion that it would be salutary for Melville studies if critics like Wenke and Spanos were more responsive to each other's work. Accordingly, though the volume is necessarily limited by the relatively small number of critical voices and perspectives that can be represented here, it nonetheless brings together critics who draw on traditional and newer approaches, and thus inevitably seeks to challenge the fixity and distinctiveness of such categories. We need our bookworms *and* our creative readers, and typically the differences between these two groups aren't as pronounced as Emerson (or the divide between Wenke and Spanos) might suggest. Yet there are differences, and rather than looking forward to a blithe future in which some sort of grand consensus emerges on how best to approach Melville, I would propose that the current critical debates and divergencies are a good thing: a sign of the vitality of Melville studies. For readers who are receptive, competing and conflicting views can help to challenge complacency and thus inspire further creative interactions with Melville's writings.

Melville states in the "Cetology" chapter of *Moby-Dick*: "I promise nothing complete; because any human thing supposed to be complete, must for that very reason infallibly be faulty" (136). I make a similar promise for this *Companion*. That said, an effort has been made to provide a relatively comprehensive overview of Melville's career. *All* of Melville's novels are discussed in the course of the volume, as is much of the poetry and short fiction. An effort has also been made to cover key historical and thematic issues in his writings. Though the contributors all have their principal subjects of focus, they have been encouraged to "trespass" on other contributors' domains. Various works and issues are thus viewed from a number of critical perspectives. Readers interested in *Moby-Dick*, for example, may wish to turn first to the essay by John Bryant, but they will also find relatively lengthy discussions of Melville's masterwork in the essays by Sterling Stuckey, Jenny Franchot, and Robert Milder; readers interested in Melville's critical reception might want to turn first to the essay by Cindy Weinstein, but they will also find issues of critical reception central to the essay by Paul Giles; and readers interested in race and slavery in Melville's writings will find the essays by Samuel Otter and Sterling Stuckey particularly helpful, but they will learn about these topics from a number of other essays in the volume as well.

Because of the importance of race to his early fiction, considerations of Melville's racial representations provide a useful starting point for the collection. In " 'Race' in *Typee* and *White-Jacket*," Samuel Otter explores how Melville conjoins the discursive, the corporeal, and the ideological in his inquiries into the constitution and boundaries of human bodies, the science and politics of race, and the structures of racial and individual identity. Melville's fascination with race, particularly with the terms, claims, and procedures of the influential "American school" of ethnology, whose aim was to make flesh and bone reveal human difference, provides the focus for Otter's reexaminations of *Typee* and *White-Jacket*. In "The Tambourine in Glory: African Culture and Melville's Art," Sterling Stuckey recovers and re-creates the African and African-American cultures that Melville would have known and experienced as a young man in the antebellum United States. In doing so, he offers a new perspective on the African-American presence in Melville's fiction, particularly the ways in which his encounters with black culture helped to shape his antislavery politics. An African-American aesthetic, Stuckey argues in his readings of *Redburn*, *Moby-Dick*, and "Benito Cereno," is crucial to Melville's American art and to an increasingly complex and diverse American scene.

The next three essays provide comprehensive readings of Melville's major novels of the 1850s. In "*Moby-Dick* as Revolution," John Bryant develops two narratives of historicism: a "genetic" narrative that tells of an artist's discovery of voice as an inherently ambivalent revolutionary act, one that in its embrace and purgation of Shakespeare serves as a model for the artistic revolutionary's anxious moment of personal and cultural independence; and a "responsive" narrative that, in telling and enacting the reader's dilemma in getting meaning out of a truly fluid text, recapitulates a revolutionary experience of being caught between equally desirable but seemingly mutually exclusive responses: Ahab's monological dramaturgy and Ishmael's dialogical lyricism. Multiplicity as a thematic and mode of reading is also central to Wyn Kelley's "*Pierre*'s Domestic Ambiguities," which studies the novel in its biographical, literary, and discursive contexts. Situating *Pierre* in relation to Hawthorne's *The House of the Seven Gables*, Kelley shows how Melville in his own domestic novel offers a utopian version of domesticity based not on family and marriage but on the risks of fraternity. Melville's unwillingness to offer a consoling vision of middle-class culture and family religion helped to ensure the novel's commercial failure. Several years after that failure, Melville wrote *The Confidence-Man* (1857), perhaps his most perplexing, difficult, and (for some) nearly unreadable work. In " 'A————!': Unreadability in *The Confidence-Man*," Elizabeth Renker takes the novel's perplexities and difficulties as its informing subject. Arguing that throughout his career Melville was frustrated by the ways in which the act of writing stifled rather than enabled his efforts to apprehend and tell great truths, Renker suggests that in *The Confidence-Man* Melville turns his frustrations on his readers. Hence the energetic (even delighted) concern in the novel with the tendencies of letters, characters, and tautologies to block and occlude meaning. Melville's increasing interest in the page, Renker posits, made his move to poetry after the publication of *The Confidence-Man* all but inevitable.

In "Melville the Poet," Lawrence Buell argues that the Civil War poems of *Battle-Pieces* (1866), the epic *Clarel* (1876), and other works reveal Melville as one of the great nineteenth-century poets writing in English. The poetry is neglected, Buell suggests, because of its apparent use of traditional poetic languages and prosody, its seeming emotional restraint, and its knotty language and jagged metrics. In response to a tradition of denigration and neglect, Buell makes the case for Melville as an experimental and, perhaps more significantly, as a cosmopolitan poet who, like his English contemporaries, is concerned with probing systems of belief in an increasingly scientific world. Though the Civil War certainly contributed to Melville's emergence as a poet, Buell ultimately presents us with a transnational writer who, even more so than the "international" Henry James, develops what could be termed an "ethnographical" perspective on history, culture, and religion.

Ethnography is central to Jenny Franchot's "Melville's Traveling God," which investigates the ways in which Melville's theological concerns connect to the relativistic, anthropological domain of ritual and historically contingent belief. Linking the trope of travel in Melville's writings to a rhetoric of ethnographical questing, Franchot, in her revisionary consideration of the place of religion in Melville's writings, explores how Melville's narratives, through their representation of the "exotic," ultimately endow Christianity with new life as metaphor, allusion, and source. In "Melville and Sexuality," Robert K. Martin also addresses questions of culture and otherness as he discusses Melville's writings in relation to shifting cultural definitions of sexuality. As Martin observes, Melville's representations of the problematics of sexual identity always take place in a political context – whether the colonialism and missionary activity of the South Seas novels or the <u>industrial capitalism of *Moby-Dick*</u>. Melville's recognition of the complex relations between desire and power is signaled most tragically in his posthumous *Billy Budd*, which addresses, in part, the persecution of the homosexual in the cultural context of the persecution (or regulation) of the sexual.

Essays by Cindy Weinstein and Paul Giles share an interest in Melville's critical reception. Focusing on nineteenth-century discourses of labor, Weinstein's "Melville, Labor, and the Discourses of Reception" studies the relationship between Melville's literary labors and contemporaneous evaluations of his texts, showing how Melville reproduces in his writings the problematics of the marketplace. Melville, Weinstein notes, hardly seeks to separate his own labors from the typical productions of other laborers; rather, he examines in his fiction the value of his own and others' labors, as well as the class structures motivating those valuations. Whereas Weinstein focuses on Melville's response to his American critics, Paul Giles, in " 'Bewildering Intertanglement': Melville's Engagement with British Culture," examines how Melville has been conceptualized by English critics and how he has responded to those conceptualizations. More broadly, Giles considers Melville's sometimes perverse and parodic engagement with various forms of British culture, ranging from the representation of Liverpool in *Redburn* to the ironic conceptions of national identity in *Israel Potter* and the ambiguous accounts of English justice in *Billy Budd*. Recent work by Lawrence Buell and others has found in Melville a "postcolonial" idiom that implicitly serves to compromise the nationalist ethos with which Melville has often been associated. One large purpose of Giles's essay is to analyze how such postcolonial anxieties mediate Melville's accounts of slavery, cultural independence, sexuality, and national differences.

At a time when a bewildering number of "old" and "new" Melvilles confront us, Robert Milder's synthesizing essay, "Melville and the 'Avenging Dream,' " argues that a relatively coherent romantic quest pattern informs Melville's major works, joining his questers and god defiers as complementary figures in a private and compulsively reenacted drama. In one variation or another, Milder shows, <u>the myth lies at the imaginative</u> center of *Mardi*, *Moby-Dick*, *Pierre*, *Clarel*, and the late poem "Timoleon." This essay brings the myth to the forefront, traces its sources in some of the patterning impulses (literary and psychological) in Melville's imagination, and contextualizes it historically within the transatlantic moment when romantic exuberance shaded into Victorian paralysis and doubt. Though not self-consciously "transnational" in its approach, Milder's essay complements Giles's, Buell's, and several other of the essays in the collection in the way its literary-historical approach works to dislocate Melville from the nationalistic particularities of his time. In his Afterword, Andrew Delbanco points to other connections among the essays as he takes stock of Melville at century's end.

In *Mardi*, Babbalanja expounds on his impassioned reading of his beloved Bardianna: "For the more we learn, the more we unlearn; we accumulate not, but substitute; and take away, more than we add."[6] Though some of the contributors to this volume may have qualms about my putting them into an antipositivistic camp, it is my belief that all of these essays help us as much to "unlearn" as to learn. In this respect, it is my hope that this volume, while inevitably contributing to the cultural monumentalization of Melville, will also help to stimulate creative encounters with an author whose writings both invite and resist interpretation. A figure of such interpretive dualism, what Melville in "The Whiteness of the Whale" calls "a dumb blankness full of meaning" (195), can be found on Melville's grave in Woodlawn Cemetery in the Bronx. Carved onto the granite headstone is a blank stone scroll – a haunting testament, perhaps, to the mysteries of silence but a tantalizing invitation as well to further inscription.

NOTES

1. The epigraph is from Herman Melville, *Correspondence*, ed. Lynn Horth (Evanston and Chicago: Northwestern University Press and The Newberry Library, 1993), p. 174. See also Melville, *Pierre or the Ambiguities: "The Kraken Edition,"* ed. Hershel Parker (New York: HarperCollins, 1995); and Philip Weiss, "Herman-Neutics," *The New York Times Magazine*, 15 December 1996, pp. 60–5, 71–2. The Melville special, "Great Books: *Moby-Dick*," produced by Judith Hallet, premiered on the Learning Channel on 14 September 1996. Complete bibliographical references to the Melville studies mentioned in this paragraph may be found in the Selected Bibliography at the end of the volume.
2. Ralph Waldo Emerson, "The American Scholar," in *Essays and Lectures*, ed. Joel Porte (New York: Library of America, 1983), pp. 57–9.
3. Melville, *White-Jacket, or The World in a Man-of-War*, ed. Harrison Hayford, Hershel Parker, and G. Thomas Tanselle (Evanston and Chicago: Northwestern University Press and The Newberry Library, 1970), p. 169; Melville to Evert A. Duyckinck, letter of 3 March 1849 (on Emerson's risk-taking philosophical explorations), in *Correspondence*, p. 21; and Melville, *Moby-Dick, or The Whale*, ed. Harrison Hayford, Hershel Parker, and G. Thomas Tanselle (Evanston and Chicago: Northwestern University Press and The Newberry Library, 1988), p. 112. Future page references to this edition of *Moby-Dick* will be cited parenthetically.
4. Melville, *The Confidence-Man: His Masquerade*, ed. Harrison Hayford, Hershel Parker, and G. Thomas Tanselle (Evanston and Chicago: Northwestern University Press and The Newberry Library, 1984), p. 71.
5. John Wenke, *Melville's Muse: Literary Creation and the Forms of Philosophical*

Fiction (Kent, Ohio: Kent State University Press, 1995), pp. xiv, 23; William V. Spanos, *The Errant Art of Moby-Dick: The Canon, the Cold War, and the Struggle for American Studies* (Durham, N.C.: Duke University Press, 1995), pp. 4, 12.

6. Melville, *Mardi, and A Voyage Thither*, ed. Harrison Hayford, Hershel Parker, and G. Thomas Tanselle (Evanston and Chicago: Northwestern University Press and The Newberry Library, 1970), p. 389.

I

SAMUEL OTTER

"Race" in *Typee* and *White-Jacket*

In the first phase of his career, the extended fiction from *Typee* (1846) through *Pierre* (1852), Melville is fascinated with "race." This fascination animates his literary practice, fueling his rhetorical excess and provoking questions about identity and intersubjectivity that he pursues across his texts. Melville inquires into the science and politics of "race," the constitution and the boundaries of human bodies, and the deep structures of identity. In a remarkable series of texts excessively linking bodies, discourse, and ideology, Melville examines the ways in which human bodies have become written and overwritten with racial meaning.[1]

Melville offers neither a transcendent critique nor a symptomatic recapitulation of racial beliefs. In his fiction, he insists that this is a false choice and that racial assumptions, presumptions, and investments are not so portable or divestible. In Melville's representations, individuals think and feel the strange and often destructive ways they do not because they are benighted or deluded, but because their responses have a history, give definition, fulfill needs. Melville is critical but does not claim, or rather comes to realize that he cannot sustain, the privilege of an outsider's position. Rather than dismiss contemporary beliefs about race, nation, and self, he acknowledges his attractions to those beliefs and examines their sources and sway. He provides an inside sense of the power of racial ideology, its satisfactions and incarcerations. Melville both inhabits and manipulates contemporary racial discourse, giving a material sense of its structures and functions.

"Race" seems in several ways to have shaped the first phase of Melville's writing career, the seven extravagant books published between 1846 and 1852: *Typee* (1846), *Omoo* (1847), *Mardi* (1849), *Redburn* (1849), *White-Jacket* (1850), *Moby-Dick* (1851), and *Pierre* (1852). In writing these books, Melville drew upon and was inspired by his experiences in the years between 1839 and 1844 as a sailor on trading ships, whalers, and frigates and as a sojourner in Liverpool, the Marquesas, Tahiti, and Hawaii. The encounters with people of various races and classes on these trips helped to define the reach, range, sympathies, and anxieties of Melville's imagination. In writing these books, the young Melville also reflected upon the roles played by his own illustrious family in establishing and reinforcing United States national and racial boundaries. His family included two Revolutionary War grandfathers and a father-in-law who, as Chief Justice of the Massachusetts Supreme Court, ruled on several important segregation and fugitive slave cases. The years of Melville's early writing career were politically volatile, charged with debate about racial identity, character, and rights. These were the years of growing United States and European missionary and military activity in the South Pacific, of victory over Mexico and massive national expansion, of the 1850 "compromise" between southern and northern states over the issue of slavery, and of a clarifying consciousness of "whiteness" among European American citizens and immigrants. During these years there was increasing political agitation over the treatment of African Americans under slavery and freedom, Native Americans in the newly acquired territories and on the frontiers, and European American male and female laborers. These are all issues that Melville addresses in his fiction.

Yet I would like to suggest still another perspective from which "race" helped to shape Melville's literary career. "Race" not only gave him a personal, family, and political content, it also provided him with the forms, scenes, figures, and assumptions of his fiction. "Race" stimulated the obsessions about character and characteristics and identity and intersubjectivity that preoccupied his omnivorous, overwrought imagination. In this sense, Melville's rhetorical excess and epistemological concerns are intimately related to the extraordinary nineteenth-century effort to gain access to the depth and difference of human character: the racial quest epitomized in the "American school" of ethnology, which achieved international prominence in the 1840s and 1850s.

American ethnologists hailed the United States as the preeminent arena for the study of human racial differences, in which at least three of the five major racial groups lived in close proximity. The archaeologist and ethnologist Ephraim George Squier announced in 1849 that "Ethnology is not only the science of the age, but also . . . it is, and must continue to be, to a prevailing extent, an *American science*." Aligned with the justifications for African American slavery and Native American "removal," American ethnology transformed scientific thinking and political and popular culture. What was "American" about the "American school" was the obsessive nationalistic insistence on finding physical evidence for the "fact" of the separate and unequal capabilities of human beings. As the result of the meticulous, encyclopedic efforts of such ethnologists as Samuel George Morton, Josiah Nott, and George Gliddon, by the 1850s the claim that American racial groups were inherently unequal and that the physical characteristics of the body specifically, literally, and permanently revealed hierarchical differences in racial character was approaching the status of fact.[2]

Nineteenth-century ethnology in America and Europe magnified the overdetermined attractions of the human body: philosophical, psychological, theological, erotic, and economic. "Race," declared the Scottish anatomist Robert Knox in 1850, "is everything: literature, science, art – in a word, civilization depends on it."[3] In the midcentury United States, many observers saw the racialized human figure as embodying the answers to crucial questions about divine intention, social structure, human origins and history, and national destiny. Thus to suggest that "race" played a significant role in shaping Melville's literary interests and practices is not to reduce Melville's texts to narrow questions about human characteristics but to acknowledge the sweep and urgency of the nineteenth-century ethnological quest. It was a quest in which the racial body was seen to contain the secrets of the world and the effort to decipher its parts was seen as essential for the articulation of the national order.

In the first phase of his career, Melville examines the ways in which the human body became invested with graded meaning and charged with mystery and revelation. He indicates how a world of definition, coherence, and difference became located in the face, skin, and skull. He insists that readers acknowledge "race" not as the abstract property of others but as the grammar book of palpable and hierarchical meanings United States culture has assigned to the features of human bodies. Literalizing his figures and probing the violence performed by and through the figures of antebellum ethnology, Melville gives us a substantial sense of how ideology became inscribed on antebellum eyes, hearts, and minds.[4]

In the pages that follow, I sketch the ways in which Melville renders strangely material the premises, terms, and structures of antebellum racial discourse in two key texts of his first phase: *Typee* and *White-Jacket*. In these books Melville restages crucial scenes, and he turns and twists conventional figures. In the destabilizing encounters between European American and South Pacific cultures in *Typee*, and particularly the scenes of tattooing, Melville examines the art and science of corporeal marking, in which tattooing comes alarmingly to look like the penetrations and delineations of ethnology. In *Typee* the human face, seen as the guarantor of personal integrity and coherence, is under assault from both Polynesian and Western attacks. In the scenes of flogging and the attention lavished on the narrator's supersaturated white jacket in *White-Jacket*, Melville examines the meanings of skin. He tests the limits of the analogy between sailor and slave, both marked by the whip. Although there is no space in this essay to discuss *Moby-Dick*, in this book Melville climaxes his investigation of racial bodies and racial discourse. In *Moby-Dick*, the narrator, Ishmael, neither fears losing his face nor attempts to jump out of his skin. In the many scenes of cranial contemplation, which restage the scrutinies of phrenology, physiognomy, and craniometry, Melville gets inside the head of antebellum ethnology. He criticizes the obsession with defining, ranking, and separating human types and analyzes how ethnology composes its objects. He attempts to imagine alternative forms of knowledge and contact.

Melville is an immanent, not a transcendent, manipulator of antebellum ideas about race, subject to all the dangers of entanglement and complicity such a position implies. Melville's primary object of inquiry is not the form or features of another. Ultimately, the face whose contours he outlines, the skin whose substance he examines, the head whose contents he inventories, and the heart whose motions he traces are his own. He lays himself open and exposes shared structures of feeling and belief. Across *Typee*, *White-Jacket*, and *Moby-Dick*, we can see a diminishing of anxiety about racial contact and exchange, a broadening understanding of his own racial position as a European American man in the mid-nineteenth-century United States, a developing mastery of form and rhetoric, an increasing figurative intensity, and a deepening self-reflection over the intimate and powerful links between his literary subjects, objects, and practices.

Part autobiography, part anthropology, part travelogue, part adventure story, part social criticism, *Typee* is the account of an American sailor's four-month stay among a group of islanders on Nukuheva in the east central Pacific Ocean.[5] The narrator, who calls himself "Tom" and is later dubbed "Tommo" by the islanders, is a crew member on the American whale ship *Dolly*. Along with his friend Toby, he breaks his contract to serve because he feels that the captain has violated the agreement by permitting abuses to flourish in the shipboard society. Coming to the Marquesas with a set of expectations about the "civilized" and the "savage," the narrator is transfixed by the question of cannibalism. Has he landed in the valley of the ferocious Typee or the friendly Happar? This question is posed over and over again during the first part of the narrative.

Typee or Happar? The anxious refrain echoes the founding European trope of colonial encounter in the Caribbean: Carib or Arawak? Fierce cannibal or noble savage? Yet from the start of *Typee*, the refrain echoes with a difference. Both tribes, Typee and Happar, are cannibals. The choice, as the narrator Tommo points out, is no longer the clear one (at least in Western eyes) between flesh eater and noble savage, but the less reassuring alternative posed by two varieties of cannibal. This unsettling of terms is the first of many gestures in *Typee* that question the naming of "savages." After situating a narrative of Typee ferocity in the context of American military atrocity, the narrator concludes: "Thus it is that they whom we denominate 'savages' are made to deserve the title." Melville argues that savagery is not innate but a product of the "fatal embrace" of islander and European. In Chapter 17, Tommo, in the style of Montaigne's "Of Cannibals," juxtaposes savage cannibalism with civilized barbarity and suggests that the savage version might be preferable, or at least should be judged in a framework that is not centered in European assumptions.[6]

In Melville's representations, cannibalism is not the ultimate sign of difference, as it is in previous narratives of cultural encounter in the South Seas, such as those written by A. J. von Krusenstern (1813), G. H. von Langsdorff (1813–14), and David Porter (1815), all of which Melville used as sources for *Typee*.[7] Melville manipulates the specter of cannibalism to probe American and European ideas about "savagery" and to build narrative suspense. In a scene in Chapter 12, a resonant joke about his characters' and audience's expectations, Melville describes how Tommo and Toby watch the preparation of a large fire, increasingly worried that they will become the main dish. Finally, to their great relief, they are invited to partake in a feast of pig flesh. In Chapter 32, Tommo returns unexpectedly to the dwelling of Marheyo, where he has been housed during his stay. He finds his companions examining three "mysterious packages" wrapped in tappa cloth, which had been suspended over his sleeping place and often had excited his curiosity (232). The "mysterious packages" function as both device and joke in *Typee*. They are suspended not only over Tommo's bed but also over the course of the narrative. They are bundles that incite Tommo's curiosity and provoke his horror, and they also represent the looming specter of cannibalism that quickens reader interest and creates tension: cannibalism as stage property. Before the Marquesans can conceal the contents of the packages, Tommo glimpses three preserved human heads: two Marquesan heads and one "white" head. Tommo fears that the "white" head belongs to his lost friend Toby, and is terrified that he himself will be devoured and his own head preserved as a souvenir. A week later, after a battle between the Typee and the Happar, Tommo lifts the lid on a curiously carved vessel in the temple precincts, and he and the reader are greeted with a glimpse of human flesh and bones, a stagy peep into a flesh pot.

Yet this peep at carnivorous Polynesian life is not the reason that the narrator Tommo flees his South Sea island paradise. It is not cannibalism, not the eating of human flesh, but tattooing – writing on flesh, or, as Melville refers to the practice, the "fine art" of skin design (217) – that deeply unsettles the narrator. The profound danger on Nukuheva is not that the Typees literally will eat Tommo but that they figuratively will consume his identity by writing upon his skin.

Strolling with his companion Kory-Kory, Tommo stumbles upon a scene of plein-air tattooing in which the Marquesan artist Karky is repairing the canvas of an old man's skin:

> I beheld a man extended flat upon his back on the ground, and, despite the forced composure of his countenance, it was evident that he was suffering agony. His tormentor bent over him, working away for all the world like a stone-cutter with mallet and chisel. In one hand he held a short slender stick, pointed with a shark's tooth, on the upright end of which he tapped with a small hammer-like piece of wood, thus puncturing the skin, and charging it with the coloring matter in which the instrument was dipped. (217)

Melville here emphasizes the violence of tattooing. (The word "tattoo" itself derives from Marquesan and Tahitian verbs meaning "to strike.") The body is compared to a sculptor's blank, composed not of marble but of a soft and sensitive material subjected to the blows of a hammer. Yet for Melville, the most exquisite instrument of torture is not the mallet and chisel but the short, slender stick. Tommo is less afraid of the blunt physical blow that would rend large pieces of flesh than he is of the delicate inscription that penetrates and contaminates the interior. Thus the artistic analogy that Melville uses to define the tattooing process more sharply is printing rather than sculpture: the body is a surface to be cut and inked. In Melville's extended analogy between tattooing and intaglio printing, the tattoo artist's instruments are described as being like the graduated tools of the etcher or engraver. Melville gives an accurate account of tattooing techniques, drawing heavily from Langsdorff's *Voyages and Travels*. The skin is punctured, and coloring matter is injected into a deeper layer.

The violence that Tommo witnesses is rendered somewhat comically. The tone changes abruptly, however, when Tommo's gaze is returned and the positions of observer and observed are reversed. Karky the tattoo artist brandishes his tools at Tommo: "Horrified at the bare thought of being rendered hideous for life if the wretch were to execute his purpose upon me, I struggled to get away from him" (218). To be tattooed is to be the object of "execution." At the core of Tommo's "bare thought" is the fear of being covered, of being "rendered hideous for life" by indelible and invidious marks, the stark fear of having his bare skin written upon for all to read.

In the illustrations we have of Marquesan tattooing from the nineteenth and early twentieth centuries, the intricate tattooing on male bodies is almost like a new skin. The surface of the body is divided into zones that are heavily marked, filled with circles, rectangles, and lozenges. The forehead is mapped, traversed by lines and arcs. The face is composed of bands of color. This charting of the human surface is visually reminiscent of the corporeal mappings in late-eighteenth and early-nineteenth-century ethnology, beginning with Enlightenment European and American efforts to investigate human anatomical differences and climaxing in the efforts of the antebellum "American school." We can see ethnologists trace their lines and inscribe their messages of separation and hierarchy in the graduated facial angles of the Dutch anatomist Petrus Camper; the physiognomic grids of the Swiss pastor Johann Lavater; the phrenological diagrams of Orson and Lorenzo Fowler; the craniometrical plates of the premier American ethnologist, Samuel George Morton; and the charts of comparative anatomy in the leading antebellum American ethnology textbook, Josiah Nott and George Gliddon's *Types of Mankind* (1854).[8]

To draw these ethnological lines on the human body is to interpret them. The angle formed by the forehead and the jaw; the distance between hairline, eyebrow, and nose tip; the cranial swells and depressions – to mark these lines on the face and head and to imagine them as measures of an interior state is to make visible a new kind of knowledge. In nineteenth-century racial theory and aesthetics, there is a standard for the angles, the inches, and the contour lines, and deviation is made explicit. Knowledge is conceived in visual and spatial terms, and the linear is seen as giving access to the depth of human character and human difference. The racial body is known and owned through reading the lines engraved on its surface.[9]

Again and again, travelers to the Marquesas expressed an ethnological interest in the bodies of the islanders. Krusenstern, Langsdorff, Porter, Charles S. Stewart (1831), Frederick Debell Bennett (1840), and Melville himself praised the light color, symmetrical proportions, and "European" features of the islanders.[10] According to Langsdorff, his companion, Counsellor Tilesius, "who unites the eye of a connoisseur and an artist," was so impressed by the form of one native that he measured every part of the man and forwarded his results to the famous ethnologist Johann Blumenbach. Several travelers compared male Marquesan bodies to classical sculptures, as though the journey to the Marquesas traced a path to the heart of whiteness, where the observer would discover models of pristine Caucasian beauty.

Yet complicating this classical vision was the vivid evidence of difference inscribed on Marquesan skin. Travelers were struck by the color transformations worked by the tattoo artist. Krusenstern, Stewart, and Bennett commented on the extensive Marquesan tattooing, suggesting a racial conversion from Caucasian to Negro. Langsdorff wrote that in later years the symmetry and clarity of Marquesan tattooing designs deteriorated into the obscure disorder of a "Negro-like appearance." Many writers described the meticulous procedures and intricate designs by which light skin was colored. Marquesan skin seems to have served as an uncanny screen upon which European and American observers projected their desires and anxieties.[11]

In *Typee*, the observer does not remain in a privileged vantage point. The tattoo artist Karky traverses the insulating distance between observer and observed. He turns toward Tommo and seizes hold of him. And what part of Tommo's body does Karky specifically threaten? His *face*:

> The idea of engrafting his tattooing upon my white skin filled him with all a painter's enthusiasm: again and again he gazed into my countenance, and every fresh glimpse seemed to add to the vehemence of his ambition. Not knowing to what extremities he might proceed, and shuddering at the ruin he might inflict upon my figure-head, I now endeavored to draw off his attention from it, and holding out my arm in a fit of desperation, signed to him to commence operations. But he rejected the compromise indignantly, and still continued his attack on my face, as though nothing short of that would satisfy him. When his fore-finger swept across my features, in laying out the borders of those parallel bands which were to encircle my countenance, the flesh fairly crawled upon my bones. . . . This incident opened my eyes to a new danger; and I now felt convinced that in some luckless hour I should be disfigured in such a manner as never more to have the *face* to return to my countrymen, even should an opportunity offer.   (219)

The flesh "crawls" on Tommo's bones at the prospect of having his white skin marked by tattoos. Tattooing here is described as "encircling" the countenance, like a garrote or a noose. Tommo explains to the reader that his resistance to being tattooed hardened when he learned the fact that the Typees regarded tattooing as a badge of religious identity. Yet this "fact" is nowhere corroborated either in Melville's sources or in twentieth-century anthropological accounts, which emphasize the ornamental functions of the designs. The religious fear seems to be an artful dodge. Tommo is afraid not of theological but of racial conversion. Tattoos are "engrafted . . . upon white skin" – as though the process involved blending the living tissues of Polynesian and American.

Tommo's face is under "attack." The piercing anxiety here registers the literal and figurative importance of the head and the face, as made explicit in Melville's pun: "I now felt convinced that . . . I should be disfigured in such a manner as never more to have the *face* to return to my countrymen." Here "face" means both the sense of dignity and, literally, the surface of the front part of the head. Tommo's sense of dignity and his reputation – his identity – are bound up with his unmarked face. The face is the conspicuous surface of contact between the individual inside and the social outside, the only such surface, with the exception of the hands, regularly exposed in Western fashion. It is the " 'face divine,' " exalted by poets, as Tommo reminds his readers (220). The face is the site of the expressive features, the eloquent features targeted by antebellum ethnologists and saturated with meaning: the chin, the mouth, the nose, the brow – signatures of the interior. The "parallel bands" that Karky desires to draw across Tommo's countenance threaten to etch lines of deviation on a face that had been imagined as composed of standard lines. They threaten to color a face that had been imagined as uncolored. Confronted by Karky, Tommo is in danger of losing his face. This vital surface will be imprinted permanently with degrading lines of difference for his countrymen to see and to read. No longer will Tommo have a face that permits him to move undetected through American society. He will be a marked man. Take my arm, he offers Karky, tattoo my arm – but leave me my *face*. Yet Karky is not "satisfied" with the limb. The more he looks into Tommo's face, the more his appetite and his ambition increase. Karky displays an artist's hunger to delineate the body, a "painter's enthusiasm."

When Karky sweeps his index finger across Tommo's features and when he brandishes his tattooing instruments, the gestures of antebellum ethnology are made palpable and ominous. In Chapter 30 of *Typee*, tattooing looks like the line cuts of ethnology, and Tommo becomes the object of this kind of inditing knowledge. Yet these lines also look different, drawn by Karky's hand. Karky is an artist and a scientist performing his operations on the human body, but he is a Marquesan artist and scientist. He is such an unsettling figure for Tommo as a result of his multiple, overlapping figurations. In the parallel bands that encircle the faces of Karky's victims, Tommo sees a reflection of the fate of his own face. W. C. Handy's illustrations of tattoo face patterns for men convey the extent of Marquesan facial marking (Figure 1). The extreme attention to zoning resembles the division of the body's surface into specific, densely inscribed areas in racial ethnology. Yet in contrast to the lines and angles, the latitudes and longi-

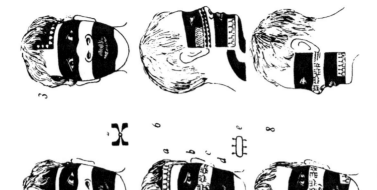

Figure 1. Tattoo designs in the Marquesas.(Bishop Museum)

tudes, of physiognomy and phrenology, which construct the Caucasian face in a firm grid of proportioned features, Karky's designs threaten to unfix the face. The segmenting and patterning divide the male face into interchangeable parts and colors. Unlike the numbered phrenological faculties in Fowler, which signify permanent locations, the denotations in Handy correspond to design motifs, which are transposable. The positions and colors of facial features appear arbitrary; the relationship among features seems unstable; the foundation for the color uncertain. The artistry and the artifice in the composition of tattooed Marquesan faces are apparent. Tommo is threatened not only with having his face permanently marked and "rendered hideous for life" but with the dissolution of the face as he knows it.[12]

In Marquesan tattooing, the ethnologist's dream of definitive facial geometry decomposes into an indeterminate, illegible nightmare. This incoherence is much more unsettling than the confusion described by Langsdorff as characteristic of aged tattooing designs that impart to some Marquesan bodies a "Negro-like appearance." While visually disordered, such an appearance is cognitively precise, conveying the stable imperfections of blackness. Marquesan faces, on the other hand, are unpredictable. Marquesan facial tattooing severs the link forged by antebellum ethnology between individual and collective character. While the markings on individual Marquesans are permanent, the location and arrangement of these marks do not persist from face to face. The ethnological guarantee that the individual recapitulates the race is invalidated. Marquesan faces offer the horrifying prospect of indelibility *and* insecurity. On Marquesan faces, it becomes impossible to chart the lineaments of character.

Marquesan tattooing is so disturbing because, in the mid-nineteenth-century imagination of *Typee*, it represents a native artistic retribution for the Western science of racial ethnology. Karky wants to decorate Tommo's body, and Tommo goes to pieces. Tattooing is at the same time ethnology and antiethnology – or ethnology as revenge. The ethnologist sought to trace lines on the body in order to read racial character and separate and rank human types. In *Typee*, in a case of measure for measure, the Polynesian tattooist turns to the American observer, seizes him, brandishes his instruments – not the scalpel and the calipers but the shark's tooth and the small wooden hammer – and threatens to return the stroke of drawing lines. And Karky's lines *are* lines. They are not the figurative tracings on Camper's faces or Fowler's heads. Karky threatens to literalize the lines drawn by ethnologists and to carve them on the body of the observer.

The scene of tattooing in *Typee* contains a violent assault, a revolution in perspective. Tommo, "unmanned," runs away (232). Melville, too, seems to flee. That is, the distance between narrator and writer seems slight. Tommo's response is validated by the subsequent account of escape and culminating fury when he delivers the ultimate retort to Karky's facial assault by hurling a boat hook at the throat of a pursuing Marquesan chief. The tattooing scene has not been staged so that the reader perceives the limits of Tommo's cultural horizons and racial perceptions. Instead, the scene as written and positioned invites the reader to share those limits. In the end, the narrative descends into scenes of contrived sentiment and spurious adventure. Yet before these final protective gestures, the reader is given a glimpse of profound cultural encounter – profound if not in its critical transcendence or dramatic irony, then in its revelation of the depth and the sources of American anxiety. Karky's assault on Tommo is a raw and vibrant textual moment.

In this first book, Melville demonstrates an intimate knowledge of the shaping obsessions of antebellum racial discourse. He offers a telling scene of reversal in which the observer's body is threatened with being scarred by the object of study. Yet the detail and the force of the representations do not indicate a critical distance from the observer's anxieties about having his own body invidiously marked or the observer's distress at being dislodged from his privileged position. For all the compelling comparative anthropology, the domestications of cannibalism, the reversal of expectations about civilization and savagery, and the perspectival shifts achieved through juxtaposing American and Polynesian cultures, Melville wishes to save his face. Relativism has its limits.

Yet these are revealing limits. *Typee* is a text structured by reversals. In a minor reversal, the ferocious Typee and the gentle Happar change positions. In the major double reversal of the book, the savage islanders switch places with the civilized Europeans and Americans, and then switch again, as native practice is revealed to be savage indeed at its core and the narrator seeks to escape to "Home" and "Mother" (248). Yet these reversals conceal a fundamental similarity between the two spheres and a recognition that there is no escape, whose full acknowledgment is postponed until the lacerating incarcerations of Melville's *White-Jacket*. The savagery of the Typee is artistic, and the conjunction between Marquesan artistry and Western science suggests that in both Marquesan and American cultures there is no refuge from inscription, no safe haven for whiteness. The "ghastly" aspect of "whiteness," to use Melville's language from Chapter 42 of *Moby-Dick*, lies in its failure to live up to its pristine promise. Imagined as the visible absence of color, white at the same time is the concrete of all colors – not blank but fraught with meaning. Embedded in the crucial twist of the narrative – the revelation of tattooing in the Karky scene – is a deeply unsettling insight. On the island of Nukuheva, Tommo has discovered civilization, and its mark, whether in the nineteenth-century Marquesas or in nineteenth-century America, is the tattoo.

Melville's *White-Jacket* is a book about the extension of black slavery to the decks of United States naval frigates and to the backs of white sailors. As Melville indicates in his subtitle, *The World in a Man-of-War*, his book takes as its subject an entire set of analogies that links ship to shore. These analogical ambitions are the ambitions of the genre in which *White-Jacket* was written, the popular antebellum seaman's narrative. The seaman's narrative detailed the structures of order, the varieties of labor, and the social relations in ship and state. It was a subgenre in a wider cultural effort to analyze the political and social constitution of the United States during the decades of crisis before the Civil War. This effort included slave narratives, political oratory, and the polemical comparisons between northern and southern society made by the opponents and defenders of slavery.

In *White-Jacket*, Melville takes the seaman's narrative as the synecdoche for this effort to analyze America, and he probes to the core of the genre. At the core, he discovers a crucial analogy, that between the white and the black "slave." He locates a defining scene: the scene of flogging, in which the similarities and the differences between the bodies of white and black men are exposed. In both seamen's narratives and slavemen's narratives, flogging is represented in explicitly theatrical terms, with actors, victims, audiences, and intricate spatial arrangements. The flogger is represented as having the power to define and convert human skin. These scenes display the textures, properties, and limits of different skins. On the decks of the frigate *Neversink*, Melville shows how the national drama of freedom and slavery is enacted on and in the skins of black and white slaves. (The frigate on which Melville served between August 1843 and October 1844, and which he used as the model for his fictional *Neversink*, was named, with an allegorical redundancy Melville must have appreciated, the *United States*.)

The analogy with slavery was at the center of antebellum political debate. It was made by northern labor radicals, slavery apologists, women's rights advocates, and nationalists. Many seamen narrators employed the analogy between sailors and slaves, including William McNally (1839), Richard Henry Dana, Jr. (1840), Samuel Leech (1843), and John Ross Browne (1846), all of whom Melville used as sources for *White-Jacket*. African American writers who had been slaves, such as Frederick Douglass and William Wells Brown, refused to remain the silent term in such analogies. They argued for the incommensurability of the comparison between American chattel slave and American, English, or Irish laborer. The presence of chattel slavery shaped antebellum political discourse.[13] Yet the analogy, while pervasive, was not self-evident. What did it mean to be "like a slave"?

In *White-Jacket*, Melville scrutinizes the analogy between sailor and slave. He embodies this analogy in characters on board his man-of-war. He presses the analogy to its limits, revealing its terms and relations. Melville tells the story of the analogy in antebellum culture: a story of white attraction, bondage, and release in which the resemblances between white sailor and black slave become too intimate and unruly. It is the story of an analogy that gets out of hand and threatens to confound the distinctions between terms and to mark its user, and then must be disciplined.

Melville's examination of antebellum American society is excruciating. *White-Jacket* describes how order is established and regulated in a U.S. man-of-war. In chapter after chapter, Melville describes the techniques through which discipline is maintained: the duration and rotation of deck watches; the allocation and withholding of alcohol; the beneficences of shore leave; the obsession with neatness and unobstructedness on the three decks; the omnipresence of punishment for the slightest infraction; the spectacle of flogging; the monthly muster around the capstan and ritual reading of the Articles of War; the mock-tragic "Massacre of the Beards" according to army standards by which sailors' facial hair was to be "accurately laid out and surveyed," showing how military authority extends to the most personal spaces.[14] Over the course of the book, the narrator describes several scenes of flogging. Four sailors are each lashed with the cat-o-nine-tails for fighting on the gun deck. The black sailor May-Day and the mulatto sailor Rose-Water are scourged for engaging in unsanctioned combat. (The captain only permits fighting at his command for the pleasure of the crew.) The old sailor Ushant is given twelve savage strokes for refusing to shave his beard. The narrator White-Jacket himself is brought to the mast on a charge of having failed to be at his proper station during the tacking of the ship. Yet just at the moment when the captain commands that White-Jacket be tied to the gratings in preparation for flogging, just as White-Jacket prepares to hurl himself against the captain and propel both of them overboard in a desperate act of murder and suicide, he receives a miraculous reprieve. Corporal Colbrook and then the main-top-man Jack Chase defend White-Jacket's reputation. The captain, in an unprecedented move, releases him from punishment.

According to White-Jacket, some of the evil effects of flogging include its indiscriminate, frequent, and severe application; the lack of proportion between punishment and offense; the absence of any trial or court of appeal; its restriction to sailors and the exemption of officers from the penalty;

and the absolute authority it confers on the captain, who becomes legislator, judge, and executive (139–49). The most evil effect of flogging in the American Navy is, as Melville puts it in a resonant pun, "an ever-lasting suspension of the Habeas Corpus" (144). Not only is the writ guaranteeing the right of an accused man to be brought before a court suspended, or rendered void, on naval ships but the body of the accused is literally suspended: hung from the gratings, stripped, its flesh bared to the eyes of the entire crew and to the whip of the boatswain's mate. The writ of Habeas Corpus isn't simply ignored on United States men-of-war; it is rewritten, sadistically, on the exposed backs of the class of men called sailors.

The subjection to authority, the vulnerability, the scarring – all these conditions sharpen the analogy between sailor and slave in *White-Jacket*. The narrator describes the legacy that endures on the body of a flogged sailor, "a penalty the traces whereof he carries to the grave; for to a man-of-war's-man's experienced eye the marks of a naval scourging with the '*cat*' are through life discernible." Although White-Jacket affirms the "untouchable" zone of a sailor's "true dignity," this insistence is qualified by his identification with the seeping body: "But what torments must that seaman undergo who, while his back bleeds at the gangway, bleeds agonized drops of shame from his soul!" (142). The whip cuts the body, and drops of the soul leak out. The slice of the whip gives the assembled viewers access to what the narrator earlier refers to as the "inmost soul" (47) and later as the interior "man's manhood" (280). The whip produces an intimate blood knowledge. The sailor's scars signify his degradation, a visceral exposure rendered permanently legible in the ruptures of his skin. White-Jacket describes a typical defense of corporal punishment by naval officers: "it can be inflicted in a moment; it consumes no valuable time; and when the prisoner's shirt is put on, *that* is the last of it" (139). The narrative of *White-Jacket* goes to great pains to show that that is *not* the last of it. The putting on of a shirt does not conceal the scars. This moment of punishment lasts a lifetime.

In this sense, flogging in *White-Jacket* presents a danger similar to tattooing in *Typee*: the prospect of indelible, invidious marking. In *Typee* the narrator fixates not on the melodrama of cannibalism but on the horror of tattooing. Similarly, in *White-Jacket* the narrator focuses not on the dismemberment of the body – which is satirically rendered in a series of chapters describing the bungled operations of the naval ship's surgeon, the eager Dr. Cadwallader Cuticle – but on the outrage of flogging. Dr. Cuticle identifies, isolates, and amputates. A "Morbid Anatomist" fascinated with diseased parts (249), he does not recognize systemic conditions. The good doctor is literally and figuratively an artist of the cuticle, the superficial integument. His knife passes through the dermis to the muscle and the marrow, but the marks are fleeting. With a slash, the patient is separated from his distressed flesh. The horror in *White-Jacket* is not the severing of amputation but the eloquent line cut of flogging.

White-Jacket draws the analogy between sailor and slave, and over the course of the narrative that analogy eludes its author. The analogy was often used by naval reformers and labor activists to appropriate the figure of the black slave and the experience of chattel slavery in order to advance the politics of white oppression and to establish a hierarchy of suffering. Attention was directed from the south to the north and from black slaves to white workers. Flogging represented such a violation in sailor narratives in part because the narrators imagined that unscathed white bodies were threatened with a disfiguring conversion. The term "slave" was definitive, endowing the term "sailor" with vitality and clarity and turning public concern to the imperiled figure of the white worker. Comparing sailor or worker with slave, many reformers articulated a racial choice for sentimental response and political action.

In *White-Jacket*, the analogy is not so easily mastered. Rather than aggrandizing the figure of the sailor while protecting him from the taint of racial slavery, the analogies in *White-Jacket* threaten to expose the sailors as slaves. The distance sustained in the hierarchical comparisons threatens to collapse. The flow of meaning is no longer conducted through contrived channels. Instead, the floodgates open and the figure of the sailor is inundated. Melville renders this condition not only through the accumulating burden of exposition (the impositions, regulations, and inscriptions in a man-of-war world) but also through plot and figure: White-Jacket's loss of balance on the yardarm, his fall into the ocean, and the almost fatal saturation of his white jacket.

The first chapter opens with the narrator describing how he manufactured his white jacket in order to protect himself from the harsh weather ahead in the trip around Cape Horn. Unable to obtain a regulation pea jacket from the purser's steward, he devises his own garment. He folds a white duck frock double at the bosom, slits it open, and pads it with old scraps of clothing. One in a series of Melville's overwritten symbols, White-Jacket's white jacket has been read as an emblem of personal alienation and illusory independence, a marker of class superiority, and a self-reflexive metaphor describing the weave of Melville's own texts: "bedarned and bequilted," "well-patched, padded, and porous" (4–5).[15]

Yet the jacket also has a more corporeal dimension. It is padded, porous – and white. The jacket is skin. It has a structure that contains secrets and invites inscriptions: "There were, also, several unseen recesses behind the arras; insomuch, that my jacket, like an old castle, was full of winding stairs, and mysterious closets, crypts, and cabinets; and like a confidential writing-desk, abounded in snug little out-of-the-way lairs and hiding-places, for the storage of valuables" (36). This skin is an "arras," a tapestry whose weave is intricate and eloquent. In *White-Jacket* the skin is represented as a surface filled with recesses of meaning. So inviting a prospect is this surface and so eager are the other sailors to investigate those recesses and to pilfer their contents that the narrator takes drastic action:

> I noticed a parcel of fellows skulking about after me, wherever I went. To a man, they were pickpockets, and bent upon pillaging me. In vain I kept clapping my pockets like nervous old gentlemen in a crowd; that same night I found myself minus several valuable articles. So, in the end, I masoned up my lockers and pantries; and save the two used for mittens, the white jacket ever after was pocketless. (37)

The narrator seeks to close the apertures that make him vulnerable to greedy eyes and intrusive hands. He seeks to shield himself from pickpockets of the skin. Even with sealed pockets he is not safe. The very texture of the jacket exposes him to danger. Stuffed and quilted and not waterproofed, the jacket acts like a "sponge" and becomes a "universal absorber" (4). Its pockets may be sealed, but its pores are open: "Of a damp day, my heartless shipmates even used to stand up against me, so powerful was the capillary attraction between this luckless jacket of mine and all drops of moisture" (4). In wet weather it drips, releasing liquid that is reminiscent of the "agonized drops of shame" (142) that bleed from the soul of the flogged victim. Soaked and heavy, the jacket is a continuous burden to bear.

Yet it is not just the structure and texture of the jacket but also its color that becomes filled with meaning and exposes the narrator to danger. As in the chromatic reversals of *Moby-Dick* ("The Whiteness of the Whale"), Melville here represents whiteness as subject to the kind of anxious regard usually associated with blackness. Unable to obtain a standard navy-blue jacket, the narrator repeatedly tries to requisition some black paint in order to waterproof his garment and to change its "complexion" to a "dark hue" closer to that of his comrades (78, 120). Again and again, his request is denied by the first lieutenant. The resonant joke here is that White-Jacket wishes to darken his skin so that he can conform to the appearance of the majority. The darker color will protect him and enable him to assimilate. Yet the narrator is unable to change his color and remains subject to the abuse of his peers. His mess mates "nourished a prejudice" against his white jacket (61). Neither blue nor black, White-Jacket is vulnerable. His whiteness makes him uncomfortably visible: "And thus, in those long, dark nights, when it was my quarter-watch on deck, and not in the top, and others went skulking and 'sogering' about the decks, secure from detection – their identity undiscoverable – my own hapless jacket forever proclaimed the name of its wearer" (120). Like Tommo in *Typee*, White-Jacket desires the freedom to move through his society undetected and unknown, but White-Jacket's own white skin, not the prospect of an alien tattooed skin, betrays him. Unlike Tommo, he is already a marked man.

In the chapter "The Jacket Aloft," White-Jacket becomes a target of interpretation and the victim of an almost lethal misreading. Seeing him high on the main-royal-yard, where he has gone to stargaze wrapped in his white jacket, the narrator's shipmates mistake him for the ghost of the recently deceased ship's cooper and they collapse the sails, nearly causing him to fall:

> . . . after hailing me, and bidding me descend, to test my corporeality, and getting no answer, they had lowered the halyards in affright.
> In a rage I tore off the jacket, and threw it on the deck.
> "Jacket," cried I, "you must change your complexion! you must hie to the dyers and be dyed, that I may live. I have but one poor life, White Jacket, and that life I can not spare. I can not consent to die for *you*, but be dyed you must for me. You can dye many times without injury; but I can not die without irreparable loss, and running the eternal risk." (78)

The narrator's white jacket invites the testing of his corporeality. The punning on "dye" and "die" extends the serious joke about the danger in which his white skin places him. A dye – a change of complexion – will, he hopes, save him from death. To dye is to live. Yet the wordplay is not the most notable feature of this passage. In this scene, the character has a jacket but the jacket also has a character. The narrator tears off his skin in a rage and speaks to it. The articulate skin, which "proclaims the name of its wearer" (120), here is personified only to be shouted down. The narrator has a close, quarrelsome, punning relationship with his skin. It's either you or me, he warns his skin. "Jacket! jacket!" the narrator both laments and threatens later in the book, "thou hast much to answer for, jacket!" (334). His skin defines and endangers his character. The name of his skin is, after all, the name of his character – the only name he has – and the name of his story.

White-Jacket tells the story of the struggle of a man with and in his skin. The book presages the meditation on skin in *Moby-Dick*, especially in the chapter titled "The Blanket." White-Jacket's cutaneous dispute in "The

Jacket Aloft" ends in a draw. His request for black paint is again refused by the first lieutenant, and he dons the white jacket once more. According to the log books of the *United States*, the frigate on which Melville served, there was an ample supply of blue naval jackets, one of which Melville himself certainly wore. In Melville's source for the final chapter about the jacket, *Life on Board a Man-of-War* (1829), the sartorial encumbrance is easily removed.[16] The white jacket on display in Melville's book is not the result of biographical exigencies or literary pilferings. Melville's emphasis on the jacket – its confinement, its capillary attraction, and its color – evokes the treatments of skin color and texture in narratives of slavery and in antebellum African American fiction.

Like black skin, the narrator's skin renders him visible and vulnerable. Like black skin, the narrator's skin becomes ominous, the sign of his difference and his degradation. White-Jacket's skin, like the white paper and the white skin produced in the factories of Melville's sketch "The Tartarus of Maids" (1855), is not blank. It bears the imprint of the man-of-war factory in which it was made. In *White-Jacket*, the white skin that was supposed to protect the narrator becomes a trap. The insulating distance between sailor and slave collapses, as the white sailor's skin becomes infected by association with blackness. His skin no longer erects a barrier, no longer defines and preserves the distance. His skin betrays him. Or, rather, it at first betrays him but then it saves him. In the end, White-Jacket's skin *does* die for him.

At the close of the *Neversink*'s journey, near the Virginia coast, while the narrator is up in the rigging working the sails, his jacket fails him for the last time. The ship tilts in the swell of a wave and the narrator, mistaking the jacket which has blown over his head for the sail, tries to support himself by grasping the white fabric. He leans on his skin, and it falters. He plunges a hundred feet into the ocean and, like Pip, the castaway in *Moby-Dick*, he undergoes a watery epiphany, suspended between life and death. Yet while Pip's epiphany drives him mad – "The sea had jeeringly kept his finite body up, but drowned the infinite of his soul" – White-Jacket's experience produces the opposite effect.[17] It results in the submersion of his skin and the buoying of his soul:

> I essayed to swim toward the ship; but instantly I was conscious of a feeling like being pinioned in a feather-bed, and, moving my hands, felt my jacket puffed out above my tight girdle with water. I strove to tear it off; but it was looped together here and there, and the strings were not then to be sundered by hand. I whipped out my knife, that was tucked at my belt, and ripped my jacket straight up and down, as if I were ripping open myself. With a violent

struggle I then burst out of it, and was free. Heavily soaked, it slowly sank before my eyes.

Sink! sink! oh shroud! thought I; sink forever! accursed jacket that thou art!

"See that white shark!" cried a horrified voice from the taffrail; "he'll have that man down his hatchway! Quick! the *grains*! the *grains*!"

The next instant that barbed bunch of harpoons pierced through and through the unfortunate jacket, and swiftly sped down with it out of sight.

(394)

"The gash being made," Melville writes in the first chapter, describing the incision that changed white shirt into white jacket, "a metamorphosis took place, transcending any related by Ovid" (3). The gash made at the end of the book enables an even grander transformation. It heals the wound inflicted by the exposure of the affinities between sailors and slaves. It reorients the sailor who has lost his bearings. White-Jacket violently frees himself from the "shroud" of his skin. In a final act of misreading, his fellow sailors interpret the sloughed jacket as a white shark and pierce it with a barrage of harpoons. The life of the jacket ends in ritual slaughter, a celebration of the regenerative powers of white skin.

The wrangle of man with skin in *White-Jacket* culminates in this chapter, "The Last of the Jacket." Here the fall into the ocean that earlier had been averted is now endured, and the flogging that had loomed is elevated into an act of liberating self-evisceration. The fantasy of murder and suicide that the narrator had directed at his captain is now turned toward himself as, breathtakingly, he murders his own skin and then is transfigured. When he could not unburden himself of his white jacket during a shipboard auction, the narrator compared his garment to the white shirt of Hercules, which, steeped in the centaur Nessus's poisoned blood, had burned his skin and which, when Hercules attempted to tear it off, had taken large pieces of flesh with it: "So, unable to conjure it into the possession of another, and withheld from burying it out of sight forever, my jacket stuck to me like the fatal shirt on Nessus" (203). Yet this allusion seems more appropriate to the protagonist of Melville's *Pierre*, who is consumed by a searing consciousness of living in his own skin and in the skin of beliefs about genealogy, gender, and desire. White-Jacket, on the other hand, has the ability to cast off his vestments. When the joke about the narrator's articulate skin goes too far, he cuts it. These are the astounding properties of white skin as represented at the end of *White-Jacket*: its owner can silence it, dye it, remove it. White skin can be wiped clean.

If in the polemics of naval reformers and the narratives of seamen the lash inscribes the analogy between sailor and slave on the backs of white sailors, then *White-Jacket* ultimately offers a fantasy by which that inscription may be erased: the vulnerable, revealing surface can be shed. White-Jacket rips himself open and steps outside of his skin. He can detach himself from his blighted parts. Unlike Ahab in *Moby-Dick*, who asks the blacksmith Perth if he can smooth the seams and dents in his forehead and is told that such damage cannot be repaired, White-Jacket does not need an artisan to effect his bodily reconstruction. He has his own tools. In the course of Melville's analysis of martial society, the narrator realizes that his own body has become degraded, overwritten with meaning by the lash. Since it is no longer pickpockets that endanger him but his skin itself, White-Jacket turns from sealing his pockets to slashing his garment. In a spectacular scene of self-flagellation, White-Jacket, the white slave, flogs himself free.

Melville shows the reader how a white man was almost made a slave and, incredibly, made a man again. He follows the logic of racial conversion threatened in antebellum political discourse and especially prominent in seamen's narratives: "I'm no Negro slave. . . . Then I'll make you one!" (Dana, *Two Years before the Mast*); "There are thousands of enterprising young men in this country who would be glad to find employment in the whale fishery, if they could do so without becoming slaves" (Browne, *Etchings of a Whaling Cruise*); "[the naval code] should not convert into slaves some of the citizens of a nation of freemen" (*White-Jacket*, 144).[18] Reflecting on the representations of writers like Dana and Browne, Melville explores the ways in which anxieties about likeness generate efforts at discrimination. He examines the hinges in the articulation of the analogy between white men and black slaves. He shows the reversals and renewals enabled by that analogy. And he reveals at the pivot, at the preposition "like" around which the meanings turn, a crucial difference that the analogy clarifies and reinforces. In the comparative anatomy laid bare in *White-Jacket*, to be "like" a slave is to be encased in skin that you cannot remove. To be unlike a slave is to possess a white jacket that is portable and divestible. *White-Jacket* ends with a vehement fantasy of erased marks and regenerated flesh: an emancipation from one's own skin.

In *Typee* and in *White-Jacket*, Melville represents prominent scenes in the drama of antebellum racial discourse, in which the male body becomes charged with meaning. Melville's prose registers, amplifies, explores, and recoils from this charge. In *Typee*, he examines and draws back from the scene of tattooing, in which a Caucasian body is threatened with invidious markings that previously had been confined to human types seen as deviating from the standard. In *White-Jacket*, and particularly in the scenes of flogging, the distinction between unmarked and marked bodies collapses under the pressure of the extended analogy between sailors and slaves. In both books, the hierarchies between subject and object are disturbed, as the body of the observer becomes vulnerable to being marked by and as the body of the observed. Yet the unsettling of distance and rank in the two books is different. In *Typee*, Tommo's position is reversed when he is menaced by Karky's gaze and by the touch of his needles. He flees to the decks of an American whaling vessel, and regains his status. Unlike Tommo in *Typee*, the sailors in *White-Jacket* have no place to hide. The United States *Neversink* itself is the domain of disfiguring authority. In *White-Jacket*, the hierarchies of position are collapsed rather than reversed. The collapse of the difference between sailor and slave precludes the possibility of literal flight and restoration. Such dangers require extreme measures.

Yet the solution offered at the end of *White-Jacket* is too easy. If *Typee* ends with a physical flight from racial encounter and corporeal inscription, then *White-Jacket* climaxes with a figurative flight. In *Typee*, Tommo's effort to go native is cut short by the specter of punctured skin, and he violently takes his leave from Nukuheva. In *White-Jacket*, the prolonged encounter between the terms "sailor" and "slave" played out by the narrator is ruptured by the prospect of lacerated flesh, and White-Jacket bloodlessly flees from his skin. White-Jacket removes the taint of the lash through a series of incisions made "straight up and down" his abdomen (394). White-Jacket's knife is an obstetrical instrument, enabling a self-inflicted and self-generating cesarean section performed in the cleansing amniotic suspension of the sea.

In the final chapter, Melville suggests that the corporeal escape performed in "The Last of the Jacket" is illusory. At the beginning of a valedictory sermon otherwise composed of commonplaces, White-Jacket offers an eerie melding of cryptography, incarnation, and incarceration:

> And though far out of sight of land, for ages and ages we continue to sail with sealed orders, and our last destination remains a secret to ourselves and our officers; yet our final haven was predestinated ere we slipped from the stocks at Creation.
>
> Thus sailing with sealed orders, we ourselves are the repositories of the secret packet, whose mysterious contents we long to learn. There are no mysteries out of ourselves. (398)

The sailors in *White-Jacket* prefigure the Polynesian harpooneer Queequeg in *Moby-Dick*, whose tattooed skin offers the viewer a mystical treatise on truth that Queequeg himself cannot read, and the young American heir Pierre Glendinning in *Pierre*, whose coat, between the cloth and the heavy quilted lining, contains the worn yet still legible philosophical pamphlet

"Chronometricals and Horologicals," whose insights Pierre had been carrying within himself all the time he was searching for them. The sailors in *White-Jacket*, themselves the repositories of the mysterious contents they long to learn, form part of Melville's astonishing gallery of legible, tantalizing bodies, texts in flesh that contain, despite their owners' ignorance or efforts at divestment, a world of secrets for the viewer. There are no mysteries out of ourselves because, in Melville's anatomy of antebellum racial discourse, the deepest mysteries lie in ourselves, waiting, longing to be read on the surface of our bodies.

NOTES

1. For interpretations of Melville's career as closely tied to issues of race and slavery, see Sidney Kaplan, "Herman Melville and the American National Sin: The Meaning of 'Benito Cereno,'" *Journal of Negro History* 41 (October 1956): 311–38 and 42 (January 1957): 11–37; and Carolyn L. Karcher, *Shadow over the Promised Land* (Baton Rouge: Louisiana State University Press, 1980). See also my *Melville's Anatomies*, forthcoming from the University of California Press.

2. E. G. Squier, "American Ethnology," *American Whig Review* 9 (April 1849): 386. On the "American school," see William Stanton, *The Leopard's Spots* (Chicago: University of Chicago Press, 1960); Reginald Horsman, *Race and Manifest Destiny* (Cambridge: Harvard University Press, 1981); George Frederickson, *The Black Image in the White Mind* (New York: Harper and Row, Publishers, 1971); and Robert E. Bieder, *Science Encounters the Indian* (Norman: University of Oklahoma Press, 1986).

3. Robert Knox, *The Races of Men* (1850; 2nd ed. London: Henry Renshaw, 1862), v.

4. In *The Corporeal Self* (Baltimore: The Johns Hopkins University Press, 1981), Sharon Cameron argues that Melville conceived of philosophical problems of identity in corporeal terms and was preoccupied with questions of bodily boundaries and bodily size. Toni Morrison and Hortense Spillers have suggested ways to talk about race in literature that avoid the reductiveness of earlier approaches such as cataloguing the images of "others," celebrating an author's egalitarianism, or castigating his racism. Morrison writes about the construction of race in language and Spillers about the grammar of meanings attached to different bodies. See Toni Morrison, "Unspeakable Things Unspoken: The Afro-American Presence in American Literature," *Michigan Quarterly Review* 28 (Winter 1989): 1–34, and *Playing in the Dark* (Cambridge: Harvard University Press, 1992); and Hortense Spillers, "Mama's Baby, Papa's Maybe: An American Grammar Book," *Diacritics* 17 (Summer 1987): 65–81.

5. In *Melville in the South Seas* (New York: Columbia University Press, 1939), Charles Roberts Anderson describes the differences between Melville's actual four-week stay on Nukuheva from July 9 to August 9, 1842, after deserting

the whaler *Acushnet* with his companion Richard Tobias Greene, and his narrator Tommo's fictional four-month visit. See also T. Walter Herbert, *Marquesan Encounters* (Cambridge: Harvard University Press, 1980), for analyses of the Marquesan context and the interpretive perspectives of different travelers.

6. Herman Melville, *Typee; A Peep at Polynesian Life*, Vol. 1 of *The Writings of Herman Melville*, ed. Harrison Hayford, Hershel Parker, and G. Thomas Tanselle (Evanston and Chicago: Northwestern University Press and the Newberry Library, 1968), 26. These passages criticizing American and European barbarism and other similar passages were excised from the second, revised American edition of *Typee* published in July 1846 as the result of negotiations between Melville and his publisher, John Wiley. See Leon Howard, "Historical Note," in the Northwestern–Newberry edition of *Typee*, 277–301. Subsequent references to *Typee* are given in parentheses in the body of this essay.

7. A. J. von Krusenstern, *Voyage Round the World* (2 vols., London: Printed by C. Roworth for John Murray, 1813); G. H. von Langsdorff, *Voyages and Travels* (2 vols., London: Printed for Henry Colburn, 1813–14); David Porter, *Journal of a Cruise Made to the Pacific Ocean* (2 vols., Philadelphia: Bradford and Inskeep, 1815).

8. For illustrations of Marquesan tattooing, see Langsdorff, *Voyages and Travels*, and Willowdean Chatterson Handy, *Tattooing in the Marquesas* (Honolulu: Bernice P. Bishop Museum, 1922). For ethnological illustrations that chart the terrain of the human body, see Petrus Camper, *The Works of the Late Professor Camper*, trans. Thomas Cogan (London: Printed for C. Dilly, 1794); Johann Caspar Lavater, *Essays on Physiognomy*, trans. Thomas Holcroft (London: William Tegg and Co., 1848); Orson S. Fowler and Lorenzo N. Fowler, *The Illustrated Self-Instructor in Phrenology and Physiology* (New York: Fowler and Wells, 1849); Samuel George Morton, *Crania Americana* (Philadelphia: J. Dobson, 1839) and *Crania Ægyptiaca* (Philadelphia: John Pennington, 1844); and Josiah C. Nott and George R. Gliddon, eds., *Types of Mankind* (1854; rpt. Miami, Fla.: Mnemosyne Publishing Co., Inc., 1969).

9. On the linked scientific and artistic investigations of the human body in the late eighteenth and nineteenth centuries, see Michel Foucault, *The Order of Things* (1966; New York: Pantheon Books, 1971); Hugh Honour, *From the American Revolution to World War I*, Vol. 4, parts 1 and 2, of *The Image of the Black in Western Art* (Houston: The Menil Foundation, Inc.; Cambridge: Harvard University Press, 1989); and Barbara Maria Stafford, *Body Criticism* (Cambridge: MIT Press, 1991).

10. Charles S. Stewart, *A Visit to the South Seas* (2 vols., New York: John P. Haven, 1831); Frederick Debell Bennett, *Narrative of a Whaling Voyage* (2 vols., London: Richard Bentley, 1840). Melville remarks upon the "European" appearance of the Marquesans through his narrator, Tommo, in *Typee*, 180–4.

11. Langsdorff, *Voyages and Travels*, 1:108–9, 119.

12. Handy, *Tattooing in the Marquesas*, Plate III. Although Handy's depiction dates from 1922, eighty years after Melville's visit to the Marquesas, mid-nineteenth-century observers such as Bennett confirm the traditional aspect of the designs. See Bennett, *Narrative of a Whaling Voyage*, 1:284.

13. William McNally, *Evils and Abuses in the Naval and Merchant Service Exposed* (Boston: Cassady and March, 1839); Richard Henry Dana, Jr., *Two Years Before the Mast* (1840; New York: Penguin Books, 1981); Samuel Leech, *Thirty Years from Home* (Boston: Tappan and Dennet, 1843); John Ross Browne, *Etchings of a Whaling Cruise* (1846; Cambridge: Belknap Press of Harvard University Press, 1968); Frederick Douglass, *My Bondage and My Freedom* (1855; New York: Dover Publications, 1969); William Wells Brown, *Clotel; or, The President's Daughter* (1853; New York: Carol Publishing Group, 1969). For discussions of the analogy with slavery, see Patricia Allen Zirker, "Evidence of the Slavery Dilemma in *White-Jacket*," *American Quarterly* 18 (Fall 1966): 476–92; Marcus Cunliffe, *Chattel Slavery and Wage Slavery* (Athens: The University of Georgia Press, 1969); Myra C. Glenn, *Campaigns Against Corporal Punishment* (Albany: State University of New York Press, 1984); Karen Sanchez-Eppler, "Bodily Bonds: The Intersecting Rhetorics of Feminism and Abolition," *Representations* 24 (Fall 1988): 28–59; Jean Fagan Yellin, *Women and Sisters* (New Haven: Yale University Press, 1989); Robert S. Levine, *Conspiracy and Romance* (Cambridge and New York: Cambridge University Press, 1989); David Roediger, *The Wages of Whiteness* (New York: Verso, 1991); and Richard Brodhead, *Cultures of Letters* (Chicago: The University of Chicago Press, 1993).

14. Herman Melville, *White-Jacket; or The World in a Man-of-War*, Vol. 5 of *The Writings of Herman Melville*, ed. Harrison Hayford, Hershel Parker, and G. Thomas Tanselle (Evanston and Chicago: Northwestern University Press and the Newberry Library, 1970), 356. Subsequent references to *White-Jacket* are given in parentheses in the body of this essay.

15. For interpretations of the jacket, see Howard P. Vincent, *The Tailoring of Melville's White-Jacket* (Evanston: Northwestern University Press, 1970); James E. Miller, Jr., *A Reader's Guide to Herman Melville* (New York: Farrar, Straus and Cudahy, 1962); Larry Reynolds, "Anti-Democratic Emphasis in *White-Jacket*," *American Literature* 48 (March 1976): 13–28; and Wai-chee Dimock, *Empire for Liberty* (Princeton: Princeton University Press, 1989).

16. In *Melville in the South Seas*, Anderson describes Melville's experience on the *United States* and how he transmuted this experience and his source accounts into the voyage of the *Neversink* in *White-Jacket*. See also Vincent, *Tailoring of Melville's White-Jacket*.

17. Herman Melville, *Moby-Dick; or The Whale*, Vol. 6 of *The Writings of Herman Melville*, ed. Harrison Hayford, Hershel Parker, and G. Thomas Tanselle (Evanston and Chicago: Northwestern University Press and the Newberry Library, 1970), 414.

18. Dana, *Two Years Before the Mast*, 152; Browne, *Etchings of a Whaling Cruise*, 496.

2

STERLING STUCKEY

The Tambourine in Glory:
African Culture and Melville's Art

I pushed on my way, till I got to Chapel-street, which I crossed; and then
going under a cloister-like arch of stone. . . . I emerged into the fine
quadrangle of the Merchants' Exchange.

Herman Melville, *Redburn*

I walk a world that is mine; and enter many nations, as Mungo Park rested
in African carts.

Herman Melville, *Mardi*

In his first eleven years, Herman Melville lived in an environment in which
slavery was being gradually legislated out of existence, its shadow receding
across New York State. Despite the movement to abolish slavery, however,
denials of freedom less severe but no less real were much in evidence. There
was, for that matter, little indication that racial equality was being considered by northern whites, most of whom did not oppose southern slavery.

Melville was born in August 1819, a time when slave music and dance
enjoyed brilliantly ironic expression in public and private, North as well as
South. In New York City and across the state, slaves were observed dancing
and making music on street corners and in marketplaces, as if preparing
for the Pinkster Festival that, once a year in May for several days and at
times in multiple locations, engaged the attention of white spectators. As
in expressions of black culture in America generally, participants in festivals revealed but a portion of their art because it was dangerous to com-
municate clear signs of African spirituality.[1]

The appreciation of irony allowed slaves to conceal, beneath a protective
covering of improvisation, that which was unpalatable to whites, thereby
preserving what was proper to them by almost endlessly changing its face.
In other words, harsh reality encouraged experimentation to alter cherished
values in order to protect them at their core. Slaves, then, mainly perceived
reality as flux artistically, and therefore in a religious sense as well, for the

37

distinction between the sacred and the secular was not often drawn by them and has long been the least understood quality of their culture.[2]

Melville's family was wonderfully placed, residentially, to be exposed to black celebrations in nineteenth-century New York City. The address at which he was born, No. 6 Pearl Street, faced the "tip of Manhattan Island, on one side, and on the other the wharves and shipping offices of the South Street waterfront." Though slaves were known to entertain whites along the wharves of New York and to reach such destinations in skiffs, only in time did such settings, with respect to African culture, become important to Melville.[3] However, celebrations of blacks along Broadway were, from an early age, impossible for him to ignore, the music alone commanding attention, as did the rhythmic march/dance of those in processions.

Until he was ten, Melville's addresses were located in sections of the city either near or on Broadway, with one at 55 Cortlandt that was ideal for hearing or attending Broadway celebrations. From that address a procession celebrating the coming abolition of slavery in New York almost certainly was heard, for its path brought it within hearing distance of the southern Broadway area in which the celebrants made music that to the young might seem as natural as the sound of rain or the play of sunlight. Melville's exposure to black music was especially full in his youth: he was but six in 1825 when the "great procession of negroes, some of them well-dressed" paraded, "two by two, preceded by music and a flag . . . down Broadway." The parade held the attention of onlookers:

> An African club, called the Wilberforce Society, thus celebrated the . . . abolition of slavery in New York, and concluded the day by a dinner and ball. The colored people of New York, belonging to this society, have a fund, contained of their own, raised by weekly subscription, which is employed in assisting sick and unfortunate blacks. This fund, contained in a sky-blue box, was carried in the procession; the treasurer holding in his hand a large gilt key; the rest of the officers wore ribands [sic] of several colors, and badges like the officers of free masons; marshals with long staves walked outside the procession. During a quarter of an hour, scarcely any but black faces were to be seen in Broadway.[4]

This was part of the cultural world of New Yorkers, who had little inclination to deny that the music of blacks was substantially different from that of white Americans. The Wilberforce Society was known to march with its own band, and its style of marching in 1825 did not substantially differ from what it was before or following the celebration of that year. In this regard, it is more than coincidence that many of its members, whether born in Africa or in America, referred to themselves as "Africans."[5]

The 55 Cortlandt address was but a ten-minute walk from City Hall and the Commons, the latter a staging area for parades and for celebrations like Pinkster. Moreover, the Negros Burial Ground, in which 20,000 African women, men, and children were buried, was part of the Commons, a sacred place revered by people of African descent that attracted African dancers and musicians and storytellers throughout the year. It is doubtful that Melville, when no more than six or seven, would have been unaware of Pinkster activity at the Commons, or at its burial ground, since both were in his own neighborhood.[6]

Reports of firearms and displays of firecrackers announced 4th of July celebrations for whites in New York City, signaling for blacks their own day of celebration or regret to follow, except that in 1827 their celebration was special. On that July 5, the New York Emancipation Day parade, beginning at City Hall near 55 Cortlandt and continuing down Broadway to the Battery, won the attention of most who glanced in its direction: The Grand Marshal for the day was Samuel Hardenburgh, "a splendid looking man, in cocked hat and drawn sword, mounted on a milk-white steed . . . his aids on horseback dashing up and down the line. . . ." A sacred occurrence and a time of jubilee, the participants assembled just a block from the Negros Burial Ground, around which hundreds of Africans gathered while waiting for thousands more before following the line of march toward the southern terminus of Broadway.[7]

It does not greatly matter whether Melville observed this particular celebration of the abolition of slavery, for many white children in attendance were his cohorts, and just as black youth remembered the event long after it occurred, it also remained a part of the consciousness of young whites who saw and heard the jubilant marchers. Yet Melville might have been standing, chaperoned, among them on the Broadway sidewalk, hearing and observing resplendently dressed – "in scarfs of silk with gold-edgings" – members of black mutual aid societies "with colored bands of music and their banners appropriately lettered and painted: 'The New York African Society for Mutual Relief,' 'The Wilberforce Benevolent Society,' and 'The Clarkson Benevolent Society.' " Then followed "the people five or six abreast, from grown men to small boys." Also marching were members of the various African marine societies, who when not at home were at sea on ships out of New York port.[8]

News accounts preceding and following Emancipation Day were in various New York newspapers and known to literate New Yorkers. *The New York Statesman* reported that "a large body of coloured people from Brooklyn and other towns in this state" made their way "through the principal streets . . . under their respective banners."[9] They were heard for many blocks, East and West, North and South, especially since, in the heat of summer, windows were up as the joyous celebrants moved along their rather suburban route. A participant in the parade described the scene:

> The side-walks were crowded with the wives, daughters, sisters, and mothers of the celebrants, representing every State in the Union, and not a few with gay bandanna handkerchiefs, betraying their West Indian birth: neither was Africa itself unrepresented; hundreds who had survived the middle passage and a youth in slavery joined in the joyful procession. The people of those days rejoiced in their nationality and hesitated not to call each other Africans, or descendants of Africa. . . . It was a proud day for Samuel Hardenburgh, Grand Marshall, splendidly mounted, as he passed through the west gate of the Park, saluted the Mayor on the City Hall steps, and then took his way down Broadway to the Battery.[10]

Black school boys fell "into the ranks of the great celebration" of "between 3 and four thousand." Stating that "the concourse was very great," the *New York American* added: "The music was unusually good: there were four or five bands, comprising a great variety of instruments, played with much skill, as will be readily believed, from the acknowledged talent for music of the African race."[11]

Few families could ignore a celebration of such dramatic quality, described by one source as a "shouting for joy . . . with *feet jubilant* to songs of freedom," which suggests a procession to improvised dance movements characteristic of black marchers in Africa and America. From what we know of black processions in nineteenth-century America, improvising dance while marching was the rule in the North as well as the South, and nowhere were the ingredients of such processions more pronounced than in Albany, whose slaves were second to none for improvisation in music and dance and known to parade on Pinkster Hill.[12]

One of the great festivals of New York, Pinkster was thought to be more robust in Melville's mother's hometown, Albany, than anywhere else in New York State.[13] His mother's family knew the festival from the time Africans began dominating its cultural forms in the late colonial period. More especially, Maria Gansevoort's patrician family was connected to Pinkster as few others were. Though one cannot speak of the connection with great certitude, the most noted Pinkster drummer, Jackie Quackenboss, may well have been owned by the Quackenboss family that married into the Gansevoort family in the late eighteenth century, when "every family of wealth and distinction owned one or more slaves."[14] Jackie was such a dramatic figure in Albany's cultural history that family lore concerning him would have been relished by one of Melville's imagination, and there is no reason to suppose it would have been withheld. In allowing Jackie to drum at Pinkster, the Quackenboss family provided crucial support to the festival and must have been proud that he bore their name.

We have a description of his drumming and the play of rhythm in early Pinkster days, probably in the early 1770s, when the whole Albany community was said to have observed the celebration:

> The principal instrument selected to furnish this important portion of the ceremony was a symmetrically formed *eel-pot*, with a cleanly dressed sheep skin drawn tightly over its wide and open extremity. . . . Astride this rude utensil sat Jackie Quackenboss, then in his prime of life and well known energy, beating lustily with his naked hands upon its loud sounding head, successively repeating the ever wild, though euphonic cry of *Hi-a bomba, bomba, bomba*, in full harmony with the thumping sounds. These vocal sounds were readily taken up and as oft repeated by the female portion of the spectators not otherwise engaged in the exercises of the scene, and accompanied by the beating of time with their ungloved hands, in strict accordance with the eel-pot melody.[15]

The dancers danced to such sounds, at times encircling Pinkster king Charley, who was from the Congo where circularity was the principal symbol of a subtle Bakongo faith that affirmed the spirituality of dance rhythms not unlike those considered "secular" by westerners. What was sacred for the African was regulated by such rhythms, which contributed to a form of spiritual recreation for the hundreds of slave participants in the festival. Drum rhythms and rhythmic cries from Jackie Quackenboss, joined by the chanting cries and hand clapping of African women, satisfied both the sacred and "secular" needs of Africans. But most whites thought they were viewing the dance and music of heathens bereft of spirituality.[16]

In 1793, arson in Albany caused such devastation that "the heart of the city was enveloped in smoke and flames." Munsell reports that such was the seriousness of the fire that, of Albany's 5,000 residents, "every man, woman and child able to handle an empty leather fire bucket was pressed into service." There is no question that Melville's mother's family contributed to the fire brigades: the fire flared first at the home of his great-uncle, Leonard Gansevoort, who was targeted by a suitor either forbidden to see one of his daughters or rejected by her. A slave named Pomp, said to have been offered a gold watch to put the Gansevoort residence to flames, allegedly enlisted the support of two slave women to that end. All three were executed on Pinkster Hill, first the women and later Pomp, and buried in its cemetery for blacks. The fire was a searing reminder to whites of their connection to the festival, to slaves at Pinkster of shadows in the light.[17]

Had Melville's mother, grandmother, and other relatives elected to discuss the conflagration with the youngster during his visits to Albany in the
1820s, or when he later lived there, they would have had much to talk
about. The number of slaves in the ward in which the Gansevoorts lived
at the time – they made up close to 26 percent of the ward – meant that
they and other whites there shared living quarters with, and moved among,
a higher percentage of slaves than usual. Still, the relative paucity of slaves
in Albany County and New York State – 5.41 and 7.64 percent in 1790,
respectively – undercuts the assumption that slaves, in a given county or
state, had to constitute the majority or a large minority of the population
to have power in the cultural sphere.[18]

By the time Melville was eight, he was taking dancing lessons and becoming more sensitive to forms of dance that might be seen near his New
York City home. No less exciting was New York's Catharine Market,
where challenging dance drew slave artists from Long Island, from New
Jersey, and, as the competition for honors became more intense, from the
city itself. Given the rigor of the competition, dancers from New York
could not afford to perform only in the market for a few days annually.
Just as dancers from Long Island practiced year round "on the barn floor,
or in a frolic," those from the city could not have excelled at Pinkster, as
they did in time, without much practice before coming to the market in the
spring.[19]

Though Pinkster in Albany was said to have ended in 1811, a matter
that remains to be resolved, the more important point is that slave dance
and music defined Pinkster rather than the reverse, which means that dance
and music brought to Pinkster would have been practiced following Pinkster as before. Regarding the end of Pinkster in Albany, the opposing argument is that Pinkster there lasted beyond King Charley's death in 1824,
after which it "was observed with less enthusiasm, and finally sank into
such a low nuisance as to fall under the ban of the authorities."[20] In this
view, more than the memory of Pinkster lived in the springtime, perhaps
into the mid-1830s, which was well after the Melvilles took up residence
in Albany in 1830. But under no circumstances could Melville, in the
1820s, have missed black dance and music during summer visits to Albany,
for Munsell writes that, during that time, "*every* corner was vocal with the
concerts of whistling negroes."[21]

When living in Albany, Melville was enrolled in the Albany Academy,
which his grandparents helped endow and establish in 1813 to educate all
but those "in an absolute state of penury." Just "a few rods" from Pinkster
hill and its burial grounds, the Academy was in a large park surrounded
by a picket fence.[22] Consequently, on his way to and from school, and

while there, Melville saw Pinkster hill and the grounds that spread out around it. Indeed, the Academy practically shared those grounds. While he later appreciated the significance of that location, his preparation for such understanding began with exposure to Pinkster music and dance on Albany corners in the previous decade.

Pinkster's special relationship to his family on his mother's side in Albany, together with his family's location in New York near Pinkster Commons and its burial ground, meant that it was virtually impossible for Melville to avoid, over nearly twenty years, contact with African culture – and issues – before first voyaging from the United States. Moreover, he enriched his knowledge of black culture by reading travelers' accounts of African culture, which gave him special insight into how blacks were affected by life in America and how their values affected others. His interest in foreign places, through travel no less than through reading, is convincing evidence that Melville was more prone than most Americans to immerse himself in different values: Newton Arvin writes that names of travelers such as Captain Cook, Krusenstern, Ledyard, Vancouver, and Mungo Park "scintillated before him like constellations during his whole boyhood, as the names of great soldiers do before other boys. . . ."[23]

Melville found in Park's *Travels in the Interior Districts of Africa* revelations of African humanity so at odds with conceptions of Africa held by whites and free blacks in America that a dramatic shift in his thinking about Africa occurred. However favorably disposed toward Africans he may have been before reading *Interior Districts*, what is revealed there concerning their work skills must have startled him, for the thought that Africans brought any skills into slavery clashed violently with the prevailing thesis that, as a people, they were by nature ignorant, hopelessly inferior to whites.

While reading the works of Park and other travelers in Africa, Melville confronted in a highly personal way his relationship to African people, and through them people of African descent in America. Contesting another young man for intellectual leadership of a youth organization in Albany, he was accused of being a "moral Ethiopian," a charge not unrelated to a companion reference to him as a "Ciceronian baboon," both of which sought to place him among the despised blacks of Africa and America.[24] The injustice of the attacks made him feel something of what blacks in Albany and the nation routinely were made to feel. But, beyond all personal considerations, his grasp of the economic value of slavery to the nation, derived from travel accounts of Africa, was at least as certain as his awareness, derived from experience, that dance formed the radiating core of slave culture in America, a force of such power even in the North that it met needs of whites as well as blacks. Such understanding was crystallizing in his Albany years as a teenager and, in little more than a decade thereafter, took impressive form in *Moby-Dick*.

But first, Melville went to sea and reflected on certain questions from his floating university: "Beware of enlisting in your vigilant fisheries any lad with lean brow and hollow eye," he has written, "who offers to ship with the Phædon instead of Bowditch in his head."[25] Had there been no blacks on the *Saint Lawrence*, the ship on which he first sailed at nineteen, the fact that its cargo was cotton bound for Liverpool, once a major slave trading port, would have excited interest in slavery not unrelated to T. E. Bowditch's travels in Africa in one as sensitive and bright as he. More precisely, movement of the principal product of antebellum slavery to a port from which ships once sailed to deliver Africans to the slave fields of the South was not lost on young Melville, whose father had also sailed to Liverpool and taken an interest in the city.

While there, Melville's imagination was seized by statuary honoring the memory of Lord Nelson, erected twenty-three years before his arrival on the *Saint Lawrence*. The figure of Nelson, triumphant though dying, looms above four suffering victims chained around the base which reminded young Melville of slaves, his thoughts reverting "to Virginia and Carolina. . . ." During this initial stay in Liverpool, he returned to this statuary many times to see the "woe-begone figures of captives . . . with swarthy limbs and manacles" so prominently represented, and he later put the statuary to use in both *Redburn* and "Benito Cereno."[26]

Tracing the footsteps of his father through Liverpool, Redburn had come upon the statuary. There is reason to believe that his father was drawn from Allan Melvill, Melville's own father, who had himself, like his fictional counterpart, befriended the distinguished abolitionist described by Redburn: "the good and great Roscoe, the intrepid enemy of the [slave] trade; who in every way devoted his fine talents to its suppression," writing a poem about it – "*The Wrongs of Africa*" (R, 156). Thus, with his guidebook in search of the spirit of his father, Redburn identified that father, and hence Melville's father, with the values of a leading opponent of slavery and the slave trade.

Despite its moving treatment of poverty and slavery, *Redburn* has not been considered particularly important in Melville's corpus, Melville himself asserting that it was written primarily because he needed money, that such a need defined its value.[27] But just as he accumulated material in youth from which he later fashioned a stunning dance scene in *Moby-Dick*, his Liverpool experience provided thoughts on how to later fashion, in "Benito Cereno," perhaps as complicated a symbol as has been discussed in literature. His Harvard, his Yale – his time at sea – gave him time to consider how he might transform what he was learning into art.

His presence on the *Acushnet* during a later voyage afforded him an opportunity to explore cultural interaction between black and white sailors. The *Acushnet* had "the usual mixture of free Negroes, Portuguese, and strays from the north of Europe" together with a majority "with good New England names," which made for a cultural laboratory in which Melville might thrive as a student of that difference he increasingly came to value.[28] Being at sea tested, in a highly focused manner, his cultural as well as other perceptions. In this regard, one must not underestimate the degree to which African influences in music and dance remained with free Negroes, resulting in artistic and spiritual qualities that, in some instances, clearly distinguished them from other sailors.

When in his mid-twenties, with his years at sea behind him, Melville witnessed Pinkster at Catharine Market in New York City. In addition, there was the opportunity, through reading James Fenimore Cooper, to more than glimpse the festival historically. That is because Cooper, one of his favorite writers, having witnessed Pinkster while growing up in New York, projected something of its spirit back into the colonial period in which he situates the festival in *Satanstoe*. Melville must have had strange feelings about Cooper's description of thousands of blacks and whites on the Commons, but minutes from his old Cortlandt address, for Cooper refers to excitement that, from early morning, started white youth on long walks through New York to the Commons where, within a few hours,

> nine-tenths of the blacks of the city, and of the whole country within thirty or forty miles, were collected in thousands in the field, beating banjoes, singing African songs, drinking, and worst of all, laughing in a way that seemed to set their very hearts rattling within their ribs. Everything wore the aspect of good-humor in its broadest and coarsest forms. Every sort of common game was in requisition, while drinking was far from being neglected. Still, not a man was drunk. A drunken negro, indeed, is not a common thing. . . . Hundreds of whites were walking through the fields, amused spectators. Among these last were a great many children of the better class, who had come to look at the enjoyment of those who attended them, in their ordinary amusements. . . . A great many young ladies between the ages of fifteen and twenty were also in the field, either escorted by male companions, or, what was equally certain of producing deference, under the care of old female nurses, who belonged to the race that kept the festival.[29]

Around the time of the appearance of *Satanstoe*, Charles Dickens published his masterful description of dance in *American Notes*, in which Melville read about William Henry Lane, a free black from Rhode Island considered by Dickens, without qualification, "the greatest dancer known." We learn that as he entered a night spot in the Five Points district, Dickens and his party were asked by the proprietor: "What will we please to call for? A dance? It shall be done directly, sir: 'a regular break-down.' " Every effort was made to please the whites, with Lane, according to Dickens, never ceasing to make "queer faces . . . to the delight of all the rest, who grin from ear to ear incessantly." And, writes Dickens: "The fiddler grins, and goes at it tooth and nail; there is new energy in the tambourine; new laughter in the dancers; new smiles in the landlady; new confidence in the landlord; new brightness in the very candles." Then he immortalizes Lane:

> Single shuffle, double shuffle, cut and cross-cut; snapping his fingers, rolling his eyes, turning in his knees, presenting the backs of his legs in front, spinning about on his toes and heels like nothing but the man's fingers on the tambourine; dancing with two left legs, two right legs, two wooden legs, two wire legs, two spring legs, – all sorts of legs and no legs – what is this to him?

As applause "thundered about him," Lane "finished by leaping gloriously on the bar-counter, and calling for something to drink. . . ."[30]

Some dances seen in New York City probably were done even earlier in Albany. We know, for example, that Charley of Pinkster fame, one of the great dancers of the eighteenth century, influenced dancers in and out of Albany, that he was a master of the extremely inventive breakdown – described by Dickens – and superior to his imitator, John Diamond, a superb white dancer at times seen in New York.[31] Simple logic holds that Albany slaves, after Charley began his decline as a dancer, extended his dance style into the nineteenth century, for they were not less attentive to the master than Diamond and hardly less gifted. According to Munsell: "Charley generally led off the dance, when the Sambos and Philises, juvenile and antiquated, would put in a double-shuffle heel and toe breakdown, in a manner that would have put Master Diamond and other *cork*-onions somewhat in the *shade*."[32] Thus we have some indication of the superiority of the dancers close to Charley and active in the ring dance and double shuffle tradition that he helped pioneer.[33]

Ring dance to juba rhythms – William Henry Lane was known as *Mr. Juba* – was performed in New York City, but with few students as sensitive as Melville observing them. While there was juba circular dance at Catharine Market, a less often remarked dance attracted the attention of Thomas De Voe, who described the music to which it was done: "There music or time was usually given by one of their own party, which was done by beating their hands on the sides of their legs and the noise of their heels."

He then refers to a popular form of dance to juba rhythms on "spring" boards held down at each end that narrow – yet heighten – possibilities for improvisation crowned by one astonishing display after another. There is evidence that Melville made his way to Catharine Market before the appearance of *Moby-Dick*.[34]

In fact, his sustained presentation of slave music and dance in *Moby-Dick* enables us to bring together much of the dance and music that we have been considering. In doing so, we find confirmation that Melville was exposed to a great deal of African cultural practice. When reading the chapter "Midnight, Forecastle," for example, one thinks of his long proximity to black performance art and of what he read concerning it. We are reminded of his youth in New York City and Albany and are persuaded that he read *American Notes*.

In Melville's fiction, African culture reaches beyond the black community to dazzle even those not particularly friendly toward blacks. To be sure, there is a sense in which, in "Midnight, Forecastle," through sailors from numerous points on the globe, the universal appeal of African dance and music – of instrumentation through the tambourine – is suggested despite marked insularity: "They were nearly all Islanders in the Pequod, *Isolatoes* too, I call such," he writes, "not acknowledging the common continent of men, but each *Isolato* living on a separate continent of his own." The entire crew of the ship is aware of the appeal of the music and dance, "federated along one keel" in that sense as well, alive to the fleeting if somewhat threatening possibility of a common, universal dance and musical culture – "belike the whole world's one ball, as your scholars have it; and so 'tis right to make one ball-room of it" – regulated by the rhythms of Pip's tambourine (*MD*, 121, 175 [emphasis in the original]). As we shall see, African dance is not the only dance in this chapter, but it is the dance on which Melville mainly focuses.

After the French sailor's "let's have a jig or two before we ride to anchor. . . . Stand by all legs! Pip! little Pip! hurrah with your tambourine!" Pip's "don't know where it is" elicits an exhortation that he "Beat thy belly, then," a reference to juba-like rhythms before the French sailor exhorts: "Throw yourselves! Legs! legs!" Yet another remark, one from the Long-Island sailor, brings Dickens to mind: "Hoe corn when ye may, say I. All legs go to harvest soon. Ah! here comes the music . . ." (*MD* 174).

When the Iceland sailor finds the floor on which dance will take place "too *springy*" for his taste, the Azore sailor throws Pip's tambourine to him and, as half the sailors dance, calls out: "Go it, Pip! Bang it. . . . Rig it, dig it, stig it, quig it, bell-boy!"(*MD* 174–5 [emphasis added]).[35] The Azore sailor's voice is itself improvisational. Fast and percussive, it not only invites dance rhythms but prefigures the scat singing of jazz: "Rig it, dig it. . . ." The sophisticated West African conception – to *dig*, that is, to understand or like – acquaints one with what was, outside a certain segment of the slave community, highly esoteric knowledge.

And so, at midnight, when asked to expend much energy, to "make fireflies," to "break the jinglers!" Pip is equal to the occasion: "Jinglers, you say? – there goes another, dropped off; I pound it so." As sparks from Pip's tambourine, riding jagged currents of sound, light the night, Melville has the Manx Sailor remark: "Dance on, lads, you're young; I was once" – very likely an utterance that resonated in Melville's consciousness not simply because he danced when young but because he took dancing lessons as well in youth (*MD*, 175).

As sailors dance, comical antics are expected of Pip, raising the specter of minstrelsy. When Pip is urged, for example, to "wag thy ears" and to "rattle thy teeth," one is reminded of the great William Henry Lane making strange faces. But nothing so simplistic as mere minstrelsy is depicted by Melville, for perceived insults are rejected a number of times in the chapter (*MD*, 174, 175). Even when Pip is urged, relatively mildly, to "hold up thy hoop . . . till I jump through it!" the response from Tashtego is: "That's a white man; he calls that fun: humph! I save my sweat" (*MD*, 175).

Ring dance enters gracefully when the Maltese sailor introduces the reader to a diverse set of dance relationships:

> It's the waves' – the snow-caps' turn to jig it now. They'll shake their tassels soon. Now would all the waves were women, then I'd go drown, and chassee with them evermore! There's naught so sweet on earth – heaven may not match it! – as those swift glances of warm, wild bosoms in the dance, when the over-arboring arms hide such ripe, bursting grapes.   (*MD*, 176)

As we imagine the left foot followed in the same direction by the right and the right by the left on the ocean floor, as waves jig above, Melville revisits, with remarkable subtlety in *Moby-Dick*, dance in *Omoo*, in which women, doing the "Lory-Lory," "fly round and round: bosoms heaving, hair streaming." Then later: "Presently, raising a strange chant, they softly sway themselves, gradually quickening the movement, until, at length, for a few passionate moments, with throbbing bosoms and glowing cheeks, they abandon themselves to all the spirit of the dance. . . ." Though a different dance, its circularity calls to mind ring dance at Pinkster, which was the principal form of dance there.[36]

Once more Melville relates dance in the Pacific Isles to African dance and slave culture when the China sailor calls to Pip to "make a pagoda of thyself," for in *Omoo* he writes of the clearing where the dance took place,

"Near the trees, on one side of the clear space, was a ruinous pile of stones, many rods in extent; upon which had formerly stood a temple . . ." (*MD*, 175; *O*, 240). Beyond that, movement first slowly and then swiftly occurred in the Ring Shout, the most influential slave dance, North as well as South, in nineteenth-century America. That Melville has sailors doing black dance steps, even improvising, to the rhythms of Pip's tambourine reflects a reality of his time.

An extraordinary passage in *Moby-Dick* that concerns African cultural influence in America is the French sailor's command: "Form now Indian-file, and gallop into the double-shuffle?" (*MD*, 174).[37] White missionaries in America applied "Indian-file" to the Ring Shout, a sacred dance characterized by counterclockwise movement in a circle to complex rhythms of the heels, hand clapping, chanting, and singing – the context in which the Negro spiritual was created. The rhythms of the Ring Shout, and the rhythms of black dance generally in *Moby-Dick*, are the rhythms that influenced the development of jazz and jazz dance.

Interestingly, the knowing French sailor's urging his fellows, after they have formed the dancing circle, to "gallop into a double-shuffle" suggests the essential unity of the sacred and the "secular" in the Shout, the double-shuffle being an extension, as it were, of the former. This could well be the best description available of the initial stages of the evolution of "secular" from sacred dance in African culture in America, a description informed by what Melville knew of dance in Albany and New York City. In fact, for generations young and old slaves in Albany, following Pinkster King Charley, did the double-shuffle, and Charley's primary dance movement was ring or Indian-file. And with William Henry Lane and his followers' mastery of the double-shuffle, placement of the double-shuffle after juba circular dance of the kind done at Catharine Market would achieve an effect similar to that of the Ring Shout and double-shuffle with respect to form.

What Melville observed in Albany and New York City, then, was the model for the French sailor's "Form, now, Indian-file and gallop into the double-shuffle. . . ." For Melville, as for others of his time, the phrase "Indian-file" was hardly confined to Indians. In particular, it appears in the literature in relation to African dance and marching style, indicating the counterclockwise movement of the African Circle dance as well as that of the Ring Shout on the plantations of the South and in the cities of the North.[38]

The Ring Shout was the principal African ritual in America. There is little doubt, when the sailors are urged to form themselves "Indian-file" before double-shuffling, that both the Shout and the double-shuffle are being depicted in a highly secular, as opposed to sacred, context. While some of the sailors dancing on board the *Pequod* encourage minstrelsy, it is small wonder that nonwhites are not greatly moved by their racist comments and attitudes. In this respect, neither Tashtego nor Pip is alone. In fact, such is the resistance to anything bordering on racism that there is a real danger of violence. Even so, the controlling sentiments are for fairness.

As winds cross swords before "lunging," the Manx sailor remarks that the sky is "pitch black." Daggoo responds: "What of that?" and adds: "Who's afraid of black's afraid of me! I'm quarried out of it!" To which the Spanish sailor, advancing toward Daggoo, challenges, "Aye, harpooner, thy race is the undeniable dark side of mankind – devilish dark at that. No offence" (*MD*, 177). It is perhaps foolish of him, for Melville establishes Daggoo's power at a glance: "There was a corporeal humility in looking up at him; and a white man standing before him seemed a white flag come to beg truce of a fortress" (*MD*, 121). Still, when the 5th Nantucket sailor asks, "What's that I saw – lightening?" the Spanish sailor replies that it is "Daggoo showing his teeth," which leads Daggoo, springing forth, to counter: "Swallow thine, mannikin! White skin, white liver!" When the Spaniard responds: "Knife thee heartily! big frame, small spirit!" the English sailor insists: "Fair play! Snatch the Spaniard's knife! A ring, a ring!" (*MD*, 177–8). The dance scene ends when the sailors form themselves into a ring around Daggoo and the Spanish sailor. A looming storm distracts them all, leading Pip to comment:

> Hold on hard! Jimmini, what a squall! But those chaps there are worse yet – they are your white squalls, they. White squalls? white whale, shirr! shirr! Here have I heard all their chat just now, and the white whale – shirr! shirr! – but spoken of once! and only this evening – it makes me jingle all over like my tambourine. . . . Oh, thou big white God aloft there somewhere in yon darkness, have mercy on this small black boy down here; preserve him from all men that have no bowels to feel fear. (*MD*, 178)[39]

"Poor Alabama boy!" Melville called Pip, remarking that his beating of the tambourine was "prelusive of the eternal time, when sent for, to the great quarter-deck on high, he was bid strike in with angels, and beat his tambourine in glory; called a coward here, hailed a hero there!" (*MD*, 121).

And so in "Midnight Forecastle" Melville translates his knowledge of black dance and music into literary art. Moreover, when reading *Moby-Dick*, we revisit with him scenes of his youth in Albany and in New York City and rediscover what scholars have largely failed even to reflect on – the presence of black culture in the North and the African aesthetic that informs it. While we encounter whites who are fascinated by the culture of people said to be their inferiors, it is now clear that Melville's depiction of African music and dance is a convincing representation – and here is the great irony – of Amercan art in *Moby-Dick*.

But in "Benito Cereno" there are aspects of African culture, including music and dance, so elusive and abstruse that we may never know why Melville made them so. What we know is that Africans in that work did not believe that God was white, which helps explain the militancy of their dance in a novella largely based on an 1804 slave revolt off the coast of South America that, for ironic subtlety, remains as brilliant as anything recorded in history.[40]

In the novella, dance inspires those resisting oppression to acts of valor, a practice but dimly remembered by old Africans in America when Melville was writing "Benito Cereno." It should be noted, in fact, that Melville bases his treatment of *dance purpose* in "Benito Cereno" on an African tradition seldom if ever drawn on in America. It is not likely, therefore, that when creating "Benito Cereno" he had before him examples of African dance, apart from their rhythms, still being practiced in America. Thus, he carried subtlety beyond the bounds familiar to his readership, a development related to his creation of the novella's governing symbol by fusing models from widely divergent cultural worlds before concealing them deep beneath surface appearances, which calls to mind a cardinal principle of his aesthetic: "I love all men who *dive*. Any fish can swim near the surface. . . ." Melville was thinking "of the whole corps of thought-divers who have been diving and coming up again with bloodshot-eyes since the world began." In fact, in the novella's creation, like "the great whale," he goes "down stairs five miles or more" to defining depths to complicate what is read on the surface.[41] The very nature of dance in the work, then, barely suggests the complexity of its most important symbol, without understanding of which there is no knowing that African values are crucial to the formation of the novella's finest art.

The reader will remember that slaves allowed to sleep unchained on the deck of the *San Dominick*, under their leader Babo's direction, suddenly revolt, tie up and throw overboard a number of Spaniards, stab others to death, and spare captain Don Benito Cereno's life in exchange for a promise to navigate them back to West Africa.[42] But weeks later, the *Bachelor's Delight*, captained by Amasa Delano, an American from Duxbury, Massachusetts, appears in the distance. Concluding that the *San Dominick* is in trouble, Delano decides to row toward her to see if he can be of assistance. Seeing him coming, the supremely confident Babo allows him to board, convinced that with everyone acting as he directs, the whites under penalty of death, the stranger will not discover the true state of affairs on the *San Dominick* (*BC*, 108–9). In such a situation, the possibilities for improvisation are nearly limitless.

Delano might have seen something of the complex future he was destined to partake of, but does not, for there is no evidence that he notices the *San Dominick*'s "shield-like stern-piece, intricately carved with the arms of Castile and Leon, medallioned about by groups of mythological or symbolical devices; uppermost and central of which, was a dark satyr in a mask, holding his foot on the prostrate neck of a writhing figure, likewise masked." Nor does he notice until the very end, if at all, a canvas covering a hideous object that might be the ship's figurehead, an object that bears a legend that even he might have pondered in that stark context (*BC*, 49). He entered a world in which revolution was concealed in the folds of art.

Melville's masterly creation is an expression of artistic irony of a type before unknown to the world of fiction. Such irony is possible because the impulse to art in the novella, as in the historical revolt, is indistinguishable from the impulse to be free, and both are sustained on nearly every page of the novella. From beginning to end, Babo directs each actor to determine his or her character in light of changing realities but consonant with the new power relations, as when Delano boards and whites and blacks "in one language, and as with one voice, all poured out a common tale of suffering"; as when, immediately after Delano has a brush with death, "the work of hoisting in the casks was resumed, whites and blacks singing at the tackle" (*BC*, 49, 79–80).

In the novella, martial intent is hidden behind the rhythmic play of hatchets, a regular reminder to the Spaniards that the hatchets are in hand for more than musical purposes. But the rhythmic play of Ashantees at times takes the complex form of eerie comment on vague suspicions. For example, when Delano thought Don Benito and Babo were somehow plotting against him, the "sound of the hatchet polishing" might fall "on his ears," causing him "to cast another swift side-look at the two." Not long thereafter, "passing from one suspicious thing to another," his "mind revolved the strange questions put to him regarding his ship." Of this Melville writes: "By a curious coincidence, as each point was recalled, the black wizards of Ashantee would strike up with their hatchets, as in ominous comments on the white stranger's thoughts" (*BC*, 66, 67). But even those comments should be considered together with more disturbing and decisive strains of improvised, martial rhythms. Melville writes that

> the six hatchet-polishers neither spoke to others, nor breathed a whisper among themselves, but sat intent upon their task, except at intervals, when,

with the peculiar love in negroes of uniting industry with pastime, two and two they sideways clashed their hatchets together, like cymbals with a barbarous din. All six, unlike the generality, had the raw aspect of unsophisticated Africans.   (BC, 50)

The rhythms were so orchestrated that at precisely the right time the hatchets are clashed side by side, indicating Melville's more than passing knowledge of African rhythm in the Americas. But the more complicated issue is whether such knowledge was acquired mainly from exposure to slaves in America or from Africans recently arrived in the Americas. The evidence suggests that his sense of African culture in this respect was cultivated in places no more exotic than New York City and Albany. In other words, Ashantee rhythms were not noticeably different, despite the ends to which they were directed, from those of northern slaves and their descendants. Hence Melville drew on travel accounts and his personal exposure to African performance style, mainly in America, to create the classic "hatchet polisher" scene.

The degree of slaveholder dependence on the slave in the historical revolt recounted by Delano is related to master class dependence on African work skills. Having both forms of dependence in mind when creating the novella made it easier for Melville to depict a master–slave relationship that resonates with Hegel's position on the subject. In fact, his knowledge of African work skills enabled him to sweep away spiritual and intellectual cobwebs that blinded other Americans when attempting to determine who, in that relationship, was dependent on whom. He was able to do so because he knew that there was no greater myth, cherished in his day, than that Africans were unable to take care of themselves and, consequently, had to be taught how to labor in workshop and field in the plantation South. Mungo Park's *Interior Districts* offered him a more informed view of African labor since the American Revolution. From reading Park, it was evident that thousands of Africans entered America with prior knowledge of tobacco cultivation and in even larger numbers knowing how to cultivate cotton, major crops in the development of the American economy. But the list of skills does not stop there, for the working of leather, iron, and gold was common, Park discloses, in many parts of black Africa affected by the slave trade.[43]

It was not lost on Melville that an African named Karfa, according to Park, on "observing the improved state of our manufactures, and our manifest superiority in the arts of civilized life . . . would sometimes appear pensive, and exclaim with an involuntary sigh, 'black men are nothing.' "[44] Apparently Park made no attempt to disabuse Karfa of that sentiment, though he owed his life to the humanity and work skills of African women, which calls to mind Babo's response to a remark from Don Benito:

> "But it is Babo here to whom, under God, I owe not only my own preservation, but likewise to him, chiefly, the merit is due, of pacifying his more ignorant brethren, when at intervals tempted to murmurings."
>
> "Ah, master," sighed the black, bowing his face, "don't speak of me; Babo is nothing. . . ."
>
> "Faithful fellow!" cried Captain Delano. "Don Benito, I envy you such a friend; slave I cannot call him." (BC, 57)

Melville offers numerous examples of Babo holding up the unstable Don Benito: Don Benito "fell heavily against his supporter"; "but the servant was more alert, who, with one hand sustaining his master. . . ."; "his vital energy failed, so that to better support him, the servant, placing his master's hand on his naked shoulder, and gently holding it there, formed himself into a sort of crutch"; "His servant sustained him and drawing a cordial from his pocket placed it to his lips"; "As he mentioned this name, his air was heart-broken; his knees shook; his servant supported him"; "As he saw his meager form in the act of recovering itself from reclining in the servant's arms, into which the agitated invalid had fallen"; "Presently master and man came forth; Don Benito leaning on his servant"; "And so, still presenting himself as a crutch, [Babo] walking between the two captains" (BC, 55, 60, 70, 80, 88, 97).

A decade and a half ago, Joshua Leslie and I wrote, though it was Leslie's brilliant thesis, that Melville was under Hegelian influence in one vital respect: he argues in "Benito Cereno" that the slave is the creative force, the master parasitic, adding: "We have been unable to find a specific reference to Hegel in Melville's work. However, the earliest reference to freedom as the recognition of necessity is from Hegel, and Melville, introducing 'The Bell Tower' with lines of poetry 'from a private MS.,' tells us: 'Seeking to conquer a larger liberty, man but extends the empire of necessity.' " "The Hegelian echo," we concluded, "is deafening."[45]

With the appearance of the Melville *Journals* in 1989, what we argued was confirmed. There is this entry, in 1849, from Melville:

> *Monday Oct 22* Clear and cold; wind not favorable. I forgot to mention, that *last night* about 9:30 P.M. Adler and Taylor came into my room, and it was proposed to have whiskey punches, which we *did* have, accordingly. . . . We had an extraordinary time and did not break up until after two in the morning. We talked metaphysics continually, and Hegel, Schlegel, Kant and others were discussed. . . . [46]

One is reminded of Edward Margolies's observation that since "ambiguity sits at the center of Melville's metaphysics, would not this hold for his vision of a people whom he could not have known very well." Since Hegel's philosophical consideration of the master–slave relationship is hardly ambiguous, and since Melville provides the finest expression in literature of this relationship, the first part of Margolies's argument is no more convincing than his assertion that Melville did not know blacks well. On the contrary, that he knew them well made Hegel of great assistance in so brilliantly imagining Don Benito's dependence on Babo. Moreover, knowing that he read Hegel gives new resonance to Redburn's remarks concerning the slave trade and the wealth of Liverpool.[47]

Hence, *Redburn*'s connection to "Benito Cereno" on the deepest levels of meaning. In fact, what appear to be relatively unimportant ties between the two works merit serious consideration. For example, Melville reveals a link between "Benito Cereno" and the *Highlander*, the ship in *Redburn*, writing that Jackson, in *Redburn*, "used to tell of the *middle passage*, where the slaves were stowed, heel and point, like logs, and the suffocated and dead were unmanacled, and weeded out from the living every morning. . . ." (*R*, 57). For those who doubt *Redburn*'s connection to "Benito Cereno," apart perhaps from the horrid conditions of passage resembling the slave trade, there is a more elusive connection that is related to Scottish Highlanders. Melville's naming the ship in *Redburn* the *Highlander* suggests that, if not as early as *Redburn*, then perhaps not long thereafter, he was associating the carving of flesh from the backs and thighs of Africans, reported in Delano's *Voyages and Travels*, with the Highlanders' deadly use of sharp blades against the British at Preston Pans.[48]

The reader will recall that weeks before Delano boarded the *San Dominick*, Babo had two Ashantees go below deck and stab Alexandro Aranda, the owner of the slaves, then bring him to the deck and stab him again before the Ashantees disappeared below deck with the mortally wounded Argentine. As they would prepare the body of an Ashantee king for burial, they removed the flesh from Aranda's body down to the skeletal remains, which were riveted to the prow of the ship, with Babo writing the legend beneath it.[49] To reinforce its meaning, again before the ship was boarded, Babo personally directed a number of Spaniards to look at Aranda's bones. The sovereign and, in its conceptual relatedness, most far-reaching symbol of the novella, Aranda's skeleton hovers over the novella from the start, and most dramatically when, just before the final battle, it casts "a gigantic ribbed shadow upon the water" (*BC*, 102).

Ashantee rites, treated by Bowdich, provided the source of the legend beneath Aranda's skeleton and inspiration for the novella's greatest scene, the one in which Babo uses the flag of Spain as an apron while shaving Benito Cereno.[50] Moreover, the Ashantee king's attire and surroundings lead the student of Bowdich to reflect on humor in the novella – to consider the source of Don Benito's appearance as a "Harlequin Ensign" (*BC*, 87). It is likely that Melville read *Mission to Cape Coast Castle and Ashantee* before going to sea. Whether before his trip to Liverpool on the *Saint Lawrence* or sometime later, he began making connections that are at the heart of "Benito Cereno."

Redburn is far more important to Melville's art than has long been as- sumed. There is, above all, the passage in which he describes the Nelson monument:

> The ornament in question is a group of statuary in bronze, elevated upon a marble pedestal and basement, representing Lord Nelson expiring in the arms of Victory. One foot rests on a rolling foe, and the other on a cannon. Victory is dropping a wreath on the dying Admiral's brow. . . . At uniform intervals round the base of the pedestal, four naked figures in chains, somewhat larger than life, are seated in various attitudes of humiliation and despair. . . . These woe-begone figures of captives are emblematic of Nelson's principal victories; but I could never look at their swarthy limbs and manacles, without being involuntarily reminded of four African slaves in the market-place. And my thoughts would revert to Virginia and Carolina. . . .   (*R*, 155)

This treatment of the Nelson statuary is subtly tied to a description of the *San Dominick*'s appearance near the beginning of "Benito Cereno":

> Whether the ship had a figure-head, or only a plain beak, was not quite certain, owing to canvas wrapped about that part, either to protect it while undergoing a re-furbishing, or else decently to hide its decay. Rudely painted or chalked . . . along the forward side of a sort of pedestal below the canvass, was the sentence "*Sequid vuestro jefe*," (follow your leader); while upon the tarnished head-boards, near by, appeared, in stately capitals, once gilt, the ship's name, "SAN DOMINICK," each letter streakingly corroded with trick- lings of copper-spike rust; while, like mourning weeds, dark festoons of sea- grass slimily swept to and fro over the name, with every hearse-like roll of the hull.   (*BC*, 49)

The reference to the pedestal in both passages is not the only analogue to be found, for Melville writes in the same paragraph of *Redburn* of one of the chained and swarthy figures, "his head buried in despondency," looking "mournfully out of his eyes," which brings to mind the "mourning weeds" in "Benito Cereno." And Redburn notes that "Victory is dropping a wreath on the dying admiral's brow; while Death, under the similitude of *a hideous skeleton*, is insinuating his bony hand under the hero's robe, and groping after his heart," which led Melville to have Ashantees strip Aranda's body down to its skeleton before covering it with canvas (R, 155 [emphasis added]). It should be noted that the skeletal Death in the Nelson monument is actually emerging from under the canvas folds of a fallen sail.

Delano is as ignorant on leaving the San Dominick as when boarding. As he puts his oars into the sea, Don Benito leaps screaming into the boat, followed by Babo, dagger in hand: "Seeing the negro coming, Captain Delano had flung the Spaniard aside, almost in the very act of clutching him . . . shifting his place, with arms thrown up, so promptly grappled the servant in his descent. . . ." (BC, 98). "At this juncture, the left hand of Captain Delano, on one side, again clutched the half-reclining Don Benito . . . while his right foot, on the other side, ground the prostrate negro . . ." (BC, 98–9). It was then that he "saw the negroes, not in misrule, not in tumult, not as if frantically concerned for Don Benito, but with mask torn away" – Babo beneath his foot. Meanwhile, like "delirious black dervishes, the six Ashantees danced on the poop" (BC, 99).[51] Their leaping, counterclockwise movement was not the only instance of dance being used to encourage resistance. Ashantee women, at critical junctures during the struggle, used song and dance to support the fight for freedom. As the final battle began, with "sealing-spears and cutlasses" crossing "hatchets and handspikes," the women "raised a wailing chant, whose chorus," Melville writes, "was the clash of steel" (BC, 102). In his deposition, Don Benito testified that, during the fighting, Ashantee women

> sang songs and danced – not gaily, but solemnly; and before the engagement with the boats, as well as during the action, they sang melancholy songs to the negroes, and that this melancholy tone was more inflaming than a different one would have been, and was so intended; that all this is believed because the negroes have said it. (BC, 112)

Melville's recognition of recondite aspects of Ashantee culture in Delano's account of the historical revolt, in which there is no mention of Ashantees, is the best indication of his knowledge of their culture.[52]

While there is no doubt that, by the end of the novel, the masked satyr figure on the stern-piece, with his foot on another figure, represents Delano, until now it has not been argued that Melville modeled him after Lord Nelson, who in Redburn has "one foot resting on a rolling foe" (R, 155).[53] This argument, the reader will recall, is more persuasive in context, for the chained figures at the base of the pedestal reminded the young Melville of slaves. More than that, Melville knew that Delano, on reaching the Perseverance in the historical account, ordered "the ports run up and the guns [cannon] run out as soon as possible," which reminded him of Nelson, cannon at his side, with his foot on a foe.[54]

In "Benito Cereno," Melville has Delano hail the *Bachelor's Delight* and "order the ports up, and the guns run out." But the *San Dominick*'s cable had been cut, and the lashing out of the fag end had "whipped away the canvas shroud about the beak, suddenly revealing, as the bleached hull swung round towards the open ocean, death for the figure-head, in a human skeleton; chalky comment on the chalked words below, '*Follow Your Leader*.' " "At the sight," Benito Cereno, "covering his face, wailed out: 'Tis he, Aranda! My murdered, unburied friend!' " (*BC*, 99–100). If Delano noticed Aranda's skeleton, there is no mention of it in the novella.

There enters another dimension of the Nelson statuary to which young Wellingborough Redburn returned so many times when in Liverpool, for Babo was not finished:

> Glancing down at his feet, Captain Delano saw the freed hand of the servant aiming with a second dagger – a small one, before concealed in his wool – with this he was snakishly writhing up from the boat's bottom, at the heart of the master, his countenance lividly vindictive, expressing the centered purpose of his soul; while the Spaniard, half-choked, was vainly shrinking away, with husky words, incoherent to all but the Portuguese. . . .   (*BC*, 99)

Just as Melville uses the skeletal Death from Nelson's statue as a model for Aranda's, and Lord Nelson for Delano as the masked figure on the stern-piece with his foot on another, also masked, he depicts Babo, determined that Don Benito follow his leader, choosing a design, as we have seen, no less striking than the one in the statuary in which "Death . . . is insinuating its bony hand under the hero's robe, and groping after his heart" (*R*, 155).

Seized at the neck by Delano, Don Benito was in a "speechless faint," and we cannot be certain that he even saw Babo aim the dagger at him (*BC*, 99). But with Babo bound in rope and raised to the deck of the *Bachelor's Delight*, then "put below out of sight," Don Benito was willing to be assisted up the side of the ship. And though there would be a heart-to-heart talk between him and Delano on the voyage to Lima, a "decided relapse" quickly came after apparent victory, so when Delano asks, "But these mild trades that now fan your cheek, do they not come with a human-like healing to you?" Don Benito responds: "With their steadfastness they but waft me to my tomb, Senor." "There was silence," we are informed, "while the moody man sat, slowly and unconsciously gathering his mantle about him, as if it were a pall" (*BC*, 116).

Babo was chained in the hold with the others, and Don Benito "did not visit him." To be sure, neither then nor later did he look at Babo. Even before "the tribunal he refused."

> And when pressed by the judges he fainted. On the testimony of the sailors alone rested the legal identity of Babo. . . . Some months after, dragged to the gibbet at the tail of a mule, the black met his voiceless end. The body was burned to ashes; but for many days, the head, that hive of subtlety, fixed on a pole in the Plaza, met, unabashed, the gaze of the whites; and across the Plaza looked towards St Bartholomew's church, in whose vaults slept then, as now, the recovered bones of Aranda: and across the Rimac bridge looked towards the monastery, on Mount Agonia without; where, three months after being dismissed by the court, Benito Cereno, borne on the bier, did, indeed, follow his leader. (BC, 116–17)

A year after the appearance of "Benito Cereno," Melville returned to Liverpool and wrote in his journal: "After dinner went to exchange. Looked at Nelson's statue, with peculiar emotion, mindful of twenty years ago."[55] Despite the lapse of time, he had used details of the statuary together with his knowledge of African culture, derived from Park and especially from Bowdich, to create some of his greatest literary scenes. We can be certain that while standing there that day, he recalled how the statuary inspired the mythological figures on the stern-piece and the scene, near the end of the novella, of Delano and Babo in the boat. That together with the creation of Aranda's skeleton, modeled after Lord Nelson's and the Ashantee king's, and its link to Babo using the flag of Spain as an apron when shaving Don Benito, modeled after the flags around the shoulders of the Ashantee king, caused Melville to marvel as he reflected on the process of creation the statuary helped set in motion.

In some ways as stunning an achievement, his depiction of music and dance in "Midnight, Forecastle" was made possible by formative experiences in Albany and New York City that also led him to combine, in his art, cultural materials from Europe, the South Seas, and Africa while concealing, in most unusual ways, much that was African in the process. In his genius and moral courage, Melville gives primary attention, in *Moby-Dick*, to an African aesthetic that captures the tempo of an increasingly complex American civilization as the language and rhythms of jazz and jazz dance are prefigured. While Pip is the bearer of a musical tradition of which change, in the form of improvisation, is the great constant, Albany and New York City dance is affirmed by sailors from across the earth. With black culture in the North and South joined in this universal setting, we discover that Melville is capturing, in the process of their formation, music and dance that are now emblematic of American culture.

NOTES

1. Sterling Stuckey, *Slave Culture* (New York: Oxford University Press, 1987), especially chapters 1–4. This essay is dedicated to Melvillean Viola Sachs and to the memory of my mother, the poet Elma Stuckey.

2. For discussion of the religious origins of "secular" forms of art in black America, see Sterling Stuckey, "The Music That Is in One's Soul: On the Sacred Origins of Jazz and the Blues," *Lenox Avenue: A Journal of Interartistic Inquiry* 1 (1995): 73–88. Such transforming qualities are at the heart of an African aesthetic in which there is no apparent opposition between mind and body, emotion and intellect, the sacred and the secular. These qualities of culture, together with an extraordinary emphasis on improvisation, define African culture in this essay. Great irony resides in the fact that slave artists did not regard themselves as American even as they defined for others, especially later generations, what is native to America in artistic terms.

3. Thomas F. De Voe, *The Market Book* (1862; reprint, New York: Burt Franklin, 1969), p. 344.

4. Bernhard, Duke of Saxe-Weimar Eisenach, *Travels in North America* (Philadelphia: Carey, Lea & Carey, 1828), p. 133. For a general discussion of celebrations and parades in the North, see Shane White, "It Was a Proud Day: African American Festivals and Parades in the North, 1741-1834," *Journal of American History* 81 (June 1994): 13–50.

5. James McCune Smith, *A Memorial Discourse, by Henry Highland Garnet* (Philadelphia: Joseph M. Wilson, 1865), p. 24.

6. For details on the Negros Burial Ground, see *The New York Times*, October 9, 1991 pp. B1, B5.

7. Smith, *Memorial Discourse*, p. 24.

8. Ibid. We are just beginning to understand something of the richness of black music in New York City in the nineteenth century and earlier. Not only did the principal mutual aid societies among blacks have their own bands, there were "Associations" of black musicians as well. In an "Oration Commemorative of the Abolition of the Slave Trade in the United States," delivered before the Wilberforce Philanthropic Association on January 2, 1809, Joseph Sidney outlined the procession, noting that it marched "through Broadway, down Pearl street...." Dorothy Porter, ed., *Early Negro Writing* (Boston: Beacon Press, 1971), p. 363. Pearl Street was, of course, Herman Melville's birthplace and first residence in New York.

9. *New York Statesman*, July 6, 1827.

10. Smith, *Memorial Discourse*, p. 24.

11. *New York Statesman*, July 6, 1827; *New York American*, July 6, 1827. July 5 and other parades of blacks to music in New York City were a well-established tradition by the 1820s.

12. Smith, *Memorial Discourse*, p. 24. Five instances of such improvised dance/marching, drawn from as many states, are cited by Stuckey in "Music That Is in One's Soul," 79–83.

13. Originally associated with the Dutch observances of Whitsuntide (the week following Pentecost), the day after Whitsunday was a holiday for slaves and

servants, known as Pinkster Monday. Throughout the eighteenth century, the holiday grew in length and came eventually to be a week of celebration distinctly yet covertly expressing African spirituality, on the grounds of the town commons which became known as Pinkster Hill.

14. Herman Gansevoort, a maternal uncle of Melville's, married a Catherine Quackenboss or Quackenbush. Since more than one family in Albany and the surrounding area had Catherine's surname, her connection to Jackie remains, for now, a tantalizing possibility. Eleanor Melville Metcalf, *Herman Melville: Cycle and Epicycle* (Cambridge, MA: Harvard University Press, 1953), "Gansevoort" Family Tree, back endpapers; U.S., Department of Commerce and Labor, Bureau of the Census, *Heads of Families at the First Census of the United States taken in the year 1790: New York* (Washington, DC: Government Printing Office, 1908), pp. 14, 43, 52. Quote from Edwin H. Miller, *Melville* (New York: George Braziller, Inc., 1975), p. 60.

15. James Eights, "Pinkster Festivals in Albany" in Joel Munsell, *Collections on the History of Albany*, 4 vols. (Albany, NY: J. Munsell, 1865), II, pp. 323–7 [emphasis in the original].

16. The theoretical basis of "spiritual recreation," first adumbrated by W. E. B. Du Bois, is discussed by Stuckey in "Music That Is in One's Soul," 76–7.

17. Joel Munsell, *Collections: History of Albany* (Albany, NY: J. Munsell, 1867), pp. 378–83.

18. The percentages cited for New York State and the Gansevoorts' Third Ward of Albany were calculated from U.S. Department of Commerce and Labor, Bureau of the Census, *Heads of Families . . . 1790*, pp. 8, 9.

19. De Voe, *Market Book*, p. 344.

20. Joel Munsell, quoted in headnote to Eights, "Pinkster Festivals," in Munsell, *Collections on the History*, II, p. 323.

21. Munsell, *Collections: History of Albany*, p. 12 [emphasis added]. Slaves danced to whistling, which suggests that whistling and dance were sources of instruction in improvisation for Melville, who passed Albany corners in the summer. Leon Howard, *Herman Melville* (Berkeley and Los Angeles: University of California Press, 1967), p. 5.

22. Munsell, *Collections: History of Albany*, p. 381.

23. Newton Arvin, *Herman Melville* (1950; reprint, Westport, CT: Greenwood Press, 1972), p. 39.

24. Howard, *Melville*, p. 12.

25. Herman Melville, *Moby-Dick, or The Whale*, The Writings of Herman Melville, vol. 6 (Evanston and Chicago: Northwestern University Press and The Newberry Library, 1988), p. 158 (hereafter pages cited parenthetically in the text). Here one suspects a play on words – that Melville was referring to Thomas Edward Bowdich (1791–1824), the African explorer, as well as Nathaniel Bowditch (1773–1838), author of *The American Practical Navigator*.

26. Herman Melville, *Redburn: His First Voyage*, The Writings of Herman Melville, vol. 4 (Evanston and Chicago: Northwestern University Press and The Newberry Library, 1969), p. 155 (hereafter pages cited parenthetically in the text).

27. The most extensive treatment of *Redburn* is William H. Gilman, *Melville's Early Life and Redburn* (New York: New York University Press, 1951), but

perhaps its weakest aspect is its analysis, such as it is, of the Nelson statuary, which Gilman argues inspired pleasant feelings in young Redburn. Of the long line of *Redburn* critics, only Carolyn Karcher, focusing on the statuary's chained figures, gives serious attention to the statuary in relation to slavery and racism. See her *Shadow over the Promised Land* (Baton Rouge: Louisiana State University Press, 1980), pp. 28–30.

28. Howard, *Melville*, p. 42.

29. James Fenimore Cooper, *Satanstoe* (1845; reprinted, New York: American Book Co., [c 1937]), pp. 60–1.

30. Charles Dickens, *American Notes for General Circulation* (1842; New York: Penguin Books, 1985), pp. 138–9.

31. Jean and Marshall Stearns, *Jazz Dance* (1964; reprint, New York: Schirmer Books, 1979), p. 46.

32. Munsell, *Collections: History of Albany*, p. 53.

33. Munsell, *Collections*, p. 56.

34. De Voe, *Market Book*, p. 344.

35. The reference to the deck being "too springy" recalls improvisational dance on *spring* boards to juba rhythms, to the beating of one's hands on the body, at the Catharine Market in New York City.

36. Herman Melville, *Omoo: A Narrative of Adventures in the South Seas*, The Writings of Herman Melville, vol. 2 (Evanston and Chicago: Northwestern University Press and The Newberry Library, 1968), pp. 241–2 (hereafter cited parenthetically in the text). Melville scholar Michel Imbert noted similarities between the "Lory-Lory" and the Ring Shout and brought them to my attention.

37. Ring dance had by then formed the context in which the Negro spiritual was created, which early in the nineteenth century was flowering in the North as well as the South. See Eileen Southern, *The Music of Black America* (New York: W. W. Norton & Co., 1971), pp. 77–8.

38. Some examples of "Indian-file" involve universal application of the designation. Describing a procession among Ashantees, Joseph DuPuis, whom Melville read, writes: "A number of women and girls, whose employment consisted in attending upon their husbands . . . closed the order of the march, which from the nature of the path was necessarily in Indian file" Joseph DuPuis, *Journal of a Residence in Ashantee* (1824; reprint ed., London: Frank Cass and Co., 1966), p. 10. A similar reference, from Melville after the publication of *Moby-Dick*, appears in his *Journals* under the heading "Voyage from Liverpool to Constantinople": "Peddlers of all sorts and hawkers. Confectionary carried on head. A chain of malefactors with iron rings about their necks – Indian file." Herman Melville, *Journals*, The Writings of Herman Melville, vol. 15 (Evanston and Chicago: Northwestern University Press and the Newberry Library, 1989), p. 65. Another example of circularity that does not involve Indians was used by white missionaries in referring to the Ring Shout, equating it with dance "Indian file." Ezra Ely describes a camp meeting in which blacks and whites were "commingled" while "wheeling around in Indian file." Rev. Ezra Stiles Ely, Review of "Methodist Error," *The Quarterly Theological Review* 2 (April 1819): 226, 228–9.

39. To "beat" the tambourine is an African percussive move, similar to beating

the banjo, which Stuckey discusses in "The Skies of Consciousness: African Dance at Pinkster in New York," in his *Going Through the Storm* (New York: Oxford University Press, 1995), pp. 53–80.

40. Amasa Delano, *Voyages and Travels* (1817; reprint ed., New York: Praeger, 1970), chapter XVIII.

41. Quoted in Metcalf, *Herman Melville*, pp. 58–59.

42. Herman Melville, "Benito Cereno," in *The Piazza Tales and Other Prose Pieces, 1839–1860*, The Writings of Herman Melville, vol. 9 (Evanston and Chicago: Northwestern University Press and The Newberry Library, 1987), pp. 104–5 (hereafter cited parenthetically in the text).

43. Mungo Park, *Travels in the Interior Districts of Africa* (London: W. Bulmer and Co., 1799), pp. 196, 198, and especially chapter XXI.

44. Ibid., p. 359.

45. Joshua Leslie and Sterling Stuckey, "The Death of Benito Cereno: A Reading of Herman Melville on Slavery," *The Journal of Negro History* 67 (Winter 1982): 301n.

46. My gratitude to David Roediger for calling Melville's reference to Hegel to my attention with the appearance of Herman Melville, *Journals*, The Writings of Herman Melville, p. 8. There are numerous references to Adler in Melville's *Journals*, which suggests that he and Adler, while in Europe in the fall of 1849, spent many hours discussing German philosophers.

47. Edward Margolies, "Melville and Blacks," *CLA Journal* XVIII, no. 3 (March 1975): 364; G. W. F. Hegel, *The Phenomenology of Mind*, trans. J. B. Baille (New York: Harper Colophon, 1967), pp. 238–40. Redburn's thoughts reverted "to the historical fact, that the African slave-trade once constituted the principal commerce of Liverpool; and that the prosperity of the town was once supposed to have been indissolubly linked to its prosecution," Melville *Redburn*, 222.

48. Delano, *Voyages and Travels*, p. 328.

49. This Ashantee practice is treated by Sterling Stuckey in " 'Follow Your Leader:' The Theme of Cannibalism in *Benito Cereno*," in Stuckey, *Going Through the Storm*, p. 181.

50. For discussion of these rites, and of the Ashantee king with flags wrapped around him, see Stuckey, "Follow Your Leader," 172–5, 178.

51. Bowdich's description of Ashantee circular dance appears to be the source of the "black dervishes" reference: "A band of Fetish men, or priests, wheeled round and round as they passed with surprising velocity. . . . [Some] danced . . . with a gesture and carriage of defiance. . . ." T. E. Bowdich, *Mission to Cape Coast Castle and Ashantee* (1819; reprint third ed., London: Frank Cass & Co., 1966), p. 40.

52. For a discussion of the uses of Ashantee dance in "Benito Cereno," see Leslie and Stuckey, "The Death of Benito Cereno," 290.

53. The skeletal symbol of Lord Nelson's death, the foundation of Aranda's as figurehead, calls into question "Benito Cereno" criticism that depicts the "new world" as the source of energy in the novella and the old world as largely drained of vital energy. See, for example, Max Putzel, "The Source and Symbols of Melville's 'Benito Cereno' " *American Literature* 34 (1962): 191–206. Nelson's victories at the Nile and at Trafalgar laid the basis for more than a

century of British supremacy at sea that greatly spurred imperialism and c
lonialism in Asia and Africa. Thus for Christopher Colon, as figurehead,
have been replaced by Aranda is emblematic of European brutalities global

54. Delano, *Voyages*, p. 325.
55. Melville, *Journals*, p. 50.

3

JOHN BRYANT

Moby-Dick as Revolution

I. TWO *MOBY-DICKS*: LEGEND AND FORM

Legend has it that there are two *Moby-Dicks*. The story varies, depending upon who tells it, but the facts behind this theory of composition are constant. Returning home in February 1850 from London, where he had peddled *White-Jacket*, Melville contemplated basing his sixth book on the neglected Revolutionary War hero Israel Potter. He had retrieved Potter's autobiography from a London bookstall and thought a narrative of the luckless patriot (like that of alienated White-Jacket) would allow him to question democratic hero worship and revolution itself. But the heated events of 1848 might have persuaded him to avoid politics for a while. He put Potter and the seeds of his revolutionary critique aside and turned to what he told his British publisher, Richard Bentley, would be nothing more than "a romance of adventure founded upon certain wild legends in the Southern Sperm Whale Fisheries."[1]

Melville began this new book by writing out of himself. Still, he was quick to invent. Although he could describe the ports of Manhattan and New Bedford from personal experience, he had never been to Nantucket, so he made his own Nantucket. And even though he would be on more familiar "ground" when his narrative took to sea, he knew enough about whaling to know that he did not know it all: not its history, science, practices, or lore. Inevitably, he needed facts. He got himself a library card, checked out William Scoresby's tome on whaling, and began mixing fact and fancy.[2] Or, as he put it on May Day 1850 to Richard Henry Dana, Jr., this "strange sort of book" would pull "poetry" out of "blubber." Given "the nature of the thing," it must itself be as "ungainly as the gambols of the whales themselves" (*Correspondence*, 162). Moreover, "the thing" was already halfway done, so that when he wrote Bentley on June 27, he said it would be ready for publication by late autumn. The "thing" was *Moby-Dick*.

But something happened. First, Melville moved his family from New York City to Arrowhead, a farm in the Berkshires. Second, he met Nathaniel Hawthorne; and that, or so the legend goes, delayed and changed the course of Melville's progress.

Before moving in early August 1850, Melville proposed a week-long party at his uncle's nearby homestead. He invited good friends, neighbors, and literary figures including his editor Evert Duyckinck, the audacious scribbler Cornelius Mathews, the humorist-sage down the road Oliver Wendell Holmes, Holmes's editor James T. Fields, and another of Fields's clients, Nathaniel Hawthorne. On the party agenda was a Monument Mountain picnic during which Hawthorne and Melville finally met, snapping together like magnets. Herman had prepared for the encounter by reading Hawthorne's *Mosses from an Old Manse* and ended up blasting out a praiseful essay, "Hawthorne and His Mosses." Duyckinck read the manuscript and, upon returning to New York, quickly published it in *Literary World*. At this time, Melville also informed Duyckinck that his Whale Fishery romance was "mostly done." Melville, then, seemed on schedule.

However, it would take another year before *Moby-Dick* was ready to print. Surely, the autumn move and subsequent spring planting in 1851 inhibited his writing. And Melville continued to research more whaling books. But, according to legend, the real delay was Hawthorne. Melville discovered in his neighbor those "elective affinities" for aesthetics, metaphysics, and politics that make deep friends. After years of writing tales for the monthlies, Hawthorne, in his mid-forties, had just made his national reputation with *The Scarlet Letter*, and while residing in nearby Lenox, he was working on *The House of the Seven Gables*, which would seal that reputation. Melville, just thirty-one, was also making his bid for national acceptance. In Hawthorne, he had finally found someone with whom he could talk about God, Being, and Fiction. Hawthorne was to him an American Shakespeare, or better: for while Elizabethan politics had kept Shakespeare from speaking the truth, Hawthorne, and Melville too, could speak more frankly in their age of democracy: "the Declaration of Independence makes a difference," Melville had told Duyckinck the year before (*Correspondence*, 122). But though the Revolution may have erased courtly repression, it also placed the "great Art of Telling the Truth" in the hands of the masses,[3] and as Melville complained to Hawthorne, "try to get a living by the Truth – and go to the Soup Societies. . . . Truth is ridiculous to men" (*Correspondence*, 191). Creating a book true to oneself and one's nation required forging a new relationship with readers or even creating readers anew: it required a revolution.

Scholars have long speculated that Melville's friendship with Hawthorne,

as well as his absorption of Shakespeare, triggered a significant reorienta-
tion of *Moby-Dick*. The view is that Melville began to write a narrative of
whaling fact (like his naval documentary *White-Jacket*) to be completed by
fall 1850. This would involve Ishmael, Queequeg, and such strange characters as Peleg, Bildad, and Bulkington, but not Ahab. However, sometime
after the August encounter with Hawthorne, Melville recast the book entirely to include the Shakespeareanized story of Ahab. By the spring and
summer of 1851, it is surmised, Melville polished the two stories, adding
certain interpolated chapters – "shanties of chapters and essays" he called
them (*Correspondence*, 195) – in order to enhance the splicing of the two
narrative strands into a seamless whole. Try as he might, the seams still
showed, but with a deadline to meet and family to feed, Melville surren-
dered the novel to his printer, telling Hawthorne that all his works were
"botches," *Moby-Dick* included.

I call this theory of the two *Moby-Dick*s a "legend" to emphasize that
it is, in fact, only a theory, for beyond the few letters revealing Melville's
time frame for a "whaling book," a few chapters whose internal references
allow us to date them during the period of composition, and several other
Ahabian chapters written in a Shakespearean mode, there is little concrete
evidence, and nothing at all conclusive, to show that Melville radically
altered the structure or conception of his book.[4] Quite possibly Melville
had the heavily Shakespeareanized Ahab story in mind from the beginning;
after all, his first serious acquaintance with Shakespeare had occurred in
1849 just before his London trip, well before he met Hawthorne. Melville
might have gotten his idea of Ahab from Mary Shelley's *Frankenstein*,
which he read aloud with his family as he was planning his novel. Or he
may have developed Ahab out of his own earlier creation, the angry but
sympathetic Jackson in *Redburn*; and there is ample precedence in *Mardi*
for the novel's "ontological heroics" without Melville's having to find their
inspiration in Hawthorne.[5]

Even so, one cannot read *Moby-Dick* without recognizing that the book
is structurally problematic. We begin with a comedy: anxious Ishmael and
serene Queequeg bed down, get "married," and take off on a whaling
adventure come-what-may. Then, Enter Ahab (Chapter 29): the captain
stumps about, throws his pipe overboard, "kicks" Stubb below decks; and
suddenly the novel is a play with dialogue, speeches, asides, soliloquies,
stage direction, and no Ishmael. But in Chapter 41, Ishmael returns transformed; no longer a central character, he becomes the novel's central consciousness and narrative voice, able to report an interior life in Ahab that
he cannot possibly witness. Nevertheless, as his role as a character erodes,
his life as a lyrical, poetic meditator upon whales and whaling transforms

the novel once again, converting Ahab's drama into a vast essay on things cetological. Along about Chapter 96, "The Try-Works," Ishmael realizes that he cannot follow Ahab's fiery ways, that he will instead seek "attainable felicities" and fly like a Catskill eagle low and high, balancing darkness and light. But Chapter 99, "The Doubloon," returns us to the drama "Ahab," as crew members pull meaning out of the gold coin the captain has offered as a reward to the one who sights Moby Dick. Quickly now the novel gears up its dramatic machinery. Ahab soliloquizes once more in Chapter 114, "The Gilder," about the unendurable cyclicity of human feeling. Conflicts with God and the crew, melodramatic confrontations with his quadrant and the pale fire of "The Candles," the hope of a reversal through the agency of Starbuck and, most significantly, the black cabin boy Pip – all of these theatricalities intensify our anticipation of the coming catastrophe, as if we were caught up in *Lear* or *Macbeth*. Then with three chapters called "The Chase" and their seemingly voiceless, almost cinematic description, and with the brief but symphonic return of Ishmael in the "Epilogue," *Moby-Dick* is done.

There is no wonder that a person reading this book would conclude, as Evert Duyckinck did: "There are two if not three books in *Moby-Dick* rolled into one."[6] And it is also no wonder that, given its flip-flopping from Ishmael to Ahab – from comedy to tragedy and from lyric meditation to drama – scholars might locate the cause of the novel's structural oddities in its actual composition and assign differently structured sections to different phases of composition. Hence, the theory that Melville wrote two *Moby-Dick*s. And it is perhaps only human for readers trying to make sense of this book to take Melville's dedication of *Moby-Dick* to Hawthorne as a sign of one author's debt to another. Out of such desire, theories become legends.

In fact, the structural peculiarity of *Moby-Dick* is not so peculiar if you consider Melville's formal habits. There is a persistent lub–dub heartbeat built into his works, a large-scale transcendental two-ness of form that derives not from external contingencies of composition but from a deeper personal necessity, a need to discover within our actual world a primal other world of ideality. As Melville put it in his poem "Art," creation pulls meaning out of the sullen matter of existence; it is a wrestling with "Jacob's mystic heart" requiring "Audacity [and] reverence"; it is the fusing of self and other, whether that other be man or God.[7] This essentially Platonic view of creativity relishes the material dust and blubber of our subjectivity (lub) in order to seize a life that transcends all that (dub). In turn, Melville's oscillating literary structure is a mapping of the artist's ontological condition, his physical struggle to experience Being.

Beethoven achieved a similar moment of transcendental form. Deafness let him hear in new ways, and he composed his last piano sonata (Opus 111) in two movements, not the conventional three. Anton Schindler thought the work was a botch. But in fact, the two-part structure embodies a revolution in form and idea, a pairing of two worlds of emotion, linked in contrast and yet combined. The first movement has been called "Sansara": forceful, conflictual, and sullen. The second is "Nirvana," a transcendent heaven of mounting trill upon trill from which there is no return. Melville's structure also confronts us with two phases of our being; he does in literary form what Beethoven does musically.

Melville was not a card-carrying transcendentalist. In a famous letter, he reassured Duyckinck, who had little affinity for Idealism, German or American, that he did not "oscillate in Emerson's rainbow" (*Correspondence*, 121); but he admired the philosopher for his ability to dive and compared him to Shakespeare. Indeed, *Moby-Dick* depicts the struggle to understand the relation between the promise of transcendental thought and its abnegating opposite, the fear of nothingness, which like a jackal gnaws at Idealism: it is the relation of Nirvana to Sansara. And the novel's problematic two-part structure embodies this struggle in its seemingly adventitious but inescapably logical pairing of the bloody world of whaling and the higher world of whale as symbol of being.

This two-part invention was not new for Melville. In earlier works, we often find a "Narrative A" giving way to a "Narrative B," and usually the A-Tale figures an anxious world of work and economy, whereas the B-Tale grasps at ideality. Such structuring is found in *Typee*, *Mardi*, *Pierre*, and *The Confidence-Man*. And though in all cases the transcendental view of Tale B is not so much promoted as darkly critiqued, we can see the inherent desire in Melville's fictional structuring to confront, if not resolve, the problems of ideality as lub gives way to dub. If there seem to be two *Moby-Dicks*, an Ishmaelean and an Ahabian Tale, it is because Melville's literary form recapitulates the revolutions of a mind forced into elemental confrontation with the nature of its being.

My complaint with the two *Moby-Dicks* theory is its presumption that Melville needed Hawthorne or Shakespeare to move from the Ishmaelean Tale A to Ahab's very Shakespearean Tale B. Charles Olson was the first to give gnomic utterance to the idea: "Above all, in the ferment, Shakespeare, the cause."[8] The poet's professor, F. O. Matthiessen, considered the influence to be "almost an unconscious reflex," believing that Shakespeare's phrasings had "hypnotized" Melville and that Melville was "subconsciously impelled to emulation."[9] Leon Howard attempts a more complex chemical argument in saying that Hawthorne "served as a catalytic agent for the precipitation in words of a new attitude toward human nature which his mind had held in increasingly strong solution for some years," and this catalysis allowed Melville his "Shakespearean heights of expression" (Howard, 169). What ties these three positions together is the belief that Shakespeare swept Melville away. The submerged bardolatry in this compositional view has subverted the deeper intertextual enterprise of exploring how Melville used Shakespeare ironically and critically rather than as merely unconscious "emulation."[10]

To be sure, Melville's Shakespearizing shapes some of the deepest moments in *Moby-Dick*. Nevertheless, Melville places the mantel of Shakespeare on Ahab who lives and breathes but also dies by Shakespeare; he takes Shakespeare down with him. If *Moby-Dick* might be reduced to a duel between two idioms – Ahab's relentless Shakespearizing and Ishmael's lyrical poeticizing – it is Ishmael's voice – Homeric yet homely, more biblical than Shakespearean – that survives. Thus, while Melville exploits, even tries to outdo, Shakespeare, he also works the narrative to get him off his back. It is all part of the book's larger cultural declaration. As a purgation of Shakespeare, *Moby-Dick* figures forth a revolution of politics, sexuality, and mind – not only for Melville but also for the reader.

II. TRANSCENDENTAL DOUBT: TRANSCENDENTAL FORM

At first glance, *Moby-Dick* seems a revolution almost exclusively in its aesthetic modernity. The long, rhythmic lines, the prose poetry, the mixture of genres and multiplicity of voices, the experiments in point of view, symbolism, and psychology, the dramatization of interior life in Ishmael and Ahab, even the novel's tragicomicality – all prefigure the literary sensibilities of James, Joyce, and Faulkner. But the novel's radical politics seem strangely submerged. Surely, we can extract from the novel's veil of allegory a prophetic warning that the American ship of state is heading toward the disaster of Civil War.[11] We can even trick out certain political readings: Ahab as hunter is the capitalist whose rapacity commodifies nature and destroys the communal values; or Ahab as individualist is the demagogue who coopts the culture's expansionist idiom to manipulate the masses and undermine the democracy's fragile community of factions; or Ahab the abolitionist is the extremist eradicating racism in his pursuit of the white whale (its whiteness a symbol of supremacy) despite Pip's healing hand.[12] But these modern political extractions were largely unrecognizable to Melville's contemporaries. And yet, while *Moby-Dick* lacks the overt political agenda of Harriet Beecher Stowe's more popular *Uncle Tom's Cabin*, its covert message of resistance lies in the rhetorical strategies of its transcendental structure. Finally, *Moby-Dick* is most political in that it makes readers read in ways that politicize and radicalize.

The novel's two-tale narrative is a part of this radicalization. A book is most like revolution when it places the reader in the condition of one caught between deeply felt but conflicting ideologies. Boston-born Ben Franklin arrogantly thanks God for his vanity, claiming it promotes success, but then reverently thanks Providence for giving him success. A utilitarian who cannot get free of puritan rhetoric, he voices the ambivalence of being situated in a moment in history in which new thoughts vie with old and old vocabularies are bent to express new ideologies. No revolt is complete: the tissues of the past obtain. Such nostalgia is a necessity of mind, for desire cannot expel memory. Thus, the revolutionary's necessarily uncertain articulations bespeak an unavoidable condition of conflict and doubt.

In *Moby-Dick*, not only do characters demonstrate these instabilities, but the narrative itself destabilizes readers; it puts us in a revolutionary condition of doubt. As revolution, it makes us inhabit the passions of conflicting ideologies. And this explains the strategy behind the novel's double form. The reader is always caught between Ahab and Ishmael: between the sullen tragedy of vengeance, pride, and authority and the desperate comedy of being; between autocratic sea and domestic shore; between the "other" and the masses, demagogue and cosmopolite.

In Melville's doubled transcendental structure, one cannot programmatically assign Ishmael to material and Ahab to ideal realms, for both inhabit both, each seeking a separate resolution to the same metaphysical and political problems of being and nothingness. The two operate in different modes – one lyrical and comic, the other dramatic and tragic. But, finally, the narrative promotes the more resolvent mode, for just as Beethoven leaves us suspended in his oscillating transcendent trills, Melville ends with Ishmael. And more, Ishmael's comedy frames Ahab's tragedy, so that in fact Ahab's tragic drama is a projection out of Ishmael's comic sensibility. In short, Ahab grows out of Ishmael; his tale is the dramatization of a burning doubt that Ishmael needs to get into and out of, if only to control something deeply self-destructive within him. He is casting out a demon. But the demon Ahab is compellingly sympathetic. Thus, even though we return confidently enough to Ishmael and survive the Ahab tale, we are unnerved by the struggle. Through reading, we become pragmatic idealists left revolving on the edges of Ishmael's maelstrom, staring into the vacant suction of Ahab's political and philosophical idealism.

But rather than allegorizing these experiential modes, our reading places us in the essentially revolutionary condition of "The Transcendentalist," who, as Emerson tells us, must struggle with self-doubt. The problem is not in achieving a mystic transcendence – that momentary sense of oneness like Ishmael's mast-head reveries – but in living on after the experience, returning from ideality to actuality and the "old tricks . . . of a selfish society." Adopting the anxious voice of doubt, Emerson concludes, "My life is superficial, takes no root in the deep world; I ask, When shall I die, and be relieved of the responsibility of seeing a Universe which I do not use? I wish to exchange this flash-of-lightning faith for continuous daylight, this fever-glow for a benign climate."[13]

Ahab voices the same feeling in "The Gilder" (Ch. 114) when he laments the continual flipping between mindless faith and cerebral doubt. If only one could harbor in a final port of balanced repose (aware but calm), but life is a retrogression, and we relive the stages of ideological growth – faith, doubt, repose – repeatedly. Ahab would rather progress linearly in "unretracing gradations," but he spins day for night perpetually, and the revolutions drive him mad.

Emerson's advice to the transcendentalist who cannot and never will experience "continuous day" or Ahab's longed-for "repose of If" is to find a Quakerly contentment in waiting for the light, or as Thoreau would put it, to "anticipate" the day. And this requires a perpetual balance between self-reliance and communality: "the great man is he who in the midst of the crowd keeps with perfect sweetness the independence of solitude" (Emerson, "Self Reliance," 135). Or as Ishmael puts it in a chapter on blubber: "Do thou, too, live in this world without being of it" (307). Ahab, all "fever-glow" and "flash of lightning," cannot, for all his political machinations to gain metaphysical ascendancy, find faith or balance. But Ishmael can.

Ishmael knows the transcendental problem. He begins in crisis, seeing death and the blackness of darkness everywhere. Faith, like a jackal, gnaws at hope. But his deepest fear is not death; he fears that there is nothing beyond our shell of existence; there is no ideal reality beyond the material; there is nothing. This ultimate doubt pushes Ishmael to ask questions not even God can answer: Where does being come from? How does consciousness happen?

Ishmael takes to sea democratically to confront his fear of nothingness, just as Ahab takes to sea autocratically to kill that fear in the form of the white whale. The two approach the matter differently. Ishmael's ideology grows and embraces growth. It begins with a hopeful proposition: "Nothing exists in itself" (53). The postmodern assertion is the seed of his salvation, for if it is true, then all actual things connect, and ideality exists in the connectiveness of actuality. And not only does everything take its being and meaning from everything else, but each thing – you, me, a whale – also connects to a higher reality – the idea of Us. This is the happy, social, Platonic view that denies any threat of nothingness. Ishmael knows he has an inner warmth because his outer nose is cold. He knows he exists because he feels Queequeg's hug; Ishmael defines himself in terms of Queequeg, and vice versa, and the two affirm each other's consciousness. Significantly, Ishmael's democratic politics grow out of his therapeutic exorcism of his fear of alienation.

But Ishmael's punning text belies his confident metaphysics, for his "Nothing exists in itself" contains a deconstruction which may be read thusly: " 'Nothing' exists in itself." That is, the "Idea of Nothingness" exists in and of itself: Nothingness is a universal constant with no higher reality. Of course, this inversion prompts another revolution in meaning. The very idea that "Nothingness exists" is a paradox. If Nothingness *exists*, then Nothingness is a something, beyond which a higher reality may in fact be operating.

Such ironic revolvings and doubts upon doubts drive Ahab to distraction. But they are Ishmael's blood. In "The Mast-Head" (Ch. 35), he finds himself in a transcendental reverie in which all reality becomes one flowing rhythm of life, and yet the moment he yields to this rhythm, he becomes a nonidentity, a nothing. This very awareness triggers a counterimpulse to retain his personal being, his little self in the midst of the larger universal self; and at that moment, he imagines himself falling to his death, his identity returning to him but "in horror," at the very moment (ironically) he has envisioned his nonexistence. In "The Whiteness of the Whale" (Ch. 42), Ishmael contemplates why the color white strikes terror, and the same cycle of identity and negation spins him toward atheism, nihilism, alienation, and even the impossibility of gaining solace from symbolism. But in a later, resolvent mode, Ishmael stares into the fire of "The Try-Works" (Ch. 96) and recognizes that his obsession with Ahab's dilemma of being and nothingness is self-destructive and politically dehumanizing. Instead, as he asserts in "The Squeeze of a Hand" (Ch. 95), whose masturbatory images hearken back to the image in "Loomings" (Ch. 1) of a phantom holding Ishmael's hand and giving solace, he will seek out the attainable felicities of "the wife, the heart, the bed" (416). Ishmael cannot explain this connective, sexual/metaphysical hand that holds him, but it is enough to pull him back from the fire. It does not remove nothingness, but it gives him something to hold (amusingly enough) while continuing to contemplate. It is Melville's version of maintaining a perfect Emersonian "sweetness" of solitude.

Ahab's approach to the problem of nothingness is denial. In "The Quarter-Deck" (Ch. 36), he rallies the crew by playing fast and loose with transcendental ideas, making the whale out to be a "pasteboard mask" or symbol of an evil and yet reasoning force. Ahab's rhetoric is bad transcendental thinking on two counts. In "The Poet," Emerson argues that we come closest to transcendence when we do what nature does. Since nature is our most immediate example of the creative force of Ideality, doing what nature does means creating, and what nature creates are palpable symbols of universal concepts. Thus, to approach transcendence we must create symbols. Ahab's double heresy, however, is that he attempts to transcend by breaking through and reducing symbols (the whale's pasteboard mask), and does so assuming that destruction, not creativity, is the universal ideal.

Ahab can appear to be performing an authentic act of self-discovery by cutting through nature's surfaces in order to apprehend its ideal reality, but his method is destructive rather than re-creative. Even more problematic is Ahab's pathological denial of the possibility of nothingness. "Sometimes I think there is naught beyond," he admits, "But 'tis enough." This dramatic aside reveals more than Ahab would allow. Ahab is an atheist in denial. His core awareness is that behind the pasteboard mask of Moby Dick, there is no god, evil or otherwise; and this primal doubt he cannot bear: "'Tis enough." To deny this fearful nothingness, he erects as a psychological crutch an inverted and shallow form of transcendentalism in which symbol is mere matter (not thought playing upon matter, or fancy upon fact, or poetry upon blubber) and the ideality behind matter is a force of malice, not the Good, or the True, or (as Emerson would have it) Beauty.

Soliloquizing after his speech to the crew, Ahab brashly proclaims, amid images of his iron-railed, locomotive will to destroy the whale, that "Naught's an obstacle" to "the iron way." As with Ishmael's "Nothing exists in itself," this Shakespearean play upon nothingness has multiple meanings. On the surface, the trope states that "nothing can get in my way." But the punning reality beneath the surface is a conflicting philosophy: "the '*Idea* of Nothingness' is an obstacle." That is, Ahab's denial of nihility stands in the way of his achieving true self-awareness. Both Ishmael and Ahab pun upon Nothingness, but Ishmael is aware of his multiple meanings – indeed, his cetological chapters are a further enactment of both the promise of something beyond and the fear of "naught beyond" – whereas Ahab's double meaning seems more of a slip he does not perceive.

Here, then, are the two tales in Melville's transcendental structure: Ishmael gives us a meditation on doubt, Ahab a play about denial. But the two are not simply two sides of the same coin; rather, Ahab's play grows out of Ishmael's meditation. The drama called "Ahab" is a manifestation of Ishmael's own fear of the tragic impossibility of a transcendent reality, just as his counterpoised poeticizing of cetology, a lyrical essay we may call "Whale," conveys his comic desires of transcendence.

Evidence of Ahab's being a projection of Ishmael occurs when we find Ahab mimicking ideas and images that Ishmael has already voiced. In Chapter 42 Ishmael relentlessly, almost Ahabistically, pursues the cause behind our fear of whiteness. The analysis takes Ishmael further than he wants to go. As a symbol maker, he celebrates the "godly gamesomeness" (126) we enjoy in building symbols and playing with meaning. But in analyzing the symbol of whiteness, Ishmael destroys the very foundations of symbolism itself and undoes the only means he has (i.e., his creativity) of counteracting his fear of nothingness. For in following the symbol of whiteness to its ultimate meaning, he finds himself "stab[bed] . . . from behind with the thought of annihilation" (169). Rather than making whiteness into an easy allegory of death, he discovers an "absence of color," and from that absence he leaps into the vacuum: "a colorless, all-color of atheism." As a symbol of nothingness, whiteness symbolizes paradoxically that symbols do not exist. Two chapters later, Ahab mimics this same revelation. In "The Chart" (Ch. 44) he experiences that shattering form of sleepwalking dream we now call "night terror," a separation of soul from body, and becomes, says Ishmael, "a vacated thing, a formless somnambulistic being, a ray of living light, to be sure, but without an object to color, and therefore a blankness in itself" (175).

Clearly, Ishmael in Chapter 44 uses the same vocabulary of "blankness" to talk about Ahab's psychological fear of nothingness that he uses in Chapter 42 to seek the source of his own fear of whiteness. More than just replaying his idea of nothingness, Melville is framing Ahab's psychosis within Ishmael's vision. He is having Ahab emerge as a fearful dramatic enactment of Ishmael's poetically derived fear. Thus the two tales are interwoven, with Ishmael acting as the novel's hidden stage director. In short, *Moby-Dick* not only demonstrates revolutionary states of mind, as revealed in the thoughts of Ishmael and Ahab, but its structure, with Ahab's world projecting out of Ishmael's, puts readers into a destabilized condition of transcendental doubt. Whose language do we hear more passionately? Whom do we follow: Ishmael or Ahab? And how, to raise the stakes, is this revolutionary transcendental structuring at all political? The answers lie in sexuality and dramaturgy, which if pursued will bring us back to Shakespeare.

III. SEXUALITY AND POLITICS

Melville's two-part transcendental structure bids us take an ontological plunge from the risky but finally safe Socratic *questioning* of Ishmael into the disastrous *questing* of Ahab. Just as Ahab says he is "darkness leaping out of light," Melville has us leap from Ishmael's warm, meditative mode into Ahab's dramatic Shakespearizing. In this double search for the nature of being, we are asked to connect down to the determinants of our identity, and in particular our sexuality. It is problematic to say that "*our* sexuality" is at issue when, in this famously male-oriented text, the female gender is barely represented. But just as Melville's pursuit of identity – and how being emerges out of nothingness – invariably leads to sexuality, his representations of sexuality invariably promote a gender-crossing politics. In fact, *Moby-Dick* is not so purely male. To know what it means to Be, Ishmael must know what it means to be male; and to know the meaning of maleness requires his knowing other males. And to know others he must know the Other, and thus Queequeg becomes the perfect mate. He is quite male and quite other in that his paganism stands in contrast to Ishmael's conventional Christianity; he is self-possessed, unlike the neurotic Ishmael; he is like a husband as, astonishingly, Ishmael plays the wife. Ineluctably, Melville portrays sexuality as a gendered cosmopolitanism wherein (to borrow from the period's definition of "cosmopolite") one "is nowhere a stranger" in either sex. This "pansexuality" is the seed of a political ideology designed to call authority and capitalism into question and to bring apparent opposites – female and male, "civilized" and "savage" – together. Unlike Stubb, Starbuck, and even Ahab, who reminisce about women or wives, Ishmael creates women in meditation, as if to infer the otherness of "female" from his own male being.

From the start, Ishmael researches the feminine side of being. He is drawn to water, like so many other Manhattanites, although for him its magnetism reveals not only the warm and shapely allurements of femininity but also the threat of narcissism. What attracts this "metaphysical professor," this "artist," this "healthy boy"? It is the Phantom of Being beneath the water, and, he remarks, "meditation and water are wedded forever" (13); they are boy and wife. Soon enough Ishmael beds down with Queequeg, struggling (but not too hard) to unloose the islander's "bridegroom clasp" (33); thus, the metaphysical wedding in "Loomings" becomes the more sensual coupling in "The Counterpane," and with "A Bosom Friend," the two are "married" (53). But this matrimonial state is nothing more, Ishmael argues, than a Polynesian version of blood brothers swearing to die for one another. Even so, in Chapter 72 Ishmael returns to the wedding metaphor to describe the whaling phenomenon of the "Monkey Rope," in which Ishmael and Queequeg are tied together by a safety line designed to keep Queequeg from falling into shark-infested waters. Actually, the seamen roped together is Melville's concoction, a convenient adaptation of whaling practice that resituates the sexualized male bonding of the bedroom in the alienating world of work. Ishmael restates that he and Queequeg "were wedded, and should poor Queequeg sink to rise no more, then both usage and honor demanded that instead of cutting the cord, it should drag me down in his wake" (271). From the point of view of the whaling industry, Melville's fictional version of the monkey rope binds two workers, two commodified beings absurdly roped in to actualizing profit, and yet the human and sexual ligature transcends alienating capitalism, or at least achieves "honor" despite capital.

By transferring the previously metaphysical and sexual idea of wedding to the symbol of rope, Melville is able to expand his meditation further into politics. Earlier, in "The Line" (Ch. 60), hempen ropes surround the oarsmen of the whale boats, as if to stress the machinery of whaling as well as the moral "self-adjusting buoyancy and simultaneousness of volition and action" required by each sailor to avoid those ropes (280–1). These are the same ropes that hang Ahab. And these lines connect harpooners to live whales as well as dead whales to "waif poles" that signify ownership. Ishmael explains the latter process in "Fast-Fish and Loose-Fish" (Ch. 89) but quickly moves from whaling law to divorce law and whether a divorced husband has any claim to the assets of his remarried former wife. The facile analogizing of women to whales ironically undercuts the law's more pernicious assumption that women are property. Before the chapter ends, Ishmael has converted an offhanded meditation on possession into a more sanguine, indeed calamitous, tirade on such imperialistic thefts as Britain's rule of India and America's taking of Mexico, a tirade that ends with the question of whether the rights of man, our very words and thoughts, and indeed readers themselves are fast fish or loose (334).

The chain of images – from weddings metaphysical and homoerotic to lines that bind us one to another in cosmopolitan interdependency to lines that commodify humans in the workplace and enslave women in courts of law – allows Melville to extract politics out of sexuality just as he infers sexuality out of being. In doing so, his message of revolt is by necessity subsumed within the lyric strains of Ishmael's meditation rather than openly announced. It has been argued that Melville is practicing an art of concealment, that he hides his political agenda so as not to incur the wrath of less liberal readers and the snippings of censorious editors, both of which he had endured in previous books, most notably *Typee*. But Melville's strategy goes deeper than this, for in following the logic of Melville's symbols, readers are encouraged to tie meanings together for themselves, made to read creatively (as Emerson would have it), and drawn to the root political determinants of our lives. We hug others, we love them, we attach ourselves to them. But to hug is to grab and take and possess: we enslave. And this happens because we fear that our being is a nothing; thus, we seek either companionship or control. Rather than have his characters spout politics, Melville has us dig for their politics in the subterranean recesses of being and sexuality, all the more to show us the human necessities of certain ideologies. Thus, readers experience in their reading why Ishmael chooses freedom and love; why Ahab demands control.

Ahab's politics stems from his wounded sexuality. Ahab is democracy's worst nightmare: the charismatic, single-issue demagogue who can sway the masses away from mutual and communal contractarian democracy to self-destructive individualism or separatism. He is a John Brown or Calhoun; a McCarthy or Buchanan; or any of a number of supremicists, white or black. What makes Melville's psychological study of Ahab's monomania so politically compelling is Melville's locating the causes of his destructive charisma – his vision of disunity, social chaos, and death – in sexuality. In "Ahab's Leg" (Ch. 106), the captain suffers a painful blow to the groin when his whalebone pegleg snaps under his weight. The pain, Ishmael says, is "the direct issue of a former woe" (385). In dancing around this delicate fact, Ishmael finally intimates that more of Ahab is missing than his leg, and part of the verbal dance that he reports happening in Ahab's mind is an intricate argument concerning castration, ontology, and genealogy. It is essentially this: Ahab's "heart-woe" is connected genealogically to "the sourceless primogenitures of the gods." That is, there is a tragic, "sourceless" source that pre-exists even God. If this is so, then "the gods themselves are not for ever glad," and the "heart-woe" pain descends to us collaterally beside God's. We are not children of God; we are cousins related to one grandparent, Grief. What is this grief? Later, in "The Candles" (Ch. 119), Ishmael dramatizes Ahab's logic. He has Ahab modify the earlier genealogical argument as a way of claiming superiority to God. Since the gods are "unbegotten," he argues, they exist without a sense of genealogy and therefore cannot know, as Ahab does, that there is "some unsuffusing thing beyond," a source for God and man's mutually shared, collateral grief. Ahab cannot reach that "thing," but he knows it is there. But instead of working out this sense of grief the way Ishmael might work out his anxiety, he uses his awareness of a higher sense of being as a means to seize a rhetorical superiority to God. Since God's "unbegotten" status makes God unaware of the higher "thing" or grief source, Ahab's ontological self-awareness gives him ascendancy over God's nonawareness. But, again, what is this heart-woe grief source? Like Goethe's "Mother Night," it is essentially the incomprehensible idea of being or consciousness itself, which precedes all. It is not Ahab who is blind (says Ahab) but our silent, impersonal God, which cannot see that the mystery of being pre-exists divinity. Ahab calls this unreachable mystery "my sweet mother" and reserves for himself a motherless, orphan, foundling status.

Ahab's argumentation is compelling but tragically flawed. On the one hand, we recognize not only that Ahab's physical loss is a sexual impotency, but also that this sterility is in addition a loss of creativity, as manifested in his longing for his lost, nurturing "mother." But Ahab has compressed his sexual loss into a desperate ontological affair. He has set up God as an unknowing, father-figure version of himself, sans personality, sans self-righteous anger; and he allows his own putative superior self-awareness to stand for a fuller recognition of being, a return to Mother Night. In defying God, he manages to ignore the fact that "the unsuffusing" mother-like "thing" beyond us all – being itself – is also an impersonal symbol of our own devising, just a rhetorical trope. Ahab's defiance of the Father God is an appeal to the absent Mother Being, as though such a verbal victory would give him an edge over God in resolving the ultimate question of his identity. The futility of all this is that Ahab's genealogical metaphor gets him no closer to resolving the real dilemma of our grief: that we can never comprehend where consciousness comes from or what being is. Thus, Ahab's repressed sexual wound leads him to rig up a defiant response to the problem of being that simultaneously gives gender to being (mother) and then takes her away (nothingness). And that response strikes us as both poignant and sadly pathological, if not delusional.

Ahab is defiant and worshipful ("defyingly I worship thee!"), and this angry male's charisma is located in his search for a mother and wholeness. Ahab's callous commodification of whales and crew bespeaks his role as unregenerate demagogue, capitalist, and imperialist. But beneath this surface politics is an agenda of personal reclamation that makes his anger so dangerously alluring: "Our souls," Ahab says, "are like those orphans whose unwedded mothers die in bearing them: the secret of our paternity lies in their grave, and we must there to learn it" (492). Finally, what is political in *Moby-Dick* lies not in its allegories of freedom or slavery, but in the novel's analysis of the deep sexual necessities of our being, both integrative and nihilistic, that make us political beasts. We are Ishmaelean cosmopolites or Ahabean tyrants because our sexuality is conditioned by our need to fill a Nothing through communality or dominance.

IV. POLITICS, DRAMA, AND MELVILLE'S "SHAKESPEHERIAN RAG"

Rather than making *Moby-Dick* a call to arms in support of an Ishmaelean or Ahabian ideology, Melville places us in the condition of experiencing the tug of both: one multicultural and inclusive, the other separatist and divisive. Thus, readers become revolutionary to the extent that they inhabit the debate, oscillating between Ahab's righteous but pathological resolve and Ishmael's deep but finally domestic creativity. Concomitantly, by offering these variant worlds in radically different voices – Ahab's dramaturgy and Ishmael's lyricism – Melville enhances the novel's revolutionary effect, for we constantly feel the switching of rhetorical modes as we read. Even so, the shifting is not indifferent or nondirectional. Ahab may be a good hater, but it is always Ishmael who contains and controls. Moreover, Melville's rejection of Ahab's railed and railing way is manifested in Melville's ultimate rejection of Shakespeare. To be sure, Melville's Shakespearean dramatics magnify Ahab's tragic bearing, but he also uses Shakespeare to purge himself of Shakespeare, as a blow for both his own artistic freedom and America's cultural independence. Indeed, *Moby-Dick*'s revolutionary politics lies in the deconstruction rather than emulation of Shakespeare.

To clarify, we need to consider the role of theater in Melville's America, and in particular the attitude Melville and his contemporaries had toward Shakespeare. We also need to consider that drama *is* politics.

Drama is a ritual of political response. As with the Greeks, who pulled performance out of communal dance, America's antebellum drama was not just an evening's diversion or a slice of life but a ritualized enactment, a symbolic re-presentation through staged event, of the culture's doubts about the democracy. To "do drama" was to "act out" race, region, and class tensions, to affirm or deny difference in the context of the nation's great Equality. This was true of formal productions such as Royall Tyler's *The Contrast* (1787), James K. Paulding's *The Lion of the West* (1830), the stage versions of *Uncle Tom's Cabin*, and even various Shakespearean plays (the most popular being *Richard III* and *Macbeth*), where manners and governance were explicit issues. But this was even truer with the more spontaneously contrived burlesques and commedia dell'arte theatricals performed by such ever-popular acrobatic mime troupes as the Ravels, in which unscripted jabs at public figures, factions, or events were the daily fare, and audiences – newsboys, workers, families, blacks, and whites (in separate sections) – hurled taunts, cheers, furniture, and overripe comestibles without restraint. Theatergoing had all the edge of a political rally; it

was physically perilous and mentally destabilizing. Given this cultural context, putting Ahab on stage was not simply Melville's aspiring to Shakespearean heights; rather, his conversion of narrative into drama was in itself
a political statement.

William A. Jones, an articulate spokesman for the liberal faction called
"Young America" (with which Melville was aligned), saw the theater as
democracy's most effective art form, for on stage the diversity of America's
factions and character types – Yankee, backwoodsman, black minstrel –
could perform and work out the nation's evolving political tensions over
its inchoate national identity.[14] It would serve as a cosmopolitan colloca-
tion of America itself. Or that was the hope. From the audience's perspective, the stage was not only a place to see American ideals realized, it was
itself a playing out of politics and the venting of class pressures. Thus, the
reality, despite Jones's hope, was that theater rarely achieved nationalizing
ritual but instead degenerated into mere political rally, and from rally it
even fell into riot. The most prominent case was New York City's three-
day Astor Place riot of 1849, which resulted in thirty deaths. The British
Shakespearean William Macready had, it was alleged, hissed at his American counterpart, Edwin Forrest, and when Macready appeared at New
York's newly constructed Astor Place Opera House (a theater not for the
people but the elite) to perform *Macbeth*, audiences inside and crowds
outside shouted him down. The aristocratic Macready barely escaped with
his life. Melville joined several others in petitioning Macready to continue
his tour, assuring him of the city's return to order (*Log*, 302), but a riot
ensued (ironically) on Melville's Astor Place townhouse doorstep.

Melville knew how the phenomenon of drama could body forth an immediate confrontation between audiences and the social forces that impinge
upon their lives and identities. And his decision to present Ahab's tale as
drama was itself a conscious political act and revolutionary both as a public
statement to his readers and as a moment of private resolve in shaping the
direction of his art. Publicly, Melville's act of dramatizing reinforces his
doubts about the direction of America's experiment in democracy. Whereas
his most optimistic political statements come to us through Ishmaelean
meditation, his concern for the nation's dangerous factionalism and racism
is delivered in the dramatist's idiom of speeches and stage direction, with
the novel's most dramatic character, Ahab, at the center. Ahab's memorable
entrance is in the play-within-a-novel section (Chs. 36–40), already mentioned, in which Ahab makes his quarter-deck speech bidding the crew to
pursue Moby Dick. But while Ahab commands our attention in the first
half of this little "play," it is the crew that brings the performance to its
chilling climax and quick curtain. Here the whalemen give no thought to

Ahab but turn immediately to drink, dance, and sexual desire; and out of the carousing comes a racial slur, then a fight, then a riot with the still sane Pip making the link for us between this chaos, an impending storm, and the foreshadowed encounter with Moby Dick. Rather than a comic enactment of political harmony envisioned by Young America's William Jones as the proper function of drama, Melville's play ends in the kind of theatrical and political riot the author witnessed at home in New York City. Melville's very use of the play genre – indeed, his jarring interruption of the controlled narrative of Ishmael with the stagy theatricals of both Ahab and the crew – enhances the political instability of Ahab's authoritarianism and the democratic crew's demolition of racially tolerant cosmopolitanism. The shifting modes also abruptly destabilize the reader, reminding us of the precarious nature of race and sexuality in America's democracy and placing us as well in a condition of doubt that sharpens our awareness of the risk in democratic revolution.

But Melville's use of drama, and Shakespeare in particular, had a private as well as a public function. In general, critics have stressed the author's emulation of Shakespeare, but the full story of Melville's "Shakespeherian Rag," to borrow Eliot's *Waste Land* phrase, reveals a crucial ambivalence: Melville lived for a while in Shakespeare's idiom, danced that dance but let it go. His relation to Shakespeare was a manifestation of the revolutionary iconoclasm he was building into *Moby-Dick*.

We marvel at Melville's uncanny replication of Shakespeare's voice. More than a source or "ordinary influence," Shakespeare had "grown into the fibre of Melville's thought" (Matthiessen, 435). Powerful confrontations such as "The Quarter-Deck" and "The Candles," or theatrical stagings such as "Midnight, Forecastle," or comic byplays such as Stubb's wide-awake sarcasms and "Leg and Arm" (when Ahab meets Boomer and Bunger)[15] do not in any real sense copy Shakespeare but rather do what Shakespeare, in the nineteenth century, might have done with America, metaphysics, and the sea. Melville's brilliant management of soliloquy and his invention of sequential soliloquies that focus on a single symbol (as in the contemplative "coin" chapters, "The Doubloon" and "The Gilder"), his adaptation of the fool (first Stubb, then Pip) to complex themes of comic regeneration, and his ingenious use of the gam to allow for scene shiftings beyond the limiting stations of the whaleship – these literary gambits extend beyond Shakespeare to an exuberant reshaping of the dramatic genre itself.

But the puzzle is that Melville's use of Shakespeare is as self-consciously bad as it is inventive and transforming. It flops as often as it soars, and rather than being dramatistic, certain moments in *Moby-Dick* are simply "dramaturgid." There are, for instance, the gratuitous Macbethean prophecies of Ahab's demise, the outrageous asides ("something shot from my nostrils"), the creaky transitions ("the envious billows sidelong swell to whelm my track; let them; but first I pass"), the overdone ellipses ("Down, dog, and kennel") designed to out-Lear Lear, the forced comic set pieces (Fleece's sermon to the sharks made all the more strained in contrast with Ishmael's far subtler meditations on sharks), and the utterly improbable staginess of Tashtego's hammering a red flag to the sinking mast-head and impaling a sky hawk in the process. Such "lumbering," "labored," and "derivative" passages (as Matthiessen put it) are precisely the kind of over-writing that drives modern minimalists to distraction.[16]

Our first inclination is to presume that these infelicities are the necessary lapses of an overreaching assimilation of Shakespeare or that Melville did not have time to make his inventions better. However, whereas Ishmael admits to the "careful disorderliness" (361) of similar infelicities in his lyric mode, he never explains away the relentless strut and fret of Ahab's Shake-speherian rag. A sedulous reviser and capable dramatizer from the time he wrote *Typee*, Melville was talented enough to diminish the "rag" if he had wanted to. Significantly, he did not.

The effect of Ahab's theatricality is twofold. On the one hand, it is symp-tomatic of the self-deluding con games Ahab uses to captivate crew and reader. His "sultanism" is undeniable, but the "paltry and base" methods to which he sinks – plying the crew with rum and gold (Ch. 36), playing electrical parlor games with the compass (Ch. 124) and corposants (Ch. 119) – are invariably rendered with strained theatricality to suggest the artificiality of Ahab's near-delusional egoism. Thus, Melville's parodic Shakespeareanisms undercut what Lawrence Levine identifies as an ideol-ogy of individualism invariably associated in the popular culture with Shakespearean protagonists.[17]

On the other hand, Ahab's "base" Shakespearean histrionics also suggest Melville's radical ambivalence toward his own experiments in the dramatic mode. Dramatism allowed Melville to curtail the metaphysical wanderings that he frequently permitted himself in his various first-person narrations. As if to make a point of this need, Melville underscored a passage from the Apocrypha at about the time he began *Moby-Dick*: "let thy speech be short, comprehending much in few words, be as one that knoweth and holdeth his tongue" (Sirach 32:8; *Log*, p. 370). The dramatic chapters in *Moby-Dick* – with their soliloquies, dialogue, stage directions, and histri-onics – cut Ishmael short in his lyrical meditations so that he might "holdeth his tongue." But if this dramatic self-effacement allowed Melville to disperse his ideas in diverse tongues, it necessarily denied Ishmael a dra-matic presence. That lyric voice which contained the novel's regenerative moral vision would remain disembodied in the face of Ahab and Shake-speare: it was undramatizable. Indeed, soon after *Moby-Dick* Melville ceased his Shakespearizing. Ultimately, Melville needed a narrative strategy that went beyond Shakespeare – one that could remove narrative voice from authorial personality and yet play a role in the narrative, despite such radical distancing – one that we find him continuing to seek in *Pierre*, "Benito Cereno," and *The Confidence-Man*.

There is no denying Melville's profound love of Shakespeare; he even compared him to Jesus (*Correspondence*, 127), and yet his "Mosses" essay reveals an ardent need for the artist to shake Shakespeare loose. The prob-lem was both societal and private: What was the new world writer's rela-tion to the past? How might artists invent a culture out of their own originality but maintain a regard for the received cultural standards en-dorsed by past readers? Shakespeare was a vital link to a past culture and a transcendent language, but as Emerson noted, "Genius is always suffi-ciently the enemy of genius by over-influence . . . [and we] have Shakes-pearized now for two hundred years."[18]

Following Emerson, Melville "boldly contemn[s] all imitation" and con-signs all "American Goldsmiths" and "American Miltons" to critical obliv-ion. But oddly enough, after having made his stand for independence, Melville virtually anoints Hawthorne as America's Shakespeare ("Mosses," 248), thus canonizing his new world friend with an old world halo. Finding himself caught between two ideologies, Melville quickly adopts something of an Emersonian approach. He is not interested in Shakespeare "so much for what he did do, but for what he did not do, or refrained from doing," both in text and with audience. He scoffs at the bardolatry of contemporary critics who call Shakespeare "unapproachable."[19] Melville's Shakespeare was a man, like himself, scarred by his culture, one who had to accom-modate his original genius to Elizabethan demands. Although a model of restraint providing insight in "cunning glimpses," he was also a rank pop-ularizer pandering to his audience's expectations of "noise and show of broad farce, and blood-besmeared tragedy." Melville's implication is that America's progressive liberalism removes the political restraints that forced Elizabethan writers to their blood, thunder, and farce. Finally, Shakespeare is as much a problematic model of the rhetorician as he is a model thinker,[20] and Hawthorne's achievement lies not in any imitation of Shake-speare's thought but in his doing what "Genius" does: he projects ideas in "the still, rich utterances of a great intellect in repose."

In short, Melville had as much to reject in Shakespeare as to admire. And he had support in this ambivalence from the populace's growing re-sentment of the classism inherent in Shakespeare's kings and such elitist interpretations of Shakespeare as Macready's, which could trigger a riot. The Declaration of Independence might free modern writers to tell certain metaphysical truths, but that document did not make audiences any more willing to accept them or the politics that come with them. Indeed, if Astor Place proved anything, it was that Americans were beginning to associate Shakespeare with aristocratic repression and class conflict. If, too, Shakespeare was becoming at this time, as Lawrence Levine argues, a symbol of drama's separation from the people, Melville's own ambivalent use of Shakespeare represents something more complex than an Emersonian attempt to apply the genius and insight of a Shakespeare to America. His use of "bad" Shakespeare is also a recognition that the "blood-besmeared" farce of American demagoguery and individualism he was witnessing in the streets was giving the lie to the effectiveness of drama in the culture. Ahab's theatricality, then, is the false ring of liberty's bell, signifying a society out of joint.

VI. REVOLUTION AND READER

Melville's use of Shakespeare clarifies even as it complicates the two-part transcendental structuring of *Moby-Dick*. As a dramatic projection of Ishmael's worst doubts about the sources of being and the communalizing promise of sexuality, Ahab dives deep, like Hawthorne and Shakespeare. However, Ahab's artificiality signifies his mental and political instability. And this undoing of his dramaturgy draws us back to the meditative containment of Ishmael's "intellect in repose." Thus, the journey out of Ishmael's "visible world . . . formed in love" into Ahab's sphere "formed in fright" (169) necessitates a return, and in this "essaying" of Shakespeare and dramatism, Melville purges both. Moreover, the reader partakes of this revolution in form.

Caught up in the duel between Ishmael's and Ahab's conflicting worlds, and feeling the shift in narrative modes, the reader experiences Ishmaelean doubt. The real dramatization going on is not Ahab's histrionics but Melville's guerrilla theatrics of pulling us on stage and forcing us to enact Ishmael's and Ahab's conditions of love and fright.

At times this revolutionary conditioning is programmed like a tennis match, as in "The Sphynx" (Ch. 70), when Melville has Ishmael and Ahab volley their emotions in front of a beheaded whale. Ishmael focuses on "silence," another symbol of absence, that reigns over the deck: "An intense copper calm, like a universal yellow lotus, was more and more unfolding its noiseless measureless leaves upon the sea" (263). For Ishmael the sea calm is an umbrageous tree of all-knowing: serene, Tennysonian, and transcendent. But for Ahab, the stillness, an emblem of his faithlessness, is a "deadly" impediment to his quest; and silence is all he hears from the Sphynx-like head that has all the answers but will not speak: "O head! thou has seen enough to split the planets and make an infidel of Abraham, and not one syllable is thine!" (264). His angry iambics stand in stark contrast to Ishmael's free-verse poeticizing that transforms the otherwise threatening calm into something palpable, hence containable. Of course, Ahab ends with a better line: "O Nature, and O soul of man! how far beyond all utterance are your linked analogies! not the smallest atom stirs or lives in matter, but has its cunning duplicate in mind" (264). Here the Shakespearean rhythms effectively articulate Ahab's tragic inability to believe, create, and transform. He acknowledges the existence of a two-part transcendental world in which matter is an analogical version of the soul, but the analogies are unutterable and, contrary to the symbolizer Ishmael, for whom utterance comes easy, Ahab lacks the creativity to give them voice. Ishmael's "copper calm" is his "deadly calm."

But though Ahab's verbal soliloquy recalls Hamlet, the staged imagery is really all Oedipus. Stage director Ishmael has Ahab stand before the whale's head using a cutting spade for a crutch so as to enact the iconography of not only the lame, staff-wielding Oedipus addressing the Sphynx but also the allegorized "three-legged" man of old age, which is the final part of the Sphynx's famous riddle. The irony is that old-man, three-legged Ahab stands in relation to the whale's head as Oedipus to the Sphynx, and yet he cannot answer the whale's riddle of Being even though he is (three "legs" and all) enacting the final part of the answer to that riddle: "Man." Ishmael's ironic stage crafting ensures that we shall see Ahab's Shakespearized allegorical insights in relation to Ishmael's more fluid symbolizing as misdirected. Even so, Ahab's antitranscendental revelation of the unutterability of analogies leaves us with the gnawing doubt that Ishmael's copper calm effusions are just artful words designed to fill a void that is "beyond all utterance." As Ishmael puts it later on, Ahab's insights "tarnish" Ishmael's poetic transcendencies.

Ishmael's ironic stagecraft grows stronger in "The Gilder" (Ch. 114) when Ishmael's and Ahab's distinct voices begin mystically to blend. In this "coin" chapter, Melville essentially replays "The Doubloon" by having successive characters reflect upon a single object, in this case another sea calm. Ishmael achieves a zen vision of "fact and fancy, half-way meeting, [and] interpenetrat[ing to] form one seamless whole" (406). Then Ahab delivers the famous "Oh, grassy glades" speech, easily his most poetic effusion. No longer a fist shaker, he addresses not God, the sun, a Sphynx, or the crew, but his own condition. He finds himself broken on a cycle of life which takes us through sequential stages of being – infancy's unconsciousness, boyhood faith, adolescent doubt, true skepticism, then disbelief, then finally "manhood's pondering repose of If." But this cycle never turns just once; the curse is that it continually revolves, sending us back from wisdom to former unbalanced selves; there is, Ahab complains, "no steady unretracing progress" (407). Ahab's problem is not that he never achieves the repose of If but that he cannot sustain it. He oscillates between boyhood faith and adolescent doubt and is forever an "orphan" wondering "where is the foundling's father hidden" and seeking out his mother in the grave.

Unlike Ishmael, who transforms these stages of consciousness – each one a revolution – into the very stuff of his lyricism, Ahab is dramatically confounded by the shifting and takes the "few fleeting moments" of "immortality" that he sometimes captures as an insult goading him on to seize transcendental totality. His speech is the lament of the anxious rebel unable to synthesize the ideology of his material self with the ideology of transcendental unity. In it, we hear none of his pathological denials and contrived arguments. This is Ahab's sincerest self-recognition that his anger, fear, and quest are rooted in his impotent, indeed infant-like and foundling status.

But most challenging for readers is that Ahab sounds more like Ishmael than Ahab. He speaks of "ever vernal endless landscapes in the soul," of "young horses" rolling "in new morning clover," and of the "cool dew of life immortal" (407). Rarely is iron-railed Ahab allowed such fluid pastoral rhythms. Gone is his insistent blank verse, but strains of the familiar Shakespearizing Ahab persist. After all, his cycle revises Jaques's seven-stages-of-man speech in *As You Like It*; in fact, it goes one better by making the cycle damningly repetitive and by recasting Shakespeare's finalized seventh stage (mere oblivion) as a seaman's orphanage or "final harbor, whence we unmoor no more," which tauntingly evokes *Othello*. Taken as a whole, the mixed modes of dramaturgy and lyricism adopt an Ishmaelean sensibility but in a Shakespearean idiom. Witness Ahab's transformation of Ishmael's notion of interpenetrating moods into his own blank verse: "But the mingled, mingling threads of life are woven by warp and woof." Clearly, Ishmael's and Ahab's separate voices are themselves mingling. "The Gilder" is crucial, then, not simply for what it says but for what it does. The mingled mingling of voices reminds us that stagy Ahab is the projection of stage manager Ishmael. He sounds like Ishmael because it is Ishmael speaking through him.

Curiously enough, an apparent accident in the printing of *Moby-Dick* has created a textual dilemma that problematizes the interpenetrating voices. Although Ishmael's lines preceding the "grassy glades" speech clearly set us up for a transfer to Ahab's point of view, there are no quotation marks around the speech itself to make these words undeniably his. In fact, the formal effect of the missing punctuation is that the "grassy glades" speech appears to be Ishmael's, not Ahab's. And this omission has existed in every edition of *Moby-Dick* since 1851. However, the editors of the now standard Northwestern–Newberry (NN) edition argue (on the basis of context alone rather than any textual variant) that the missing quotation marks should be supplied, and their emendation to that effect assigns the speech unequivocally to Ahab. Although the arguments for adding the punctuation are convincing, the change remains debatable because there is no physical evidence suggesting that Melville intended to supply quotation marks. The NN editors' decision is not so much a "correction" of a previously "corrupt" text as the creation of a modern variant. In effect, the "grassy glades" speech has now become a "fluid text," one that exists in significantly different physical forms for significantly different readerships. For readers of the historical editions of *Moby-Dick* (sans quotes) have and can continue to assume that the "grassy glades" speech is a continuation of Ishmael's meditation, whereas readers of the NN edition (with quotes) have no choice but to read the speech as Ahab's. In short, readers of "The Gilder" fall into Ahabian and Ishmaelite camps, depending on who they assume is speaking.

Moreover, our awareness of this editorial dilemma accentuates the destabilized revolutionary condition of the reader. For the speech itself, whether in quotes or not, sounds sufficiently Ishmaelean and Ahabian to make us consider with "equal eye" two possibilities: either Ishmael is becoming more Ahabian or Ahab, in his final dramatic moments, reveals his longing for an Ishmaelean sensibility. It is as though the editorial indeterminacy of the text signals to us the interpenetration of worlds: Ahab's anxiety and Ishmael's transcendence. Lub and dub.

Melville could not have foreseen this particular postmodern reading experience, but nevertheless it reinforces the established experience of the novel's revolutionary conditioning of the reader. Tripped up by the text itself, an errant set of quotation marks, and caught in the quandary of having to assign voices to ideas, we find ourselves revolving in and out of variant worlds – pitting Ahab's fears of nihility against Ishmael's faith, the politics of supremacy rooted in sterility against the politics of inclusion rooted in a sexualized communality, an ontology of self against other, and the rhetoric of Shakespearean theatrics against the poetics of transcendence. Surely these conflicting ideologies manifest an age of revolution in itself; but the deeper revolution is in the revolving that readers must perform in reading. That process leaves us wakeful, not confused, poised in anticipation of a synthesis we shall never fully achieve. It is the hot–cool copper calm of desire that is finally our only realizable approximation of ideality, a condition of perpetual revolving. Ahab's stage is struck. The rest is Ishmael spinning on the margin of his maelstrom. Always in revolution.

NOTES

1. *Correspondence*, ed. Lynn Horth. In The Writings of Herman Melville, Vol. 14, ed. Harrison Hayford, Hershel Parker, and G. Thomas Tanselle (Evanston and Chicago: Northwestern University Press and The Newberry Library, 1993), p. 163.

2. In addition to Scoresby, he also researched Frederick D. Bennett's *Narrative of a Whaling Voyage* (1840), J. Ross Browne's *Etchings of a Whaling Cruise* (1846), and Thomas Beale's *Natural History of the Sperm Whale* (1839). Still the best study of Melville's borrowings in *Moby-Dick* is Howard P. Vincent, *The Trying-out of Moby-Dick* (Boston: Houghton Mifflin, 1949; rpt. Kent, OH: Kent State University Press, 1980). For a broader assessment of Melville's reading habits and a list of books he is known to have read and borrowed, see Merton M. Sealts, Jr., *Melville's Reading* (Columbia: University of South Carolina Press, 1988). For a history of source studies and a checklist of Melville's sources, see Mary K. Bercaw, *Melville's Sources* (Evanston, Ill.: Northwestern University Press, 1987).

3. Herman Melville, "Hawthorne and His Mosses," in *The Piazza Tales and Other Prose Pieces, 1839–1860* (Evanston and Chicago: Northwestern University Press and The Newberry Library, 1987), p. 244. Hereafter cited as "Mosses."

4. The fullest articulation of the theory is in Leon Howard, *Herman Melville: A Biography* (Berkeley: University of California Press, 1951), pp. 150–79. See also George R. Stewart, "The Two *Moby-Dicks*," *American Literature* 25 (January 1954): 417–48, as well as James Barbour's extension of Howard's view to three compositional phases in "The Composition of *Moby-Dick*," *American Literature* 47 (November 1975); rpt. in Louis J. Budd and Edwin Cady, eds. *On Melville: The Best from American Literature* (Durham, NC: Duke University Press, 1988), pp. 203–20. Harrison Hayford supplies a helpful overview of the development of the compositional theories (including his own multiphase "Unnecessary Duplicates" theory) in the Historical Note to *Moby-Dick*, ed. Harrison Hayford, Hershel Parker, and G. Thomas Tanselle (Evanston and Chicago: Northwestern University Press and The Newberry Library, 1988), pp. 648–59.

5. Walter E. Bezanson makes this point in his argument against the received legend of the composition of *Moby-Dick* in "*Moby-Dick*: Document, Drama, Dream," in John Bryant, ed., *A Companion to Melville Studies* (Westport, CT: Greenwood Press, 1986), pp. 176–83.

6. "Melville's *Moby-Dick*; or, *The Whale*," *Literary World* 9 (November 12, 1851), as qtd. in Barbour, "The Composition of *Moby-Dick*."

7. Herman Melville, *Collected Poems of Herman Melville*, ed. Howard P. Vincent (Chicago: Hendricks House, 1947), p. 231.

8. Charles Olson, *Call Me Ishmael* (San Francisco: City Lights Books, 1941), p. 39.

9. F. O. Matthiessen, *American Renaissance: Art and Expression in the Age of Emerson and Whitman* (New York: Oxford University Press, 1941), pp. 423, 424, 416.

10. Julian Markels, *Melville and the Politics of Identity* (Urbana: University of Illinois Press, 1993), in his otherwise cogent study of Melville and Lear reverts to a rhetoric of compulsion when he asserts that Shakespeare's "political vision . . . compelled . . . Melville to rise to its occasion" (1).

11. See Allan Heimert, "*Moby-Dick* and American Political Symbolism," *American Quarterly* 15 (Winter 1963): 495–534.

12. These positions are drawn in several recent studies, including Michael Paul Rogin, *Subversive Genealogy: The Politics and Art of Herman Melville* (New York: Knopf, 1983); Wai-chee Dimock, *Empire for Liberty: Melville and the Poetics of Individualism* (Princeton: Princeton University Press, 1989); Larry Reynolds, *European Revolutions and the American Literary Renaissance* (New Haven: Yale University Press, 1988); and Toni Morrison, "Unspeakable Things Unspoken: The Afro-American Presence in American Literature," *Michigan Quarterly Review* 28:1 (Winter 1989): 1–34.

13. Ralph Waldo Emerson, "The Transcendentalist," in Stephen Whicher, ed., *Selected Writings of Emerson* (Boston: Houghton Mifflin, 1957), p. 203.

14. Largely headed by Evert Duyckinck and the loquacious Cornelius Mathews, Young America was a political and literary faction that lionized Irving and promoted the development of an American national literature. See John Bryant, *Melville and Repose: The Rhetoric of Humor in the American Renaissance* (New York: Oxford University Press, 1993), pp. 47–8.

15. Edward H. Rosenberry, *Melville and the Comic Spirit* (Cambridge: Harvard University Press, 1955), pp. 132–3.

16. Matthiessen, *American Renaissance*, p. 435. Olson's *Call Me Ishmael* also focuses upon Melville's borrowing from Shakespeare.

17. Lawrence Levine, *Highbrow/Lowbrow: The Emergence of Cultural Hierarchy in America* (Cambridge: Harvard University Press, 1988), pp. 40–1.

18. Ralph Waldo Emerson, "The American Scholar," in *Selections*, ed. Stephen E. Whicher (Boston: Houghton Mifflin, 1957), p. 68.

19. "Mosses," p. 245. Of Chatterton's belief that "Shakespeare must ever remain unapproachable," Melville wrote, "Cant. No man 'must ever remain unapproachable' " (*Log*, 363–4).

20. Hershel Parker states the rhetorical problem confronting Melville succinctly: how can an American writer "write of real American life with a Shakespearean intensity without imitating Shakespeare – particularly Shakespearean rhetoric." See *Herman Melville: A Biography, Volume 1, 1819–1851* (Baltimore: Johns Hopkins University Press, 1996), p. 739.

4

WYN KELLEY

Pierre's Domestic Ambiguities

In the spring of 1851, Melville wrote to his Pittsfield neighbor Nathaniel Hawthorne, pretending to review his new novel:

> "The House of the Seven Gables: A Romance. By Nathaniel Hawthorne. One vol. 16mo, pp. 344." . . . This book is like a fine old chamber, abundantly, but still judiciously, furnished. . . . There is old china with rare devices, set out on the carved buffet; there are long and indolent lounges to throw yourself upon; there is an admirable sideboard, plentifully stored with good viands; there is a smell as of old wine in the pantry; and finally, in one corner, there is a dark little black-letter volume in golden clasps, entitled "Hawthorne: A Problem."[1]

This witty letter develops into Melville's famous characterization of Hawthorne as the tragic hero who "says NO! in thunder, but the Devil himself cannot make him say *yes*" (186). Melville's opening, however, lingering as it does over the household images the novel inspired, suggests his acute awareness of Hawthorne's private side. Melville clearly knew and admired the domestic Hawthorne, inhabiting *The House of the Seven Gables* with sensual pleasure, and the letter shows that even as he was writing the ocean-going *Moby-Dick*, he contemplated house and home. In *Pierre: or the Ambiguities* Melville responds to Hawthorne's novel by making his own foray into domestic literature. But rather than uphold middle-class domestic values, as Hawthorne does, Melville offers a different kind of domesticity: one founded not on marriage and family but on the riskier relations of fraternity. In this choice, Melville may well have been influenced by contemporary women's domestic novels, which often envisioned a domestic life based on brother–sister relationships. Unfortunately, his vision of the home as a community inspired by fraternal ideals was too radical for many middle-class readers, and his book failed with that audience.[2]

Melville's letter to Hawthorne suggests that he had given considerable thought to domestic subjects and that he had, indeed, a complex response to Hawthorne's literary house. On the one hand, he seems to revel in its luxurious appointments: the lounges, viands, and wine that make this "fine old chamber" look rather more like a men's club than the little red cottage where Hawthorne lived with his wife Sophia and children Una and Julian. At the same time, with its self-conscious language and exaggerated tone, his letter mocks that luxury, revealing its shadow side. Hawthorne appears not as the gracious host, but as a dark little book entitled "Hawthorne: A Problem." Biographers and critics have long speculated on the "problem" of Hawthorne, or indeed, Melville's problematic relation with him.[3] Melville doesn't elaborate on it here, but his letter goes on to hint at a deeper consideration of Hawthorne's *House*.

He could not take up the domestic subject, though, until he had finished with his whale, saying to Hawthorne, "The tail is not yet cooked" (*Correspondence*, 196). Cooking *Pierre* would send him into new literary terrain – the family, house, and home of a young American aristocrat rather than the working-class decks of American ships – and his choice has puzzled many readers. Why, one might ask, did Melville abandon the subject he knew best and which had garnered him considerable recognition for one that seemed completely unsuited to his sensibility: domestic life, family secrets, and romantic love? "HERMAN MEVILLE CRAZY" might summarize this argument.[4]

Yet Melville knew the contemporary domestic literature well. Much of it contained issues and themes that preoccupied him deeply in the 1850s, and the success of Hawthorne's *House* stimulated him to think of a new audience. More than that, the domestic novel offered an opportunity to probe a theme that runs through much of his nautical fiction, namely, brotherhood. In *Pierre* Melville moves brotherhood from the ship to the home, from a model of comradeship between men to an equally intimate "brotherhood" between man and woman.[5] *Pierre* acts as a brother to the three women in his life: his mother Mary Glendinning, his supposed sister Isabel Banford, and later his fiancée Lucy Tartan. But whereas social convention allows a man to share almost unlimited intimacy with his brothers, closeness with sisters imposes certain constraints. If he is to achieve an ideal relationship with a sister, the brother must either adopt monastic celibacy or live in incest. *Pierre* experiments with both, with ambiguous intentions and results. Either to escape from or to protest against the patriarchal institution of marriage, *Pierre* tries to renovate the middle-class household, to achieve a fraternal communion like the one that nurtured Ishmael in *Moby-Dick*. In this sense, Melville's novel shares the antipatriarchal spirit of much domestic fiction by women writers of the 1850s. Unfortunately, the pressure of gender conventions makes *Pierre*'s quest for radical domesticity doomed. And unlike Hawthorne's *House*, which, after challenging the rules of the patriarchal family, ends by reinscribing them, Melville's *Pierre* rejects marriage, offering a warped utopian alternative. These tensions in his novel create some of the ambiguities so aptly named in its title, ambiguities that continue to perplex its readers.

Melville's choice of domestic settings and themes for *Pierre*, which takes place almost exclusively in the main characters' private homes, is not as strange as it may at first appear. Melville had considerable knowledge of the world of domesticity and of women's novels. Furthermore, he recognized and used many of the themes of domestic fiction in *Pierre*, some, it must be acknowledged, in a parodic way, but others with thought and care.[6]

Melville's knowledge of domestic life and novels began in and was sustained by his own household, which, during the early 1850s, consisted largely of women. His father Allan Melvill had died in 1832, and his older brother Gansevoort died abroad in 1846. He and his brother Allan took a New York house together when both married in 1847, but that arrangement eventually broke down, and Melville moved his family from New York to the farm Arrowhead near Pittsfield, Massachusetts. By 1850 Melville, then, was the only male in the house besides his infant son. Meanwhile, his wife Elizabeth and his mother Maria, as well as his sisters Helen, Augusta, Catherine, and Fanny, generally kept house with him. Nor does this female-centered household appear to have irked the man who wrote in *Moby-Dick* that "man must eventually lower, or at least shift, his conceit of attainable felicity; not placing it anywhere in the intellect or the fancy; but in the wife, the heart, the bed, the table, the saddle, the fire-side, the country." Melville's letters from Arrowhead show that, on the whole, he took considerable pleasure in rural domestic life, at least in the early years. "My peace and my supper are my reward, my dear Hawthorne," he wrote, and Hawthorne praised Melville's hospitality: "If you were to see how snug and comfortable Melville makes himself and friends, I think you would not fail [to visit]." Letters from Melville's sisters confirm that he participated readily in the family's amusements and picnics, readings in the parlor, sleigh rides, and visits.[7]

Although it is not hard to reconstruct Melville's domestic life at Arrowhead, finding evidence of his reading or knowledge of what have been called the "literary domestics" – women who wrote family romances or domestic or sentimental novels – is more difficult. We do know, from a reference in *Redburn*, that Melville was familiar with Susanna Rowson's *Charlotte Temple*, one of the period's most sensational and popular stories of a woman's seduction and betrayal. Catharine Maria Sedgwick, a prolific writer of such novels as *Hope Leslie* and *The Linwoods* (which Helen Melville urged her sister Augusta to read), was a close neighbor of the Arrowhead Melvilles and a family friend. Augusta and Helen both read widely, mentioning Dickens and Thackeray in their letters, reading *Jane Eyre* as soon as it appeared in an American edition, but also reading the popular female authors published in the magazines they avidly consumed. Melville exchanged books and ideas with several women who loved to read, most notably Anne Lynch, who held lively literary soirees in New York, Sophia Hawthorne, who read *Moby-Dick* with singular appreciation, and Sarah Morewood, who sent him Harriet Martineau's *The Hour and the Man*. Nearly every day, Melville drove to Pittsfield for the mail, newspapers, and magazines, which he would bring home for family reading in the evenings. There is no direct evidence of the family reading Harriet Beecher Stowe's *Uncle Tom's Cabin*, Susan Warner's *The Wide, Wide World* and *Queechy*, Caroline Chesebro's *Isa*, or Alice Cary's *Hagar*, to name just a few of the popular women's novels published within two years of *Pierre*. But it is hard to believe that Melville and his family did not participate in the "parlor culture" of the day – the family circle reading aloud from current books and magazines.[8]

Whatever Melville may have thought of the popular women novelists, in some ways he had more in common with them socially than he did with respected male writers like Washington Irving, Hawthorne, Nathaniel Parker Willis, or Longfellow. Many of the literary domestics, like their male counterparts, came from elite American families. But unlike college-educated male writers, female authors were often self-taught or did not advance beyond the typical schooling for women. Melville too, because of his family's reverses and his father's death, missed having a college education. Furthermore, the female writers tended to write out of financial necessity, often to supplement a failing husband's income, rather than because they had trained themselves for an authorial career. Melville too turned to writing out of necessity, preferring not to follow the men of his family into law, business, or politics. Many women writers, laboring under the disadvantages of economic hardship and lacking professional credentials, began their careers as "Anonymous." For *Pierre*, Melville also considered publishing the book anonymously or under the pseudonym Guy Winthrop, as if aware that this new subject matter required of him a new identity. When Melville promised Sophia Hawthorne that his new book would be a "rural bowl of milk" (*Correspondence*, 219) and informed his publisher Richard Bentley that it would have "unquestionable novelty . . . treating of utterly new scenes & characters . . . very much more calculated for popularity than anything you have yet published of mine" (*Correspon-*

dence, 226), he may have meant only that *Pierre* concerns "home-born" characters from the countryside.[9] Clearly, however, the book has more in common with popular women's fiction than either of these two disingenuous comments would imply.

Pierre includes many of the themes that feminist scholars have identified with women's novels at midcentury. First, and most obviously, house and home are significant domains in the book. Scenes in *Pierre* take place in the Glendinning mansion's bedroom, dining room, and private closet; Lucy's aunt's cottage; Mrs. Tartan's drawing room; the Miss Pennies' sewing circle; Walter Ulver's farmhouse; Glen Stanly's bachelor apartment; and Pierre's meager dwelling at the Apostles Church in New York. Significantly too, the few outdoor scenes are often domesticated. For example, Pierre and Lucy's journey up the mountainside takes place inside the coach, and Lucy doesn't like heights. Furthermore, these domestic settings do not appear accidental or as mere backdrops but have considerable meaning in the way they encode class and character. The Glendinning house embodies the family's pride of place; Isabel's bleak home her poor, friendless condition; Lucy's cottage her middle-class domestic purity; and the Apostles' tenement Pierre's revolt against the expectations of marriage.

In its portrayal of women, *Pierre* also draws on popular stereotypes from women's fiction, such as the domestic angel, the dark temptress, the busybody, the proud matriarch, the abandoned woman, and even, briefly, the prostitute. Both Lucy and Isabel exhibit the independence and self-sufficiency of many spirited heroines, even as they subordinate themselves eventually to Pierre, in a pattern characteristic of nineteenth-century women's novels.[10] Furthermore, Pierre shares many of the traits of female protagonists. His mother worries about his "sweet docility": "Now I almost wish him otherwise than sweet and docile to me, seeing that it must be hard for man to be an uncompromising hero and a commander among his race, and yet never ruffle any domestic brow" (20). His heroism consists in his not assuming or displacing his father's position in the household but rather in sacrificing his own identity and wishes to his mother's social status and Isabel's needs. For this sacrifice, Lucy later in the novel calls him an angel, the name usually reserved for self-negating women.[11]

Although reviewers of *Pierre* seemed appalled at the book's treatment of incest, women's fiction frequently explored subliminal incestuous relationships.[12] Implied incest, in fact, might be seen as a primary form of socialization for women, as in many women's novels heroines learn from fathers and brothers how to submit to male authority through love. In Susan Warner's *The Wide, Wide World* and *Queechy*, for example, Ellen and Fleda marry their "brothers," the men who have brought them up when their own parents failed them. Ellen lives for a long time in her "brother's" household, learning to tame her rebellious spirit, educate her mind, and adapt to a religious domestic ideology. Pierre's later household arrangement differs from Ellen's most notably by combining marriage and brotherhood at once, whereas for Ellen, John is first a brother and then a husband.

Clearly, *Pierre* in many ways differs markedly from women's novels of the period. *Pierre*'s women do not have the autonomy or credibility of many popular domestic heroines. The book parodies the culture's idealization of domesticity. Yet at the same time, it engages and takes in quite startling directions some of the women's novels' challenges to patriarchal notions of marriage, family, and the home. The question for many of *Pierre*'s readers is, why? What was Melville trying to do in his rewriting of the romantic and domestic plots?[13]

Many of *Pierre*'s readers have assumed that the novel, like women's domestic novels, has a "cover story," that it works out sensitive personal issues or presses an urgent social agenda under a socially acceptable guise.[14] A number of critics have approached *Pierre* looking for an autobiographical subtext – about Melville's family, his sexuality, or his relation to the literary market – for which *Pierre*'s story provides the cover. According to this argument, the biographical tensions in the novel, the secrets Melville is trying to keep, help explain the book's many ambiguities.

The theory of a family plot is now well known. On the basis of a letter from Melville's uncle Thomas Melvill to Herman's future father-in-law Lemuel Shaw, scholars have speculated on the possibility of there being a real Isabel in the Melville family. The letter is frustratingly elusive, describing a visit by a woman and her daughter who came to claim money after the death of Herman's father, Allan Melvill. Whether the young woman was Allan's illegitimate daughter or not, whether the women blackmailed Thomas Melvill or simply came with a milliner's bill, is impossible to ascertain. *Pierre* remains, however, for many readers Melville's most autobiographical novel. The biographical parallels are certainly numerous, and if accurate, they suggest that *Pierre* is only a very thin cover for Melville's rage at his own family.[15]

A thicker cover might be required for another private plot, the sexual one. Edwin Haviland Miller and Newton Arvin have explored the emotional and sexual dimensions of Melville's friendship with Hawthorne as it may have colored the ambiguous sexuality of *Pierre*. But James Creech has been most straightforward in arguing that *Pierre* is a gay novel in which a heterosexual love story covers the hero's love for a man. In an incestuous twist, however, the real object of fascination is not a lover but the father, although Isabel, as the "father's flesh," provides a female cover for homoerotic passion. Melville, according to Creech, uses the portrait of his father to "wink" at the reader, showing that a hidden, subversive truth always lurks beneath the sanctioned surface. The incest in *Pierre* may be a way for Melville to deflect attention from his true concerns in the novel.[16]

Finally, the story has appeared to many readers a thin cover for Melville's attack on his publishers, editors, and audience. The book may have *begun* as a love story with a twist, but somewhere along the way – probably at about the time Melville began getting the first negative reviews of *Moby-Dick* – Melville turned Pierre into a heroic frustrated writer, slaving away at a book that was bound to fail. Family, incest, love, women, dropped out of sight as Melville mounted his assault on meretricious editors, critics, and reviewers.[17] Again the domestic plot conceals and at the same time helps to reveal a biographical imperative.

Another possibility, however, is that in *Pierre* Melville was rewriting Hawthorne's *House*; his story, then, is a cover for his reading of and relationship with Hawthorne, which was not only emotional but also literary.[18] Locating the story in the domestic sphere, as Hawthorne did in *House*, allowed Melville to focus on themes of intimacy that may have covertly alluded to his feelings for Hawthorne. At the same time, he departed from Hawthorne's domestic politics, especially on the subject of marriage. In *Pierre*, then, Melville announced his own position, and his dissatisfaction with Hawthorne's, on the domestic novel and its readers.

Melville's "Hawthorne and His Mosses" and his letters to Hawthorne exhibit worshipful devotion, which many scholars have read as explicitly sexual and personal. When Melville says that "Hawthorne has dropped germinous seeds into my soul . . . and further, and further, shoots his strong New-England roots into the hot soil of my Southern soul," it is hard to miss the erotic overtones.[19] And how else are we to read a letter like this one?

> . . . I can't write what I felt. But I felt pantheistic then . . . your heart beat in my ribs and mine in yours, and both in God's. A sense of unspeakable security is in me this moment, on account of your having understood the book. . . .
> Whence come you, Hawthorne? By what right do you drink from my flagon of life? And when I put it to my lips – lo, they are yours and not mine. . . .   (*Correspondence*, 212–13)

Although many of the surviving letters to Hawthorne are not this sexual in their imagery, they almost all contain some personal appeal for intimacy.

But we must also remember that Hawthorne was a literary celebrity, and that nearly all the erotic language surrounds the subjects of reading and writing. Hawthorne's germinous seeds are his stories in *Mosses from an Old Manse*. Melville feels their hearts beating together when Hawthorne has read and admired *Moby-Dick*. When he touches his lips to the flagon of life and finds Hawthorne's lips there, he's trying to describe the wonder he feels at being understood. He thanks Hawthorne for having "hugged the ugly Socrates" (*Correspondence*, 213), an embrace of Melville's ideas as much as of his body. As in somewhat similar pantheistic passages in Whitman's *Song of Myself*, sexual ecstasy serves as the gateway to the spirit, sexual union as a metaphor for the merging of body and soul.[20]

I am not trying to deny that Melville had erotic feelings about Hawthorne. But whatever feelings he had existed in the context of, or alongside, an intense meeting of the minds that Melville experienced as the ecstasy of reading and being read. What better way to show his gratitude to Hawthorne than, in his next book, to show that he had read *The House of the Seven Gables* as Hawthorne had read *Moby-Dick*?

As Melville began to write his own domestic romance, he would have found Hawthorne's novel inspiring and provocative on many fronts. Rereading Hawthorne's book, he would have realized that *House* consciously attempted to work with materials that the "scribbling women" had made their own: the "true woman" or domestic angel, the separation of gender spheres, and the redemption of the male sphere by domesticity. But in several instances, Hawthorne remodeled conventions of the domestic novel for his own use. The most striking of these, in terms of Melville's handling of domesticity in *Pierre*, is the way Hawthorne locates both masculine and feminine spheres on the same site.

Many midcentury female novelists portray the home as the separate domain of women, a place where men are domesticated and the forces of capitalism and patriarchy held at bay. In Stowe's *Uncle Tom's Cabin*, Mr. Bird cannot rule his household the way he can the Congress; in Rachel Halliday's kitchen, men have a place but only under her benevolent sway. The House of the Seven Gables, however, is not a protected, sanctified home. Though presided over by a woman, Hepzibah Pyncheon, it lacks domestic warmth and cheer. Because Hepzibah is a "lady," she does not perform the domestic labor that would make her house a home. But more problematically, the house cannot be a home because it lives under the curse of male Pyncheons who have stifled female and domestic influence.

Only when Phoebe, the country cousin, arrives can the house be redeemed, for she is a "true woman," whereas Hepzibah is a "lady."[21] Phoebe brings the old house back to life, restoring its kitchen, garden, and chambers with her busy, "cheerful" presence, her "homely witchcraft" (72). Although she succeeds partially with Hepzibah, Phoebe makes her greatest impact on the household's men. Clifford, whose soul is described as a "dark and ruinous mansion," learns to "kindle the heart's household-fire" (105) under her care. For "Phoebe's presence made a home about her – that very sphere which the outcast, the prisoner, the potentate, the wretch beneath mankind, the wretch aside from it, or the wretch above it, instinctively pines after – a home!" (141).

Phoebe also has a powerful effect on Holgrave, the mysterious daguerreotypist dwelling in the house. "Homeless . . . he had been – continually changing his whereabout, and therefore responsible neither to public opinion nor to individuals" (177). Phoebe gradually makes a home for this homeless man, who, as Pierre will be, is an enthusiast, a radical, and a philosopher. Holgrave would seem to be the antithesis of domesticity. Yet when he declares his love to Phoebe, he promises "to set out trees, to make fences – perhaps, even, in due time, to build a house for another generation" (307). At the end of the novel, she professes amazement at his zeal for making improvements in their new home.

Phoebe's homely influence, then, domesticates the House of the Seven Gables, overturning the patriarchal power of those who built the house, and especially of the murderous Jaffrey Pyncheon, who wants to keep it a great dynastic house and not a family home. In the end, Hawthorne asserts the power of home and of female domestic influence.

Men, however, remain at the center and ultimately in control of this home. As T. Walter Herbert has pointed out, Holgrave gets Phoebe's house with her hand and quietly, without fanfare, restores his own family's claim to the land.[22] Instead of providing a female-centered sphere opposed to or in retreat from the world, the Pyncheon house remains open to outside influence. Rather than separating the gender spheres, Hawthorne shows them meeting and competing within the same structure. The house is a site where masculine, dynastic house and feminine, domestic home work out their ideological struggle on the same ground. Melville uses a similar structure in *Pierre*, but with strikingly different results. Pierre resolves the conflict between patriarchal house and maternal home by leaving both behind.

In his first appearance, Pierre emerges from "the embowered and high-gabled old home of his fathers" (3), a house as ancient, patriarchal, and burdened with family secrets as Hawthorne's. Pierre lives in domestic bliss with a much-cherished mother, their life a "softened spell which still wheeled the mother and son in one orbit of joy" (16). But as in Hawthorne's House of Pyncheon, a curse hangs over the House of Glendinning. The intervention of Isabel reveals that in house and home, Pierre has "habituated his voice and manner to a certain fictitiousness in one of the closest domestic relations of life" (177), and he sets out for New York to correct that error. Melville's treatment of domestic life eventually works to shatter middle-class norms of marriage and home.

Pierre is presented first as the heir of an honorable house. From his father, he has inherited the name that he is the last family member to bear. Should he marry as his mother wishes, he would also receive a fine estate surrounded by a landscape that with "all its hills and swales seemed as sanctified through their [the Glendinnings'] very long uninterrupted possession" (8).[23] As in Hawthorne's House of Pyncheon, with its ancestral portrait, desk, and chair, signs of patriarchal sway appear everywhere in Melville's House of Glendinning: the General's military paraphernalia, the oversized coach and pampered horses, and finally, the dignified portraits of Pierre's parents. Pierre's house, however, is managed by a more vital female presence than Hawthorne's. Whereas Hepzibah seems undone by the task of preparing breakfast for her brother, Mary Glendinning presides over an abundant table loaded with delicacies; and she never does so "in any dishabille that was not eminently becoming" (15). Although Mary, like Hepzibah, proudly upholds her family's patriarchal legacy, she also sheds a potent feminine influence over her house and son.

But does she make the House of Glendinning a home? Pierre thinks so: "it [his life with his mother] seemed almost to realize here below the sweet dreams of those religious enthusiasts, who paint to us a Paradise to come, when etherealized from all drosses and stains, the holiest passion of man shall unite all kindreds and climes in one circle of pure and unimpairable delight" (16). Mary Glendinning works as hard as any domestic angel to create that delight. Her greatest efforts go into raising Pierre as a gentleman, a Christian, and a conscientious lord of his tenants. To that end, she showers him with "maternal tuitions" (16) about how to behave: "Never rave, Pierre; and never rant. Your father never did either . . ." (19). She measures her success in Pierre's filial devotion: "For thus sweetly and religiously was the familiarity of his affections bottomed on the profoundest filial respect" (14). As in the domestic novels, Pierre and his mother sustain a private cult, founded on worship of the absent father, love for the "lovely, immaculate" (88) mother, and obedience in the "fine, proud, loving, docile, vigorous boy" (20).

Pierre's mother's domesticity supports his father's ancestral legacy by helping to nurture the next Glendinning hero. This domesticity is her feminine legacy to Pierre and, by extension, Lucy Tartan, for Lucy participates wholly in the Glendinning vision of an elegant home. Melville shows both the Glendinning mansion and Lucy's cottage as shrines to religious domesticity, the women as saints and angels, and Pierre as the Christian knight sworn in fealty to domestic goddesses. "Truly, thought the youth, [looking at Lucy] with a still gaze of inexpressible fondness; truly the skies do ope, and this invoking angel looks down" (4). Melville draws the link between mother and beloved by showing Pierre in their bedchambers; in these zones of intimacy, Pierre behaves with total reverence. Greeting his mother in her boudoir, he helps her dress for breakfast, calling himself "First Lady in waiting to the Dowager Duchess Glendinning" (14). Placing a ribbon around her neck, he kisses it, fastens a cameo, attends to her hair, and bends to tie her slipper before escorting her down to breakfast.

Lucy's domestic influence over Pierre promises to be every bit as potent as his mother's. He seems especially overcome by her bedchamber, pausing outside the door to entertain "feelings of a wonderful reverentialness. The carpet seemed as holy ground. Every chair seemed sanctified by some departed saint" (39). The room appears to him a "secret inner shrine" to Lucy and to love. And her bed seems the altar in that shrine:

> So he advanced, and with a fond and gentle joyfulness, his eye now fell upon the spotless bed itself, and fastened on a snow-white roll that lay beside the pillow. Now he started; Lucy seemed coming in upon him; but no – 'tis only the foot of one of her little slippers, just peeping into view from under the narrow nether curtains of the bed. Then again his glance fixed itself upon the slender, snow-white ruffled roll; and he stood as one enchanted.   (39)

Lucy's bedding elicits the same kind of fervent response as Mary Glendinning's deshabille, a response at once erotic and devotional.[24] But the eroticism is fetishized, located in ribbons, slippers, and ruffles. Toward the real women, Pierre acts with the childlike respect that the domestic cult requires.

Pierre has inherited a powerful legacy from both parents: from his male progenitors a great house and from his mother a sanctified home. To these legacies, Melville adds another: the dark stain of incest. This incest, it appears, is a necessary element of the family's house and home and has been established as a family pattern even before the advent of Isabel.

The family pattern of incest seems most obvious, of course, in the domestic fiction binding Pierre and his mother: "In the playfulness of their unclouded love, and with that strange license which a perfect confidence and mutual understanding at all points, had long bred between them, they were wont to call each other brother and sister" (5). The "strange license" of this relationship invades his later bond with his supposed sister; he admits that the "fictitiousness" (177) of his connection with his mother makes possible the incestuous union with Isabel. But other, more subtle forms of incest appear in the novel, more like what Hawthorne hints at in *House*. Pierre's Aunt Dorothea's worship of her departed brother, Pierre's father, resembles the unrequited devotion that Hepzibah feels for Clifford. Dorothea and the elder Pierre are singularly close. Like Hepzibah, she lavishes ritual attention on his miniature portrait: "before a gold-framed and gold-lidded ivory miniature, – a fraternal gift – aunt Dorothea now offered up her morning and her evening rites, to the memory of the noblest and handsomest of brothers" (73). Unlike Mary Glendinning, Dorothea cherishes the chair portrait, the picture of her brother in his "bladish" (73), erotic, wooing mood. "How much comfort that portrait has been to me" (77), she tells Pierre, claiming that she sees her brother "looking at me, and smiling at me, and nodding at me, and saying – Dorothea! Dorothea!" (79). Like the love of Hepzibah for Clifford, or of Clifford for Phoebe, this one is outwardly chaste, but it takes the form of religious devotion which supersedes all other affections.

The elder Pierre also inspires devotion and love in his cousin Ralph Winwood, the painter of the chair portrait. Ralph seduces his cousin with questions about the beautiful French emigrée in order to make him sit for a painting; the men's shared confidence and intimacy produce the only truthful portrait of Pierre's father. Melville does not make as much of this cousinly attachment as he does of the one between Pierre and his cousin Glen Stanly, which "transcends the bounds of mere boyishness, and revels for a while in the empyrean of a love which only comes short, by one degree, of the sweetest sentiment entertained between the sexes" (216). But the elder Pierre shares greater intimacy with Winwood and his sister Dorothea than he ever does with his wife, a pattern that may influence Pierre's decision to look for his closest bonds within the family rather than outside it.

House and home are not at odds in the early chapters of *Pierre* because the spheres of masculine dominance and feminine influence support the same class interests. A family religion sets the terms for domestic life, which is experienced as a tacit worship of the feminine and the home. But reverence for the family produces "a certain fictitiousness in . . . the closest domestic relations" (177), a fictitiousness that conceals fetishism and incest. It also obliterates any natural sexuality, for Mary Glendinning worships her official husband, not the wooing, erotic husband. And Pierre, contemplating his future wife, wonders, "*I* to wed this heavenly fleece? Methinks one husbandly embrace would break her airy zone" (58). Suddenly aware of the dangers of the cult of domestic purity, Pierre thinks, "I am Pluto stealing Proserpine; and every accepted lover is" (59). Pierre has only just seen Isabel's face, but it has exposed to him the hypocrisy of the family domestic fiction.

Isabel's domesticity differs radically from that of the Glendinnings and Tartans. Pierre lives in a mansion and Lucy in a cottage covered with honeysuckle and roses. Isabel dwells in a "small and low red farm-house" (110) with gables at either end, covered with moss and vines.²⁵ Mrs. Glendinning presides over her table or boudoir and manages her servants and tenants. Lucy works at her painting and drawing. But Isabel makes butter and cheese, sews, bakes bread, and draws water. Like Phoebe, Isabel is well versed in the domestic arts, and like her as well, she presents a social challenge to the great family in the old house. In going to her, Pierre leaves "the brilliant chandeliers of the mansion of Saddle Meadows, to join company with the wretched rushlights of poverty and woe" (111). Not only does she come from a different social class, but also she seems a real bodily presence. Whereas to enter Lucy's bedroom or to embrace her airy zone seems to him an act of Plutonic rape ("I am Pluto stealing Proserpine" [59]), Pierre unhesitatingly enters Isabel's dark room, takes her labor-hardened hand, and kisses her. Though in no way as cheerful and lightsome as Phoebe, Isabel has a similar effect in getting the aristocratic Pierre, like Clifford, to emerge from his ancestral house and escape the confinements of his class.

Although psychically and socially homeless, Isabel also teaches Pierre what a real home ought to be. Speaking for her in their final meeting before leaving for New York, he tells her, "thou wantest not the openness [of acknowledgment]; for thou dost not pine for empty nominalness, but for vital realness; what thou wantest, is not the occasional openness of my brotherly love; but its continual domestic confidence" (192). Without necessarily foreseeing how he will make a home for Isabel, Pierre nevertheless knows that his previous domesticity, his fetishistic relations with his mother and Lucy, were false. Now houseless and homeless, Pierre staggers over the threshold of the mansion: "He seemed as jeeringly hurled from beneath his own ancestral roof" (185). Pierre flees the domestic religion of his ancestors, choosing Isabel's radical, vital domesticness instead.

Up to this point in the novel, Melville adheres to an antipatriarchal plot that shows some similarities to Hawthorne's. When Pierre leaves for New York, however, moving his family from country to city, Melville leaves Hawthorne and the world of middle-class house and home far behind. Instead Pierre commits himself to radical utopian brotherhood.

In his letter on *House*, Melville described his sense of kinship with Hawthorne: "I feel that the Godhead is broken up like the bread at the Supper, and that we are the pieces. Hence this infinite fraternity of feeling" (*Correspondence*, 212). Melville expresses the "fraternity" that he felt for Hawthorne as a spiritual union, a sacred and ideal brotherhood that resembles in some ways Ishmael's sense of divine fraternity with his shipmates: "Oh! my dear fellow beings, why should we longer cherish any social acerbities, or know the slightest ill-humor or envy! Come, let us squeeze hands all round" (416). Robert K. Martin has shown how the ethic of fraternity works to create solidarity among the *Pequod*'s crew and to resist the ship's oppressive hierarchy. Pierre similarly tries to oppose the family hierarchy by creating a spiritual fraternity that will obliterate the traditional power relations of marriage. Ironically, and perhaps not accidentally, Hawthorne was to explore the same possibilities in *The Blithedale Romance*, written at the same time as *Pierre*. Hawthorne's utopian community at Blithedale tries to base relations between the sexes on brotherhood and sisterhood. Both Hawthorne and Melville had observed a similar enterprise when they visited the Shaker community at Hancock Village in the summer of 1851.[26] After Melville's first visit to the Shakers, he bought one of their books and marked this passage: "Now let any candid person examine the causes by which associations [i.e., marriages] . . . so often fail, and he will find that it arises from the partial and selfish relations of husbands, wives and children, and other kindred relations, together with the jealousies and evil surmises naturally arising therefrom" (*Log*, 381). Melville welcomed the cultural currents challenging traditional domesticity. Brotherhood seemed preferable to the "partial and selfish" relations of marriage.

As Hawthorne shows in *The Blithedale Romance*, he may have shared some of Melville's views on marriage, but ultimately he rejected them. Erotic tensions between the Blithedale brethren and sisters destroy their community. And although marriage in this novel is nowhere near as successful or traditional as it appears in *House* – Zenobia dies seemingly out of frustrated love, Coverdale chooses a single life, and Priscilla and Hollingsworth are locked in a regressive and guilt-ridden interdependency – the fraternal experiment nevertheless fails, leaving marriage as the only alternative. Pierre, however, commits himself passionately to the fraternal ideal, joining Isabel and later Lucy in a tiny utopian community at the Apostles. As in *Blithedale*, the community fails, but in Melville's novel marriage does not take its place. Instead Pierre creates a monastic domestic sphere, a cell that replaces the house and home he had earlier revered.

Melville's choice of the city for this experiment is not accidental. Much contemporary urban fiction questioned whether a family culture nurtured in the country could survive in the city. Novelists George Lippard (*New York: Its Upper Ten and Lower Million*, 1850), E. Z. C. Judson (*The Mysteries and Miseries of New York*, 1848), Fanny Fern (*Ruth Hall*, 1855), and Walt Whitman (*Franklin Evans*, 1842) and journalists like Lydia Maria Child (*Letters from New York*, 1844) and George Foster (*New York by Gas-Light*, 1850) showed the struggles of middle- or working-class protagonists to maintain their virtue and protect their homes in the face of urban pressures.²⁷ Like many of these protagonists, Pierre and Isabel flee the country hoping to find new lives in the city. But New York, as Pierre bitterly says, is a place where "[m]ilk dropt from the milkman's can in December, freezes not more quickly on those stones, than does snow-white innocence, if in poverty, it chance to fall in these streets" (230). The realities of life in a city rapidly expanding in size and population, diversifying both socially and economically, and boldly displaying the widening gulf between the classes give Pierre's gloomy statement some basis in historical fact. But Melville also draws on urban literature describing the evils of the city – poverty, prostitution, drunkenness, and ruin – to highlight the dangers of Pierre's first foray into independent homemaking. Clearly, the conventional middle-class notions of domesticity with which Pierre was raised will prove insufficient to the economic and social challenges of New York.

Nowhere does that problem appear more obvious than in Pierre's attempts to house himself and Isabel in the city. When Pierre first announces his engagement to Lucy, his cousin Glen offers him the use of his "very charming, little old house . . . which . . . possessed great attractions for the retired billings and cooings of a honeymoon" (220). Dubbing his house the "Cooery," Glen goes on to describe how he will have it prepared for the young couple:

> . . . the venerable, grotesque, old mahoganies, and marbles, and mirror-frames, and moldings could be very soon dusted and burnished; the kitchen was amply provided with the necessary utensils for cooking; the strong box of old silver immemorially pertaining to the mansion, could be readily carted round from the vaults of the neighboring Bank; while the hampers of old china, still retained in the house, needed but little trouble to unpack; so that silver and china would soon stand assorted in their appropriate closets. . . .
>
> (121)

Glen's letter emphasizes the hard labor involved in starting up the lumbering engines of Victorian domesticity. The house filled with ancestral silver, furniture, and china weighs as heavily on its descendants as the Glendinning family history and name. In Pierre's first response, he merely thanks Glen for his trouble and reminds him to stock up on wine and coffee. After his decision to "marry" Isabel, however, Pierre writes in a different tone, thanking Glen for the offer of the house but adding that "the pre-engaged servants, and the old china, and the old silver, and the old wines, and the Mochas, were now become altogether unnecessary" (228). Pierre can no longer afford such expensive domesticity, but more than that, he now recognizes that his projected home with Lucy, the Cooery, like Saddle Meadows, is another domestic fiction that Isabel's presence has exploded.

Knowing that his marriage to her is an ingenious sham, Pierre boldly refuses to adopt the trappings of middle-class domesticity.

Instead, Pierre, Isabel, and Delly settle in a tenement, the renovated
church known as the Apostles. Melville details their domesticity there as
fully as he does in the Saddle Meadows section, and with a similar intent:
to expose the middle-class worship of house and home, this time through
a dramatic contrast. At Saddle Meadows, Pierre's being Master Pierre Glendinning of the great house made him a young lord of the manor and a
hero. At the Apostles, the houseless Pierre is suddenly free of that "loathed
identity" (171) and can enter into a new kind of home. Tenement housing
signifies the change in his social status, as he no longer owns his domestic
space but rents it and shares it with "scores of those miscellaneous, bread-
and-cheese adventurers, and ambiguously professional nondescripts" (267).
Instead of a time-honored family mansion, he occupies a former church
carved up into flats by speculators. Instead of the privacy of his bedroom
and closet, he shares three small rooms with Isabel and Delly, and from
his window he can see other tenants gazing back at him. Rather than separating his living space from the space of labor, he writes his novel in his
bedroom, and Isabel and Delly perform their sewing and other chores on
the other side of the wall. Stripped of comforts, furniture, even heat, Pierre's
flat represents the polar opposite of his former luxurious home.

At the same time, it offers a freedom he previously lacked. The creative
use of space at the Apostles, the motley assortment of "artists of various
sorts; painters, or sculptors, or indigent students, or teachers of languages,
or poets, or fugitive French politicians, or German philosophers" (267), the
transitional flow of life make for a lively culture that has created its own
identity. The old church retains its "romantic and lofty" (268) ambiance,
which exerts a unifying influence over the tenants: "the occupants of the
venerable church began to come together out of their various dens, in more
social communion. . . . By-and-by . . . they . . . became organized in a peculiar society" (269). Although only nebulously defined, this community
provides a loose brotherhood of like-minded souls, many like Holgrave and
his friends, radicals of one kind or another. Melville's narrator mocks their
transcendentalism that feasts on Graham crackers and water, presided over
by the faintly ghoulish guru, Plotinus Plinlimmon. But at least Pierre has
found a community congenial to his newly conceived revolt against house
and home.

In this environment of spiritual fraternity and philosophical radicalism,
Pierre turns to his newfound metier, writing. Whereas in the Cooery, as
Lucy's husband, Pierre would have performed no labor more arduous than
that of grinding coffee, the grim domesticity of the Apostles nurtures

Pierre's higher calling as a writer of metaphysical fiction. As at Hawthorne's Blithedale, Pierre and his small community must live simply in order to produce finer thoughts – or, in the case of Isabel and Lucy, finer music and art. His revolt against marriage finds a congenial home at the Apostles, and at the same time this revisionist domesticity proves necessary to his art.

Furthermore, in a domesticity based on fraternity rather than marriage, Pierre hopes to formulate a response to the philosophical challenge he encountered in Plotinus Plinlimmon's tract, "Chronometricals and Horologicals." This puzzling essay addresses Pierre's metaphysical condition by proposing two mutually opposed yet coexisting standards of behavior: the chronometrical, or God-given, truth and the horological, or worldly, necessity. Plinlimmon advises mortals not to fret if they can't achieve chronometrical perfection. In fact, to do so would be to upset the whole human order: "in things terrestrial (horological) a man must not be governed by ideas celestial (chronometrical). . . . A virtuous expediency, then, seems the highest earthly excellence for the mass of men" (214). By surrendering the chronometrical ideal, humans will thrive, according to Plinlimmon: "there would be an end to that fatal despair of becoming all good" (215).

Plinlimmon's ethic of "virtuous expediency" subverts Pierre on two fronts. The first is moral and philosophical, as Pierre begins to doubt his actions and to feel he may have chosen unwisely to defend Isabel's honor and to write a metaphysical novel. Feeling Plinlimmon's face gazing on him through the tenement window, he imagines it mocking his idealistic endeavors: "Vain! Fool! Quit!" (293). But on the domestic front as well, Plinlimmon challenges Pierre's enterprise, which, under his cynical scrutiny, comes to seem more horological than chronometrical in its aims: for "[w]hat was most terrible was the idea that by some magical means or other the face had got hold of his secret. 'Ay,' shuddered Pierre, 'the face knows that Isabel is not my wife!' " (293). Plinlimmon the voyeur sees into Pierre's unorthodox household, and although Pierre puts muslin over the window, he can't banish the all-seeing face from his mind. Pierre's distress over the pamphlet suggests, then, that just as his writing is intimately connected to his domestic life, his metaphysical doubts grow out of and return to his household secrets.

The sections of *Pierre* devoted to his writing likewise show a continuity between his literary and his domestic experiments. At Saddle Meadows, as a "highly respectable youth" (245), Pierre produced genteel poetry that was, in one critic's words, " 'blameless in morals, and harmless throughout.' Another [critic], had unhesitatingly recommended his effusions to the family-circle" (246). Melville ironically condemns the parlor culture that produces such amiable young men and sustains itself by nurturing their literary effusions. When reflecting on his female admirers, all urgently requesting his autograph, Pierre thinks of the danger of this domestic culture, where "the true charm of agreeable parlor society is, that there you lose your own sharp individuality and become delightfully merged in that soft social Pantheism, as it were, that rosy melting of all into one, ever prevailing in those drawing rooms" (250). In the rosy drawing room, what can one expect to write but "that delightful love-sonnet, entitled 'The Tropical Summer' " (245)?

In the brotherhood of the Apostles, however, and in his new domestic sphere, Pierre is inspired to write a very different kind of work, an attempt to "show them deeper secrets than the Apocalypse!" (273). In this endeavor, Pierre aims not only to bring a "miserably neglected Truth to the world" (283), but also to sustain his new household. Rather than the decorative domesticity of Saddle Meadows, he expects to support "the hundred and one domestic details of how their internal arrangements were finally put into steady working order" (282). This domestic life includes Delly's therapeutic labor and companionship with Isabel, Isabel's partnership as muse and copyist in Pierre's writing, and the women's democratic sisterhood with Charlie Millthorpe's hard-working mother and sisters. In this setting of shared labor and high ideals, Pierre hopes to reform the patriarchal household and to nurture literature, philosophy, music, and art. Pierre as writer sees himself as traveling in the "orbit of his book" like an "old housewife [who] goes her daily domestic round" (298). Pierre imagines that his new domesticity will support his writing and his writing a reformed housewifery.

Melville uses the imagery of religious worship, however, to show that in a corrupt materialist culture, Pierre's new domestic arrangements are just as much a fiction as the old. In Saddle Meadows, the Christian gentleman-knight worships the saint-mother and angel-wife with elaborate adoration. The Apostles, named after Christ's brotherhood of followers, also has religious resonances, suggestive of the irony of George Lippard's name for his palace of dissolution, Monk Hall (*The Quaker City: or The Monks of Monk Hall*, 1845). Melville may certainly have been aware of the common cultural associations between Catholic orders of monks or nuns and stories of Gothic licentiousness.[28] The picture of Pierre, bundled up in blankets with hot bricks tucked around him as he writes, presents an ironic inversion of the sacred ideal, and even the narrator mocks his excessive self-discipline: "Is Pierre a shepherd, or a bishop, or a cripple?" (301).

This monastic domesticity becomes ever harder to sustain once Lucy reenters the picture. Calling her "[a] very strange cousin . . . almost a nun in her notions" (313), Pierre tries to convince Isabel and himself that Lucy can take her place in their celibate household without strain. The more experienced Delly has some inkling of the truth and begins to see the domestic façade as a lie: " 'If they are not married; if I, penitentially seeking to be pure, am now but the servant to a greater sin, than I myself committed: then, pity! pity!' " (321). Lucy's presence in the house tips the delicate balance Isabel and Pierre have maintained, so that he is forced to display himself as husband rather than as brother. Meanwhile, he and Lucy have reignited their old passion and with it Isabel's resentment. The ideal of fraternity breaks down as Lucy seems to divine and by implication to expose the truth. Pierre can no longer maintain this domestic fiction, and in his despair he feels himself "a doorless and shutterless house for the four loosened winds of heaven to howl through" (339). The gothic family melodrama that has been gathering tension in the book's later sections – Lucy's dramatic break from her mother, brother, and suitor, Isabel's jealousy of Lucy, Pierre's staunch protection of the two beleaguered women – bursts into a murderous climax when Pierre kills his enemies Glen Stanly and Frederic Tartan and ends in the last of his cells, the prison.

As if to signal the end of his domestic experiment, Melville shows Pierre having a "strange vision, [that] displaced the four blank walls, the desk, and camp-bed" (346). His dream of himself as the dismembered Titan Enceladus, struggling with the gods and elements in a sublime wilderness, seems the clearest evidence that Pierre's metaphysical book has devoured his domestic life. Yet in other ways, the dream engages his domestic conflicts anew. Enceladus's story is a Titanic version of Pierre's own family romance and of many women's novels of the period. The "son and grandson of incest," Enceladus is the product and victim of monstrously bad parenting. Heroically resisting his progenitors' destructive family patterns in a spirit no less defiant than that of such female rebels as Fanny Fern's Ruth Hall or E. D. E. N. Southworth's Capitola, Pierre adopts a "reckless sky-assaulting mood" (347). Like these female protagonists, he has sought to escape the sins of his demonic fathers and grandfathers by resisting male authority and by locating his revolt in the home, creating an explicitly nonpatriarchal household.

Eventually, however, Pierre runs the ideal of domestic fraternity its full course and abandons it in despair. Exhausted by his writing labors, frustrated that he must sacrifice Lucy all over again, he finally asks the question he might have asked when he first received Isabel's letter: "How did he know that Isabel was his sister?" (353) But it is too late for him to repair the damage and for Melville to produce the conventional happy ending: "not always doth life's beginning gloom conclude in gladness; . . . wedding-bells peal not ever in the last scene of life's fifth act" (141). Rather than wedding bells, Pierre finds the dark dungeon presided over by a "squat-framed, asthmatic turnkey" (361) who jingles his bunch of keys suggestively and says, "easy, easy, till I get the picks – I'm housewife here" (361). Pierre's heroic efforts to remake middle-class domesticity run up against the law, ending in a grim joke. Midwife to an aborted experiment and housewife to his ruined family, Pierre unites himself in death with his sisters.

Although the blood-soaked ending might explain the failure of *Pierre* among "cultivated" readers in terms of literary taste, one may still ask why it produced such violent contemporary responses. And if Melville knew the market well enough to anticipate such responses, if he consciously drew from the antipatriarchal domestic novel to expose a rigid middle-class ideology, why did he destroy his own vehicle at the same time? Why does not Melville make Pierre's utopian community a triumph of ideal love and sacrifice? It is impossible to define with any certainty the intense emotional and ideological tensions in Melville that produced this self-destructive text, but clearly the novel failed with its buyers because, among other things, it could not produce wedding bells in the fifth act. Hawthorne contrives a marriage in the last few pages of *House*, reasserting the patriarchal household that the book has worked so assiduously to undermine. Fanny Fern's *Ruth Hall* goes much further than *House* in satirizing middle-class family and domestic structures, even, as in *Pierre*, replacing Ruth's marriage with a fraternal attachment to her editor John Walter. Yet in the end, Fern does not rule out the possibility of Ruth's marrying again. *Pierre*, however, boldly attacks the perversions of domesticity from within. The failure of brotherhood, Christ's own alternative to marriage, indicts the false gods and goddesses of Melville's readers. The book's revelation of corruption at the heart of the home guaranteed its commercial failure.

To readers in the twentieth century, however, *Pierre* offers a radical reading of the gender roles and domestic structures that have produced profound distress in middle-class culture. The book reveals the fault lines in the American family, not simply in extremis – in patterns of incest, abuse, betrayal, and the hypocrisy and silence that surround them – but also in the enormous and seemingly artificial labor required to maintain the illusion of ordinary, day-to-day respectability. The religion of the American family, Melville implies, demands the worship of false idols. Melville's alternative is not, as it might appear, radical individualism, for Pierre's iconoclastic writing is rooted in an egalitarian, communal domesticity. But the ideal of fraternity and sorority creates problems that neither Melville nor his fellow toiler Hawthorne could resolve. *Pierre* remains an unsettling book less because of its open defiance of conventional sexual morality than on account of its violent and ultimately inconclusive wrestling with the notion of intimacy itself and the home wherein it dwells.

NOTES

1. *Correspondence*, ed. Lynn Horth (Evanston and Chicago: Northwestern University Press and the Newberry Library, 1993), 185. Further references appear in the text in parentheses.
2. Sheila Post-Lauria, however, has argued that in *Pierre* Melville was trying to reach beyond a middle-class "cultivated" audience to target more "general" readers. See her *Correspondent Colorings: Melville in the Marketplace* (Amherst: University of Massachusetts Press, 1996), 127–47.
3. Leon Howard, *Herman Melville* (Berkeley: University of California Press, 1961); Edwin Haviland Miller, *Melville* (New York: George Braziller, Inc., 1975); Laurie Robertson-Lorant, *Melville: A Biography* (New York: Clarkson N. Potter, 1996); Hershel Parker, *Herman Melville: A Biography (Volume 1, 1819–1851)* (Baltimore: Johns Hopkins University Press, 1996), 834–6.
4. Quoted in Brian Higgins and Hershel Parker, *Critical Essays on Herman Melville's Pierre, or, the Ambiguities* (Boston: G. K. Hall, 1983), 50.
5. For the theme of brotherhood, I am indebted to Robert K. Martin, *Hero, Captain, and Stranger: Male Friendship, Social Critique, and Literary Form in the Sea Novels of Herman Melville* (Chapel Hill: University of North Carolina Press, 1986).
6. See Gillian Brown, *Domestic Individualism: Imagining Self in Nineteenth-Century America* (Berkeley: University of California Press, 1990); also Post-Lauria, *Correspondent Colorings*, 82, 140; Lora Romero, "Domesticity and Fiction," in *The Columbia History of the American Novel*, ed. Emory Elliott (New York: Columbia University Press, 1991), 110–29; and William C. Spengemann, "Introduction" to Herman Melville, *Pierre, or the Ambiguities* (New York: Penguin Books, 1996).
7. *Moby-Dick*, ed. Harrison Hayford, Hershel Parker, and G. Thomas Tanselle (Evanston and Chicago: Northwestern University Press and the Newberry Library, 1988), 416. Further references appear in the text in parentheses. *Correspondence*, 212. Jay Leyda, *The Melville Log: A Documentary Life of Herman Melville, 1819–1891* (New York: Gordian Press, 1969), 408. On Melville's life at Arrowhead, see Robertson-Lorant, *Melville: A Biography*, 239–77, and Parker, *Herman Melville*, 782–811. For Melville's domestic circle, see Hershel Parker, "*Moby-Dick* and Domesticity," in *Critical Essays on Herman Melville's Moby-Dick* (New York: G. K. Hall, 1992), 545–62. For a view of Melville's domestic tensions, see Elizabeth Renker, *Strike through the Mask: Herman Melville and the Scene of Writing* (Baltimore: Johns Hopkins University Press, 1996).
8. On domestic novels, see Nina Baym, *Woman's Fiction: A Guide to Novels by and about Women in America, 1820–1870* (Urbana and Chicago: University of Illinois Press, 1993); Baym, *Feminism and American Literary History: Essays* (New Brunswick: Rutgers University Press, 1992); Susan Harris, *19th-Century American Women's Novels: Interpretive Strategies* (New York:

Cambridge University Press, 1990); Mary Kelley, *Private Woman, Public Stage: Literary Domesticity in Nineteenth-Century America* (New York: Oxford University Press, 1984). On the Melvilles and Catharine Maria Sedgwick, see Helen Melville to Augusta Melville, Oct. 8, 1835, in Additions to the Gansevoort-Lansing Collection, New York Public Library. On *Jane Eyre*, see Parker, *Herman Melville*, 583. On Melville's connections with Sophia Hawthorne and Sarah Morewood, see *Correspondence*, 218–20, 205–6. For parlor culture, see Joan Hedrick, *Harriet Beecher Stowe: A Life* (New York: Oxford University Press, 1994).

9. *Pierre, or the Ambiguities*, ed. Harrison Hayford, Hershel Parker, and G. Thomas Tanselle (Evanston and Chicago: Northwestern University Press and the Newberry Library, 1971), 218. Further references appear in the text in parentheses.

10. Nina Baym, *Woman's Fiction*, defines an overplot in woman's fiction that emphasizes female independence; Susan Harris, *19th-Century American Women's Novels*, argues that many novels showed women who did not completely challenge the marriage conventions (9).

11. See also Post-Lauria, *Correspondent Colorings*, 137.

12. See G. M. Goshgarian, *To Kiss the Chastening Rod: Domestic Fiction and Sexual Ideology in the American Renaissance* (Ithaca: Cornell University Press, 1992).

13. Higgins and Parker argue that trying to find out the "intentions" of *Pierre* imposes a New Critical unity on the novel and ignores its biographical and compositional history. See Brian Higgins and Hershel Parker, "Reading *Pierre*," in John Bryant, ed., *A Companion to Melville Studies* (New York: Greenwood Press, 1986), 211–39. Nevertheless, as my succeeding discussion shows, this question has vexed numerous readers of the book.

14. Susan Harris has shrewdly observed that *Moby-Dick* in fact has a domestic cover story: "The subversive plot of course belongs to Ahab, who represents the antithesis of domesticity" (20). But in the overplot, Ishmael rejoins the maternal *Rachel* and learns to accept "the wife, the heart, the bed" (416).

15. Herman's brother Gansevoort changed the family name from "Melvill" to "Melville." On Thomas Melvill's letter, see Henry A. Murray et al., "Allan Melvill's By-Blow," *Melville Society Extracts* 61 (February 1985): 1–6; Amy Puett Emmers, "Melville's Closet Skeleton: A New Letter About the Illegitimacy Incident in *Pierre*," in *Studies in the American Renaissance*, 1977 (Boston: Twayne, 1978), 339–42; Philip Young, *The Private Melville* (University Park: Pennsylvania State University Press, 1993). Both Robertson-Lorant and Higgins and Parker in "Reading *Pierre*" are cautious about the conclusions of Murray et. al.

16. Newton Arvin, *Herman Melville* (New York: William Sloane, 1950); James Creech, *Closet Writing, Gay Reading: The Case of Melville's Pierre* (Chicago: University of Chicago Press, 1993).

17. See Higgins and Parker, "Reading *Pierre*." On the basis of this theory, Hershel Parker has published an edition of *Pierre, or the Ambiguities* that recovers the text he feels Melville originally wrote. Called the "Kraken" edition, this book is handsomely illustrated by Maurice Sendak (New York: HarperCollins, 1995).

18. Miller, *Melville*, argues that Melville wrote *Pierre* in order to rival Hawthorne's *House* but that "in this new contest he was no match. Melville was not a domesticated person; his artistic skills did not include the intimacies of domestication or the realistic detail of this genre" (225).

19. *Piazza Tales and Other Prose Pieces, 1839–1860*, ed. Harrison Hayford, Alma MacDougall, G. Thomas Tanselle, and Merton M. Sealts, Jr. (Evanston and Chicago: Northwestern University Press and the Newberry Library, 1987), 250.

20. See David Reynolds, *Walt Whitman's America: A Cultural Biography* (New York: Random House, 1995).

21. *The House of the Seven Gables*, in *The Centenary Edition of Nathaniel Hawthorne* (Columbus: Ohio State University Press, 1965), 2:45. Further references appear in the text in parentheses.

22. T. Walter Herbert, *Dearest Beloved: The Hawthornes and the Making of the Middle-Class Family* (Berkeley: University of California Press, 1993), 102–6.

23. Samuel Otter, "The Eden of Saddle Meadows: Landscape and Ideology in *Pierre*," *American Literature* 66 (March 1994): 55–81.

24. On the connection between the religious and the erotic, see Jenny Franchot, *Roads to Rome: The Antebellum Protestant Encounter with Catholicism* (Berkeley: University of California Press, 1994).

25. See Miller, *Melville*, on the symbolism – house, moss, and vine – surrounding Hawthorne.

26. Leyda, *Log*, 422.

27. See Wyn Kelley, *Melville's City: Literary and Urban Form in Nineteenth-Century New York* (New York: Cambridge University Press, 1996); David S. Reynolds, *Beneath the American Renaissance: The Subversive Imagination in the Age of Emerson and Melville* (Cambridge: Harvard University Press, 1989).

28. See Franchot, *Roads to Rome*, 112–61.

5

ELIZABETH RENKER

"A _____!": Unreadability in
The Confidence-Man

The Confidence-Man, Herman Melville's last novel, was a critical and commercial failure when it was published in 1857. Critics panned it as an unreadable book. The reviewer in the *New York Dispatch* finished it "wondering what on earth the author has been driving at." The London *Literary Gazette* called it "a book professing to inculcate philosophical truths through the medium of nonsensical people talking nonsense." The *London Illustrated Times* commented:

> We can make nothing of this masquerade, which, indeed, savours very much of a mystification. We began the book at the beginning, and, after reading ten or twelve chapters, some of which contained scenes of admirable dramatic power, while others presented pages of the most vivid description, found, in spite of all this, that we had not yet obtained the slightest clue as to the meaning (in case there should happen to be any) of the work before us.

Nearly a century later, after the novel was resurrected along with Melville's reputation, the complaints were similar. F. O. Matthiessen (1941) judged it to be an uncontrolled fragment and a failure, and Van Wyck Brooks (1947) complained about the book's "clutter of faceless characters and its dubious meaning."[1]

The Confidence-Man's critical fortunes have deservedly undergone a dramatic reversal in recent decades. Critics now mostly praise the complexities of the novel – even while wrestling with them – and it has been called "Melville's most nearly perfect work" as well as "the exemplary postmodern text."[2] In my estimation, *The Confidence-Man* is Melville's most fully controlled novel, the one in which he's most in command of his craft. But the early reviews were right in an important sense: the book *is* unreadable. By "unreadable" I mean that it's aggressively resistant, not only to interpretation but also to even superficial comprehension. Characters who are unnamed or whose names change without warning, long exchanges of dialogue between unidentified speakers, an almost plotless plot, and a narrator who fails to clear any of this up are among the novel's hallmarks. Why would Melville, a proven storyteller who began his career writing popular novels and whose oeuvre demonstrates his virtuosity of style – adventure, humor, philosophy, satire, and so on – produce such a recalcitrant work? The answer to this question helps us better understand not only *The Confidence-Man* but also Melville's career more generally. Though incredibly productive between 1846 and 1857, Melville was also a profoundly frustrated writer, and *The Confidence-Man* represents a pivotal shift in his writing life. There we can see him both coming to terms with his frustrations and working toward his important but still little-understood shift from writing novels to writing poetry.[3]

Melville famously referred to his books as "botches." His frustration with his work, fed by his failures in the marketplace, ran deeper: it was essentially an epistemological problem with the condition of writing itself. He conceived of writing as what he called the "great Art of Telling the Truth," but he simultaneously believed that the truth could not be told frankly. "What a madness & anguish it is, that an author can never – under no conceivable circumstances – be at all frank with his readers," he wrote in 1849. The "madness" associated with truth-telling comes up again in his 1850 review, "Hawthorne and His Mosses." There, he tells us that Shakespeare "craftily says, or sometimes insinuates the things, which we feel to be so terrifically true, that it were all but madness for any good man, in his own proper character, to utter, or even hint of them." In Melville's terms, it would thus be "madness" to speak the things that are terrifically true, but at the same time it's "madness" that an author can never do so. Melville's writing process was in fact famously discontented. He wrote: "The calm, the coolness, the silent grass-growing mood in which a man *ought* always to compose, – that, I fear, can seldom be mine." Melville himself, as well as friends and family members, noted how agonizing, how emotionally and physically destructive, the process of writing was for him. Perhaps the most immediately apparent instance, as portrayed in the fiction, of the frustration and failure he felt in his writing life is the quest narrative of *Moby-Dick*, in which Ahab's madness to pierce the Truth of the whale brings only destruction.[4]

Melville's frustration over his thwarted desire to speak the Truth through art is intimately related to the material conditions of his scene of writing. When I talk about Melville's "scene of writing," I mean his compositional process and all the forces – both mental and material – impinging on it. The words "material" and "materiality" as I use them in this chapter bring together what are for Melville two important related problems. First, I mean to call upon the philosophical opposition between materialism and idealism, which much concerned Melville. In a nutshell, this philosophical problem concerned the nature of Truth, which for the idealist was immaterial (inhering in "ideas" and often associated with transcendent categories, as in the Platonic tradition) but which for the materialist did not transcend matter itself. Second, I mean the physical aspects of writing, its "matter." In this sense the "materiality of writing" includes both the physical aspects of writing as an activity (such as Melville's compositional habits) and the physical aspects of the pages he labored over (such as the paper he wrote on, the ink he used, his handwriting, and so on).

For Melville these two kinds of materiality are tied up with one another. Philosophically speaking, Melville was, like Ahab, a frustrated idealist. In "The Quarter-Deck," Ahab laments:

> All visible objects, man, are but as pasteboard masks. But in each event – in the living act, the undoubted deed – there, some unknown but still reasoning thing puts forth the mouldings of its features from behind the unreasoning mask. If man will strike, strike through the mask! How can the prisoner reach outside except by thrusting through the wall? (164)

Melville, like Ahab, wanted to pierce the material world to reach the ultimate and enduring Truth it masked. Although this desire lay at the heart of his writing labor, he repeatedly felt he could never succeed. Here's where it's crucial to see the connection between the two senses of materiality. Melville struggled with big ideas even as he struggled with the gritty details of getting words down on paper; problems like a chronic inability to spell and illegible handwriting that made his manuscripts nearly impossible to read were part of his writing process. While for Ahab the white whale was the consummate mask both promising and blocking him from ultimate knowledge, for Melville the very vehicle of his quest for Truth also proved its greatest obstacle, since it was that vehicle – the written page – that failed to give way to the Truth he desired, despite his repeated and insistent efforts to strike through it. In this sense, Melville was at odds with his own writing process, which increasingly became a tormented one blocking his most profound desires.

Melville struggled with this agonized relation to the writing process in different ways throughout his career.[5] By the time he composed *The Confidence-Man*, the grand metaphysical gestures of *Mardi* and *Moby-Dick* were gone; the tortured lament for their failure in *Pierre* was behind him. *The Confidence-Man* instead presents a fundamental reconception of the author's relation to his text and, in turn, to his readers. Melville no longer burns, with Ahab, to strike through the mask of the dead, blind wall; instead, he turns the mask on a bewildered reader and delights in its obscuring powers. The notorious "unreadability" of the novel is the result of this shift. Melville achieved greater control in *The Confidence-Man* than he had in any of his prior novels because in it he took on and explored the obstructing page that was at the core of his own writing anxiety; as he did so, he displaced his frustration with the page onto his reader. This turn – breathtakingly effective – is what accounts both for the novel's superb self-control and for its unreadability.

CHARACTER

Note as a starting point the fact that the title character and the novel share the same name. In fact, they operate analogously: just as the Confidence-Man's constant changes of identity baffle the perceptions of the other characters, *The Confidence-Man* baffles the reader with a bewildering proliferation of characters and descriptions. For example, the characters generally lack names. They are instead identified by epithets like "the hook-nosed man," "the other," and "the stranger." But a single epithet can apply to more than one character. "The stranger," for example, refers both to the Confidence-Man and to other characters, creating confusion about exactly who is at issue. While a single epithet like "the stranger" might apply to multiple characters, it's also true that individual characters also accrue multiple epithets; for example, "the man with the weed" is also called "the unfortunate man" and "John Ringman," and "the man with the big book" is also "the Man with the traveling-cap" and the president and transfer-agent of the Black Rapids Coal Company. In this sense, the bewildered characters in the novel confronting the Confidence-Man have as their analogues the bewildered readers confronting *The Confidence-Man*.

Melville's embrace of the resistant force of the page, the very force that had once most frustrated him, is worked out most strategically in *The Confidence-Man* through the notion of "character," a word the novel meditates on insistently. It appears in chapter titles ("In which a variety of characters appear," "Inquest into the true character of the Herb-Doctor"); characters discuss it (taking as their subjects "character" references, confidence in or suspicion of someone's "character," the "character" of the landscape, a "character" seen in the theater, engraved Greek "characters," and so on); and the narrator devotes three chapters to it (14, 33, and 44). Such persistent discussion serves a twofold purpose: first, it makes it quite clear that "character" is a crucial word in this novel; second, it simultaneously stresses the fact that the meaning of the word is inconsistent. (Here it's useful to remember that the fundamental inconsistency of character is the subject of Chapter 14.) Like the Confidence-Man himself, who changes costume and physical shape constantly, the word "character" appears repeatedly but has no enduring substance – no essential meaning – beneath its changing surfaces. The problem of "character" in *The Confidence-Man* is thus an example in microcosm of the dynamic of the Melvillean scene of writing, in which writing in general failed Melville in just this way: its material nature failed to give way to the absolute Truth that Melville sought to reach through it. Melville was deeply interested in definitions and etymologies, and so it's no accident that the word "character" in particular bears so much weight in this novel: etymologically, "character" derives from "writing."[6]

As the novel embraces "inconsistency" as its own domain, it opposes itself to a contrary notion that it calls "transparency." The word "transparency" was current in Melville's time to describe, among other things, the ideal kind of personal character: an absolute sincerity that would make a person's interior thoughts and feelings perfectly legible in outward appearance and behavior.[7] Melville's presentation of "character" as inconsistent, elusive, and hard to read refutes such faith in the possibility of transparency. Chapter 14 tells us that some believe that "Always, they [authors] should represent human nature not in obscurity, but transparency" (70), even though to do so is "untrue to reality," since "in real life, a consistent character is a *rara avis*" (69). In his draft of the chapter, we can see Melville lingering over the word "transparent,"[8] so we know it was a word that was of particular interest to him here. In the same chapter, the narrator notes that readers dislike inconsistent characters "from perplexity as to understanding them." As he undercuts the possibility of transparency as foolish and impossible, he insists instead upon the compelling – and truer – problem of what he calls "obscurity" (70).

The truer thinker, he tells us, is one who recognizes the obstacles to knowledge rather than one who believes we can know clearly and completely:

> Upon the whole, it might rather be thought, that he, who, in view of its inconsistencies, says of human nature the same that, in view of its contrasts, is said of the divine nature, that it is past finding out, thereby evinces a better appreciation of it than he who, by always representing it in a clear light, leaves it to be inferred that he clearly knows all about it. (70)

To begin with, we should note the dense and convoluted syntax in this passage – classic Melville – that makes it tough to read. If we unpack it, we see that it goes something like this: The person who realizes that human nature, like God's nature, ultimately can't be known is more correct than the person who treats it as if it's thoroughly clear. Of course, Melville has chosen to write about the problem of transparency (in this passage, that which is "clear") versus obscurity (that which is "past finding out") in aggressively opaque prose, which encourages us to see that the problem of obscurity that interests him is a problem not only of human and divine nature but also of writing in itself. The focus on how to "represent" human nature in the passage is another indication that writing is at issue. And of course, the problem of how to depict written characters is the primary subject of the chapter and the narrator's main concern. He asks: "But if the acutest sage be often at his wits' end to understand living character, shall those who are not sages expect to run and read character in those mere phantoms which flit along a page, like shadows along a wall?" (69). Here he asserts that living human beings are enigmas (placing himself at odds with the notion that people should, or could, be "transparent"), and he goes on to note that written characters – "mere phantoms" – are even more opaque than living ones. Melville's critique of transparency tells us that in the world of human nature and, more pressingly, in the world of the novel, occlusion is truer than revelation. And his form, here as throughout *The Confidence-Man*, mirrors this problem of occlusion.

Those "mere phantoms which flit along a page," as described in the previous example, are not only the novelist's characters in the sense of actors or personages created in the tale; they are also written characters in the sense of marks (letters, numbers, any written signs), which are, of course, what most literally flits "along a page" to create the world of a novel. Melville's reflections on writing in this sense are reflections not only on creating a fictional world but also on the literal materials that that world is made of: paper, ink, letters, and so on, the stuff of Melville's arduous craft.

We can see Melville's reflection on written characters as marks on a page in the novel's persistent thematics of writing. The title character operates as a striking figure for writing. His first two embodiments, the starkly white "man in cream-colors" with his fair cheek, flaxen hair, and white fur hat (3) and the starkly black Black Guinea, a "grotesque negro cripple" with "black fleece," "black face," and "an old coal-sifter of a tambourine" (10), begin the novel with a black-and-white contrast that figures black writing on a white page. The speculation about Black Guinea is that his blackness is literally "put on" white: "He's some white operator, betwisted and painted up for a decoy" (14). A number of the Confidence-Man's subsequent manifestations are also associated with shades of black and white, including the agent of the Black Rapids Coal Company, the man with the weed in mourning dress, the man in a gray coat and white tie, and the herb-doctor in a snuff-colored surtout (74). "Snuff-colored," the brownish color of pulverized tobacco, here also carries the denotation of "snuff" as the black-charred portion of a wick, which foreshadows the extinguished light that concludes the novel. Other characters, too, are identified by shades of black and white, among them the gentleman with gold sleeve buttons, with his strikingly white accoutrements and Negro body servant (36), the woman in a mourning "twilight" dress (43), and the man named Pitch. The novel's preoccupation with "papers" for authentication and the Confidence-Man's fondness for books and papers as props reinforce the importance of writing to this inconsistent world.[9]

The theme of writing in *The Confidence-Man* speaks to Melville's own relation to his pages as resistant forces. That Melville in *The Confidence-Man* imagines characters scrawled across a page as resistant is figured within the terms of the plot during a discussion between Mark Winsome and the cosmopolitan:

> "I conjecture him to be what, among the ancient Egyptians, was called a _____" using some unknown word.
> "A _____! And what is that?"
> "A _____ is what Proclus, in a little note to his third book on the theology of Plato, defines as _____ _____" coming out with a sentence of Greek.
>
> (193)

The insistently unreadable dashes here represent Winsome's definition of "an operator, a Mississippi operator" (196). The unreadable dashes (the reader can't read them) stand for an uninterpretable word (the cosmopolitan doesn't know what it means) that invokes the analogously unreadable title character and the novel named for him: "Mississippi operator" is a synonym for "confidence man." By transforming the words "Mississippi operator" that we can read into dashes we cannot, the novel shows its interest in unreadable characters. By "characters" here I mean not the novel's personages, but the very writing on the page with which Melville can create a world either that invites his readers in or, as in this case, that repels them. By focusing on marks that are no longer even words (in this case, dashes), *The Confidence-Man* takes unreadability from the level of a confusing cast and bewildering plot to the verge of literal unreadability – by which I mean a hypothetical novel that would not even contain legible words.

TAUTOLOGY

The other primary way in which Melville creates unreadable text is through tautology. At the heart of tautology is repetition, specifically repetition that does not add new information because it tells us only what we've already been told. As a matter of logic, a tautology takes a statement as its own cause; as a matter of style, a tautology is a repetition of phrases or words. Tautological constructions act as mirrors, reflecting one proposition with another version of itself. The narrator's three chapters on character (14, 33, 44) all fall under tautological chapter titles: "Worth the consideration of those to whom it may prove worth considering," "Which may pass for whatever it may prove to be worth," and "In which the last three words of the last chapter are made the text of the discourse, which will be sure of receiving more or less attention from those readers who do not skip it." The mirror effect of tautology suspends language at the level of its own materiality – that is, of itself as language – refusing to penetrate its surface in order to "mean" something.[10] Tautology is a use of language with no "inside" or space of meaning. Instead, it offers itself *as* language, twice. As Charlie says to Frank – two confidence men pitted against one another, an embodiment of the tautological structure essential to the novel – "Agreeable, how we always agree" (160).

The Confidence-Man is replete with tautological devices. When the good merchant tells the agent of the Black Rapids Coal Company the story of the unfortunate man (Chapter 12), he repeats back to one incarnation of the Confidence-Man a story told to him by another, a tautological exchange of tales. One of the Confidence-Man's techniques is to authenticate his own future incarnations by recommending them in advance of their appearance, a tautological method for establishing credit. Elizabeth S. Foster points out that the structure of the novel is one in which the final scenes of the book "suggest incidents and ideas of the beginning but in reverse order mostly, as though the novel were being unrolled towards the beginning at the same time as towards the end." For example, in the first scene the lamblike man's message is juxtaposed with the barber's sign, and the barber and his philosophy return at the end; the Confidence-Man's second incarnation, the Black Guinea, mirrors the next-to-last one, the man with the brass plate.[11] The shape of the narrative is thus also tautological. We can hear Melville's interest in such structures at the beginning of Chapter 14: "As the last chapter was begun with a reminder looking forwards, so the present must consist of one glancing backwards" (69).

In Chapters 33 and 44, Melville implicates character in similarly tautological operations. Chapter 33 discusses critical readers who desire characters from "real life" (182) and refers them to Chapter 14, the narrator's first aside on character ("all such readers . . . are now referred to that chapter where some similar apparent inconsistency in another character is, on general principles, modestly endeavored to be apologized for" [183]). Here the narrator's strategy is to hand over not "real life," but instead merely another chapter, and a tautological one at that. His parting shot to readers in the last paragraph of Chapter 33 – "One word more" – gives readers who want writing to deliver "real life" only more words. Chapter 44 takes the last three words of the previous chapter, "Quite an Original," as its first three words. Although the chapter apparently discusses "original characters in fiction" (238), Melville's joke is that he repeats the letters that make up the phrase "Quite an Original" just as he tells us that originality of character is rare. In addition, note that these two tautological chapters fall under chapter numbers that repeat the same written character twice: 33 and 44. Here Melville extends the tautological game beyond even the ostensible boundaries of the plot.

Melville's focus in these instances on writing's literal "content" – not real life but marks on a page – is one the Confidence-Man plays with. In his exchange as John Ringman with the good merchant, he says: "Is it possible, my dear sir . . . that you do not recall my countenance? why yours I recall distinctly as if but half an hour, instead of half an age, had passed since I saw you. Don't you recall me, now? Look harder" (18). His distinction here between "half an hour" and "half an age" is the difference between the time of the scam, with its illusions of "half an age" (since he is pretending to know the good merchant from six years ago), and the secret time of the Confidence-Man's change of disguise in half an hour.[12] The Confidence-Man's claim that "half an age" has passed since the last encounter between the two men proffers a ruse of depth not only to his dupe, but also to the reader who enters into fiction ready to believe that "half an age" can pass in "half an hour" with a few turns of the page. The narrative similarly insists upon itself as mere paper in the title of the tautologically numbered Chapter 11, "Only a page or so," and in another title Melville drafted but did not use: "Less than a page."[13] In these ways Melville brings his "page" to the foreground of a narrative from which, he implies, gullible readers will expect something entirely different – and be thwarted in their expectations.

P

For example, they will be thoroughly lost in the exchanges in the novel in which the narrative takes words *as words* – particularly as constructed by letters, or characters – as its subject. Chapter 29 presents an illuminating example. Frank and Charlie sit down together over a bottle of wine:

. . . a common quart bottle, but for the occasion fitted at bottom into a little bark basket, braided with porcupine quills, gayly tinted in the Indian fashion. This being set before the entertainer, he regarded it with affectionate interest, but seemed not to understand, or else to pretend not to, a handsome red label pasted on the bottle, bearing the capital letters, P.W.

"P.W.," said he at last, perplexedly eyeing the pleasing poser, "now what does P.W. mean?"

"Shouldn't wonder," said the cosmopolitan gravely, "if it stood for port wine. You called for port wine, didn't you?" (160–1)

The quick solution to the mystery of the characters "P" and "W," after which the cosmopolitan comments, "I find some little mysteries not very hard to clear up," is subtly derailed throughout the chapter, which takes the bottle's label for its unstated subject. John T. Irwin has pointed out that " 'P.W.' could stand for any number of two-word combinations with these initials," and in fact the chapter's subsequent discussions of "pure wine," poison wine ("He who could mistrust poison in this wine would mistrust consumption in Hebe's cheek"), and promising wine ("this wine with its bright promise") present other candidates for the "meaning" of the characters in question.[14]

The permutations of the "P" in Chapter 29 spin well beyond port, pure, poison, and promising wine. The letter "P" in fact pervades the extensively alliterative chapter throughout. When Charlie reports, "I saw a good thing the other day; capital thing; a panegyric on the press" (165), the alliteration of the particular "capital thing" he cites, the panegyric on the press – here presumably meaning "capital" as "first-rate" – also focuses our attention on the letter "P" that dominates these alliterative words. The alliterative "capital thing" thus recalls "the capital letters, P.W." earlier in the chapter, which also foreground a "P." The panegyric is, of course, itself a text – "I got it by heart at two readings" (165) – thus literally a thing made of letters.

Melville's interest in written characters as such motivates his choice of the bizarre and seemingly arbitrary topics of conversation in Chapters 29 and 30, from Charlie's pledge, Aristotle's "Politics," the panegyric on the press, and the apostle Paul to Polonius, the Puritans, Pizarro, and Peru. The character "P" also gives rise to the content of the dialogue (which features the words "Pardon, pardon," "practical punning," "panacea"), the secondary events in the chapter (Charlie laughs, "pointing to the figure of a pale pauper-boy" [163]), and the narrator's descriptive language ("placidly pleased," "princely kindness," "perplexedly eying the pleasing poser"). (We should remember, too, the setting of the novel on a steamer on the Mississippi, with emphasis on the sound of the last syllable.) This exuberance with the letter "P" – as a consistent written character that refuses to mean anything consistent – suggests that the narrative is one in which characters, in the sense of written marks, are primary in importance.

Melville's playfulness with written characters also illuminates other exchanges between the "characters" of Frank and Charlie. When Frank recollects the story of Phalaris, the capricious tyrant of Sicily, he and Charlie simultaneously exclaim opposite sentiments:

"Funny Phalaris!"
"Cruel Phalaris!"

Just as Melville sets up the contrast here between the boon companions who profess to share identical sentiments, he juxtaposes the characters (in the sense of letters) beginning their names: "F" and "C," "Funny" and "Cruel," "Frank" and "Charlie." The letters "C" and "F" are also associated with the constant (although variable) "P": " 'Cruel Phalaris!' 'Funny Phalaris!' " Although neither line of dialogue is attributed to a speaker, Charlie's laughter at the "pale pauper-boy" at least suggests that it is he who finds humor in suffering and thus is the one who says Phalaris is "Funny," while Frank says he's "Cruel" – a chiastic shift that associates Frank with "C" and Charlie with "F," a version staged in written characters of their other shifts and exchanges of identity. (At times, for example, both are referred to as "the other," making them nearly impossible to distinguish from one another.) But of course, the lines are specifically not attributed to speakers; the two letters and the two men are equivalent tokens in a confidence game of characters. Frank, after all, is also the cosmopolitan, and so remarks to Charlie (known at this point as "the stranger"), "[O]ur sentiments agree so, that were they written in a book, whose was whose, few but the nicest critics might determine" (158).

Other letters also extend the confidence game of characters. "W," for example, motivated by the "P.W." label, appears in formulations like "western pottery" (168). The "W" that in part suggests "wine" or "western" also represents writing in a chapter self-consciously obsessed with written letters. If we substitute "writing" for "wine" in all the phrases spun out of "P.W." earlier, we get "pure writing," "poison writing," "promising writing," and "port writing" – all of which are signatures for Melville's writing career. His frustrated relation to writing (pure when it was going well, poison when it wasn't) and his early success (promising) are written into the first three formulations, while "port" suggests his career as a writer of sea stories, including this one, in which the *Fidele* makes port stops throughout. That writing can fall under the rubric of "poison" is clear elsewhere in the novel, when the man with the weed dismisses the book the collegian is reading as "poison, moral poison" (26). The "W" as "writing" also suggests a "P" that is print on a page of paper in a world – like the world of this novel – in which characters are made of black print on a white page. Earlier in the novel, when the Black Guinea is asked to produce the "papers" to prove that his case is not spurious, he bemoans that he "haint none o' dem waloable papers" (13). Here "waloable papers" transposes the letters "P.W." and this time "p" stands for "papers."

According to the *Oxford English Dictionary* (*OED*), the letter "P" is an abbreviation for proper names beginning with "P"; and "p." and "pp." are also abbreviations for "page" and "pages," respectively. The phrase "P's and Q's" meant, in nineteenth-century usage, one's words or one's letters. The *OED* suggests that this construction might have sprung from the difficulty with which a child, in learning to read and write, discriminates the letter "p" from the letter "q," its mirror image. "P" is thus a particular letter, the child's written letter "p," as well as the prototype of the letter, standing, as in "P's and Q's," for any letter. Another possible origin for the need to mind one's "p's and q's" would be the compositor's imperative, while typesetting, to return types for particular letters to the section of the case in which they belonged – the letters "p," "q," "b," and "d" being especially tricky because they could be mistaken for one another if the types were turned the wrong way.[15] The letters "p" and "q" also follow one another in the alphabet, and thus face each other like mirror images in the chain of alphabetic characters, looking forward and backward like the image with which Melville opens Chapter 14. The *OED* tells us that "P" "presents probably a greater number of unsolved etymological problems than any other letter." Etymology, word relationships, and, as the present discussion contends, letters as such held great interest for Melville. But while he spins many connotations out of the characters "P.W.," they importantly remain, finally, inconsistent: we are never told their ultimate meaning; they have none. Thus the "P" operates, at the level of the individual character, as "character" does at the level of the word: as a persistent but inconsistent bit of writing. This inconsistency speaks to what was for Melville the tormenting heart of writing itself as a tautological force that blocks penetration to a realm of Truth. In *Pierre*, the narrator refers to "the dread of tautology" as "the continual torment of some earnest minds" (227). Because tautology is writing that gives back only itself, it emblematizes for Melville his failed efforts to dissolve the materiality of writing into ideal Truth. But what torments the earnest minds in *Pierre* is what delights the narrator of *The Confidence-Man* – and what has clearly tormented all too many readers.

Melville's vision of the "P" as specifically a written character, and a central one at that, is further suggested by one scrap of paper among the manuscripts of *The Confidence-Man*. On one side, we find a draft for the title of Chapter 40 (the story of China Aster) in Melville's customary hurried and illegible script; on the other side, in uncharacteristically careful and even ornamental print, we find the large, centered words "First Part." Centered beneath them appears a precisely formed capital letter "P" (see Figure 1). This sole "P" is inscribed differently from the "P" in "Part," as if it were a different character, and its central and lone placement on the page suggests that it was written not as the first letter of a word or paragraph, but rather as the character "P" as such. These handwritten letters are formed and laid out with a care unlike those on any of the other manuscript fragments, a discovery of particular interest because it illustrates not only Melville's awareness of the page as a white space on which he placed written characters to create the world of his novel, but also his particular interest in the letter "P."[16]

MODELS

Melville presents an image of his own writing methods in the deaf-mute's appearance with his slate. He traces a series of phrases combining the constant initial word "Charity" with changing complements:

> " 'Charity thinketh no evil.' "
> " 'Charity suffereth long, and is kind.' "
> " 'Charity endureth all things.' "
> " 'Charity believeth all things.' "
> " 'Charity never faileth.' " (4–5)

"The word charity, as originally traced, remained throughout uneffaced, not unlike the left-hand numeral of a printed date, otherwise left for convenience in blank" (5). The word "charity" appears as a constant initial word producing a series of different sentences just as elsewhere the character "P" appears as a constant initial character attached to endlessly shifting companion characters ("port," "pure," "poison," "promise"). Melville works with the same structure when "a charitable lady" begins "twenty different sentences, and left off at the first syllable of each. At last, in desperation, she hurried out, 'Tell me, sir, for what do you want the twenty dollars?' " (45). Her twenty sentences become twenty syllables and then twenty dollars in the space of a paragraph as Melville offers several variations on the initial word "twenty." He plays this game not only with whole words ("charity," "character") and with individual characters ("P," "W," "F," "C"), but also with syllables. The syllable "char," for example,

Figure 1. Manuscript fragment from *The Confidence-Man*: "First Part/P." (By permission of the Houghton Library, Harvard University [bMS Am188(365)])

is repeated in the key words "Charity," "Charlie," "Charlemont," "charming," "charlatan," and "character," all of which appear frequently in the novel.

The model for writing that I've been mapping at the level of the character, the syllable, and the word is one that also generates the novel's stories-within-a-story. Just as the deaf-mute's word "charity" spins off a series of sentences, Melville's tale of the Confidence-Man spins off a series of other narratives and narrators embedded in the larger tale. We've seen that the word "character" and the letter "P" insist finally on their own anti-transparent nature as written marks, "mere phantoms which flit along a page" rather than windows to Truth. As one story spins off a series of other tales and other narrators, Melville catches us in layers of text that are finally impenetrable. This "impenetrability," a word I borrow from Chapter 26, is a bewildering mediation of information through multiple sources and narrators that undercuts the truth of the story in question (while incidentally gumming up such additional matters as exactly who is speaking in whose words based on what evidence). The story of the unfortunate man (Chapter 12), for example, is told by the unfortunate man himself and again by the man in a gray coat, both personae of the Confidence-Man, to the good merchant, who then tells the story to another Confidence-Man, the transfer agent of the Black Rapids Coal Company, making the circulation of this story a tautological exchange. The story of China Aster is told "at second-hand" (208) by Egbert, playing Charlie, narrating in the style of the unnamed "original story-teller," whose style has "tyrannized" over him (207). It is in these terms that we can understand why Chapters 11 and 33, two of the novel's three tautologically numbered chapters, set up stories-within-a-story: Chapter 11 introduces the story of the unfortunate man, and Chapter 33 sets up the story of Charlemont.

The chapters on Indian-hating (25–8), another story-within-a-story, have attracted a great deal of commentary. Disagreements have raged around two questions in particular: Did Melville side with the Indian or the hater? Are Melville's Indians metaphysical symbols for devils or some evil principle, or actual victimized human beings who had been abused and sometimes exterminated in the name of "civilization"?[17] To address these questions, we need to begin by noting that the chapters on Indian-hating, too, insist primarily upon the textuality of their subjects. The "acquaintance" tells the story of Colonel John Moredock as told by Judge James Hall, a chain of storytelling already hard to follow but further complicated by the suggestion that the acquaintance, who later identifies himself as Charlie, is a confidence-man. (It is he who wears a violet vest and thus seems to represent one of the "ge'mmen" on Black Guinea's list – a list of persons whose descriptions largely but not completely match those of the confidence-men to come [13] – who otherwise never appears.) It is thus with great irony that the cosmopolitan, awaiting the tale of Colonel John Moredock, inclines his ear "so disposed towards the speaker that each word came through as little atmospheric intervention as possible" (143), a parodic reference to the labyrinthine multiple layers of narrative that make up the story.

Hall, a historical figure, was well known for his habit of using the same material repeatedly in his writings; he told the story of the Indian-hater in at least three publications. Melville in fact adapted his chapters on Indian-hating from Hall's *Sketches of History, Life, and Manners, in the West* (Philadelphia 1835), often borrowing directly from Hall's wording,[18] so it's important to note the subtle presence of printed text in this chain of ostensibly oral tales. Hall's text describes Indian-hating as an animosity that springs from stories about the Indian's nature rather than from the Indian's nature itself. He writes of the Indian-hating backwoodsmen, "They know the story only as it was told to them. They have only heard one side, and that with all the exaggerations of fear, sorrow, indignation and resentment."[19] Melville follows Hall: " 'Still, all this is less advanced as truths of the Indians than as examples of the backwoodsman's impression of them' " (146). Thus Melville's Indian-hating chapters and all their sources and narrators do not provide "truths of the Indians"; they give us only an "impression." "Impression," a printing term, suggests that the Indian is known only as a text written by the backwoodsman from a text written by Hall in a text written by Melville. Furthermore, the figure of the backwoodsman was a notorious masquerader and teller of tall tales in nineteenth-century American culture; hence he was an additionally problematic point of departure for any reliable tale.[20]

Melville's claim here – that the Indian-hater's image of the Indian is an image, not a truth – resembles his treatment of the mutinous slave Babo in "Benito Cereno." The true face of Babo, the character called "the black" (as if archetypal), remains impenetrable, his true voice unspoken. Like Babo, Black Guinea plays the role of subservient darkie in a racial game of black and white roles, even as his blackness simultaneously plays into the black-and-white game of writing on a page. Melville's interest in the textuality of the Indian and Black Guinea does not make his treatment one that avoids or ignores the historical or political realities of his time. In both cases, his emphasis on the inescapable layers of fiction associated with these racialized figures ironizes the stereotypes that fed such enterprises as Indian-hating.

Like the Indian, the Indian-hater is presented as a finally inaccessible text. He, too, is a type of character that comes from written accounts and for which "a special word has been coined" (141). We've been considering how words operate in this novel as antitransparent forces. In the case of the Indian-hater, we find that, like the "P" that finally remains an obscure mark, the character of the Indian-hater remains fundamentally impenetrable. " 'The career of the Indian-hater *par excellence* has the impenetrability of the fate of a lost steamer' " (150), says the acquaintance quoting the judge. All known examples of the Indian-hater necessarily "impair the keeping of the character" (150) because they dilute its pure, impenetrable form. The way the "impenetrability" of the "character" of the Indian-hater and the "impressions" of the Indian both render the truth inaccessible helps us to see why Melville presents such information in a chapter claiming to offer "the metaphysics of Indian-hating." Metaphysics, the branch of philosophy concerned with the nature of reality, is the type of inquiry into ultimate truths that *The Confidence-Man* presents as futile. Although the chapter promises a metaphysics, the substance of the chapter undercuts those promises. Thus the generations of critics who find that the Indian and hater are symbols of good and evil principles fall into Melville's metaphysical trap.

Taken as a group, Melville's stories-within-a-story are related not only to one another (as examples of the same genre) but also to other printed sources as a chain of tales. His playfulness with the layers of text in these chapters is apparent when Charlie (at this point not yet so named) describes hearing the tale of Moredock from Hall:

> . . . you would have thought he spoke less to mere auditors than to an invisible amanuensis; seemed talking for the press; very impressive way with him indeed. And I, having an equally impressible memory, think that, upon a pinch, I can render you the judge upon the colonel almost word for word.
>
> (142)

"Press," "impressive," "impressible": the game with the word "press" here (like "impression," discussed earlier), quickly following the reference to an amanuensis, shows the preoccupation with writing – in this case, writing in the form of printed sources ("press" and "impression" are printing terms). And of course, Melville borrows Hall's written (published) words for the unnamed Charlie just as Charlie reports that he can "render you the judge upon the colonel almost word for word."

Other printed sources also figure into the stories-within-a-story as further layers of textuality. For example, the protagonist of the story-within-a-story of Charlemont, the gentleman-madman, alludes to William Gilmore Simms's novel *Charlemont; or, The Pride of the Village* (1856). Simms's *Charlemont* is dedicated to James Hall, the same figure at the center of the chapters on Indian-hating. Texts by Hall and Simms were also printed sources for Melville on the lives of the outlaws Meason, Murrel, and the brothers Harpe,[21] whose printed lives are hawked in Chapter 1. The network of associations Melville weaves here among specific printed sources ultimately points to a specific aspect of Melville's own history as an author: Simms, Hall, and Melville were among the sixteen authors who published in an 1845–7 series called the "Library of American Books" (as was Poe, who appears in Chapter 36); Egbert has been widely interpreted as Henry David Thoreau, who had tried to publish *A Week on the Concord and Merrimack Rivers* in the series; and Mark Winsome has been widely interpreted as Ralph Waldo Emerson, whom Evert A. Duyckinck, the series editor, went to great lengths to entice into contributing, unsuccessfully.[22] Melville published his first book, *Typee* (1846), in the series, which made him a famous author overnight. By weaving specific references to his own publishing history into his broader philosophical reflections, Melville reflects – bitterly – on the career that began as such "promising writing."

The Confidence-Man distills issues of "content" – whether of wine, or charity, or character, or Indians and their haters – to the written character and the "novelist's page" as such. In its distillation of prose fiction to the level of the character, and in its focus on letters and words as things, it's a particularly appropriate last novel before Melville's full-scale change in genre to poetry.[23] In the manuscript for *Weeds and Wildings Chiefly: with A Rose or Two*, for example, a volume of poems Melville left unpublished at his death, he engages in extensive alliterative wordplay sprung from the title of the volume, with the words "rose," "rosary," "Rosamond," and "Rosicrucians," for example. Perfect rhyme, a poetic technique Melville often worked with, hinges upon changing initial characters and preserving those at the ends of words (such as "book"/"took"). His interest in the manipulation of characters as one of the primary ingredients of poetry is thus closely related to his interests in *The Confidence-Man*. Later still, in *Billy Budd*, the prose work he left unfinished at the time of his death in 1891, we see that his explorations of character give form to Billy Budd's famous stutter, in which a repetition of characters as such ultimately produces words: " 'd-d-driving,' " " 'g-g-go,' " " 't-t-toss' " are three such examples.[24] In the *Billy Budd* manuscript, we can see Melville adding and deleting characters that create the stutter. In the passage that reads in manuscript, " 'If you d-d-dont start, I'll t-t-toss you back over the rail!',' " Melville strikes through a "d" preceding "dont" and carets in a single "r" preceding "rail!"[25] – clear indications of his meticulousness with individual characters that don't in themselves mean anything. In this sense, we can see that *Billy Budd* did indeed spring from Melville's poetry, not only in its order of composition (the narrative of *Billy Budd* probably grew out of what is now the poem that concludes it, "Billy in the Darbies"[26]) but also in its relation to words on the page. This connection helps to explain *Billy Budd*'s repeated references to the poetic.

I pointed out earlier that writing failed Melville in a most crucial sense, in fact in the sense that mattered most to him: in enabling him to penetrate the world of the material in order to attain a transcendent realm of Truth. In *The Confidence-Man*, he's already given up this hope and has turned his frustrations with the page on his reader. After publication of *The Confidence-Man*, Melville wrote poetry almost exclusively for the rest of his life. Poet James Galvin recently commented on writing his own first book of prose: "As a poet, I – I spend probably an unhealthy amount of time staring at blank pieces of paper and not touching them. And so then doing this prose book was almost like being someone else for a while in relation to the page, which is part of its attraction."[27] Melville's change in genre – the reverse of Galvin's – also signaled a new relation to the page. His experiments with character in *The Confidence-Man* laid the ground for this important but still little-understood shift in Melville's writing career.

NOTES

1. Some of the contemporary reviews are collected in the Norton Critical Edition of the novel (ed. Hershel Parker, 1971). See also F. O. Matthiessen, *American Renaissance: Art and Expression in the Age of Emerson and Whitman* (London: Oxford UP, 1941), 411–12; and Van Wyck Brooks, *The Times of Melville and Whitman* (E. P. Dutton, 1947), 169.
2. H. Bruce Franklin, *The Wake of the Gods: Melville's Mythology* (Stanford: Stanford UP, 1963), 153; A. Robert Lee, "Voices Off, On, and Without: Ventriloquy in *The Confidence-Man*," *Herman Melville: Reassessments*, ed. A. Robert Lee (Totowa, NJ: Barnes & Noble, 1984), 160.
3. My argument in this essay is based on my study of Melville's career, including but not limited to *The Confidence-Man*, in *Strike Through the Mask: Herman Melville and the Scene of Writing* (Baltimore: Johns Hopkins UP, 1996).
4. The phrase "the great Art of Telling the Truth" appears in "Hawthorne and His Mosses" (*The Piazza Tales and Other Prose Pieces 1839–1860*, ed. Harrison Hayford, Alma A. MacDougall, and G. Thomas Tanselle [Evanston and Chicago: Northwestern UP and the Newberry Library, 1987], 244). The other quoted phrases appear in Melville's correspondence with Evert A. Duyckinck, 2 and 14 December 1849, *Correspondence* (ed. Lynn Horth [Evanston and Chicago: Northwestern UP and the Newberry Library], 1993), 149; "Hawthorne and His Mosses," 244; to Nathaniel Hawthorne, [1 June?] 1851, *Correspondence*, 191.
5. See my *Strike through the Mask* for a fuller account.
6. The word "character" derives from a Greek word that signifies an instrument

for marking or graving, and its denotations derive from its etymological association with writing.

7. Karen Halttunen, *Confidence Men and Painted Women: A Study of Middle-Class Culture in America, 1830–1870* (New Haven: Yale UP, 1982), 51–2.

8. My readings of Melville's revisions are based on my examination of the manuscript at the Houghton Library, Harvard University (bMSAm188 [365]). The first lines of the page, eventually struck through, seem to stutter over the word. You can also consult the reproduction of this page and the genetic transcription in the Manuscript Fragments appendix to the Northwestern–Newberry edition of *The Confidence-Man*, 454–5.

9. Several studies have pointed out the novel's prevalent motifs of writing and of blackness and whiteness. See, for example, Rebecca J. Kruger Guadino's "The Riddle of *The Confidence-Man*," *The Journal of Narrative Technique* 14 (1984): 124–41; Henry Sussman's "The Deconstructor as Politician: Melville's *Confidence-Man*," *Glyph: Johns Hopkins Textual Studies* 4 (1978): 32–56; and Khalil Husni's "The Confidence-Man's Colourful-Colourless Masquerade: Melville's Theatre of the Absurd," *Studia Anglica Posnaniensia: An International Review of English Studies* 17 (1984): 219–31.

10. Melville's prose style in general features elaborate subordinate clauses and rhetorical devices such as litotes, a figure of speech in which an affirmative proposition is expressed by the negative of the contrary (*OED*), creating dense resistance at the surface of his language.

11. Elizabeth S. Foster, Introduction, *The Confidence-Man* (New York: Hendricks House, 1954), xci–xcii.

12. Watson G. Branch also points out that "half an hour" is the time elapsed between these two manifestations of the Confidence-Man ("The Genesis, Composition, and Structure of *The Confidence-Man*," *Nineteenth-Century Fiction* 27 [1973]: 431–3, note 16).

13. See the genetic transcription of Fragment 21, a list of chapter titles, in the Manuscript Fragments appendix to the Northwestern–Newberry edition of the novel, 480–1.

14. John T. Irwin, *American Hieroglyphics: The Symbol of the Egyptian Hieroglyphics in the American Renaissance* (New Haven: Yale UP, 1980), 337.

15. My thanks to Michael Winship for pointing this out.

16. This fragment is also reproduced in the Manuscript Fragments appendix to the Northwestern–Newberry edition, 483–4.

17. For a summary of criticism about these chapters, see Branch et al. in the Historical Note to the Northwestern–Newberry edition, especially 340–2.

18. See Foster in the Explanatory Notes to the Hendricks House edition, 338, and Branch et al. in the Historical Note to the Northwestern–Newberry edition, 281. See also the appendix to the Northwestern–Newberry edition, "Melville's Indian-Hating Source," 501–10, for a reproduction of one of Hall's chapters. Lucy Maddox argues that the number of Melville's allusions in the Indian-hating chapters is a reminder that Hall constructed his stories out of bits and pieces from other writers (*Removals: Nineteenth-Century American Literature and the Politics of Indian Affairs* [New York: Oxford UP, 1991], 86–7).

19. Hall, 78, reproduced in the Editorial Appendix to the Northwestern–Newberry edition, 506.
20. Halttunen, *Confidence Men and Painted Women*, 30.
21. Foster, Explanatory Notes 2.7, 291–2.
22. I am indebted here to Winship's description of Wiley and Putnam's Library of American Books for The Program in the History of the Book in American Culture at the American Antiquarian Society, 14–26 June 1992; on Hall and Simms, see Branch et al., Historical Note to the Northwestern–Newberry edition 282; see also Ezra Greenspan, "Evert Duyckinck and the History of Wiley and Putnam's Library of American Books, 1845–1847," *American Literature* 64 (1992): 683–4, 685, 686; William Charvat, *The Profession of Authorship in America, 1800–1870*, ed. Matthew J. Bruccoli (1968; New York: Columbia UP, 1992), 168–89. On Emerson's recommendation of *A Week* to Duyckinck and Thoreau's subsequent exchanges with Duyckinck on the subject, see Steven Fink, *Prophet in the Marketplace: Thoreau's Development as a Professional Writer* (Princeton: Princeton UP, 1992), 143–7. Emerson and Hawthorne both pressed Duyckinck to include *A Week* in the Library; Melville dined with Duyckinck just as he was deciding in the negative (Branch et al., Historical Note, 286). On the identification of Egbert as Thoreau and Mark Winsome as Emerson, see Branch et al., Historical Note, 285–6, 332.
23. I am indebted to Robert Schreur for suggesting this to me.
24. *"Billy Budd Sailor" and Other Stories*, ed. Frederick Busch (New York: Viking Penguin, 1986), 332.
25. Based on my analysis of the manuscript at the Houghton Library, Harvard University (MSAm 188 [363], leaf 158). See also Harrison Hayford and Merton M. Sealts, Jr.'s *Billy Budd Sailor (An Inside Narrative). By Herman Melville. Reading Text and Genetic Text, Edited from the Manuscript with Introduction and Notes* (Chicago: U of Chicago P, 1962), 349.
26. See Hayford and Sealts for the genetic theory that *Billy Budd* began with "Billy in the Darbies."
27. James Galvin, interview with William Marcus, *Morning Edition*, National Public Radio, WOSU, Columbus, Ohio, 3 August 1992.

6

LAWRENCE BUELL

Melville the Poet

Melville is justly said to be nineteenth-century America's leading poet after Whitman and Dickinson, yet his poetry remains largely unread, even by many Melvillians. Most major studies of premodern American poetry have given him short shrift;[1] the recent *Columbia History of American Poetry* limits itself to a few passing references. The old impression persists that Melville was "a poet of shreds and patches" who never mastered the art.[2] Such is the curse of being only second best. Among American premoderns, next to Whitman, Melville wrote the best series of Civil War lyrics, *Battle-Pieces* (1866),[3] and the second-best long poem, *Clarel* (1876), which indeed is *the* great Victorian epic of faith and doubt.[4] Only Emily Dickinson surpassed Melville in her development of a gnomic, intellectualized rhetoric that gained intensity by working within the confines of rhymed verse while bending those forms to the limit. Most tellingly, Melville's poetry was second best to his own best prose fiction, which also came first chronologically. Hence it is all too easy to type Melville as "essentially" a prose writer who wrote verse with the left hand.

True, even more than most Victorians, Melville turned to poetry as an instrument of meditation rather than for the sake of melody or linguistic play. Among his contemporaries, he tended to value the work of poet-essayists like Bryant, Emerson, James Thomson, and especially Matthew Arnold over writers who specialized in poetry, like Tennyson and Longfellow.[5] Yet Melville's late-life transition from fiction to poetry was no mere afterthought. His quantity of output shows this. He composed twice as much poetry as Dickinson and probably as many lines as Whitman; and the span of time during which each of the three wrote poetry of distinction was almost identical, a little more than a quarter of a century – twice as long as Melville's career as novelist.

More important, although Melville doubtless turned to poetry partly out of disillusionment at the reception of his serious fiction after *Moby-Dick*, the turn was a logical one given the trajectory of his development. As Nina

Baym has stressed, from an early point in his career Melville developed a "quarrel with fiction" as being at cross-purposes with art's highest mission of prophetic truth-telling.[6] Within less than a decade, his novels had moved irreversibly away from quasi-autobiographical protagonist-centered initiation narratives in the direction of ruminative meditation presided over by a much more detached narrative consciousness. The reflexive, fabulizing style of *The Confidence-Man* (1857), Melville's last published work of prose fiction, shows a sensibility pushing at the outer limits of the genre and ready to exchange it for another form that the persona can dominate more fully – that is, either poetry or nonfictional prose. Melville tried both. If there is a mystery about the turn at this point in Melville's career, it is not that he ceased to write prose narrative (except for the posthumously published *Billy Budd*), but that he chose poetry over essay, in which he might have been equally formidable and which he also attempted at this time. Perhaps his unsuccess as lyceum lecturer helped him decide. However that may be, the three novels of the 1850s in which Melville invested the greatest intellectual effort – *Moby-Dick*, *Pierre*, and *The Confidence-Man* – are drawn away from conventional tale-telling into reflection to such a marked degree as to make either philosophical poetry or nonfictional prose seem a much more logical next step in Melville's development than additional works of narrative fiction, quite apart from reversal of fortune in the marketplace. So too with Thomas Hardy several decades later.

One of the telltale signs of the underdeveloped state of commentary on Melville's poetry is a tendency to acknowledge the infelicities of the autodidact, in a way reminiscent of Whitman and Dickinson commentary half a century ago. The fact is that Melville was as deeply read in both traditional and modern poetry as they;[7] and that scarcely more allowance needs to be made for Melville's poetry than for theirs, or, for that matter, Melville's own fiction. Melville, Dickinson, and Whitman were all uneven writers, at worst dully self-imitative of their own mannerisms. The deeper reasons for neglect of Melville's poetry are probably the comparatively traditional character of its language and prosody relative to Whitman's and Dickinson's; its severe emotional restraint; and the deliberate entanglement of the larger narrative continuities of Melville's two most significant books of poetry in the knottiness of individual cantos, passages, sentences, couplets, and lines. Very likely, then, Melville's poetry will forever be less popular, less anthologized, less assigned. But those who ignore it will have overlooked a major poet.

Even when Melville's verse stumbles, the underlying approach often justifies the lapse. Take, for example, the sudden end of the fourteenth canto of Part III of *Clarel*. Several pilgrims, who have been tippling clandestinely at the Mar Saba monastery, are interrupted by a harrowing "Lord have mercy" that seems to come from the "belly of the whale" many chambers below:

> Arrested, those five revelers there,
> Fixed in light postures of their glee,
> Seemed problematic shapes ye see
> In linked caprice of festal air
> Graved round the Greek sarcophagi.
> (III.xiv. 139–43)

With this the canto abruptly ends. The terminal "there" and "ye see" are all too obviously positioned so as to pad out the rhythm and the rhyme; yet awkwardness is crucial to the underlying purpose both to disrupt and to enchain. This the rhymed octosyllables (the dominant meter in *Clarel* and throughout Melville's poetry) do admirably. The first line's bunched stresses (*thòse fíve rèv*) signal the sudden arrest; the weak closing syllables here and in lines 3 and 5 leave the revelers dangling by partial disarrangement of rhythm and rhyme, while the final image completes the instant transformation of the animated, bibulous truants into frozen figures two thousand years old. That the prosodic patterning imposes a dense formal screen between us and the event it records, that the passage does no more than hint at how the culprits feel while seeing to it that the passage's one explosion of real passion occurs offstage, and in ritualized language uttered by an unseen, unknown figure – this is just as it should be. It is right that all individual emotional complexity should be flattened into enigmatic tableau. For the point of the passage is precisely to withdraw from direct presentation of feeling to a remote standpoint from which the scene's problematic character – in Melville's marvelously terse ellipsis of everything at stake here ethically and hermeneutically – can be made all the more insinuating given that expression has been restrained to the point of enigma. Such terse oscillations between half-expressions of intense feeling and vast realms of implication darkly hinted at are vintage Melville. To a limited extent they recall the insinuations of the narrative voice in his more reflexive fictions starting with *Moby-Dick* but purged of its sesquipedalian garrulity: the Doric counterpart of the Corinthian prose.

Melville's strict but broken prosodic gridworks, "Chafing against the metric bound," as he wrote of Virgil (*Collected Poems* 349), have the potential, then, to enrich through the very constraints they impose. This is a poetic ideally suited to a visionary of advancing years, a visionary who could invent such a strange diptych as the polarity/intimacy between Captain Vere and Billy Budd – a visionary who understood the austere aesthetic pleasure, the rectitude, and the pragmatic efficacy of "measured forms" while realizing full well the restrictions such forms impose: accepting such restrictions, however arbitrary he knows they are in principle, because they or something like them are the sole conditions under which intimations that otherwise would remain dumb, crude, or chaotic can be conveyed with the gravity, obliquity, and reserve they merit and require. Pushed far enough, as in the passage just quoted, "writing becomes a technique of concealment as much as communication and revelation, and the work produced is a quasi-gnostic document whose meaning is revealed only to the initiated."[8] This was the Shakespearean lesson with which Melville credited Hawthorne in "Hawthorne and His Mosses"; it was a lesson Melville himself learned during the course of his career as novelist, from *Typee* to *Moby-Dick* to *The Confidence-Man*; and it was a lesson he finally mastered in the best of his poetry. Morse Peckham rightly suggests that "poetry, far more over-determined phonically and symmetrically than nineteenth-century prose, provided the protection, the citadel which Melville needed" to express himself.[9]

Melville published poetry long before turning intensively to it. The first experiment of which we can be certain was the score of lyrics he interspersed throughout *Mardi* (1849).[10] None of these, however, are as noteworthy as "The Ribs and Terrors of the Whale" (the hymn sung in Father Mapple's church) and "Billy in the Darbies," which seems to have launched *Billy Budd* as a project and which ends the novella in the form that Melville left it at his death. By 1860, Melville had completed a book-length collection of poems, which his erstwhile literary patron Evert Duyckinck offered to Charles Scribner for review. Scribner politely declined to publish it on the ground that the firm had recently made too many unprofitable commitments to such volumes.[11] At this point, Melville seems to have lain almost fallow until, at the end of the Civil War, he composed *Battle-Pieces*, a series of seventy-two short lyric and narrative poems published by Harper's in 1866. These he grouped into two sections: a longer sequence featuring particular episodes (mostly battles, with emphasis on aftermath, result, stock-taking) and personalities (mostly officers) and a shorter sequence featuring elegies, epitaphs, and requiems.

"With few exceptions," the Preface explained, these poems "originated in an impulse imparted by the fall of Richmond"; but though "composed without reference to collective arrangement" (*Collected Poems* 446), they followed the sequence of major public events from John Brown's Harper's Ferry raid in November 1859 to the interrogation of Confederate Commander-in-Chief Robert E. Lee before the Reconstruction Committee of Congress in April 1866. The book ends with a moving prose "Supplement," written in a spirit of Lincolnian irenics, urging that Reconstruction be carried out unvengefully ("In our natural solicitude to confirm the benefit of liberty to the blacks, let us forbear from measures . . . of a nature to provoke, among other of the last evils, exterminating hatred of race toward race").[12] In this essay, Melville identifies himself as "one who never was a blind adherent" (*Collected Poems* 461), and the collection as a whole shows it. Though clearly written more from a Yankee than a southern viewpoint, *Battle-Pieces* seldom voices without irony the jingoism of the first portion of Whitman's *Drum-Taps* or the triumphalism of the closing pieces.[13] Celebration of such milestone achievements as the *Monitor*'s victory over the Confederate *Merrimac* in the first-ever skirmish between ironclad ships is quickly qualified. "What poet shall uplift his charm, / Bold Sailor, to your height of daring?" Melville apostrophizes the captain in the first of his three poems on the subject, "In the Turret" (35). But "A Utilitarian View of the Monitor's Fight" undercuts this naiveté by prophesying:

> War yet shall be, and to the end;
>   But war-paint shows the streaks of weather;
> War yet shall be, but warriors
> Are now but operatives; War's made
>   Less grand than Peace,
> And a singe runs through lace and feather. (40)

All previously sanctioned forms of military valor suddenly seem paleolithic.

Indeed, the whole collection is presided over by a sober superintending consciousness skeptical of military heroism on principle, a consciousness that obviously values peace above war, believing that "All wars are boyish, and are fought by boys" (10). Again, the comparison with Whitman is striking. Both poets, in their mid-forties when the war ended, affectionately and compassionately imagine the soldiers as "boys." But whereas Whitman was uplifted by his boys' idealism and heroic endurance of their wounds, Melville dwelt upon the irony of their innocence and the grimness of the grizzled wisdom to which the survivors were forcibly awakened ("What like a bullet can undeceive!" [*Collected Poems* 41]).

Whitman later claimed that the Civil War was crucial to the formation of *Leaves of Grass* – though in fact most of his best work was already behind him by 1861. In Melville's poetic development, the war was even more crucial. Robert Penn Warren has rightly said that the war was what "made Melville a poet" worthy of the name. Not only was it inherently a major, "overmastering subject," it was a subject that freshly reactivated the inner divisions that had given rise to Melville's best fiction. Whereas "Whitman, in his poems of the War, moves toward ritual" affirmation of democratic values, "Melville moves toward tragedy;"[14] whereas Whitman expressed his unionism sentimentally by emphasizing the heroism and suffering of northerners and southerners alike, Melville stressed the ironies of one people divided by symmetrical obsessions:

> Who looks at Lee must think of Washington;
> In pain must think, and hide the thought. (148)

Battle-Pieces, in short, makes amply clear that Melville "did not believe that God took sides in wars."[15]

The Civil War thus shaped Melville's mature poetic persona: a tough-minded albeit compassionate observer, self-consciously middle-aged rather than young, careful to weigh opposite perspectives against each other, whose controlled reserve keeps him from saying as much as it's clear he thinks and feels. The overheated rhetoric in many portions of the earlier fiction from *Typee* through *Pierre* has largely been purged from *Battle-Pieces* except as an ironic imitation of the vox populi. For example, the initially jingoistic ballad on Sherman's "March to the Sea" ("It was glorious glad marching, / That marching to the sea" [85]) turns lurid at the end:

> For behind they left a wailing,
>   A terror and a ban,
> And blazing cinders sailing,
>   And houseless households wan,
> Wide zones of counties paling,
>   And towns where maniacs ran . . . (87)

Melville emerges, then, as the patriotic Whitman's laconic opposite number. Partly this was a difference in politics (Melville being the far more ambivalent partisan), partly in degree of personal involvement. Yet such differences merely accentuated the preexisting contrast in their cast of mind. Long before war broke out, Whitman was predisposed to believe Democracy would stride on with purposeful force no matter what, Melville to fear that "the Founders' dream shall flee" (*Collected Poems* 7). After all, he had already showed its speedy degeneration in *Israel Potter*.

From his Sophoclean promontory, Melville strove for variety of perspective: southern as well as northern, enlisted man as well as officer, battle front and home front, commemoration and satire. *Battle-Pieces*' dozen or so strongest poems, however, tend to build upon ambivalence about the legitimacy of the war effort ("Misgivings," "Conflict of Convictions"), rejection of standard *dulce et decorum* pieties ("The March into Virginia," "On the Slain Collegians"), revulsion against military or civic excess ("The House Top," on the 1863 New York draft riots and their suppression; "The Armies of the Wilderness"), and grim tributes to valor where an extreme penalty was paid ("The College Colonel," "Dirge for McPherson").

Between *Battle-Pieces* and Whitman's *Drum-Taps* perhaps the most telling common denominator was that both received mixed reviews and did not sell well: in Melville's case, just 486 copies by 1868. But Melville did not acquiesce to critics who cited his jagged metrics as evidence that he should have kept to prose any more than Whitman accepted his critics' charge that his poetry was nothing more than prose. After a decade, Melville followed *Battle-Pieces* with his most ambitious poetic work: *Clarel: A Poem and Pilgrimage in the Holy Land* (1876), a massive four-part poem of 18,000 rugged octosyllables loosely based on his brief 1857 sojourn in Palestine and the *Journal* written during it.[16] The poem would probably not have been printed – at least not by a major commercial publishing house – without a subvention from Melville's uncle Peter Gansevoort. Certainly it was a most un-Centennial production, "eminently adapted for unpopularity," as Melville later remarked.[17] Books of oriental travel, particularly to the Holy Land, were profitable commodities, but dense philosophical poetry on this or any other subject was not. For Melville's odd title, to which some of the poem's few reviewers took exception, meant exactly what it advertised. Literally, *Clarel* unfolds the movements, encounters, and observations of the protagonist around Jerusalem (Part I) and thence to "the Wilderness" (Jericho, the Jordan, the Dead Sea [Part II]), Mar Saba monastery (Part III), and westward again to Jerusalem via Bethlehem for the culmination of the Christian year from Ash Wednesday through Whitsuntide (Part IV). But clearly the poem is more important as an act of pilgrimage in and of itself than are the experiences of the title figure, a pallidly indecisive young seeker-student torn between love for a Jewish-American expatriate who ironically dies while he is on his pilgrimage and the longing for some definite, secure religious belief that Hawthorne famously diagnosed in Melville himself when he stopped by Liverpool to visit and obtain a visa for his travels in the Levant.

Indeed, the poem's weakest feature is the insipidness of this Hamlet-Pierre *resartus*, who unlike his prototypes never becomes more than a device for registering the cross-currents of emotion set in play by the more distinctive, mature figures who surround him. In principle, the counterpoint of love plot and quest plot is highly suggestive for its critique of the bar-

renness of metaphysical questing and for underscoring Clarel's inchoate
conflict between heterosexual impulses (which he tends postpuritanically to
censor) and his yearning for male companionship (which he desires but
which gets rebuffed by others).[18] But what really makes *Clarel* outstanding
within the Melville canon, even by comparison to *Moby-Dick*, is the am-
plitude, erudition, and extraordinary attentiveness to geographical particularity and its mythic resonances with which the poem dovetails a
multitude of different individual and cultural perspectives, to the end of
exploring as unsentimentally and clear-sightedly as possible the nineteenth-
century (male) obsession to identify a secure foundation of belief (or unbelief) in the possibility of ultimates that might withstand the challenge of
science and cultural relativism. As Helen Vendler declares, *Clarel's* "driven
ambition to incorporate all forms of ancient and modern belief, its bitter
pasquinades and its exalted after-shine of faith, its scorn of the slippery
compromises of religious modernism, its respect for genuine faith even
while it condemns the rivalries of creeds, its refusal of any palliative morsel
for itself, its human sympathy for the life and death of Jesus, its riveting
landscapes and seascapes, and its sheer monumentality make it one of the
lasting documents of American culture."[19] Or ought to, at any rate. Indeed,
for parallels to the creativity, intensity, audacity, and intellectual range with
which *Clarel* anatomizes the problem of belief, one would have to turn to
such Anglo-European writers as Coleridge, Carlyle, George Eliot, Schopenhauer (one of late Melville's favorite authors), Nietzsche, and Thomas
Mann.

Clarel is extraordinarily hard to hold in the mind. It has more cantos
than *Moby-Dick* has chapters, more significant characters, a "plot" even
more committed to episodes and digressions, and a convolution of syntax
made all the more impenetrable by the anesthetizing effect that rhymed
octosyllables tend to have on a reader conditioned by a twentieth-century
preference for free verse who, if a Melvillian, usually comes to *Clarel* with
more of a taste for prose than for poetry. Therefore *Clarel* is often avoided
as a teaching text even by those who profess to admire it; and it has received closer attention over the years from a small but devoted group of
younger scholars in doctoral dissertations and the first books constructed
from them than from senior eminences socialized into prudential time management. Thus it remains far less studied than Melville's other major books,
although it was elegantly championed by Walter Bezanson at a fairly early
date in the American phase of the modern Melville revival.[20] Even in well-
informed discussions, the sense of the heroic effort that went into the writing of *Clarel* – and must go into any serious reading of it as well – gets

short-circuited by the critic's sense of obligation to play the clear explainer to the uninitiated.

One way to begin mining *Clarel*'s riches is simply to start quoting lines and passages of unmistakable power and originality: the archetypal wandering Jew describing himself as condemned to " 'maintain / The perilous outpost of the sane' " (III.xix.98–9); the ex-partisan of multiple lost causes imaged as "The Parsee of a sun gone out" (IV.v.54); the desert's night sky "Bee'd thick with stars in swarms how bright" (II.xi.6), or (inverting the mood) "Whose stars like silver nail-heads gleam / Which stud some lid over lifeless eyes" (IV.xxx. I 54–5). Strokes like these by the hundreds make an Aeolian harp of the tetrameter's chains. An aphoristic approach doesn't, however, get at the poem's major sources of intricacy. For that, we must turn to longer sequences.

Two from opposite ends of the poem should suffice. The first is from the history of the father of Clarel's intended bride. Nathan, a child of the New England diaspora to the Midwest, assuaged his internal restlessness by marrying an American Jew and becoming a Zionist, thereby fortuitously reclaiming the symbolic ancestry the Puritans claimed as self-styled "children of Israel." The passage describes a period of inconclusive seeking after his rickety adolescent faith was blown away by deism.

> a sect about him stood
> In thin and scattered neighborhood;
> Uncanny, and in rupture new;
> Nor were all lives of members true
> And good. For them who hate and heave
> Contempt on rite and creed sublime,
> Yet to their own rank fable cleave –
> Abject, the latest shame of time;
> These quite repelled, for still his mind
> Erring, was of no vulgar kind.
> Alone, and at Doubt's freezing pole
> He wrestled with the pristine forms
> Like the first man. By inner storms
> Held in solution, so his soul
> Ripened for hour of such control
> As shapes, concretes. The influence came,
> And from a source that might well claim
> Surprise.   (I.xvii.184–201)

– namely, his conversion to Judaism. Nathan's struggles get underscored by one of the signature devices of Melville's prosody: enjambment of selected lines so as to accentuate key initial stresses: Uncanny, good, Contempt, Abject, Erring, shapes, Surprise. The passage – and still more, the longer sequence from which I have abstracted it – renders in intense psychological and symbolic detail the inner life of this quite peripheral figure, who appears elsewhere as little more than a cartoon figure of Zionist monomania. This canto, however, unfolds as a haunting case study of the search for spiritual bedrock, quintessentially "American Protestant" in the untutored prairie loneliness of Nathan's wrestling "with the pristine forms / Like the first man," but distinctive in the idiosyncrasy of his odyssey and in his integrity relative to the vulgar sectaries of his locale. Thus Melville compensates, Walter Scott–like, for the colorlessness of his vacillating protagonist by creating dozens of striking figures like Nathan who form complicated analogical interlinkages to Clarel and to one other.

These figures get developed in mutual collision as well as in isolation. *Clarel* unfolds partly as a *Canterbury Tales* of relatively free-standing cameo portraits and individual narratives, but with a much greater amount of colloquy, which is rarely lifelike but is intellectually masterful. *The Confidence-Man* was a kind of trial run for Melville in this respect, with its series of increasingly philosophical disputations about trust. In *Clarel*, the focal issue is defined more complexly, the topical agenda and historical/ cultural range far greater, the disputants more numerous, the discussions less interchangeable, the level of intellection more sophisticated. Typically, Clarel is the troubled, quizzical witness of exchanges between older companions he only half understands. Chief among these are Rolfe, a much-traveled agnostic ex-mariner who is both outspoken in his exposure of religious and ritual formulas and respectful of real spiritual sincerity; Derwent, a wilfully optimistic English cleric of liberal bent whose cheerful worldliness conceals an anxiety about ultimates that he refuses to confess; and Vine, a recessive, fastidious aesthete, impatient with the theological and historical debates into which the other two are drawn, who seems to be kept from returning lonely Clarel's overtures of companionship by some never-disclosed secret wound or history of personal disappointment.[21] Sometimes, however, Clarel is drawn into debate, usually to his consternation.

A good example is an exchange instigated by the last significant figure the poem introduces, an epicurean Lyonese traveling salesman of luxury goods of about Clarel's own age with whom he shares a room in, ironically, Bethlehem. The Frenchman twits the prim Clarel on the theological gravity with which he treats Palestine: "You of the West, / What devil has your hearts possessed / You can't enjoy?" (IV.xxvi.149–51). Debate ensues. Clarel maintains his solemnity. At one point, he incautiously cites the authority of the patristic allegorical interpretation of the Song of Songs. This the Lyonese shrugs aside:

> Eh? so too
> The Bonzes Hafiz' rhyme construe
> Which lauds the grape of Shiraz. See,
> They cant that in his frolic fire
> Some bed-rid fakir would aspire
> In foggy symbols. Me, oh me! –
> What stuff of Levite and Divine!
> Come, look at straight things more in line,
> Blue eyes or black, which like you best?
> Your Bella Donna, how's she dressed?
> (IV.xxvi.199–209)

"Bella Donna" is a shrewd, fortuitous hit on Clarel's ambivalence about whether to abandon questing for the sake of Ruth, who is thus both belle and poison to him. His roommate's challenge – and even more the monologue with which he follows it in praise of the dark beauty of Jewish women – shows a self-conscious awareness of specious ethnic stereotyping on Melville's part that is rare in nineteenth-century American literature. Clarel's vision of Ruth is belatedly revealed to have been, all along, formulaic, not – or at least not only – through the limits of authorial imagination but by design. The irony is compounded by Clarel's guilt-fraught responsiveness to the physical attractiveness of the handsome Lyonese himself, and these theological, ethnic, and sensual nuances are again complicated, two cantos later, by the disclosure that the Lyonese is a secularized Jew whose rejection of "Levite" theocentrism likely conceals an anxiety about his own identity and destiny. At that point, we are at last in a position to redefine the Lyonese not as the simple adversary of our "student late/ Of reverend theology" so much as a counterpart in skepticism, who like Clarel, only to a greater degree, has turned away from his own tradition, to his inner cost.[22] The Lyonese's dismissive allusion to the "Bonzes" exegetical misprision of Hafiz is one of many brilliant learned ellipticisms in *Clarel* that register the double-sided awareness that, on the one hand, in the transmission of religious topoi across cultures, sensuous particularity gets lost in translation; yet on the other hand, when the topoi are reduced to their material underpinnings, spirituality gets lost. Finally, to connect this with our previous passage, we now see Clarel as something like Nathan's true heir: drawn instinctively "back" toward Jewishness.[23]

This passage's tonal complexity, its concise esoteric allusiveness, its interlinkage with previous and subsequent events – these typify the density, depth, and cosmopolitanism with which Melville interweaves dozens of Protestant, Catholic, Eastern Orthodox, Jewish, Islamic, and secularist faiths, using Clarel's pilgrimage as the occasion but ultimately all of Euroamerican history as his canvas. The guiding vision, to the extent that there is one, is neither theistic nor atheistic, but a *via negativa* committed to exposing opacity, hypocrisy, and moral cowardice while honoring the search, however quixotic, for principles whereby spiritual life, ethical behavior, and public affairs might be understood, regulated, possibly even redeemed.

By concentrating on *Clarel* as a semi-omnisciently orchestrated dialogue among contending participant-observers, I have neglected its other conspicuous strength: its attention to the physical environment of Palestine – its geography, its polyglot architecture and social life – and how these are seen through the lens of a geopiety conditioned by Bible reading, religious fantasy, and nineteenth-century travelogue and archaeologism. Melville visited Palestine, roughly speaking, halfway between the time when it became marginally safe for travel and exploration (in the 1830s) and when it became a destination for large-scale, organized tourism (beginning in the late 1860s). Clearly he experienced culture shock at the land's barrenness and poverty, not to mention the meretricious commercialism of many of the sacred sites – in which respect he was not too different from other serious-minded, Bible-literate Euroamericans of the day who disembarked at Jaffa dreaming of promised land imagery but with little or no knowledge of modern Middle Eastern history.

At one level, *Clarel* is a thinking person's attempt to make coherent sense of this disturbing gap between image and reality. It develops in a more baroque and elegant fashion the running-commentary-on-sacred-sites approach and the dystopian imagery of the region's stoniness and decrepitude found in Melville's own on-the-spot *Journal* and much other nineteenth-century travel writing and scholarship, which he mined for source material.[24] *Clarel* stands out, however, for the self-conscious physiographic sensitivity with which it exploits what might be called the "aesthetics of the not there" – the deployment of images generated from one's own cultural background as a means of bringing into focus an unfamiliar landscape in front of one, creating in the process a mirage and a powerful focusing lens through which what *is* there may be rendered in a powerful albeit subjectified way.[25] In particular, Melville repeatedly visualizes the strangeness of the desert landscape in terms of the otherworld he knew better:

> Sands immense
> Impart the oceanic sense:
> The flying grit like scud is made:
> Pillars of sand which whirl about
> Or arc along in colonnade,
> True kin be to the water-spout

– the distant, "dispirited" caravan, meanwhile, laboring

> like a fleet
> Dismasted, which the cross-winds fan
> In crippled disaster of retreat
> From battle.   (II.xii.38–43, 47–50)

Melville was hardly the first western literary traveler to image desert as sea; but *Clarel* must surely be the ne plus ultra of that tradition, so exhaustively does it pursue that sustained analogy from the first canto to the last. In order fully to understand such a passage as this, one must resist resolving it back into autobiography, travelers' commonplace, or metaphor for the sake of dramatic intensification. Although all three are surely at play here, in addition the envisionment of desert as ocean is Melville's most distinctive way of indicating the conflict between the psychological imperative to see the land "as" something and to allow that it is what it is whether one likes it or not. As a traveler, Melville wrote, despite alienation and acute physical discomfort, "in pursuance of my object, the saturation of my mind with the atmosphere of Jerusalem, offering myself up a passive object, and no unwilling one, to its weird impressions, I always rose at dawn & walked without the walls."[26] *Clarel* shows that Melville did indeed keep his eyes open, even if his mind in some respects remained closed to the full implications of what he saw. *Clarel*'s great strength in this respect is that it both conveys with telling force the perception of the land's alien strangeness (which drove Melville, like more pious disillusioned westerners, to the brink of supposing that Judea must indeed be a wasteland "Which doom hath smitten" [II.xii.93]) and signals that this and all other poetic and mythic renditions of the land are finally so much overlay – like the intellectual systems that the poem relentlessly sifts at the levels of dialogue and narratorial reflection: finally, something other than the silent land itself. Thus the geographic imagination of the poem, no less than the philosophic, follows the *via negativa*.

Earlier, I mentioned in passing *Clarel*'s un-Centennial nature. Very little at first sight marks it as an American work. In subject and form it seems more a western or Victorian than an American poem. By contrast, Mark Twain, who followed Melville to the Holy Land in the first large-scale party of American tourists but broke into print seven years earlier with *Innocents Abroad* (1869), constantly reminds us of how he sees Palestine as an American: Jerusalem is no bigger than a small American village; a typical street there looks the way an American alley would if you fastened chicken coops to every window; many American streets are twice as wide as the Jordan River, and so on. Melville's narrator and travelers rarely display their nationality. But not only are most of *Clarel's* central figures travelers or self-exiles from America, one of its dimensions is a postbellum meditation on the national destiny in light of the fate of democratic revolutions in the nineteenth century generally. First, the poem introduces a bitterly disillusioned ex-partisan of Europe's 1848 rebellions. After he dies, his place is taken by the equally disillusioned Ungar, an expatriate mercenary whose improbable but symbolically rich triple minority status as Catholic and Confederate officer with Native American blood makes him a relentless prophet of "the Dark Ages of Democracy" to come (JV.xxi.149):

> Be sure 'twill yield to one and all
> New confirmation of the fall
> Of Adam. Sequel may ensue,
> Indeed, whose germs one now may view:
> Myriads playing pygmy parts –
> Debased into equality:
> In glut of all material arts . . .
>   (xxi.131–49)

Ungar's pessimism then gets reinforced by a disillusioned Mexican ex-revolutionary, lending a pan-American as well as a transhemispheric cast to the critique of the failure of democratic movements.

The other American pilgrims (Rolfe, Vine, Clarel) by no means wholly accept the mordant diagnostic, but they too have "misgivings of their own" about "Their sanguine country's wonted claim" (xxi.158, 160):

> how far beyond the scope
> Of elder Europe's saddest thought
> Might be the New World's sudden brought
> In youth to share old age's pains –
> To feel the arrest of hope's advance. (xxi.161–5)

Whereas Mark Twain draws a firm, smug line between American energy and old world decrepitude, whereas Whitman's centennial lucubrations continued to imagine "Earth's *résumé* entire" borne grandly along by the "ship of Democracy," Melville refuses to grant the United States of the Gilded Age immunity from the usual laws of history. Up to a point, this allies *Clarel* with Henry James's *The American* and later expatriate novels, except that Melville is actually more cosmopolitan than James in organizing reflection on cultural and creedal differences not in terms of an old world–new world, Europe–United States polarity alone, but in terms of something like a globalist perspective encompassing world history, cultures, religions.

After *Clarel*, Melville published nothing for another decade; but at the end of his life he released two slim volumes, *John Marr and Other Sailors* (1888) and *Timoleon* (1891), in private printings of twenty-five copies each. He also completed a third, "Weeds and Wildings, with A Rose or Two," which was left unpublished at his death. These three collections, plus a sizable body of other poems left in manuscript (more than 100 of the 450 pages of the Hendricks House edition of Melville's shorter poems) round out Melville's poetic canon. Together with *Billy Budd* (begun in 1889), this work shows that although Melville fell into a public obscurity that he seems, if anything, to have welcomed as an alternative better than being misread, he neither lapsed into silence nor did he "soften up in his later years, as Whitman and Emerson did, but remained unsimple and hard to the end."[27] It has even been claimed, with pardonable excess of zeal to retrieve Melville's late verse from oblivion, that his last poems were his best: that only in extreme old age did he master the subtleties of poetic language and achieve the ironic obliquity of his best prose work.[28] But even if we cannot apply Yeats's dictum "Bodily decrepitude is wisdom" so convincingly to Melville as to Yeats himself, certain it is that late Melville's variety of tone, subject, and style shows a more ongoing interest in experimentation with one's medium than the comparatively self-repetitive late work of Whitman, Dickinson, Tennyson, Longfellow, and Whittier.

John Marr features maritime pieces, intermixing narrative, dramatic monologue, balladry, and symbolic lyric, intermixing attempts at chatty vernacular orality with Melville's customarily more formal personae. The title work, a prose narrative with lyric coda (in vague anticipation of *Billy Budd*), features an old sailor turned carpenter who compensates for his displacement in a "frontier-prairie" settlement by conjuring up "phantoms" of his former sea life: a bemused down-home version of the mood of elegiac retrospect that the Melvillian persona favors here. At times, as in the fatalistic dream vision of "The Berg," the phantoms become intensely nightmarish; but the gritty, aphoristic, brooding, cerebral stoicism of *Clarel* is more typical. Rarely was it so powerfully expressed in all the Melville canon as in the last of the seven epitaphic "Pebbles," with which the volume ends.

> Healed of my hurt, I laud the inhuman Sea –
> Yea, bless the Angels Four that there convene;
> For healed I am even by their pitiless breath
> Distilled in wholesome dew named rosmarine (*CP* 206)

The same Sophoclean intuition that drove Matthew Arnold from the sea in despair Melville here embraces. The awareness of the ultimate pitilessness and inhumanity of things somehow, amazingly, brings not blight but consolation.[29]

This was not Melville's final word as a poet, however, well pleased though he might have been for it to be his epitaph. *Timoleon* is actually a stronger and more diverse collection, the first of its two main sections, at any rate. Here we find the delicately satirical "The Margrave's Birthnight" (on the ritual persistence of Christmas observance); "The New Zealot to the Sun" (against religious enthusiasm, including the gospel of scientism); the touching "Monody" to an aborted friendship, generally thought to be a reminiscence of Hawthorne;[30] a pithy epigram on the difficulty of creating "Art"; and a stunning dramatic monologue, "After the Pleasure Party," in which a woman astronomer by the Miltonic and (in late Victorian discourse) sexually ambiguous name of Urania expresses her frustrated rage both that the man she desires desires instead a common woman and that her own intellectual integrity has been undermined by passion.[31] To put love and questing at cross-purposes had long been a favorite Melville strategy; but it is remarkable that one whose female characters had been so chronically stereotyped should at this late date have made such a concerted attempt to imagine that conflict in so strongly eroticized a way from the perspective of a commanding, intellectually superior woman.

Timoleon's second half is a pendant to *Clarel*, short pieces deriving from the author's Mediterranean travel in 1857, with special emphasis on sculpture and architecture in situ as windows onto Roman, Greek, and Egyptian civilization. They underscore Melville's serious interest in comparative art history and geography. Though they break little new ground thematically or prosodically, they show the emergence of the urbane, gentleman-of-culture persona that marks Melville's two other significant poetic projects.

"Weeds and Wildings," dedicated to his wife Elizabeth under the transparent disguise of "Winifred," is suffused with a mellow, pastoral, Hudson Valley localism seasoned by a slight admixture of piquant arcana through its Christian and Persian rose symbolism.[32] Likewise, the most substantial among Melville's unassembled poetic manuscripts, the "Burgundy Club Sketches," as their most careful bibliographer has called them, feature the witty, clubbable personae of the Marquis de Grandvin and his American protégé Major Jack Gentian.[33] Such figures may suggest "what Melville might have been if he had not become immersed in the insoluble metaphysical and theological problem of good and evil."[34] The unfinished Grandvin–Gentian sketches comprise two major poetic sequences interspersed with prose commentary, a hybrid genre Melville often favored in his late work. (*John Marr*, for instance, opens as a prose tale about the retired sailor's loneliness in a provincial landlocked midwestern town.) In the first sequence, the Marquis orchestrates a symposium of disputatious old masters (further evidence of the breadth of Melville's artistic interests); in the second, an innocents abroad motif is accompanied by a sinister political twist as the worthy Gentian becomes increasingly troubled during his touristical excursions around Naples by the evidence of tyranny and squalor.

This material is too inchoate to allow us to surmise what Melville might finally have made of it. It certainly shows, however, Melville's ongoing interest in stylistic experimentation; in defining his artistic practice transhemispherically, cross-culturally, and with reference to forms of art other than literature alone; and in stressing the impossibility of sealing off aesthetic experience from the history of religion, science, politics, and war.

What actual chance, then, does Melville's poetry have of obtaining the hearing that its relatively small group of devoted admirers have claimed it deserves? It will be an uphill battle, surely, despite Melville's eminence. Have his poems influenced other writers? With the possible exceptions of Robert Lowell and Robert Penn Warren, no. Of course, the same holds for, say, *The Confidence-Man*. But the latter is obviously a much more modern (nay, postmodern) work, also much more obviously the anatomy of a major "American" cultural formation than Melville's poetic masterpiece, *Clarel* – not to mention the most impressive of Melville's later poems. (The Melville of *The Confidence-Man* seems to be almost in cahoots with Mark Twain; the Melville of *Clarel* looks like a deracinated expatriate next to Twain's bumptious Yankee.) For Melville's poetry to receive its just due, I suspect, one or both of the following would need to happen: (1) At least one and preferably many latter-day poets would need to claim his verse as a major influence, or a plausible claim of a Melvillian genealogy would need to be pressed by third parties; or/and (2) influential readers would need to make the case that Melville's poetic (meaning especially his use of rhymed octosyllables, his favorite meter) is not, despite appearances, hopelessly obsolete and un-American. Although, like Melville, I have learned in my middle years that it isn't safe to hope for too much, it seems at least conceivable that headway might be made on the second front. At present, the standard myth of American poetic succession is still a Whitman-centered myth of the unfolding of a "democratic poetic" via progress from traditional bound prosody to experimental forms. This is not only a consoling myth; it seems to be ratified by the later American contribution to poetic modernism and by the homage (however ambivalent) paid to Whitman by Pound, Williams, Hughes, Ginsberg, and many others. Yet it remains true that a poetry of intellectualized, cerebral bound form (rigorously disciplined accentually and/or syllabically, if not by rhyme as well), in which Melville participates, is at least as distinguished an American tradition as the Whitmanian – if one proceeds by head count, anyhow: Edward Taylor, Philip Freneau, William Cullen Bryant, Ralph Waldo Emerson, Emily Dickinson, Frederick Goddard Tuckerman, Robert Frost, T. S. Eliot, Wallace Stevens, Countee Cullen, Hart Crane, Marianne Moore, Elizabeth Bishop, Howard Nemerov, James Merrill, William Stafford, and so on. The poets one would wish to place on any list of this sort would perforce include several distinguished figures often wishfully preempted as Whitmanian. Such being the case, it might not take so seismic an intellectual shift as is commonly thought for the map of American poetry's internal formal and thematic affinities to get redrawn so as to make Melville the poet begin to look more like a true forebear.[35]

NOTES

1. For example, Roy Harvey Pearce's classic *The Continuity of American Poetry* (Princeton: Princeton University Press, 1961) mentions Melville only as a prose writer, as does Albert Gelpi, *The Tenth Muse: The Psyche of the American Poet* (Cambridge: Harvard University Press, 1975). Hyatt Waggoner, *American Poets, from the Puritans to the Present* (Boston: Houghton, 1968), pp. 227–35, treats his poetry dismissively ("Melville never found a voice for his poetry" [227]). Alan Shucard, *American Poetry: The Puritans through Whitman* (Amherst: University of Massachusetts Press, 1988), 100, and James E. Miller, Jr., *The American Quest for a Supreme Fiction: Whitman's Legacy in the Personal Epic* (Chicago: University of Chicago Press, 1979), 20, agree that Melville's poetry does not bear comparison to his fiction. Mutlu Konuk Blasing, *American Poetry: The Rhetoric of Its Forms* (New Haven: Yale University Press, 1987), does not mention Melville. A conspicuous exception to this sidelining of Melville's poetry is Donald Barlow Stauffer, *A Short History of American Poetry* (New York: Dutton, 1974), which argues, persuasively to my mind, that it "reveals the same toughness and integrity that characterizes his best prose" (p. 131).

2. Robert Penn Warren, "Melville the Poet," *Kenyon Review* 8 (1946): 208, 213. Warren's later estimate (see note 15) was more generous.

3. Modern editions include the pertinent section of *The Collected Poems of Herman Melville*, ed. Howard Vincent (Chicago: Packard, 1947); a facsimile reprint of the original edition with an introduction by Sidney Kaplan (Gainesville, FL: Scholars' Facsimiles & Reprints, 1960); and Hennig Cohen, ed., *The Battle-Pieces of Herman Melville* (New York: Yoseleff, 1963), an illustrated edition with an introduction and extensive, illuminating notes. In quoting from *Battle-Pieces* and all Melville poems other than *Clarel*, I cite Vincent's *Collected Poems*, which incorporates the manuscript revisions from Melville's own copy of *Battle-Pieces* (Houghton Library, Harvard) into the reading text. (Cohen relegates them to the notes, and Kaplan omits them.) Cohen's edition, however, remains useful for its notes and Kaplan's for the facsimile. Robert Ryan's long-awaited edition of Melville's shorter poems for the Northwestern–Newberry edition should eventually become the definitive text, however.

4. Two excellent modern scholarly editions of *Clarel* have been edited, respectively, by Walter Bezanson (New York: Hendricks House, 1960) and Harrison Hayford, Alma A. MacDougall, Hershel Parker, and G. Thomas Tanselle (Evanston: Northwestern University Press and the Newberry Library, 1991), who pay Bezanson the just tribute of reprinting his historical introduction and using his explanatory notes as the basis for their own. Except when citing the unreprinted portions of Bezanson's apparatus, I use the Northwestern–Newberry edition.

5. Of Dickinson, Melville, of course, knew nothing since she was "discovered" only shortly before his death. Melville and Whitman were exact contemporaries who knew about each other; but there is no evidence that Whitman read past *Typee* and *Omoo* (which he reviewed), and Melville's interest in Whitman was belated and seemingly noncommittal, possibly instigated by late-century British comparisons between the two as America's neglected geniuses.

6. Baym, "Melville's Quarrel with Fiction," *PMLA*, 94 (1979): 909–23.

7. This is clear from what we know of Melville's library, annotations, and reading; see, in the first instance, Merton M. Sealts, Jr., *Melville's Reading*, rev. ed. (Columbia: University of South Carolina Press, 1988).

8. William Shurr, *The Mystery of Iniquity: Melville as Poet 1857–1891* (Lexington: University Press of Kentucky, 1972), p. 245.

9. Morse Peckham, "Hawthorne and Melville as European Writers," *Melville and Hawthorne in the Berkshires*, ed., Howard Vincent (Kent, OH: Kent State University Press, 1968), p.62.

10. Warren F. Broderick, "Melville's First Five Poems?," *Melville Society Extracts*, 92 (March 1993): 13–16, suggests that in 1838–9 Melville may have published five (callow) love poems under the signature of "H" in the *Democratic Press*.

11. Jay Leyda, ed., *The Melville Log* (New York: Harcourt, 1951), 2: 619–20.

12. *Collected Poems*, 465. Melville's desire to see white northerners and southerners reconciled obviously takes priority over his concern that African Americans be granted their rightful place as American citizens. The fact that

Melville did not in this instance resist Eurocentric racial hierarchicalism to the extent that he did in some earlier work, notably *Moby-Dick* and "Benito Cereno," has disconcerted some Melvillians.

13. "The reader that *Battle-Pieces* implicitly assumes," as Robert Milder states, "is Northern, white, middle-class, and almost assuredly male; educated but not necessarily intellectual; patriotic to the Union (overzealously at times) yet fundamentally humane; and 'empowered' in the sense that he and his like will define the moral character of the postwar America-to-be" ("The Rhetoric of Melville's *Battle-Pieces*," *Nineteenth-Century Literature*, 44 [1989]: 175).

14. Robert Penn Warren, "Melville's Poems," *Southern Review*, n.s. 3 (1976): 806, 818. Chapters 1, 2, and 6 of Timothy Sweet, *Traces of War: Poetry Photography and the Crisis of the Union* (Baltimore and London: Johns Hopkins University Press, 1990), provide the most extended comparative discussion of the war poetry of Whitman and Melville.

15. Stanton Garner, *The Civil War World of Herman Melville* (Lawrence: University of Kansas Press, 1993), p. 75. By far the fullest and most illuminating account of Melville's life during the war years, this book is invaluable in placing the individual poems of *Battle-Pieces* in their historical and biographical contexts. In particular, Garner explains fully and thoughtfully how the conservative Democrat formation with which Melville, through family alliances, was surrounded during the war kept him from the abolitionist radicalism that from a late-twentieth-century standpoint is apt to seem self-evidently the litmus test of an enlightened thinker.

16. *Clarel* may have been started even before 1860, although Parker points out that no evidence unearthed thus far proves that it was begun before the 1870s (v. *Clarel*, pp. 531, 651–5).

17. 10.10.84 to James Billson, *Log* 2: 786.

18. On these points, see Nina Baym, "The Erotic Motif in Melville's *Clarel*," *Texas Studies in Literature and Language*, 16 (1974): 325–8.

19. Helen Vendler, "Desert Storm," *New Republic* (7 December 1992): 42.

20. Bezanson, author of a groundbreaking 1943 Yale dissertation on "Herman Melville's *Clarel*," edited the 1960 Hendricks House edition of *Clarel*, the most distinguished of the generally distinguished (but unfinished) first scholarly edition of Melville's works, as well as several pertinent articles, of which the most consequential is "Melville's Reading of Arnold's Poetry," *PMLA*, 69 (1954): 365–91. Three other significant extended critical discussions of *Clarel* so far published in book form are William H. Shurr's two chapters in *The Mystery of Iniquity*, pp. 45–123; Vincent Kenny, *Herman Melville's Clarel: A Spiritual Autobiography* (Hamden, CT: Shoe String Press, 1973), which also contains a helpful history of prior *Clarel* criticism, updated in Kenny's bibliographical essay on *Clarel* in John Bryant, ed., *A Companion to Melville Studies* (Westport, CT: Greenwood Press, 1986), pp. 375–406; and Stan Goldman, *Melville's Protest Theism* (DeKalb: Northern Illinois University Press, 1992). The number of essay-length studies of enduring importance can be counted on the fingers of one hand; among them, I would include Baym's (note 19); Bernard Rosenthal, "Herman Melville's Wandering Jews," *Puritan Influences in American Literature*, ed. Emory Elliott (Urbana: University of Illinois Press,

1979), pp. 167–92; and Hershel Parker, "The Character of Vine in Melville's *Clarel*," *Essays in Arts and Sciences* 15 (1986): 91–113.

21. These and the poem's other characters, both major and minor, are usefully profiled in Bezanson's Hendricks House edition, pp. 529–49. Rolfe's combination of vehemence and circumspection, his maritime background, and his youthful memories of Polynesia have led some commentators to link him to Melville himself. Although many of the figures in *Clarel* have antecedents in Melville's 1857 travels or other life experiences, none can be resolved into any one prototype and all, conversely, are integral to the expression of Melville's many-sided vision, which, as Kenney argues, "does not allow for any single spokesman of the author's views" (p. 206).

22. Dorothee Melitsky Finklestein observes that the Lyonese's "secret rejection of Judaism represents the predicament of all humanity in the failure to pursue the mystery 'in bold quest thereof' for fear of being destroyed" (*Melville's Orienda* [New Haven: Yale University Press, 1961], p. 273).

23. "Like Nathan," as Rosenthal puts it, "Clarel, despairing of Christianity, will seek a Judaic path" (p. 187). Rosenthal's whole analysis is admirable for confronting the elements of antisemitism in *Clarel* (e.g., the secularized Jewish geologist Margoth, obsessively referred to as "the Jew") while insisting that Melville's perspective cannot be reduced to these elements, despite the fact that Melville's emphasis on the Wandering Jew as a master symbol of spiritual anomie bespeaks a post-Christian and particularly post-Protestant orientation. (Finkelstein is more severe on Melville's post-Protestant limitations [pp. 269–73].) I think Rosenthal's admirable essay finally understates the poem's breadth of cultural vision when he concludes that "Judaism offers a ghostly backdrop to the religious dialogue about the virtues of Protestantism and Catholicism" (177).

24. Melville's sources are discussed in *Clarel*, pp. 528–35, 656. For further valuable contextualizing of how Melville would have seen Palestine and what he would have gleaned from literary sources (travel books and biblical/archaeological research), see Naomi Shepherd, *The Zealous Intruders: The Western Rediscovery of Palestine* (London: Collins, 1987), and Lester I. Vogel, *To See a Promised Land: Americans and the Holy Land in the Nineteenth Century* (University Park: University of Pennsylvania Press, 1993). For assistance in interpreting this material and nineteenth-century American biblicism generally, I am indebted to Paul Charles Gutjahr, who generously shared with me portions of his dissertation in progress, "Battling for the Book: The Americanization of the Bible in the Antebellum Publishing Marketplace" (University of Iowa, 1996).

25. My *The Environmental Imagination: Thoreau, Nature Writing, and the Formation of American Culture* (Cambridge: Harvard University Press, 1995), pp. 55–82, discusses this mode of environmental envisionment with reference to pastoral writing, attempting to give due emphasis to both its "negative" potential as self-mystified Eurocentric proprietary hallucination and its "positive" aspects as a means of environmental representation and cultural affirmation. A similar problematic, I think, marks Melville's relentlessly antipastoral representation of the Palestinian environment.

26. *Journals*, ed. Howard C. Horsford with Lynn Horth (Evanston: Northwestern University Press and the Newberry Library, 1989), p. 86.

27. Bezanson, Editorial introduction to the 1960 Hendricks House edition of *Clarel*, p. ix.

28. William Bysshe Stein, *The Poetry of Melville's Late Years: Time History, Myth, and Religion* (Albany: State University of New York Press, 1970), makes many fine, penetrating observations about the late poems at the cost of overstating their "subversive" dimension and the amateurishness, as he perceives it, of *Battle-Pieces* and *Clarel*.

29. Helen Vendler remarks: "What it cost Melville to write this poem makes us pause, reading it. Alone, it is enough to win him, as a poet, what he called 'the belated funeral flower of fame' " ("Introduction," *Poetry of Herman Melville* [San Francisco: Arion Press, 1995], p. xxv).

30. Harrison Hayford, "Melville's 'Monody': For Hawthorne?" *Clarel*, 883–9, explains the grounds for questioning the certainty of this identification. No hard biographical evidence has come to light confirming that anything went sour in the personal relations between the two, although it would have been surprising if Melville had not come to doubt whether Hawthorne's sensibility was less akin to his own than "Hawthorne and His Mosses," Melville's famous review-essay on *Mosses from an Old Manse*, seems to suppose. Robert Milder, "Editing Melville's Afterlife," *Text* (forthcoming), thoughtfully poses some methodological questions about Hayford's antibiographicalist argument.

31. Robert Martin rightly characterizes the poem as preoccupied by "the yearning for a rediscovery of an androgynous self" (*Hero, Captain, and Stranger* [Chapel Hill and London: University of North Carolina Press, 1986], p. 99). Whatever its date, whatever Melville's degree of direct knowledge of the discourses of Victorian sexuality, the poem's "use of Urania," as Martin adds, "strikingly anticipates the Uranian poets of the turn of the century" (p. 137), although the poem's perspective seems to be more in keeping with, say, Edward Carpenter's usage of the term to suggest transcendence of binary sexual categorization than as equated with male homosexuality. It must also be admitted that the poem could be seen in a far more misogynistic light, as being about the fall of a prideful bluestocking. To stop there, however, would be to caricature a strenuous, unique achievement.

32. For the Christian, see Stein, *Poetry of Melville's Later Years*, pp. 200–23; for the Persian, see Finkelstein, *Melville's Orienda*, pp. 256–60.

33. On this unfinished work, see especially Merton M. Sealts, Jr., "Melville's Burgundy Club Sketches," *Harvard Library Bulletin*, 12 (1958): 253–67.

34. Stein, *Poetry of Melville's Later Years*, p. 227.

35. My sincere thanks to Helen Vendler, Alan Heimert, and Robert Milder for commenting upon a previous version of this manuscript; to Robert Milder and Paul Gutjahr for sharing their unpublished work with me; and to William Pannapacker for invaluable research assistance.

7

JENNY FRANCHOT

Melville's Traveling God

It is with fiction as with religion: it should present another world, and yet one to which we feel the tie.

The Confidence-Man[1]

Readers of Melville cannot help but notice the conjunction of generic innovation, anthropological encounter, and theological quandary that characterizes his fiction. Yet when addressing themselves to the question of Melville and religion, critics have largely viewed these domains separately, agreeing that Melville's fiction is pervasively characterized by his battle, or "quarrel," with a dying Christianity but that his interests in anthropological encounter and aesthetic experimentation are present because Christianity is absent or, at most, merely vestigial. At war with Christian theology and practice, his literature constitutes an antireligious domain of subversive indictment against a god who has failed man and whose absence has generated a modern voice of recrimination and alienation: "doth not Scripture intimate," queries the narrator in *Pierre*, "that He holdeth all of us in the hollow of His hand? – a Hollow, truly!"[2] What is new in Melville is new because it is not religion.[3]

My purpose in this essay is to suggest that, to the contrary, Melville's revolutionary impact upon the novel form does not derive from Christianity's absence – a formal experimentalism released from the grip of conventions that have their roots in a defeated Protestant orthodoxy – but precisely from its continued presence. Its "believability" having migrated from dogma into the absorbing domain of ambiguous literary narrative, Christianity is there, translated from its cultural "death" into a new ontological register. No longer inviolable creed, the dead body of Christianity is remobilized (one might even say resurrected) as metaphor by Melville's circular procedure of return and departure, a form of authorial "travel" constituted by fragmentary citation, recurrent metaphorization, and willful misreading of Scriptural and theological discourse.[4]

In that his fictional plots are generated from such recurrent and deviant translations of religious language, Melville's misreadings of Christianity form the heart of his lifelong artistic production; God's failed authorship (whether because he has abandoned his creation or simply and miserably botched it) is the generative authorial model for Melville's moody, belligerent, and quixotic passage through his own writings. As the devilish figure of the confidence man explains with reference to the narrative utility of perverted Christianity, "here on earth, true charity dotes, and false charity plots" (14). Thus while Melville's subversive readings of religious discourse and practice "kill" Christianity by exposing its hypocrisies or sheer impracticality, in another sense this repeated murder – these willful misreadings – restore Judeo-Christianity's viability as the inaccessible, authentic "other" within the "false charity" of the fictional.

This other, against and toward whom the false charity of fiction plots itself, is worked and reworked through the trope of travel – a rhetoric of questing, contact with, and meditation upon cultural others and their religions. There is no endpoint of spiritual conviction or final disillusionment reached through this travel, but rather a recurrent movement between opposed possibilities of belief and unbelief, antinarrative and successful plotting, solitude and cultural encounter. In this process, the Western God is himself rendered other – a presence just beyond travel's ultimate reach and fiction's possibilities that yet remains wholly "inside" them. This ambiguous position of God and, more generally, of religious language in Melville's narratives sheds little light on his beliefs and certainly offers the reader no coded doctrinal resolutions to life's conundrums. Instead, the disabled and remobilized Christianity encountered in Melville's writings yields, like Ishmael's view of an individual's passage through life, no final destination but instead a repetitive movement. "There is no steady unretracing progress in this life; we do not advance through fixed gradations, and at the last one pause: – through infancy's unconscious spell, boyhood's thoughtless faith, adolescence' doubt (the common doom), then scepticism, then disbelief, resting at last in manhood's pondering repose of If. But once gone through, we trace the round again; and are infants, boys, and men, and Ifs eternally."[5] In Ishmael's portrait of the individual's circuit from belief through disbelief and back again, we recognize the spiritually restless protagonists so characteristic of Melville's fiction. And next to this figure of the traveler, we can discern another, intriguing presence: that of his god, unmoored from doctrinal fixities, released along with him into the unstable spaces of empire and authorship.

Students of Melville and the question of religion have long recognized the connection between his fictions of travel and pilgrimage and his own spiritual restlessness. Hawthorne's famous description of Melville's relent-less metaphysical questing has become a locus classicus for readers inter-ested in such questions. Visited by Melville in Liverpool in 1856, Hawthorne later described in his journal their conversation on the dunes:

> Melville as he always does, began to reason of Providence and futurity, and of everything that lies beyond human ken, and informed me that he had 'pretty much made up his mind to be annihilated'; but still he does not seem to rest in that anticipation; and, I think, will never rest until he gets hold of a definite belief. It is strange how he persists – and has persisted ever since I knew him . . . in wandering to and fro over these deserts. . . . He can neither believe, nor be comfortable in his unbelief.[6]

While spiritual persistence was celebrated in John Bunyan's influential Christian classic, *The Pilgrim's Progress* (1678), as a Christian's most im-portant trait, Hawthorne's mid-nineteenth-century appraisal indicates how such persistence had come under suspicion; for Hawthorne, Melville's te-nacity is "strange," less a crucial action for the Christian pilgrim than a symptom of psychological delusion, of a searching for a God no longer hidden but simply not there. Following in the wake of Hawthorne's as-sessment, critical efforts have sought to extract an essence of Melville's beliefs from the ambiguous domain constructed by this metaphysical per-sistence, hoping perhaps to rid us of the troubling specter of a man "wan-dering to and fro." At times such accounts have recapitulated, on a hermeneutic level, the drama of frustrated faith that is staged not only by Hawthorne in his journal account but also in Melville's fiction itself. But Melville's own appreciation of Bunyan's "most marvelous book" (*Pierre*, 342) should make us pause in our efforts to settle this restlessness or, more generally, to view this persistence as the mere mark of a dying religious world and a man's futile desire for it. Instead, we might consider this per-sistence as a form of travel crucial to the production of Melville's seafaring fictions and to the production of a new god who emerges within them: a deity who is no longer a fixed point, a "presence" who will bring final quiet, but is instead also on the move.

Through their wanderings, Melville's characters encounter the seemingly insuperable conflicts represented by the warring factions of Christianity: the schism between Catholicism and Protestantism initiated by the Protestant Reformation; the sectarian battles within Protestantism, particularly the de-bates between Calvinism and liberalizing Protestant and post-Protestant movements like Unitarianism and Transcendentalism; and finally the battle between Christianity entire and atheism. But alongside this well-documented defiance of a fraught Christianity is Melville's sustained effort to reanimate a faith exhausted by the challenges of the Enlightenment and, in the nineteenth century, by those of the higher criticism, of liberalizing Protestantism, and finally Darwinism. Accordingly, Christianity has a double valence throughout his writings: as a potent, vindictive, and contradictory force, it bears down on outraged humanity like Moby Dick, the "breathless hunter" (549) whose "vengeful wake" (552) drags Ahab and crew down to their deaths; as a depleted force stripped of its powers, it appears as impoverished landscape and mute character, ceaselessly interrogated, mourned over, and ambivalently resuscitated by the narrative voice. From *Typee* to *Clarel*, Melville's fiction explores this dual heritage of the potent/impotent god by traveling from the New World of the Pacific gradually back to the Old World of the Holy Land – a regressive arc that measures a flight "outward" from a repressive Protestantism into the "exotic" territories opened by Western imperialism and eventually "backward" to the site of Christianity's birth in Palestine, itself a terrain, as Clarel discovers, of disturbing otherness. At once flight, pilgrimage, and touristic travel, Melville's art investigates this doubled and paradoxical religious inheritance – struggling against its power while lamenting its death. Rather than pondering whether Melville ultimately found answers to his religious questions or chose route "a" or "b" in response to his spiritual predicament, it is more fruitful to consider how his narratives and poetry construct this duality, coupling belief and unbelief, force and exhaustion, the deity's simultaneous oppression and abandonment of humanity. The encounters with cultural difference and exotic others that are so fundamental to Melville's writings voice this interior struggle with the home theology of a paradoxical Protestantism, dispersing that theology across the spaces of empire, estranging it from the suffering protagonists while seeking to uncouple its unbearable contradictions.

From the early Polynesian encounters of *Typee: A Peep at Polynesian Life* (1846) and *Omoo: A Narrative of Adventures in the South Seas* (1847) through the global travels of *Moby-Dick or, The Whale* (1851) (and its sequel of sorts, *Pierre*, 1852), down the Mississippi in *The Confidence-Man* (1857) and, finally, to Palestine in his 20,000-line epic, *Clarel: A Poem and Pilgrimage to the Holy Land* (1876), Melville's authorial project involves the translation or forced travel of his religious inheritance into fiction, a translation which abases *and* reanimates the sacred by bringing it down into the horizontal trajectory of fictional narrative. Beginning with his early Polynesian fictions, Melville's lifelong narrative and poetic investigation into the nature and limits of religious belief is entangled with the dynamics of cultural encounter. His writings braid the incomprehensibilities of cultural and religious otherness to those of the Judeo-Christian God and indeed draw their characteristic style and energy from this awkward, passionately allegorical union. A way to expel the inner voice of Protestant deity into the spaces of Western expansion, this braiding splices "Jehovah" to native "other" in an ironic version of missionary outreach; Melville does not aim to convert cultural others but to author an urgent narrative of Western searching through and against them.

Under siege in antebellum America, "God" was itself a category of transcendental meaning *and* institutionalized religious power regulating Protestant Americans – a contradictory discursive site of mystery, intimately familiar theology, and national identity. Throughout Melville's writings, invocations of deity play upon this rich discourse of biblical and national religious identity while summoning a wholly silent Other who refutes this discursive play, even its most self-aware, ironic voicings. Melville's questing characters – Tommo, Ishmael, Pierre, Clarel – accuse this first, discursive deity for "his" punitive mandates (or hypocritical followers) while simultaneously seeking his doubled and silent Other within the same language. Hailing this divine double through a petitionary rhetoric of accusation, mockery, and sheer negation, these characters try to provoke this Other into dialogue. The most crucial language at issue here is that of providence, the Christian doctrine affirming that an omnipotent God supervises humanity for the good. The initial movement in this travel from known god to silent Other occurs through the release of anger against this providential deity of nineteenth-century Christianity, a figure who not only allows for evil and suffering but authors it. In disputing the validity of this doctrine of providence, Melville's variously voiced anger refuses Christianity its providential narrative and, in effect, refuses Christianity *as* narrative.

Actual travel is crucial to this rhetorical voyage, for the hero's movement through the heterogeneous space of cultural otherness releases an otherwise dormant multiplicity of voice. Travel, wondrous contact with others, convivial masculine conversation on shipboard or shipwreck, and the reimagination of that experience into fiction constitute Melville's grappling utterance, a rhapsodic voicing of contradictions woven out of the sacrificed narrative of Scripture, particularly its providential voicings. An avid student not just of South Seas cultures but also of Protestant theology and tradition, Melville develops an anthropological gaze upon Christianity, one that voices itself through satire and insinuation, rhetorical stances that reduce Christianity from the unseen, punitive immensities of ideology to visualizable fragments open to authorial citation and appropriation. In effect, Melville slips out from the "hollow" of God's hand – as described by the tormented Pierre – to hold "him" in turn. Religion – like the "native" before the imperial traveler-anthropologist – becomes subject *of and to* his art. Thus Melville's translations of Christianity into his fictions subjugate religion to his imperial art, deconstructing it into a repository of analogies and images that form the body of his plots and characters that together then dispute Scripture's ability to author anything authentic.

Particularly in the New World quests of *Typee* and *Moby-Dick*, the space of the unknown god's silence is demarcated by this elaborate language of anthropological difference *and* existential accusation and summoning. Repeatedly, Melville situates his characters within the dynamics of this braided anthropological-theological encounter: the ethnographic moment lures the hero to decipher the native, offering the tempting prospect of understanding others in order to overturn his home god and thus finally grasp the divine Other. But while rhetorically and even metaphysically brilliant, such Melvillian travelers as Tommo and Ishmael are ultimately situated between two ungraspable languages: the minimalized voice of the cultural other, a noise on its way to articulateness – a "not yet" – and the minimal voice of divine otherness, a silence that has transcended language as the "no longer."[7] Narrative and characterological voices struggle to assert their mastery over and against both of these silences.

Melville's deconstruction of religion converts Christianity to a dead but wondrous body that then yields itself to a probing literary gaze of dismemberment and appropriation; narrative verve and representational dimensionality are achieved through repeated invocations of Christianity's implausibility. Yet Melville's citational travels through Christianity's fragments also endow them with a new, uncanny life as metaphor, allusion, and literary source; subtended to the life of the text, these Christian fragments are both meaningless phantoms (doctrinally or ideologically speaking) and newly potent presences in their aesthetic serviceability.[8] As these anthropological and theological questings unfold inside the container of fiction, characters' struggles against theology and toward a cultural and divine otherness must contend with the revitalized religious allusiveness of the narrative voice, one which allies fragmented religious meaning to the well-documented elusiveness of the Melvillian text itself. Narrative voice, point of view, plot, and imagery all participate in this rivalry between the hero's metaphysical questing and the uncanny religiosity of the narrative voice that insinuates the futility of metaphysics while insisting upon its obligation to persevere, to travel, to wander "to and fro."

THEOLOGY, ANTHROPOLOGY, AND THE DIVINE OTHER

When Tommo, the hero of Melville's first novel, *Typee*, jumps ship, his newfound freedom promptly degenerates into a captivity among the Typees, a Marquesan tribe who include tattooing and cannibalism among their religious rituals. The first in a long line of Melvillian characters beset by problems of theology and anthropology, Tommo scrutinizes his captors' religious practices in the hope of staving off the unsavory prospect of being tattooed or eaten. But as our amateur ethnographer periodically admits of Typee religion, "I saw everything, but could comprehend nothing" (210).[9] Longing to break the taboo prohibiting women from canoes, Tommo at one point threatens to take his paramour, Fayaway, aboard, only to confront again the problem of theological obscurity. Alarmed at Tommo's insubordination, the chief, Mehevi, treats him to a "long, and I have no doubt a very learned and eloquent exposition of the history and nature of the 'taboo' . . . employing a variety of most extraordinary words, which, from their amazing length and sonorousness, I have every reason to believe were of a theological nature. But all that he said failed to convince me: partly, perhaps, because I could not comprehend a word that he uttered" (159). Tommo's delicate lampooning of theological rhetoric suggests that in any language theology is an indecipherable discourse, given to rhetorical inflation and resistant to translation. The mark of Tommo's racial and national difference, this elusive text of Marquesan religion entices him into ever more intimate, transgressive contact with the Typees in order to comprehend their otherness fully and thus underscore his difference from them. Typee religion (and its theological explanations) are everywhere before his eyes and yet nowhere, for they remain hidden from his comprehension. Yet theology's indecipherability only amplifies its power as the ubiquitous, tempting unseen. "But in sober seriousness," Tommo confesses after several weeks' captivity and intensive scrutiny of the Typees, "I hardly knew what to make of the religion of the valley" (209).[10]

Tommo's exclusion from Typee religion reenacts his sense of alienation from Western Christianity, a loss that fuels his melancholia and his critique of missionary Protestantism in the South Seas, especially for its imposition of Calvinistic melancholia upon native populations. Undertaken in the wake of the Ages of Exploration and Enlightenment, the anthropological study of man (which Tommo practices in amateur fashion) was both disillusioned and triumphant in its discovery of humanity's different gods. The encounter with the otherness of divinity was a powerful stimulant both to Western secularization and to a renewed search for transcendent meaning. As suggested by Tommo's prolonged effort to make sense of Typee culture, secularization in the West occurred alongside the anthropological project of supplying meanings to the "primitive" – the creation of ethnological meaning coinciding with the erosion of European theological meaning. That man's proper subject of study was no longer God but humanity also registers the melancholic new "truth" that man's *only* subject of study was himself.[11] There is no divine Other, but simply other human beings; the "space," then, of anthropological investigation is ample in the variety it reveals but also diminished by this melancholic constraint.

While the Typees have not been evangelized, their religion seems as baffling and grotesque as Calvinism, thwarting Tommo's effort to assign meaning to the "primitive." Tommo's ethnographic interpretations are symptoms then of his ailing religious identity, as well as of the ailing body of religion, considered from the universalist viewpoint of Enlightenment critique. And yet the Typees, in their elusive primitivism, promise to overcome the greater incoherence of Tommo's home deity, featured in his declared omnipotence over a world of suffering, his denunciation of his own creation, and his recent abandonment of humanity. The Typees might even cure Tommo's specifically Protestant melancholy, the legacy of this paradoxical deity who has both disappeared and continues to punish with his estimation of humanity's depraved status. "I will frankly declare," Tommo gingerly admits, "that after passing a few weeks in this valley of the Marquesas, I formed a higher estimate of human nature than I had ever before entertained" (238).

But if Tommo cannot quite attain a coherent ethnography, his failures do produce a new whole, that of his narrative. Sacrificing Scripture to the fresh if relative truths of anthropology, Tommo's comparativist vision supplies his narrative with novel and partially compensatory wonders. While these wonders secularize his and the reader's consciousness, they also incite a religious impulse to assign transcendent meaning – a contradictory gesture resolved by supplanting theological and anthropological mystery with that of literary mystery, a mystery that can reach a denouement. Thus Tommo's efforts to decipher what is to him the Typees' unintelligible religiosity motivate the production of his own "new world" – that of his venturing, antitheological subjectivity and its literary narration. In this other world of the EuroAmerican colonial adventure tale, fragments of cultural otherness are organized into a fiction whose coherence is contingent upon the religious incoherence of both home and native cultures, of both interior self and the interior/exterior of the cultural other.

Debilitated by theology, Tommo, with his mysteriously swollen leg, assembles his anthropological understanding from a variety of disabled postures that mime his spiritual malaise. Carried on the back of Kory-Kory or reclining in his hut, his bodily ailment prevents that lofty, comprehensive perspective that will later prove so enchanting to Melville's mast-climbing heroes. His is a captive ethnography that rejects missionary Protestantism while rummaging through Typee religion for answers to the mystery of being: tattooing, feasting, dancing, cannibalism spring out at him, threatening to ambush his stationary body, daring him to decipher their intentions. The other is both ethnographic subject and Tommo's interior subjectivity (and body), rife with contradiction, plunged into its own unseen.

Although infantilized by injury and confinement, Tommo thrills to the imperial power promised by the emptiness of the indecipherable Typees and their lands. The island of Nukuheva promises Tommo escape from Western culture and particularly from Christianity, its landscape initially appearing as "one unbroken solitude, the interior of the island having apparently been untenanted since the morning of the creation" (58). Tommo's post-Christian gaze upon the paradisal landscapes of Nukuheva allows a momentary recuperation of a pre- and post-Christian emptiness, an imagination of the world thoroughly, mercifully vacant of other Europeans and, most important, of Christianity itself. This emptiness is sustained by exterior and interior violence, animated by the proselytizing religion that is momentarily absent from it. But as Tommo soon discovers on Nukuheva, paradise is not empty but inhabited by warring cannibal tribes and by Western military powers: in the harbor stand French ships to claim possession of the island, while in the heart of the temple, the Typee elders hand Tommo a rusted gun to repair. Some European has always been there before the hero. This imperial presence even lurks within the antimissionary Tommo, whose romantic primitivism is close cousin to the Western imperial and evangelical powers he ostensibly deplores.[12]

Inventing a Protestant imperial imaginary for the English novel that proved central to Melville's fictions, Defoe's *Robinson Crusoe* (1729) formulated this paradoxical topography of inhabited emptiness. Crusoe's narrative of religious conversion in his island solitude suggests that the English God, in the wake of the Reformation and European religious wars, must be built from scratch elsewhere. The radical emptying that marks Defoe's novelization of Nonconformist piety, one that is ever anxious to cleanse itself of human mediations, is best performed by becoming a castaway into an "empty" space. But this spiritual process, coinciding with the developing reach of English empire, is made possible only through the mediation of imperialism. Crusoe is shipwrecked onto his island after attempting to purchase slaves in Africa for his Brazilian plantation, the island serving as momentary punishment for his greed (Crusoe will eventually leave it and garner handsome profits from his Brazilian holdings) while offering a purified Protestant version of Roman Catholic monastic retreat from the world.

Crusoe's spiritual retreat exemplifies the worldly asceticism that Max

Weber would later isolate as the preeminent trait of a Protestant piety dedicated to being "in the world" but not "of it," a piety at once capitalist, abstemious, and otherwordly.[13] Crusoe's is an imaginary exodus, for he has left the world only in order to rebuild it. By the novel's conclusion, both the visible and invisible domains are neatly aligned, thus assuring readers that the two (with a good deal of anxious ingenuity) will prosper in the age of British imperialism. His cleansed island space, where he reconstitutes English culture (down to the detail of fashioning a goatskin umbrella), is also the site of his greatest manufacturing triumph: the rebuilding of Christianity from nothing but himself, his Bible, and one native subject, the docile Friday. Readers of Defoe's novel are faced with the revolutionary eighteenth-century Protestant proposition that true Christianity can be re-created anywhere – that the truest Christianity, in fact, finds in the "nowhere" of other peoples the most adequate site for its reproduction. Moving inexorably toward submission to his interior voice of conscience and thence to the subjugation of Friday, Crusoe's is an ascetic retreat of interior and exterior colonization – a flight to the margins of empire and to the margins of introspection that is simultaneously an invasive retreat into the world of others, a pilgrimage that enables him to find his hitherto distant god in and through the wondrous encounter with and subjugation of New World natives.

This metaphysical fantasia is a central convention in Melville's voyaging fictions that repeatedly isolate the male hero from "civilization," bidding him to generate new spiritual worlds within and through the domain of the "native." While Tommo disdains Crusoe's missionary imperative, he nevertheless follows in his steps, comparing his own surprised discovery of a footpath to Crusoe's paradigmatic moment of astonishment: "Robinson Crusoe could not have been more startled at the footprint in the sand than we were at this unwelcome discovery" (58). Tommo still moves within the terms of Crusoe's religious drama that promise spiritual recovery through imperial travel, a repossession of home through the artifice of the castaway's dispossession.

Thus while the effort on the part of the Typees to "conceal every trace" (271) of their cannibal practices underscores Tommo's search for the *deus absconditus* of Western Christianity, their apparently idyllic existence provides escape from the oppressive presence of Protestantism's God.[14] In dubious flight from American civilization, Tommo consistently imagines a boundary, an endpoint to this emptiness of the indecipherable other: he will finally discover the proof of cannibalism and/or he will ultimately be devoured. Human depravity will reappear, Eden will again recede, and the comforting boundaries of Western religious alienation will be reborn.

Tommo finds this elusive presence of cannibalism his best help in his theological quandary, for it provides tension to the idyll, a plot to the narrative. Ironically, only by imagining his extermination can Tommo lend
coherence to his experience – what is religious otherness about except my
being eaten by them? As suggested by Tommo's eventual glimpse of cannibalized flesh that precipitates the novel's denouement, being devoured is
the exit from mystified religious inquiry. What it all means is that they are
about to eat me, grisly death the "answer" to alienation and to baffled
anthropological interpretation.[15]

Yet this resolution of the mystery of otherness involves not just death
but literal incorporation into the "religious other" – an annihilation so
extreme, so intimate that it lends an obsessive, homeward cast to Tommo's
anthropological "gaze": analogizing wherever he can to EuroAmerican culture, Tommo's attempts at interpretation construct the novel's readerly
space as one of comic, failed communion, the Typees speaking an inept
English which Tommo scrupulously reproduces, as does Crusoe of the broken English he has taught Friday. Thus Tommo translates: "Ki-Ki, nuee
nuee, ah! moee moee mortarkee (eat plenty, ah! sleep very good)" (109).
Like Crusoe's fluent representation of Friday's handicapped English,
Tommo genially conveys this Typee "gibberish" (126) in supple English to
his readership.

As suggested by Tommo's startled encounters with tattooed bodies and
carved idols, the sheer materiality of cultural difference recorded in this
novel of Polynesian adventure initially fills his spiritual vacancy, renewing
conversation between the Western seeker and otherness by reaffirming, first
and foremost, that there is an other whom the hero can see and even, in
the looming scale of its altars, begin to measure. But this ethnographic
moment also extends the emptiness of secular space, fashioning a domain
that is not so much devoid of language as filled with the "gibberish" of
the Marquesans *and* the discredited discourse of Protestant theology. The
exterior imperial space of exploration and conquest, like the vast interiors
of Melville's characters, is cluttered with languages that no longer speak,
silence more the sign of invalidation and cultural incommensurabilities than
of literal emptiness.

Thus anthropological encounter and the ethnography it generates dis-
lodge the discursive Christian God from his primacy, not only silencing
him but reproducing him as illegitimate, silenced other to the disenchanted
Western traveler: Tommo, stranded on Nukuheva, is finally far enough
from Jehovah to visualize him as reduced, nonsensical other. No longer the
omnipotent unseen, the Judeo-Christian God is made to suffer the vulnerability of foreign peoples subjected to the anthropological gaze. When

Tommo stumbles upon a decomposed wooden idol in the woods, his is the abusive stare of disillusion with a former god, now exposed as "nothing more than a grotesquely shaped log, carved in the likeness of a portly naked man with the arms clasped over the head, the jaws thrown wide apart, and its thick shapeless legs bowed into an arch" (210). What follows from this discovery of the cast-off idol is a fascinating revenge play upon religion: Kory-Kory, attempting to straighten the carving for Tommo (who is in "one of my inquiring, scientific moods"), grows furious at its refusal to stand and begins "beating the poor image," and finally "whirled the idol about most profanely, so as to give me an opportunity of examining it on all sides" (211). Arms lifted, mouth wide open, the idol's body is sprawled to the gaze and subject to Tommo's rage. While Tommo's cool perusal of the beating could also be said to mimic the gaze of the disembodied Jehovah, who jealously interdicts all images of himself as idolatrous, his view of Kory-Kory's violence is also directed against his monotheistic heritage. Tommo's fascination is not with the beating of the idol so much as with the beating of divinity.

Tommo's account of the religious other, built upon repeated assertions of his inability to decipher Typee language, customs, or religion, establishes an antiethnographic strain that will characterize much of Melville's future writing.[16] Like Tommo imagining the Nukuhevans reading ethnography produced about them by a "scientific voyager" and finding it simply incredible (*Typee*, 202), Melville consistently turned an estranging anthropological perspective back onto American Protestantism, not simply in order to reveal the hypocrisies of Christianity but, more profoundly, to propose (to his characters and his readers) that the cultural and racial other cannot possibly be as strange as the god who had raised them back home. But in addition to perplexity, ethnography potentially yields renewed substance for an ideologically depleted Christianity. Behind the tattoos that mark the extraordinary cultural encounters of Tommo and later of Ishmael, who in the opening pages of *Moby-Dick* stares in astonishment at Queequeg's legs, "marked, as if a parcel of dark green frogs were running up the trunks of young palms" (23–4), lies the glimmer of a Christianity made valuable again through estrangement.[17] That is, Christianity draws upon the uncanniness of anthropological encounter to be seen again in all the original oddity of its claims. Imperial expansion and the pilgrimages it makes available to the American seeker traveling across the "wonderfreighted, tribute-rendering waves" (*Moby-Dick*, 459) can potentially reanimate a desiccated theology diagnosed by Ishmael as "somehow dreadfully cracked about the head" (*Moby-Dick*, 86).

Thematically speaking, we encounter this ethnographic reanimation at brief moments over the course of Melville's writings when Christ surfaces in tattooed form. Yillah, the Polynesian spirit-girl of Melville's third novel, *Mardi*, is astonished, for example, at the Scandinavian Jarl's "characteristic device upon the arm of the wonderful mariner – our Saviour on the cross, in blue; with the crown of thorns, and three drops of blood in vermilion, falling one by one from each hand and foot."[18] Traveling in the world's emptiness beyond the reach of Scripture, the Christ on Jarl's arm emerges from within the space of the colonial imaginary as anthropological wonder, a sign *from* but also *beyond* the Western world: it astonishes rather than converts the "native" girl. The tattoo provides Christ a new context, one that at least partially removes him from the contaminations of a worldly, imperializing Christianity and its "cracked" theology and recontextualizes him as a marvelous sight from an unseen (yet antitheological) world. The Western reader is invited to see Christ and, for once, not understand – to share Yillah's experience of him as exotic trinket, a miniature wonder instead of an enormous but deadened meaning. We encounter this same reversal of perspective in *Clarel* when Agath stretches forth his arm, revealing his tattoos to the startled, ever-superficial Derwent: "A thing of art, vermil and blue, / A crucifixion in tattoo, / With trickling blood-drops strange to see" (4.2.50–2).[19]

These moments of Christ's emergence in tattooed form – the same tattoo described in works thirty years apart – articulate Melville's fascination not just with crucifixion and its visual reproduction but with its dissemination, even literal incorporation, into the text of imperial adventure and discovery. Closer perhaps than Tommo's grotesque idol in the woods, these tattooed Christs reknit the incarnate god of Christianity to the flesh he reportedly transcended, thus restoring to the Western deity the uncanny attraction of the idol, the sacrilegious entrapment of invisible divinity into body. The tattoo's trickling blood drops – moving and yet always there – reanimate the deadness of the story of crucifixion: exposed not so much in the name of Christ as in the name of travel, Yarl's and Agath's tattoos are fragmented allusions, souvenirs even, that invite us to consider Christ as idol and thus as a "wonder" of European consciousness. More generally, these tattoos literally emblemize Melville's larger literary practice of Scriptural citation and appropriation. Detached from church and state, the tattooed Christs and their discursive equivalent – the numerous allusions to Christianity throughout Melville's writings – constitute a dispersal of Christianity through the space of colonialism, a dismemberment and reattachment to the body of anthropological and literary spectacle. Thus positioned within the colonial uncanny, the tattoo mutely questions: Is there a new form of belief obtainable through contact with native worlds? Can belief leave its deadened self behind and produce itself anew? Or is the Western traveler caught forever in a tautological movement of persistence, "wandering to and fro over these deserts" of belief and unbelief?

Dedicated to never resolving these questions of belief, Melville's fiction establishes religion's impotence as fiction's power; the futility of spiritual questing signals the resistance of implied author and reader to the temptation to believe. It is this resistance (coupled with occasional surrender) to belief that forms the essence of Melville's narratives and metanarratives. "Do you have confidence, my friend? Only have confidence" the confidence man murmurs as he strolls the decks of the *Fidele,* the Mississippi steamboat that has forgone the *Pequod*'s teleological pursuit of the whale for domestic transit "to and fro" on the river. Tempting passenger after passenger to believe in his investment schemes, his quack medicines, his comforting view of humanity, it is the devilish confidence artist who tempts people to belief, to subscribing to any one narrative. Resisting this temptation, the narrative voice oscillates between sharply variant viewpoints and interpretations, forging its fiction against belief and, in so doing, braiding them together as twinned manifestations of an unreal reality, of "another world, and yet one to which we feel the tie."

THE QUESTION, AGAIN, OF EVIL

The coupling of theodicy and colonial encounter that characterizes Melville's fiction can be traced back, as we have seen, to the imaginative world constructed by Defoe's *Robinson Crusoe.* But if we are to understand fully the connection between the labor of belief and the work of empire, we must realize that Crusoe's manufacture of Christianity is not only ingenious but anxious. For out on the margins of empire, Crusoe encounters the anxiety at the heart of Christianity itself – the problem of evil. Listening to his self-styled "master's" account of Jehovah's omnipotence, Friday suddenly interrupts to ask what every student of Christianity soon enough does: "Well, says Friday; but you say, God is so strong, so great, is he not much strong, much might as the Devil? Yes, yes, says I, Friday, God is stronger than the Devil. . . . But, says he again, *if God much strong, much might as the Devil, why God no kill the Devil, so make him do no more wicked?*"[20] Although Friday's broken utterance is shaped, as we have discussed, by Crusoe's authorizing, imperial discourse, the native's radical challenge is still audible enough. Friday's enunciation of the problem of evil under an omnipotent God leaves Crusoe literally speechless, reduced to pretending he hasn't heard the question. This rupture in the missionary dialogue marks a pivotal moment, for it signals anthropology's ultimate challenge to theology: to travel is to meet those who will show you not just other gods but, more disturbingly, the otherness, the incomprehensibility within your own.

Friday's question doesn't erupt from the outside so much as from inside the discourse of a transmitted Christian theology; it recoils upon the European, suggesting to him that his theology has failed to master its own god. That Friday should render Crusoe speechless over the question of evil registers the scope of its scandalous presence. Christianity's problem with evil is the crevice through which the subjugated native almost makes his escape (Crusoe sends him on a long "errand" so that he can "fabricate" an answer). Released into the New World and projected onto the "savage" through the expansion of European empire, the Pauline "mystery of iniquity" reemerges before the Protestant subject, debasing him into speechlessness.[21] The emptied space of other cultures – arrived at across the vast, ascetic reach of the oceans – permits the release of the voices of evil *and* its questioning, permits the emergence of voice in all its hostility and multiplicity. The repressive grip of an allegedly providential, monotheistic god, of deity as jealous single voice, is broken and a polytheism of voices – a heteroglossia – erupts, with evil as its central and celebratory theme.

In the opening pages of *Moby-Dick*, we see the masterly achievement of the polyvocality that emerges from an intensification of these converging discourses of an ailing theology and a resplendent anthropology. Unlike Tommo's, Ishmael's process of "getting away" is a laborious one. He must wade through various emanations of Christianity and its religious other (especially in the form of Queequeg's worship) before boarding ship – a reverse pilgrimage of sorts that uncovers the layers of fabrication glossed over in the earlier adventure novel where the hero so easily "falls" into the space of colonial adventure and religious investigation. In the first of repeated overturnings of monotheism, Ishmael, a melancholic like Tommo, promptly encounters the "savage" Queequeg, whose presence in New Bedford, "sellin' human heads about the streets when folks is goin' to churches" (*Moby-Dick*, 20), brings the outside of the imperial imaginary back home. Cultural inversion produces a sly and skilled anthropological observer in the figure of Ishmael. Adept at sounding the various registers of idolatry, Ishmael proffers both Queequeg and the Calvinist Father Mapple as infinitely decipherable; subject to his punning acumen, their otherness is usurped by his voluble narrative voice that continually alludes to "vague wonderments and half-apprehensions . . . and a hundred other shadowy things" (98) in a language of dazzling precision and flexibility.

Volubility and mystery are reenacted in the tension of Ishmael's reach into the empty space of unseen worlds, a reach that arcs back to home. An urge for the unseen motivates the urge toward authorship, toward the creation of an imaginative world that will enclose those of theology and anthropology. Viewing the walls of the Spouter Inn before he sets sail, Ishmael proposes these two worlds of anthropological wonder and indistinct spiritual questing as suspended before him: on one wall, a "heathenish array of monstrous clubs and spears . . . set with glittering teeth" and "tufted with knots of human hair" (13) confronts him. Opposite this display of native artifacts, redolent with the titillating specter of cannibalism, hangs a grimy oil painting that emanates "a sort of indefinite, half-attained, unimaginable sublimity about it that fairly froze you to it" (12). Displayed across from this composition of romantic sublimity is the composition of empire: the distinct and appalling "heathenish" (13) artifacts, mixed in with old whaling equipment, confront the painting's storminess, not so much as an alternative composition or a destination but as the ground for its being. The Spouter Inn's hallway suggests to Ishmael that the colonial pilgrim and heathen native will together manufacture the sublime – and that this colonial sublime will burst open the enclosure of Christianity.

The heteroglossia that emerges from this rupture floods the mimetic space of the novel with the curiosities and splendors of a dissenting language that disobeys novelistic convention and religious and political orthodoxies. It is this disobedient language which constitutes the ultimate anthropological wonder in *Moby-Dick*. Pronouncing himself finally "a savage, owing no allegiance but to the King of Cannibals" (277), Ishmael's internalization of Queequeg's cosmopolitan, native viewpoint lies behind his conversion from traveler to author. With the fragmentation of monotheism into his new polytheistic perspective, Ishmael releases a multiplicity of voices within him that authorizes him to speak. As the Jonah narrative is dispersed through *Moby-Dick* by Ishmael's multiple voices, so Jehovah becomes ubiquitous as fragment. There is nowhere that he is not as metaphor, allusion, echo. Thus this region of anti-Christian metaphysical questing, defined by its geographical and cultural distance from institutionalized monotheism, is a departure that yields no distance. The wondrous encounter with disobedient language supplies the seeker a material sublimity that measures Ishmael's disavowal of a parched Christianity, rendered abject and empty by the problem of evil. But this "other" body of speech points back to itself rather than forward to any "truth." The pure God whom Ishmael seeks, one undefiled by imperialist violence and Christian dogma (or the dogmatic fixities of any religious tradition), can be reached only *through* empire and the touristic voyages to "nowhere" that America's prowess affords.

This rich, disobedient, evil language (that is, one might argue, "native" to the West but long repressed) ultimately alienates both language and the self

from Ishmael. Conventional description yields, in *Moby-Dick,* to an erup-
tion of new, previously censored voices – of imprecation, innuendo, insinuation, reminiscence, lamentation. In this rupture, religion emerges *as*
rhetoric, its interior exposed to the authorial gaze and its parts cannibalized,
translated from the invisible interiority of the single voice of conscience into
a visible, manipulable, fragmented body of words. It is not simply that the
Judeo-Christian god who swooped on Jonah and "swallowed him down"
(49) has been subversively renamed as cannibal but that this accusation
against deity constructs a new form – the heteroglossic novel whose infinite
variety swallows "god" in turn, an incorporation at once vengeful and am-
orous. Estranged from its representational obligations, Ishmael's language
exceeds its object just as humanity's awareness of suffering exceeds its gods.
To this extent, then, the exuberant language of *Moby-Dick* is authored by
the problem of evil and voices its presence. The sheer pleasures of a transgressive literary language dramatize the failure of theodicy.

But while this polytheistic language resists the implausible, self-
proclaimed providential god of Christianity, it bears the trace of monotheism's imperial practice. Indulged yet confined, both Tommo and Ishmael
are figures of America's nascent imperial prowess, questing abroad for the
pleasures of the "primitive," and, to the extent that their escapes from
civilization succeed, questing abroad to retreat from American military and
religious power. *Typee* and *Moby-Dick* mark a moment in antebellum
America's postcolonial status as a nation struggling against continued British cultural dominion while forging its own nascent imperial identity under
the aegis of "Manifest Destiny."[22] Thus Melville's heroes criticize imperialist expansion across the world's seas while appropriating an imperial language of discovery, exploration, and conquest for their interior spiritual
quests. This importation of an imperial language of discovery to the interior
life lends a characteristic violence to these private religious quests, as Melville's heroes, with a force commensurate to Ahab's pursuit of the white
whale, assault themselves with theological interrogatives. Ishmael's salute
to Bulkington is suggestive here; hailing his elusive double, Ishmael gives
vent to his characteristically hyperbolic, interrogative, dialogic style that
edges between self-contempt and rage: "But as in landlessness alone resides
the highest truth, shoreless, indefinite as God – so, better is it to perish in
that howling infinite, than be ingloriously dashed upon the lees, even if that
were safety! For worm-like, then, oh! who would craven crawl to land!
terrors of the terrible! is all this agony so vain?" (*Moby-Dick,* 111). Ishmael's vocal space mimes cultural invasion, creating a motion of ceaseless
imperial summoning and negation that creates in turn an immense, yet
abstract, materiality of language.

Shortly after completing *Moby-Dick*, Melville returned to this idea of the metaphysical travel made possible by negation. Writing appreciatively to Hawthorne of his capacity to say "NO! in thunder," Melville unfolded (in a considerably less inflated language than in his novel) an interior "colonial" topography of spiritual discovery. "For all men who say *yes*, lie; and all men who say *no*, – why, they are in the happy condition of judicious, unincumbered travellers in Europe; they cross the frontiers into Eternity with nothing but a carpet-bag, that is, the Ego . . . You see, I began with a little criticism extracted for your benefit . . . and here I have landed in Africa."[23] For Melville, saying "no" constitutes a form of internal travel, even colonization, in which the self cordons off a region within, marking it as other, as "Africa." Unlike the ascetic negation of the European world signaled by Crusoe's shipwreck in New Spain, a negation that in turn produces the presence of an internal voice of conscience to which he submits ("methought it spoke to me like a Voice; WRETCH!"),[24] Melville's narratives of inner travel replace the subjugated Christian self with an "unincumbered" subjectivity. In both *Moby-Dick* and the famous letter to Hawthorne, Melville reproduces the exoticized domain opened to the Western gaze by European imperialism as interior to the questing subject; this internal topography is a place of continued negation, "Africa" an imaginary site for inquiry that is authored by but in turn resists Christianity's imperial construction of subjectivity. To the extent that the Christian God emerges from language, is language (in that God contains all attributes), the heteroglossia of *Moby-Dick* beats again against the mute otherness of divinity.[25]

SILENT DIVINITY, TALKATIVE VOICE, AND CONTAINMENT

While *Moby-Dick*'s heteroglossic, "evil" representation of being subverts the social and religious conventions regulating national and personal identity, it is indebted to the "shore" doctrines of original sin, salvation through faith in Christ, and the resurrection of the believing body. Like Ahab's metaphysical rivalry with the white whale, Melville's art – simply by virtue of its verbal brilliance – salutes and does battle with this mystery of a being which is and is not Scripture and is at once mute and heteroglossic. While his fictions repeatedly invoke the dire workings of fate and the hopelessness of deciphering ultimate meaning, his art is nonetheless an enormous assertion of authorial free will, creative experimentation, and enunciation. The stunning contrasts between the spiritual anxiety, even barrenness from which his characters suffer and the exuberant materiality of his literary style suggest not only a cannibalistic relation to the "body" of religion, as I have discussed, but a new conception of literary character as limitless, ascetic interior.

Even in Melville's often discussed collapse from the masterpiece of *Moby-Dick* to the reviled absurdities of *Pierre*, we still confront an immense talkativeness, an alliterative prose that in its excess challenges the believability of the novel form that contains it: "Bind me in bonds I can not break," Pierre thinks to himself, trying to urge himself forward to the self-sacrificial gesture of recognizing his illegitimate sister; "remove all sinister allurings from me; eternally this day deface in me the detested and distorted images of all the convenient lies and duty-subterfuges of the diving and ducking moralities of this earth" (107). Pierre utters his petition to be freed from conventional morality in language so absurd that it disrupts the mimetic illusion of the narrative that sustains him, his alliterative "d's" mocking the novel's ostensible commitment to realism (or at least to the urgent believability of the parodic subversion of convention).[26] These shifts in ontological position, like *Mardi*'s "ascent" from realistic narrative to sheer allegory, dissolve the novel from mimetic to self-consuming narrative, to the same level of imbecility visited upon the main character by the plot.

Melville's novel of life on land imports *Moby-Dick*'s discourse of sublimity and incarcerates it as Pierre's subjectivity: "He felt," the narrator explains of Pierre's reaction to Isabel's appearance, "that what he had always before considered the solid land of verifiable reality, was now being audaciously encroached upon by bannered armies of hooded phantoms, disembarking in his soul, as from flotillas of spectre-boats" (49). Invaded by the very terms through which Ishmael authored his triumphant narrative – of hooded phantoms and spectre-boats – Pierre struggles to reformulate them into his own masterpiece, his mutilated efforts driven by his ambition to write the perfect novel. Pierre's novel, which fails to materialize beyond certain fragments which the reader glimpses toward the end of Pierre's doomed authorship, is defined not only by deference to its "prequel" but also by defiance of the novel form. After Pierre has learned of Isabel's existence and abruptly forsakes his idolatrous worship of his father, the narrator inserts a critique of "common" novels for impudently solving the unsolvable mysteries of being, that is, for unfolding plots that have conclusions. Nothing less than "false, inverted attempts at systematizing eternally unsystemizable elements," fictional narrative betrays an "intermeddling impotency" (141).

Significantly, this critique of the falsity of the novel form emerges from the midst of Pierre's religious conversion; New Light enthusiast that he is, his sight of God ("He saw that human life doth truly come from that, which all men are agreed to call by the name of God" [141]) releases an icono-clastic fury against the novel form. God, newly recognized author of Pierre's reborn life, does not lend plots or conclusions to life or art but instead casts a sublime destruction on all forms.[27] Divinity cannot be un-raveled into plot, no matter how delicate the theological or novelistic effort or how combative Pierre's "deadly feuds with things invisible" (41). Central to Pierre's religious insight then is that aesthetic form, to be metaphysically authentic, must be deformed, must turn a religious rage against its own body. Uncommon, true, religiously authentic novels cannot have "proper endings" (141); they can only be imperfect sequels to the one before – hilarious, tormented imperfection the closest equivalent to the perfection of no-form.

Thus, like Tommo and Kory-Kory pummeling the grotesque idol, Pierre's narrative voice castigates the fallen materiality of any book *and* the hero who views such fallen materiality seriously. So painful is this willed aes-thetic imperfection that the narrator describes true narratives as "mutilated stumps" – extending the imagery of amputation and deformity from the one-legged Ahab to Moby-Dick's imperfect sequel, Pierre. Authentic rela-tion to divinity results, must result, in the abyss of parody where "mutilated stumps" are made, deliberately and absurdly, to "hurry." Pierre's icono-clasm then ("From all idols, I tear all veils; henceforth I will see the hidden things; and live right out in my own hidden life!" [66]) deforms this sequel to the masterly Moby-Dick, as if to purify the story of the whale of any lingering "impotency." In Melville's alternation between elegant fictions like "Bartleby, the Scrivener," "Benito Cereno," and Billy Budd, Sailor (An Inside Narrative), narratives that keep quiet about their inauthenticity, and noisy, self-abnegating, indigestible works like Mardi and Pierre, we watch this oscillation between generativity and an iconoclasm that is a willed if "silent" pronouncement of the divine. The narrative voice's ascetic refusal of the resolutions offered by polished literary form demands the continued, tempting presence of perfected fictions as the other by which it knows its own purity, the form by which it knows its deformity.

In place of the widening distance, artifice, and absolutism of Christian dogma, Melville's prose, in both its polished and indigestible manifesta-tions, offers an improvisational, idiosyncratic voice imparting, so it avers, deeper truths than those conveyed by the linear sequences of organized religion or conventional literary narrative. The reader of this literature will be supplied not only "more entertainment," as the narrative voice promises in the midst of The Confidence-Man, "but, at bottom, even more reality, than real life itself can show" (183). This defense of fiction is later devel-oped on board the Fidele when the implied author turns to ruminating on the difficulty of creating original literary characters – a feat he compares to God's genesis of the world: "the original character, essentially such, is like a revolving Drummond light, raying away from itself all round it – everything is lit by it, everything starts up to it (mark how it is with Hamlet), so that, in certain minds, there follows upon the adequate conception of such a character an effect in its way, akin to that which in Genesis attends upon the beginning of things" (205). Fiction, when it manages to create an original character, can be its own cosmic beginning, negating any ordinary literary lineage, throwing author and reader back onto the mystery of being ("But, if original, whence came they? Or where did the novelist pick them up?" [*The Confidence-Man*, 204]). In the repetition of God's creative act, the author will return us to the beginning of time itself, and together we will gain access to an emptiness otherwise impossible to attain through travel and imperial adventure. Yet the struggle to repeat Genesis with original literary characters inevitably reproduces dumb mystery as sign of its originality.

It is toward this dumbness, then, that Melville's ornate literary language points as it gives itself again and again to the self-canceling project of voicing silence: "for how can a man get a Voice out of Silence?" (208) the narrator asks us in *Pierre*. This effort to vocalize silence is thematized in the struggle of the Melvillian narrator to provoke silent characters like Jarl, Bartleby, and Billy Budd into speech, to decipher a silence whom their author has created and knows all about. Ahab punching through the "pasteboard mask" of reality dramatizes Melville's larger authorial gesture of creating surfaces of fiction that his narrative voice seeks to rupture, excavate, or coyly refuse to break through. Melville's repeated efforts to gain access to a mystery he simultaneously makes distant is the generative artifice behind his literary characters. Ironically, these processes of characterization reenact the artifice he so detested in organized religion; in that his narrators and major characters seek an ultimate rationale for life's suffering and union with an abiding presence, his plots are imitated religious acts. To the extent that Melville's stories argue for truths available only to those who, like his much admired Shakespeare, make "short, quick probings at the very axis of reality,"[28] his prose and poetry rival Scripture, ingesting it into his own innovative, post-Scriptural voice that uses biblical sublimity against itself. But the signature of Melville's literary spirituality is that these fictional probings and postbiblical sublimities fail or, at best, conclude inconclusively, resisting the very quest they narrate, denying the access they *could* author. Thus, Melville's posthumous novel, *Billy Budd*, is as answerless as his early adventure novels in which the young hero confronts the challenge of religious otherness. Is the story of Billy Budd's execution an allegorical testament to Christ's abiding presence or a darkly ironic account of a pointless execution in a universe abandoned by god? Is it a Christian or an anti-Christian allegory or does it refute the premises of allegory altogether?

Throughout his art, then, Melville's narrators are never clearly inside or outside Christianity, for Christianity has itself been repositioned as a dispersed fragment subject to recurrent citation. No longer an invisible "out there" into which the self must enter and lose its "self" by forsaking its individual perspective, Christianity is materialized as a deadened substance, one subject to multiple perspectives, voicings, and borrowings. Even when Melville forgoes a polytheistic narrative perspective, turning from the colossal novels of *Moby-Dick* and *Pierre* to his precisionist short stories, the narrating self performs these borrowings through repeated punning on inside and outside, spatial representations of belief and nonbelief.

This spatialized topography of belief is most wittily constructed in Melville's short story "The Two Temples," where the religious seeker's hopping into and out of religious spaces provides a playful variant to Hawthorne's melancholic image of Melville "wandering to and fro" between belief and unbelief. "Here I am, I say," opens the narrator of "The Two Temples" as he stands outside a fashionable New York church, having just been denied entrance by the church's beadle, "and, after all, I can't get in."[29] "The Two Temples" is a diptych whose doubled structure mimes this dual religious stance of incarceration within a punitive theology and exclusion from a redemptive one. "Temple First" situates the narrator in a hidden perch observing a religious service in New York, while "Temple Second" takes him to a London theater where he finds a holiness conspicuously absent from the Manhattan congregation. This doubled narrative stance recapitulates the Jonah motif in *Moby-Dick* that continually questions: who is inside whom? Excluded from what he seeks, the narrator of "The Two Temples" battles to gain entrance. But once inside, he seeks desperately to escape the fallen interior, rhetorically negotiating his yearning, contemptuous relation to the interiority of belief through a punning biblical allusiveness that creates out of language a container holding doubled, or "inside," meanings. Sneaking inside the church in the hope of "gaining that one secret window where I might, at distance, take part in the proceedings" (305), our anonymous religious voyeur finally establishes himself in an aerial perch where he can look down upon the Episcopalian service in progress beneath him. Those far below, "so snug and cosy in their padded pews" (305), are poor Christians by contrast to the narrator, who enjoys a panoramic perspective – the otherness of the prophet gazing upon the fallen urban congregation in its "sumptuous sanctuary" (306).

If Tommo and, even more so, Ishmael are disabled by their encounter with cultural otherness and thus reborn into polytheistic voice, this narrator, confronting his own countrymen, can expertly summarize them from his lofty, "summary" position. Enjoying the fact that he remains unseen as he participates in the service, he pointedly reminds the reader of his superior spiritual status: "Depend upon it, no Pharisee would have my pew" (306). Melville's repeated punning on exclusion and inclusion allows him to position his outcast narrator "inside" in order to unleash the outsider's perspective of an "inside prowler" (308). But on trying to leave the church, this closet Christian finds himself locked in, the church now his prison. Returning to his aerial perch, he looks down on the now deserted church interior and imagines himself as another famous outcast, Moses, "gazing from Pisgah into the forests of old Canaan" (308). Like his predecessor, this midcentury American Moses cannot get into what now seems the Promised Land of the church, but he consoles himself by discovering within it not insiders but fellow outcasts. He perceives these outcasts disguised beneath the Catholic imagery of the stained glass: "A Puseyitish painting of a Madonna and child, adorning a lower window, seemed showing to me the sole tenants of this painted wilderness – the true Hagar and her Ishmael. – " (308). Satirically adept at deploying religious analogies against the tradition that literally houses them, Melville's narrator demonstrates his contact with an inaccessible "belief" by traveling inside it and out again.

Melville's engagement with this contained and containing Christianity finds its most powerful trope, as we have seen, in that of travel. The self's progress through space offers a linear reprieve from the enclosure created by the oscillation between belief and unbelief. In the flight to ostensibly emptied regions, meditation will replace the impossibility of enunciation, the linguistic sign of surrender to dogma. Melville frequently imagined such statements of belief as claustrophobic architectural interiors. The wittiest of Melville's dogmatic structures is the madhouse from which Isabel is rescued in *Pierre*, where "some were always talking about hell, Eternity, and God; and some of all things as fixedly decreed; others would say nay to this, and then they would argue, but without much conviction either way" (121). Isabel's madhouse of Calvinist lunatics debating predestination while indifferent to the conclusions they arrive at is echoed by repeated imagery in Melville's fiction of Catholic confessionals and monasteries. In "Benito Cereno," the hapless Amasa Delano is so drenched in his Protestant suspicions of the *San Dominick*'s fearful Catholic interiorities that he cannot see the real horror at work before him, the presence of slavery in the New World and the slave mutiny it inspires.[30] While the narrative voice subtly parodies Delano's anxious ruminations about the "ship-load of monks" (48) commanded by a "hypochondriac abbot" (52), these images of Catholic monastic interiors, like Isabel's Calvinist madhouse or the Episcopalian prison of "The Two Temples," express a pervasive symbolism of theological dogma as a closeted space from which the religious hero must break free. But as suggested by the monastic imagery at the conclusion of "The Encantadas," one cannot ever really flee these dogmatic enclosures; rather, one must disperse them in the form of analogies across the spaces opened by travel. "It is but fit that like those old monastic institutions of Europe, whose inmates go not out of their own walls to be inurned, but are entombed there where they die; the Encantadas too should bury their own dead, even as the great general monastery of earth does hers."[31]

Melville's expansion of the monastic image into a metaphor of the entire earth not only eloquently phrases the boundedness of our mortality but also images religion as such as an oppressive interior that it encloses all of humanity's space. When Melville traveled to the Middle East during 1856–7, these symbolics of anxious containment were made suddenly literal by his encounter with the Egyptian pyramids, which to him "authored" the idea of monotheism. At their "heart," Melville recorded in his travel journal, was "conceived the idea of Jehovah. Terrible mixture of the cunning and awful."[32] At the base of Melville's imagery of closeted religious otherness – whether of an abandoned Roman Catholicism that serves as American Protestantism's most intimate "religious other" or of Polynesian "idolatry" – lies the profound and "cunning" otherness of the Judeo-Christian God. In one sense, this monotheistic god's emergence from the built space of the pyramid demotes him from his transcendental, uncreated origin. But in another sense, Melville's perception that Jehovah is an "idea" authored by humanity vastly increases this deity's strangeness and reach: he now becomes Western humanity's true other, like and unlike us, the uncanny fictional character whom we have authored to represent and to answer us.

The culminating figure in Melville's series of pilgrim-travelers, Clarel occupies all these nested spaces of religious otherness as he tours the Holy Land, seeking god in his "home" in the Old World. The culmination of Melville's anthropological disruptions of theology, *Clarel* represents a turning away from the wonders of the New World to encounter those of the Old as the young and spiritually tormented Clarel rifles through Jerusalem and its environs in search of theological evidence. When, a decade or so after the publication of *Typee*, Melville sat in Jaffa waiting for a steamer home, he recorded in his journal that waiting there gave him that "old – genuine, old Jonah feeling."[33] Impelled like Jonah to speak the word of a god whose existence he doubted, Melville changed literary forms and set about his Old World religious epic on returning to America.

If in *Moby-Dick* the ample, undulant space of representation submerges the crisis of religious severance – the loss of a monotheistic god – *Clarel* brings the hero full circle in the quest for a "primitive" religious understanding, sending him eastward to Christianity's beginnings, to the very site of monotheism's birth. Unlike Melville's earlier travelers, who draw upon the uncanny wonders encountered through travel to rearticulate divinity, Clarel looks for the Christian God in his own terms, at his self-professed place of origin. Thus when he travels to Jerusalem from America, Clarel confronts, as does Pierre, the beseeching countenance of mystery, but now it is no longer manifest in the countenance of the cultural other but rather in that of the most intimate self: that is, in *Clarel*, tropes of exoticism, primitivism and imperial questing that had proved so central to Melville's colonial-religious symbolics are now aimed at Christianity's birthplace. Appropriately, the others whom Clarel first meets are not cultural "exotics" but simply other characters whose difference from Clarel has nothing to do with New World racial and cultural difference. Instead, it has to do with an Asia that Melville hardly saw as a site of anthropological wonders, but rather as "sort of used up – superannuated."[34]

Entering at the Gate of Zion, Clarel immediately meets one of the poem's most powerful expressions of this obsolescence: a group of lepers whose "faces, yet defacements too, / Appealed to them; but could not give / Expression. There, still sensitive, / Our human nature, deep inurned / In voiceless visagelessness, yearned" (1.26.4–8). Like Tommo's sight of the uncanny, tattooed bodies of the Typee elders, whose skin is so scrawled by tattoos and time that it betrays a "frightful scaly appearance" (*Typee*, 114), Clarel's appalled gaze on these Jerusalem lepers precipitates an anxious meditation on humanity's uncanniness and the fearsome prospect of silence which that uncanniness implies. In their disfigurement, these defaced, voiceless persons are radically open to scrutiny: they are idols to be stumbled over and fled from by the American tourist-pilgrim. While Clarel's sight of the lepers repeats the earlier encounters with anthropological otherness, it does so in order to reverse its logic: the leper is not a cultural other but instead, simply and horribly, has shed all culture and thus figures the abyss that separates humanity from god. All of Melville's art faces toward this abyss that dwells behind anthropological encounter, a changeless, abiding presence of emptiness that thwarts rational explication and literary meaning, dissolving, like leprosy, the boundaries of form. In its dumbness it disdains dialogue, even parodying, as we have seen in *Pierre*, the very fictions which attempt to voice its presence; it is an antiredemptive presence that speaks an ethic of endurance rather than of glory.[35]

As we might expect, then, *Clarel* concludes inconclusively with a struggle between two authors, Despair and Faith, who inscribe their competing versions of truth on very different writing surfaces. Against the backdrop of Western culture's troubled development from "Luther's day" to "Darwin's year" sits the Sphinx, on whose "adamantine brow" Despair "scrawls undeterred his bitter pasquinade" (4.35.7). Faith turns away from this satirical graffiti, choosing a considerably more sensitive writing surface and medium, her own broken body and blood. Like nineteenth-century sentimental heroines, whose tears drop their purifying power onto ink and page in order to move the reader to a deeper, more feelingful piety, Faith's authorship is a bodily one in the service of an eventual and triumphant disembodiment: "With blood warm oozing from her wounded trust, / Inscribes even on her shards of broken urns / The sign o' the cross – *the spirit above the dust!*" (4.35.9–11). While Faith's hieroglyphic points to a resurgent spirit, the sign of the cross written with her own blood transcending the fallen language of Despair who "scrawls" his lampoon without interruption, we cannot ignore the desperation of her dwindling, self-enclosed authorial resources. Reduced to writing on herself with herself, Faith is a self-consuming text, crucifixional, sacrificial, and barely decipherable.

Mirroring Christianity's post-Darwinian ruination, Melville's image of Faith metonymically transfers Christ's sacrificial death to the "body" of Christianity entire. While Faith has read (indignantly) the writings of Despair, there is no indication at the conclusion of *Clarel* that Despair has returned the courtesy by reading Faith's bloody, vanishing sign. Instead, Melville, as the third author in this concluding scene, the one who ventriloquizes both Faith and Despair, scrawls his "pasquinades" (in the form of parodies of organized religion and "common" fiction) *and* parsimoniously inscribes traces of unread, redemptive meaning in the midst of his exuberant, satirical transgressions. Speaker of both voices, Melville's narrative voice in *Clarel* is the greater immensity that knows both Christianity and its cancellation. The poem's concluding juxtaposition of the ballooning discourse of despair with faith's cramped script echoes its formal structure – an immense length unfolding in cramped sequences of metrically difficult versification. On the one hand, the exacting trial of Melville's chosen verse form mimics the labor and tribulation of Clarel's religious inquiry. But on the other, the readerly trial imposed by the verse form, as it impedes and renders painful the telling of Clarel's despair, as it mimics and requires perseverance, is also the very trace of faith.

Spanning the second half of the nineteenth century, Melville's fiction and poetry are scrawled pasquinade on the sphinx's brow of the page, volumes of words, characters, conflicting points of view provoked into existence by the silence that is divinity, insinuating blasphemy and confessing religious longing – an uninterrupted but, over the course of his career, increasingly unread conversation with the divine other. Can the individual, reawakened by solitude and various figurations of the other, travel finally to God? Will theology yield to a newer, more persuasive anthropological meaning? Or will wondrous contact allow belief to speak again? In circling back to a desiccated Asiatic origin, *Clarel* renounces the illusion of travel, the illusion that there is a space of belief, of otherness, into which one can journey and lose the burden of unbelief and of self.

NOTES

1. Herman Melville, *The Confidence-Man: His Masquerade*, eds. Harrison Hayford, Hershel Parker, and G. Thomas Tanselle (Evanston and Chicago: Northwestern University Press and The Newberry Library, 1984), 183. Further citations from this edition appear parenthetically in the text.

2. Herman Melville, *Pierre or The Ambiguities*, eds. Harrison Hayford, Hershel Parker, and G. Thomas Tanselle (Evanston and Chicago: Northwestern University Press and The Newberry Library, 1971), 139. Further citations from this edition appear parenthetically in the text.

3. Early critical treatments of Melville and religion that established future lines of critical investigation include William Braswell, *Melville's Religious Thought: An Essay in Interpretation* (Durham: Duke University Press, 1943); Nathalia Wright, *Melville's Use of the Bible* (Durham: Duke University Press, 1949); and Lawrance Thompson, *Melville's Quarrel with God* (Princeton: Princeton University Press, 1952). The best study of Melville's debate with Calvinism remains T. Walter Herbert, *Moby-Dick and Calvinism: A World Dismantled* (New Brunswick: Rutgers University Press, 1977). A useful recent overview of critical treatments on the subject of Melville and religion is Rowland A. Sherrill, "Melville and Religion," in John Bryant, ed., *A Companion to Melville Studies* (New York: Greenwood Press, 1986), 481–513.

4. For an informative discussion of Melville's treatment of Scripture within the larger context of Scripture's relativization by liberal Protestants, see Lawrence Buell, *New England Literary Culture: From Revolution through Renaissance* (New York: Cambridge University Press, 1986), 166–92. See also Buell, "*Moby-Dick* as Sacred Text," in Richard H. Brodhead, ed., *New Essays on Moby-Dick* (New York: Cambridge University Press, 1986), 53–72.

5. Herman Melville, *Moby-Dick; Or, The Whale* (Berkeley: University of California Press, 1979, pp. 498–9). Further citations from this edition appear parenthetically in the text.

6. Nathaniel Hawthorne, *English Notebooks*, as quoted in Jay Leyda, *The Melville Log: A Documentary Life of Herman Melville, 1819–1891*, 2 vols. (New York: Harcourt, Brace and Co., 1951), 529.

7. I borrow this formulation from Donald Wesling and Tadeusz Slawek, *Literary*

Voice: The Calling of Jonah (Albany: State University of New York Press, 1995), in their discussion of two forms of minimal voice: "The first minimal is that of the not yet of the speaking subject, and the second minimal is the no longer" (10).

8. I am indebted to Michel de Certeau for the idea of a novelist's return to his or her sources as an act of travel. See his "Writing the Sea: Jules Verne" in *Heterologies: Discourse on the Other* (Minneapolis: University of Minnesota Press, 1986), 139.

9. Herman Melville, *Typee, or a Peep at Polynesian Life*, in *Typee, Omoo, Mardi* (New York: The Library of America, 1982), 263. For a discussion of Tommo's specifically racial fears about being tattooed, see Samuel Otter, *Melville's Anatomies: Rhetoric, Discourse, and Ideology in Antebellum America* (Berkeley: University of California Press, forthcoming).

10. On questions of epistemological bewilderment and "wonder " in the Age of Exploration, see Stephen Greenblatt, *Marvelous Possessions: The Wonder of the New World* (Chicago: University of Chicago Press, 1991).

11. Talal Asad has recently argued that Western anthropology has close affiliations with the Christian exegetical tradition; see *Genealogies of Religion: Discipline and Reasons of Power in Christianity and Islam* (Baltimore: Johns Hopkins University Press, 1993), 60. For a superb ethnohistory of the discursive interactions between the English and the Polynesians, see Greg Dening, *Mr. Bligh's Bad Language: Passion, Play and Theatre on the Bounty* (Cambridge: Cambridge University Press, 1992).

12. Mitchell Breitwieser, "False Sympathy in Melville's Typee," *American Quarterly*, 34 (1982), argues that the novel is so solipsistic that Tommo, caught within his "imaginative imperialism" (398), is able to "use" but never to "comprehend" Typee culture.

13. Max Weber, *The Protestant Ethic and the Spirit of Capitalism*, trans. Talcott Parsons (New York: Charles Scribner's Sons, 1958).

14. For an influential discussion of *Typee* in the context of American Calvinism, see T. Walter Herbert, *Marquesan Encounters: Melville and the Meaning of Civilization* (Cambridge: Harvard University Press, 1980).

15. Greenblatt underscores how cannibalism was viewed as the "other" to the Eucharist, an "inverted, metaphoric representation of the central rituals of Christian culture" (*Marvelous Possessions*, 45).

16. See Mary Lousie Pratt, *Imperial Eyes: Travel Writing and Transculturation* (London and New York: Routledge Press, 1992). I have developed my understanding of Melville's antiethnography from Pratt's argument about " 'anti-conquest' . . . strategies of representation whereby European bourgeois subjects seek to secure their innocence in the same moment as they assert European hegemony" (7).

17. My discussion of the estranging effect of these tattoos is indebted to Otter, *Melville's Anatomies*.

18. Herman Melville, *Mardi and a Voyage Thither*, in *Typee, Omoo, Mardi*, p. 809.

19. Melville, *Clarel*, 389. A final manifestation of the tattooed Christ appears on Daniel Orme in Melville's late, unpublished manuscript "Daniel Orme." For a brief discussion, see *Clarel*, 821, n. 4.2.51.

20. Daniel Defoe, *Robinson Crusoe* (New York: W. W. Norton & Company, 1994), 158.

21. Crusoe's speechlessness is an early example of the loss of discursive modes to describe evil discussed by Andrew Delbanco, *The Death of Satan: How Americans Have Lost the Sense of Evil* (New York: Farrar, Straus and Giroux, 1995).

22. See Lawrence Buell, "Melville and the Question of American Decolonization," in *American Literature*, 64 (1992): 215–37.

23. Herman Melville to Nathaniel Hawthorne (April, 1851) in *Correspondence*, ed. Lynn Horth (Evanston and Chicago: Northwestern University Press and The Newberry Library, 1993), 186–7.

24. Defoe, *Robinson Crusoe*, 68.

25. Geoffrey Galt Harpham, *The Ascetic Imperative in Culture and Criticism* (Chicago: University of Chicago Press, 1987), argues that "logology would be impossible in a pagan culture, for it is only the Christian God that is modeled on language, that is, containing all attributes" (17).

26. For a discussion of the novel's parodic gestures, see Sacvan Bercovitch, *The Rites of Assent: Transformations in the Symbolic Construction of America* (New York: Routledge, 1993), 246–306.

27. Emory Elliott discusses Pierre's New Light rebirth in the context of antebellum culture; see "The Problem of Authority in *Pierre*" in Sacvan Bercovitch and Myra Jehlen, eds., *Ideology and Classic American Literature* (New York: Cambridge University Press, 1986), 337–51.

28. Herman Melville, "Hawthorne and His Mosses," in *The Piazza Tales and Other Prose Pieces 1839–1860*, eds. Harrison Hayford, Alma A. MacDougall, G. Thomas Tanselle, et al. (Evanston and Chicago: Northwestern University Press and The Newberry Library, 1987), 244.

29. Herman Melville, "The Two Temples," in *The Piazza Tales and Other Prose Pieces 1839–1860*, 303. On visual perspective (and issues of framing and containment) in this short story and in *Clarel*, see Sanford E. Marovitz, "Melville's Temples," in *Savage Eye: Melville and the Visual Arts* (Kent, Ohio: Kent State University Press, 1991), 77–103.

30. For a discussion of Catholic thematics in Melville, see my *Roads to Rome: The Antebellum Protestant Encounter with Catholicism* (Berkeley: University of California Press, 1994).

31. Herman Melville, "The Encantadas," in *The Piazza Tales*, 172.

32. Herman Melville, *Journals*, eds. Harrison Hayford, Hershel Parker, and G. Thomas Tanselle (Evanston and Chicago: Northwestern University Press and The Newberry Library, 1989), 75.

33. Herman Melville, *Journals*, 81, as quoted by Walter Bezanson, "Historical and Critical Note," *Clarel*, 523.

34. As quoted in *Clarel*, "Historical Note," 513.

35. Julia Kristeva, in "Holbein's Dead Christ" (*Black Sun: Depression and Melancholia* [New York: Columbia University Press, 1989]), observes of Holbein's art that it "opens out not on glory but on endurance" (113).

8

ROBERT K. MARTIN

Melville and Sexuality

Sexuality is a concept we owe to Melville's time. As the theorist Michel Foucault has argued, prior to some point in the later nineteenth century, there were no sexual identities, but only sexual acts that could be committed by anyone.[1] What sexuality does is to associate acts and "tastes" with identity, to say, for instance, putting it simply, that there are those who prefer the same sex and those who prefer the other sex, and that these "preferences" are crucial to the construction of the self. The effect of the creation of this binary of sexuality is at once an enlargement of possibility and the assurance of an identity that may serve to create community, as well as an augmentation of the power of social discipline through the creation of manageable, confinable groups. Melville's career coincides with these developments, both reflecting them and participating in their elaboration. The Melville of the earliest travel writings still operates largely in a realm of undifferentiated sexuality, while his final work, *Billy Budd*, is an enactment of a drama figuring the exclusion and execution of the homosexual.

Typee (1846)[2] sets up one of Melville's principal motifs, the search for a lost paradise, through the evocation of a place of apparently unbridled and polymorphous sexuality. Although the text was perceived in its time, and indeed for many years thereafter, as a veridical travel document, it is now clear that it artfully rearranges Melville's actual journey to the Marquesas Islands and constructs an image of an alternate sexuality that is at once attractive and frightening. Melville did not know the islands as well as he claimed he did, but he had an underlying purpose to construct a symbolic place that would be free from the constraints (both economic and sexual) of the civilization he yearned, with anxiety, to leave behind.

From the first glimpse of the Marquesas, the narrator sets up an opposition between what is represented as the "natural" and the "civilized," in which sexuality allegedly participates in the former category and imperialism and religion in the latter. The bay is "lovely" and looks tranquil, but the French warships are "black hulls" with "bristling broadsides" (12). In addition to setting up a nature/culture binary, these passages of cultural encounter warn of the unreliability of surface impressions, of the dangers that lurk even (or especially) in paradise. The women of the islands swim out to meet the narrator's ship, the *Dolly* (whose name indicates childishness as well as femininity), where they are perceived as "nymphs" and "mermaids," that is, as mythic creatures assimilable to a Western culture. Their erotic welcome to the crew signals an open sexuality that is immediately placed on the defensive by the narrator's judgmental comments, as he records "the unholy passions of the crew and their unlimited gratification" (15). The strategy is a complex one: the scene of "licentiousness" allows simultaneously an appeal to voyeurism and Orientalism at the sight of the "graceful" brown maidens (the text's subtitle is "A Peep at Polynesian Life") and a self-righteous complaint about the "pollution" brought by Europeans. Melville's dilemma is common to those authors who, while writing critically of colonialism, find themselves implicated in the very forces they wish to contest. The eroticizing of the brown body, in which brownness signifies the primitive other, is part of a complex and contradictory process by which the native is seen as disfigured and hence "deserving" of colonization and at the same time is seen as sexually appealing. The scene of the display of the erotic brown body, whether as object of desire or object of scorn, dramatizes the violence of the colonial encounter. Thus the anticolonial lover of the colonized darker native participates in the very objectification and possession he (or, more rarely, she) protests.[3]

The scene of erotic encounter has already been prepared for ironically in the comic tale of the missionary's wife. The islanders "regard *it* [that is, the woman] as some new divinity" (39) and seek to discover what lies behind "the sacred veil of calico." However, once she turns out to be a woman, "idolatry was charged with contempt," as she is seen to be without interest (49).

The tale is also paralleled by a series of references to an eroticized male body. This latter body marks off the originality of Melville's work, moving away from the cliché of the near-naked native woman. The first erotic male friend is the narrator's shipmate Toby, who is described as a transitional figure, halfway between the world of the ship and that of the island, and perhaps also halfway between conventional gender roles. Toby has a "naturally dark complexion," with "jetty locks" of hair (32). The two young men establish a friendship pact before jumping ship. The friendship between Tom and Toby should not only be seen in terms of the relations between men established in such homosocial environments as nineteenth-century ships. Their relationship derives more particularly from the observation of so many Western visitors that the institutionalization of male friendship constitutes one of the striking signs of difference between the South Seas and European cultures. By sealing their friendship in terms of marriage, by an "affectionate wedding of palms" (33), Tom and Toby become possible intermediaries between cultures, and Toby can serve as a guide to the difficult passage to Typee, that is, to otherness. There can be no doubt of the importance of such a concept to Melville: the relation between Tom or Tommo, the narrator, and Toby will be rewritten in *Moby-Dick* in the relation between Ishmael and Queequeg. Both of these scenes dramatize a growing openness to cultural difference, and both take male friendship as the crucial sign of that difference. If affectionate, marriagelike relations between men can be maintained in the public world of the South Seas, why are such relations always violent and oppressive in Western cultures? Much of the rest of the account of Typee is concerned to establish Tom's attraction to this alien culture, largely because of its awareness of sexual possibilities, while at the same time recording the terror that accompanies such a radical questioning of assumptions about sexuality and desire.

Although Melville's own society of the nineteenth century offered no model for adult male relations except those of competition (affectionate friendship was permitted between adolescents but had to give way as boys became adults, as *Pierre* shows), there was, of course, a model for relations between men that was not only permissible but that was indeed, in high culture, valued and praised – Greek love. Although its equivalence in Melville's day would have provoked horror, Greek love had the benefit of several centuries of cultural power, and was admired as a philosophy and an esthetics, if not as sexual practice. Although for readers at the end of the twentieth century Greek love is seen as a practice and not an identity, nineteenth-century readers had a different view of the matter. For many artists and writers from Winckelmann to Thomas Mann, Greek beauty remained a way of alluding to an idealized sexuality without necessarily offending Christian prejudices against a criminalized practice.

Much of *Typee*'s narrative is centered on problems of interpretation. Tom – or Tommo, to use his native name – and Toby are never certain whether they are in Happar or Typee territory, whether they are with the "good guys" or the "bad guys." The problem of the legibility of experience is heightened by the use of this obsessive binarism that stands in the way of a more complex perception. This need to make exclusive choices is related to the problem of sexuality and the contradictory ways it was understood and read in the culture. Greek love is pure and ennobling, while sodomy is degrading and bestial: but in the end, both are the same thing, viewed through a different lens. Stepping out of the culture, abandoning ship, means opening the possibility of discovering a new sexual freedom and a new taxonomy of desire, but it also means losing the landmarks that guide our "natural" responses. Thus the Marquesas may be an ideal, lush world in which there is no sin and where male friendship is institutionalized or a frightening, violent world of cannibals where one's identity is lost and one is held prisoner in a system one can never fully understand. In an important recent essay, Caleb Crain has read cannibalism in the nineteenth century as expressing a homosexuality not yet defined. For Crain cannibalism, like homosexuality, evokes a double bind "of horror and fascination" that has been termed "homosexual panic" by Eve Sedgwick.[4] A memorably comic dramatization of such panic structures the Ishmael–Queequeg encounter at the Spouter Inn in *Moby-Dick*. Melville characteristically seeks a middle road, with suspended judgment, one that permits him to recognize Western culture's need for a little more nature and for greater personal freedom while at the same time acknowledging the natural world's need for order. We might read the same work as an attempt to have it both ways, to possess the sexuality that terrifies and titillates.

The stranger, Marnoo, is the figure who best represents the achievement of some such balance. Tom calls him a "Polynesian Apollo," a phrase that clearly signals his cultural androgyny, at once Polynesian, or primitive, and Greek, or civilized. He has "beardless cheeks," as befits an object of Greek male desire, along with "warmth and liveliness of expression" that make him a Polynesian. He reminds Tom appropriately enough of "an antique bust" (135), perhaps the bust of Antinoüs, beloved of the Emperor Hadrian and model for Billy Budd, which Melville himself always kept in his room. The classical reference operates to ennoble the figure of the native and to suggest a heritage of male love. Faced with the apparent initial indifference of the handsome Marnoo, Tom is feminized, seeing himself as a rejected "belle." At the same time Marnoo is himself "feminine," at least by the rigid gender definitions of Western culture. His cheek shows a "feminine softness," and his hair is worn in "close curling ringlets." This androgynous figure will recur throughout Melville's work as the principal object of desire, from Marnoo to Redburn and Carlo and to Billy Budd, the final incarnation.

Typee's attempt to link Greek love to a reappropriated body faces the obstacle of cultural difference. Tom's "official" friend, Kory-Kory, is a "hideous object to look upon" (83), despite his youth and robustness, because of the tattooing that covers almost his entire body. The young Polynesian is an ethnographic oddity: a difference in conceptions of beauty renders him unattractive to Western eyes. This sense of the strange works against cross-cultural desire and requires a rethinking on Tom's part until he can see beyond his own cultural vision – as Ishamel must rethink his response to the similarly tattooed and ugly Queequeg in *Moby-Dick*. Kory-Kory is nonetheless devoted to Tom and is quite jealous during the anointing of Tom's body by the "girls." The scene of this passive enjoyment of bodily attention is followed by Kory-Kory's light-striking or masturbation scene in Chapter 14, one of the book's great comic moments, in which Kory-Kory "mounts" a stick until he reaches his "climax."

Such juxtapositions indicate the degree to which what is at stake in Melville's work is a reorganization of erotic activity to a greater range of possibility. Over and over again Melville confronts a sexuality of use or production with a generalized, less teleological sexuality. One important example of this issue occurs in Melville's description of polyandry on Typee. For Melville such a practice indicates a shift in male behavior and an elimination of male rivalry; it might also be seen to create the possibility of a triangulated desire *between* men through the intermediary of a woman. It is not a matter of seeing homosexuality opposed to heterosexuality, categories that were in any case not yet in place; instead, whatever the object of desire, the sexuality must be divorced of its links to possession and power, must be decolonized. Sexuality, like textuality, must be playful, must not only depict the erotic but also perform it. Melville's asides and digressions are often the expression of a sexual exuberance that threatens to break out of the boundaries of prose: the danger remains an ecstatic prose of power, like that spoken by Ahab.

Omoo (1847), Melville's next work, is considerably more cynical than *Typee*. Once again Melville is interested in the social construction of desire and same-sex relations. Guided by the example of Richard Henry Dana's *Two Years before the Mast*, Melville sketches the male friendships that characterize the societies of the South Pacific. In Melville's account, the *tayo*, or male friend, is "eager to form an alliance after the national custom, and do our slightest bidding."[5] There is no apparent hesitation in accepting such gestures of servitude. Indeed, they are ennobled by their classical analogues – "In the annals of the island are examples of extravagant friendships, unsurpassed by the story of Damon and Pythias" (152). The narrator's willingness to abandon his *tayo* Poky with ease suggests that a social institution of deep meaning can only be read by Westerners in a simplified manner. The chapter on the *tayo* is followed by a story of false friendship. Kooloo, although prized as "a comely youth, quite a buck in his way," quickly betrays his friend for "a smart sailor, who had just stepped ashore quite flush from a lucky whaling-cruise" (158). The corruption of friendship by money stands synecdochally for the experience of

colonial encounter. The establishment of intense male friendships manifested in a vanished Eden is Melville's gesture toward an anticolonialism
that is always already lost.

If *Typee* and *Omoo* record a passage to a culture seen as radically other
and linked to a lost childhood, the world of *Omoo*'s "simple-hearted natives" (152), *Redburn* stands in sharp contrast, depicting a misleading and
inadequate childhood that must be left behind on the path to adult consciousness. The journey to Liverpool takes Redburn to a paternal past that,
like his inappropriate belongings, cannot serve him. Redburn's loss of innocence includes a recognition of sexuality. His first view of the port of
Liverpool is idyllically erotic, a celebration of homoerotic affection, with
just enough irony to warn of Redburn's naïveté: "under the beneficent sway
of the Genius of Commerce, all climes and countries embrace, and yard-
arm touches yard-arm in brotherly love."[6] Such a scene promises a sexuality that offers no challenge whatever to the needs of commerce, to the
economic regime that ensures vast class differences and will eventually destroy Redburn's friend Harry. It also ignores a darker sexuality – the sodomy of shipboard, of course, but also the attempted seduction of the
unsuspecting Redburn by the captain of the salt-drogher. Although Redburn ultimately resists what he terms the bachelor captain's "inducements"
(168), he is unprepared to respond to the unspoken offer to stay the night,
since such sexuality, unlike his adolescent friendship with Tom, is illegible
to him, his ideal views on friendship as faulty a guidebook as his father's.
At the same time the narrator, in his reference to a "Sodomlike" look and
details that "propriety forbids that [he] should enter into" (191), makes
retrospective knowledge clear, even if it must be veiled for literary consumption.

Redburn's friend Harry Bolton is a figure of the homosexual as that
construction was emerging out of one of effeminacy in the mid-nineteenth
century. His body is small, his complexion "feminine as a girl's," his eyes
"womanly." The two young men quickly become "comrade[s]" and form
a "singular . . . couple" (216). Bolton can be Redburn's guide to the noc-
turnal pleasures of gambling and sex at "Aladdin's Palace." On board the
ship, though, Harry is a victim of enforced masculinity. Redburn recalls
how the "girlish youth" was "hunted" and "pursued" by the men who
found him lacking in virility. Harry's relation to a dissident sexuality is
signaled by his links to Orpheus, the mythic "discoverer" of homosexual
practices, according to Ovid. Harry's feminine nature provokes Redburn's
anxiety, prompting him to speak of Harry's "perfumed hand" (281), like
that of Petronius, the author of the *Satyricon*, the notorious Roman account
of a degraded Greek culture and sexuality. England and America play out

similar roles of cultural appropriation for Melville, neither providing a place for Harry, who, as a male prostitute, "sells" the culture that should have provided paternal guidance. Redburn's final abandonment of Harry once they have arrived in New York indicates a refusal to acknowledge the brotherhood that the novel wants to endorse. Harry is simply too one-sided, and perhaps too contemporary, to be introduced into Melville's imagination of desire or the Albany of his family. Melville could imagine sexual desire in exotic landscapes, and he could acknowledge a feminine man in the case of Harry Bolton, but he could not work out a way to locate these issues in contemporary America.

White-Jacket (1850) continues the theme of betrayal. The idealized relationships evoked in the earlier works are impossible in the military world of *White-Jacket*, which anticipates that of Melville's last work, *Billy Budd*. The overriding symbol of a system of unjust authority worked out on the body is flogging, which can be seen in Foucault's terms both as an outdated form of physical punishment and as a theater of power.[7] The ritual stripping of the torso and the administration of severe blows inscribed on the exposed body constitute an erotics of punishment that reinforces the disciplinary power of all authority. What personal affection can survive such pressures will, as in *Billy Budd*, have to be eliminated, for it runs counter to the concentration of all energy in obedience to and defense of the state. The attractive and humane figure of Jack Chase offers an ultimately ineffective form of resistance to the operation of power. In *White-Jacket* Melville begins to recognize what will be a major argument of *Billy Budd*, that the illusions of personal affection outside of society can only lead to destruction.

Melville returned to erotic male friendship in *Moby-Dick*, whose "framing" scenes rework themes from the earlier *Typee*. Once again, cannibalism serves as the generalized trope of difference and the threat to the autonomous self (to be eaten is the most radical form of loss of identity imaginable). There are striking shifts in presentation, however. Where Tom was only intermittently comic in his fears, the reasonableness of which is never absolutely denied, Ishmael is the constant source of humor in his naïveté and panic. Having to share a bed with Queequeg provokes Ishmael's sexual and cultural fears, even if these cannot be expressed directly. The entire episode is a lesson in cultural relativism that focuses on bodily anxieties. For working-class men, sharing a bed was a common event, but one that was in the process of becoming terrorized. Such sharing can, of course, take place only at a historical and cultural moment where there is no possibility of a glide to the sexual or where such a glide is unimportant. Ishmael's anxieties speak for the shift in male intimacy that will render homosocial relations so dangerous. Ishmael cannot even express his fears directly but must project them onto fears of cannibalism, of fire, and even of hygiene. What they amount to is the shock of an encounter with the other in which cultural assumptions are put into question. Learning to undo ethnocentric fears includes overcoming the fear of sharing a bed, even when that means admitting the possibility of sexuality. What is clear in *Moby-Dick* is that, although the fear may begin as an anxiety about sodomy (that is, fear of the loss of bodily integrity), it is resolved (not without nervous hesitation) by the affirmation of affection and a male marriage that offers the possibility of working against the forces of an aggressive phallic system of power present on the *Pequod* and inherent in a system of capitalism and colonialism.

Melville's 1851 text thus moves away from the Greek love model still present in *Typee* (at least in the figure of Marnoo) toward an exploration of a potentially politically powerful male friendship that incorporates a nonaggressive sexuality. In this world without affection, in which all is profit and loss or desire for vengeance, domesticity is provided by the couple, Ishmael and Queequeg, "a cosy, loving pair" like "man and wife."[8] Queequeg serves as a means of Ishmael's transformation from his cowardly, culture-bound self to a figure of cooperation and sharing. Over and over again in Melville's novels the order of the ship is threatened by a transgressive male who provokes a threatening erotic response. What Melville seems to recognize clearly is that the interdiction of same-sex sexuality is necessary for the maintenance of structures of power. On land Ishmael and Queequeg can lie together in bed; on sea they are subject to the authority of the captain, or the "Law of the Father," as Lacan terms it.

Melville is not suggesting that homosexuality is superior to heterosexuality but rather that transgressive sexuality of any kind, by putting conventional order and authority in question, offers a subversive, or queering, potential. Of course, many homosexual acts participate fully in the system of power and indeed exploit sexuality for personal interest. So it is, for example, with the privileged midshipman of *White-Jacket*, who "indulge[s] his capricious preferences at times in undignified familiarities with the men who, sooner or later, almost always suffered from his capricious preferences" (216). In its worst version, such desires, if unfulfilled, can lead to accusations and revenge, as in *Billy Budd*. In such cases, the differences in status and power work against any transgressive potential and indeed place the men in a feminized position of powerless passivity. In *Moby-Dick*, however, Ishmael overcomes his presumed superiority and comically decides, "Better sleep with a sober cannibal than a drunken Christian" (24). Melville's depiction of the affection between Ishmael and Queequeg is partly utopian, but this tendency is held in partial check by Ishmael's naive and comic responses. It is also situated structurally on both sides of the three chapel scenes and the events of the street that confirm racial prejudice. This structure forces the reader to recognize that the dream of a redemptive and blissful male friendship can take place only in the enclosed space of the bedroom. In the world of the ship, Ishmael and Queequeg are separated, even though Queequeg's coffin will symbolically enable Ishmael to survive the wreck of the *Pequod*.

Sexuality between men contains a subversive potential in its challenge to the isolation of the individual as a cog in an industrial machine. In many cases, such as "The Paradise of Bachelors," men's comradery both supports and is supported by the system: the lawyers enjoy the privilege of a very corrupt *Symposium*. The women of the linked tale, "The Tartarus of Maids," are cut off from human contact, their bodies subject to a regime of surveillance and production: they embody the factory system and its use of repetitive labor. The men on board the *Pequod* are also part of an industrial system, as the "Try-Works" chapter demonstrates. This chapter, which reminds us that the story of Ahab is not merely one of personal madness, but also an account of an industrial system and its waste and destruction, follows a remarkable sequence of chapters that attempts to locate the role of the phallus, and to portray its simultaneous power to control or transform.

The two central chapters to examine here are "A Squeeze of the Hand" and "The Cassock," but they are preceded by "The Castaway," which sets up the theme of human isolation and its relation to slavery and race. Pip's despair, his belief that he has been abandoned by the ship, is the product of his life as a slave, a sense that he cannot count as a human. As Stubb puts it, "A whale would sell for thirty times what you would, Pip, in Alabama" (413). Slavery makes men and women into commodities and deprives them of agency; the separation of couples and families was designed to deprive slaves of avenues of social intercourse. They were, like Pip, radically alone.

"A Squeeze of the Hand" offers a contrasting scene of fellowship in which work is transformed into sexuality. The subject of the chapter is masturbation, with a play of variations on the whale's "sperm." Throughout Melville's work, masturbation plays an essential role in male sexuality. This use of masturbation is indebted partly to his search for a nonaggressive phallicism and partly to a response to cultural pressures against masturbation as a dangerous and nonproductive sexuality. Ishmael immerses his hands in the sperm and finds himself transported to a pastoral scene of "a musky meadow." Caught up in the erotic sensations, he finds himself forgetting the "horrible oath" of vengeance obtained by Ahab (415–16). He thereby temporarily imagines his escape from his fate, but only by ignoring the reality of the hunt and the dangers of a Transcendentalist optimism. As he squeezes the sperm, he squeezes the hands of his coworkers:

> Such an abounding, affectionate, friendly, loving feeling did this avocation beget; that at last I was continually squeezing their hands, and looking up into their eyes sentimentally; as much as to say, – Oh! my dear fellow beings, why should we longer cherish any social acerbities, or know the slightest ill-humor or envy! Come, let us squeeze hands all round; nay, let us all squeeze ourselves into each other; let us squeeze ourselves universally into the very milk and sperm of kindness. (416)

This is an affectionate, comradely sexuality at its most evocative. However appealing it is, though, it cannot be sustained, for it rests upon a momentary suspension of the real. Melville is too much of a cynic about human nature and too honest about the realities of economics and labor to let this vision last; but he is also too much of a radical dreamer not to entertain the possibility of such a transformative sexuality in which men enjoy each other and, at least temporarily, abandon their place in the order of work. There is a sharp shift at the end of Chapter 94 as the narrator goes from handling the sperm to detailing the "business" of its preparation. Before the text moves to that industrial scene, it must incorporate another digression, this time to phallic worship.

Ending the previous chapter with a comic but anxiety-laden remark on castration fears about chopping off toes while preparing the sperm, Melville then shifts to a discussion of the whale's penis. Melville recalls the role of the phallus as an idol – whether Queequeg's Yojo or that worshipped by Queen Maachah in Judea. The point of these references is to offer a radically anti-Christian vision that confirms Melville's repetition of the charge of body hatred in Western culture from Plato on. The story of Queen Maachah emphasizes the role of Judaism in the suppression of the body and suggests links between paganism and Christianity. The patriarchal authority destroys the phallicism of the matriarchy as a dangerous sign of free sexual play and a tamed male sexuality. An abstract authority of putative fathers, what Nietzsche would soon label as the "Socratic order," now takes the place of the orgiastic celebration of the phallus and its playfulness. The circumcision or castration enacted in this chapter stands for a cultural disempowerment. The cassock-wearing priest conceals his own castration under his transvestite costume, condemning the sexual even while continuing to enjoy the love of "a lad for a Pope" or, punningly, "an archbishoprick" (420). In such a moment Melville is at his darkest, convinced that his culture is dedicated to the destruction of the erotic, for which the hunt of the whale may serve as a synecdoche. The persecution of the homosexual, which becomes explicit in Melville's last work, is already present in *Moby-Dick*, but it is part of a larger cultural persecution of the sexual.

Moby-Dick is already a dark, pessimistic work, brightened only by the Ishmael–Queequeg relationship. The works after 1851 are even darker, as if Melville's dream of an Eden regained had become a bitter joke. *Pierre* shows many qualities of the gothic romance, with an ancestral crime, a mysterious portrait, and a complex incest theme. James Creech has argued recently, in a brilliant and important text, that the novel's concern for the father's sexuality and the apparently repentant incest represent a transfer of "guilt for homosexual desire"[9] to other crimes. In *Pierre* one sexual transgression can stand in for another, and what is most often at stake is a transgression against patriarchy. *Pierre* records a primary incest drive not only where the novel begins, with a mother–son romance, but, more important, with a desire for the dishonored father. The desire for purity, for the expiation of the sins of the father, can only lead to other sins. The novel writes its homosexuality, Creech argues, through a series of textual winks, enabling a kind of complicity, or camp reading. The language used by Melville to describe the adolescent friendship of the two cousins, Pierre and Glen, with its contrast to "Aphroditean devotees,"[10] as well as the final allusion to Shakespeare's sonnets, indicates the presence of a concept of different loves, in other words, the emergence of a homosexual identity that can still only contribute to a general sense of a doomed search for an innocent sexuality.

In his late works, Melville seems more willing to be open about sexual desires even as he seems more distant from them. His poem "After the Pleasure Party" is one of his most sympathetic treatments of women and his only developed portrait of a woman's dissident sexuality. Most of the poem is a monologue spoken by an intellectual woman who appears to regret her dedication to scholarship. Desire, it seems, can only be repressed for so long, for "soon or late . . . one's sex asserts itself."[11] The speaker feels trapped by her body, "bound in sex" (134) in terms that clearly draw from Plato's *Symposium* and Aristophanes's account of the original split self yearning for reunion. The poem may also draw on emerging discourses of sexology, for whom the Uranian, named after the Aphrodite Urania of Plato, is the invert, or soul of one sex trapped in a body of the other. Although the speaker, who recalls the Hilda of Hawthorne's *The Marble Faun*, is tempted by withdrawal from the world into a convent life, she ultimately chooses instead the figure of the "armed Virgin" (135) who can join "power and peace" (136). The poem ends with the frame speaker recording his belief, echoing Plato, that love cannot exist outside its embodiment, although it may point toward an ideal. "After the Pleasure Party" seems in many ways a record of lost opportunities, of a sexuality largely unrealized. Other late poems, such as "To Ned," are elegiac as Melville records the loss of the "Edens" of his youth and male companionship.

The sense of lost possibility seems fundamental to the breakdown Melville apparently suffered in 1853 and for which an 1856 journey to Palestine was meant to be the cure. Some of the most moving moments of the long poem *Clarel* that ensued record Melville's lingering love for, and estrangement from, Nathaniel Hawthorne. Although the precise nature of their relationship cannot be known,[12] it is clear that the autobiographical Clarel seeks emotional and probably sexual union with the Hawthorne figure, Vine. Clarel seeks a "communion true" as a "brother" but meets with a refusal that convinces him that his feelings are "sick" (69–71). Clarel/Melville imagines Vine's response, should he have pushed the issue,

> But for thy fonder dream of love
> In man toward man – the soul's caress –
> The negatives of flesh should prove
> Analogies of non-cordialness
> In spirit. (71)

Innocence could apparently not survive in the world of Melville's later years. If *Typee* imagined a world of innocent and mutual desire, his last work, *Billy Budd*, enacts the destruction of the beautiful young man by a system of power that cannot allow for the subversion of the erotic. In this work, which was written *after* the "invention" of the homosexual, the pastoral romance gives way to a language of deceit and barely hidden allusions as homosexuality is criminalized and medicalized, illustrating Foucault's point that the emergence or creation of a new category of identity serves the interest of greater, more intense policing. At the same time that the story eulogizes the doomed Handsome Sailor, it also insists on the ways in which the title character cannot live up to the models on which he is based. Billy has the beauty of the mythic Handsome Sailor but not the force or the intelligence. He is the object of almost universal desire but seems to have few desires of his own. Melville's introduction of his hero involves a series of negative comparisons, most notably that to "the grand sculptured Bull"[13] worshipped by the Assyrians. Against such a figure of masculinity and erotic energy, Billy seems oddly feminine, lacking even the powerful androgyny of Marnoo. It is as if the emergence by the time of composition (probably in 1888–9) of a sexological model of the invert had rendered impossible any depiction of a masculine image of male love in the manner of Whitman but now required a weak figure who could be sacrificed. Billy Budd is one of the first of a long series of tragic homosexual heroes, such as Thomas Mann's Hanno Buddenbrook and Forster's Rickie Elliot, whose death is required by their inability to be incorporated into the society they inhabit.

In many ways, the homosexual in the story is not the beautiful Billy but the evil Claggart. Claggart's unfulfilled desire for Billy ultimately leads him to accuse Billy of mutiny. While Melville had actual cases of shipboard mutiny in mind, the accusation must also be taken in a symbolic sense, for Billy's visible beauty acts as a disruptive erotic force that cannot be tolerated on board ship, where desire must be subordinated to duty. Claggart's "evil nature," which cannot quite be spoken except as "dark sayings" (76), is innate, manifest in his desire for Billy that cannot be expressed as love and hence must be expressed as hatred. Claggart, the homosexual by "nature" or "depravity" (75), confronts the figure of the beautiful innocent. There can be no hope in this context of war and revolution (Billy's ship is ominously termed the *Bellipotent*) for the achievement of an erotic paradise. Melville's principal concern is to suggest the ways in which a potential for love is diverted in a homophobic order into jealousy and hatred. "Claggart could even have loved Billy but for fate and ban" (88): the unspeakability of his desire, and Billy's own literal speechlessness, transform desire into frustration. Claggart acts out the homophobia of self-hatred.

In Eve Sedgwick's provocative reading, the issue in *Billy Budd* is whether "men's desire for other men [is] the great preservative of the masculinist hierarchies of Western culture, or . . . among the most potent of the threats against them."[14] Coming to the question from Melville's earlier works, one expects to see the power of those threats; but Billy cannot speak, and his gestures can only be misread. As Sedgwick suggests, male–male desire works both ways, at least potentially: it reinforces male power at the same time that it offers a potential for disrupting the power of masculinist authority. Melville is bleak about the possibility for disruption on board the *Bellipotent*. The Captain's execution of Billy for the murder of Claggart, although presented by him as painful and unfortunate, asserts the need for cool rationality and seeming justice to prevail and insists that his own desires for Billy, whom he likes to keep under "observation," imagining him as he would appear "in the nude" (95, 94), be suppressed in the name of authority and career. Vere's "surveillance" of Billy, to borrow Foucault's term, at once expresses his (unacknowledged) desire and the need to enforce a disciplinary order. The execution of Billy is exemplary, a warning against any misrule, demonstrating the failure of rebellion and asserting the masculine over the feminine, which, Vere explains, "must here be ruled out" (111).

Billy's story will be normalized and heterosexualized. The means of that appropriation is not only Vere's self-justification; Melville intervenes with figures of authority that can speak in the name of science, enacting in this specific case the role they are being assigned in the culture as a whole as arbiters of sexuality and identity. Melville's parodies of medical incompetence include the notorious Cadwallader Cuticle of *White-Jacket*, but *Billy Budd* is not simply a comedy of learnedness. The conversation of the purser and the surgeon, obscene in its fascination with the failure of Billy to ejaculate at the moment of hanging ("the absence of spasmodic movement" [125]), testifies to the obscurantism of a scientific language but also to the ways in which medical professionals will appropriate sexuality through a taxonomic authority that coincides with the establishment of models of sexual identity. Melville, who began his career by seeking a realm of generalized sexual freedom, concludes by recording a sexuality at once visible and regulated in the emergence of the modern homosexual.

The academic canonization of Melville in the 1940s and 1950s was largely the work of gay men. In the context of the homophobia of that period, their understanding of Melville's sexuality was necessarily coded and suggested rather than stated. F. O. Matthiessen links Melville and Whitman (a reproduction of Thomas Eakins's "The Swimming Hole" is placed in the Melville section of *American Renaissance*), suggesting that Whitman "would certainly have responded to Melville's warmth of feeling for Jack Chase."[15] He might also "have come nearest to understanding what Melville was driving at in his tragedies if he had read *Billy Budd*" (499). What Matthiessen himself was "driving at" remains unstated. A decade later, Newton Arvin was slightly more direct in his account. Drawing on the psychoanalytic discourses of the period, he sees Ahab's loss of his leg "as a kind of castration" and Moby Dick as "the archetypal Parent."[16] But he also asserts the nature of Ishmael's affection: "it is love that Ishmael deeply feels toward Queequeg, and it is the imagination of an even more comprehensive love that comes to him as he sits before a tub of cooling spermaceti" (174). Arvin sets such utopian love against a social reality in which "the sailors despise [Harry Bolton] for his effeminacy and naturally persecute him without mercy" (43). It is not merely a matter of a lack of masculinity but indeed a sexual nonconformity, a feeling "irregular" or "equivocal" (44) that can be linked to the speaker of Shakespeare's sonnets, as Arvin puts it, neglecting perhaps the extent to which a construction of masculinity is crucial in the enforcement of sex and gender norms. In England the popular editions prepared by William Plomer included commentary on Melville's "appreciation of manly beauty"[17] and linked Melville's love for Jack Chase to his central mythology.

Despite this early interest, the advent of open gay criticism in the 1970s did not produce a large body of work on Melville.[18] Melville's sexuality was far too complex or too conflicted to be adopted by critics who were seeking positive models. Melville's role as husband and father made him seem inappropriate for study in a gay context as long as "gay" was understood to denote a fixed and exclusive identity. Melville's repulsion at certain forms of shipboard sex seemed to exclude him from any idealistic model at the same time that an expressed preference for a sexual equality made him seem naive in the age of Foucault. The adoption of a queer model that proposes contingency instead of certainty seems likely to offer the best future for the study of sexuality in Melville's texts. Billy Budd does not need to be gay in order for us to understand his condemnation as the product of a sexual dissidence that is read by others as subversive and of the sexual terror that produces proper gender and authority. Similarly, as James Creech has shown, sexual crimes in *Pierre* operate metonymically, with one easily standing in for another. What matters in the end are not the specifics of Melville's sexuality but rather the sense of difference and the price exacted for it by a patriarchal, homophobic society. Most of his career gives expression to a sense of isolation that grows increasingly desperate, to his desire to find both a place for love and a suitable partner. It would appear that he found neither except, perhaps, in memory.

NOTES

1. See Foucault's *Histoire de la sexualité*, vol. 1, *La volonté de savoir* (Paris: Gallimard, 1976). Foucault's influence has been widespread. It is most important in the work of David Halperin, *One Hundred Years of Homosexuality* (New York and London: Routledge, 1990).

2. *Typee: A Peep at Polynesian Life*, ed. Harrison Hayford, Hershel Parker, and G. Thomas Tanselle (Evanston and Chicago: Northwestern University Press and the Newberry Library, 1968). Subsequent quotations from this edition are cited parenthetically in the text.

3. See Mary Louise Pratt, *Imperial Eyes: Travel Writing and Transculturalism* (London: Routledge, 1992).

4. Crain, "Lovers of Human Flesh: Homosexuality and Cannibalism in Melville's Novels," *American Literature* 66 (March 1994), 25–53. Eve Kosofsky Sedgwick, *Between Men: English Literature and Male Homosocial Desire* (New York: Columbia University Press, 1985).

5. *Omoo: A Narrative of Adventures in the South Seas*, ed. Harrison Hayford, Herschel Parker, and G. Thomas Tanselle (Evanston and Chicago: North-

western University Press and the Newberry Library, 1968), 152. Subsequent quotations from this edition are cited parenthetically in the text.

6. *Redburn: His First Voyage,* ed. Harrison Hayford, Herschel Parker, and G. Thomas Tanselle (Evanston and Chicago: Northwestern University Press and the Newberry Library, 1969), 165. Subsequent quotations from this edition are cited parenthetically in the text.

7. See *Surveiller et punir* (Paris: Gallimard, 1975), trans. Alan Sheridan as *Discipline and Punish* (New York: Pantheon, 1977).

8. *Moby-Dick or The Whale,* ed. Harrison Hayford, Hershel Parker, and G. Thomas Tanselle (Evanston and Chicago: Northwestern University Press and the Newberry Library, 1988), 52. Subsequent quotations from this edition are cited parenthetically in the text.

9. James Creech, *Closet Writing/Gay Reading: The Case of Melville's Pierre* (Chicago: University of Chicago Press, 1993), 122.

10. *Pierre or The Ambiguities,* ed. Harrison Hayford, Hershel Parker, and G. Thomas Tanselle (Evanston and Chicago: Northwestern University Press and the Newberry Library), 217.

11. *Selected Poems,* ed. Hennig Cohen (Carbondale: Southern Illinois University Press, 1964), 133. Subsequent quotations from this edition are cited parenthetically in the text.

12. Some biographers have been emphatic in their reading of the relationship. Particularly overdetermined is the reading of Edwin Haviland Miller in *Melville* (New York: Braziller, 1975).

13. *Billy Budd, Sailor (An Inside Narrative),* ed. Harrison Hayford and Merton M. Sealts, Jr. (Chicago: University of Chicago Press, 1962), 44. Subsequent quotations from this edition are cited parenthetically in the text.

14. *The Epistemology of the Closet* (Berkeley: University of California Press, 1990). Subsequent quotations from this edition are cited parenthetically in the text.

15. *American Renaissance* (New York: Oxford University Press, 1941), 498. Subsequent quotations from this edition are cited parenthetically in the text.

16. Arvin, *Herman Melville* (New York: Sloane, 1950), 171–2. Subsequent quotations from this edition are cited parenthetically in the text.

17. *White Jacket,* ed. William Plomer (London: John Lehmann, 1952), viii.

18. The first full-length study of sexuality in Melville's writings is Robert K. Martin, *Hero, Captain, and Stranger: Male Friendship, Social Critique, and Literary Form in the Sea Novels of Herman Melville* (Chapel Hill: University of North Carolina Press, 1986).

9

CINDY WEINSTEIN

Melville, Labor, and the Discourses of Reception

This essay is not, strictly speaking, about Melville's reception in the nineteenth century, but rather about the discourses constituting that reception and what those discourses have to say about certain fundamental aspects of antebellum culture and Melville's relation to them. Labor is the crucial category which organizes readers' responses to Melville as well as Melville's replies to his readers. I should like to begin with two brief examples that illustrate the symbiotic relations between labor and reception in Melville's writing: the first, an unsigned *Boston Post* review (though we know Charles Gordon Greene to be the author) of *White-Jacket* (1850), and the second, a letter written by Melville to his father-in-law, Lemuel Shaw. Greene's review questions Melville's ability to discuss naval discipline and the Articles of War, and of particular interest is the language he uses when denying Melville's credentials as a cultural critic: "The mind as well as the body is subject to the 'Division of Labor,' and, in most cases, those gifts and acquirements which enable one to produce a good romance unfit him for the calm, comprehensive and practical consideration of questions of jurisprudence or policy."[1] Here *White-Jacket* is attacked on the grounds that Melville's labors as author not only should be, but emphatically are, subject to precisely those divisions of labor that pertain to any other mode of labor, literary or otherwise.

It is quite possible that Melville, in the case of *White-Jacket* (and *Redburn*), would agree, at least in principle, with the notion that certain divisions of labor are desirable. In a famous 1849 letter to Shaw, Chief Justice of the Massachusetts Supreme Court and presumably someone whose "gifts and acquirements" were in the sphere of "jurisprudence or policy," Melville confided: "No reputation that is gratifying to me, can possibly be achieved by either of these books. They [*Redburn* and *White-Jacket*] are two *jobs*, which I have done for money – being forced to it, as other men are to sawing wood. . . . Being books, then, written in this way, my only desire for their 'success' (as it is called) springs from my pocket, & not from my heart."² Melville clearly separates or divides the labors of these two books, which were for the most part completed in the summer of 1849, from his other literary productions such as *Mardi* or *Moby-Dick*, a division nicely characterized by the distinction between pocket and heart. This letter suggests another division as well, that between his own labors and "other men's," which might best be characterized as the difference between intellectual and manual labor or between the upper and lower classes.³ To be sure, many of Melville's texts insist upon the inseparability between various kinds of labor. "The Paradise of Bachelors and the Tartarus of Maids" (1855) immediately comes to mind in its unflinching depiction of both the legal profession and the art of fiction as wholly dependent upon the corporeal and psychic violations of working women in the paper factory. But Melville's letter to Shaw suggests that different kinds of work elicit different evaluations of work as well as competing class identities. By paying particular attention to *Mardi*, *Moby-Dick*, "The Paradise of Bachelors and the Tartarus of Maids," "Bartleby the Scrivener," and *Billy Budd*, it becomes clear that Melville doesn't simply wish to separate his own labors from the typical productions of "other men"; rather, he tries to imagine in his own work a way to reimagine the value of other men's labor, as well as the class structures informing those valuations.

Mardi (1849) is Melville's first attempt to think through the relation between his literary labors and antebellum attitudes toward labor in general. The novel is a far-reaching inquiry into the workings of the northern market economy in the mid-nineteenth century, and it is only by getting a sense of how that economy operated that we can begin to see the complicated place *Mardi* occupies in both Melville's career and antebellum culture. For Melville, this economy affects workers of all sorts, including readers and writers, and constructs the divisions of labor upon which that economy depends for its survival, the most important being the separation between labor and leisure. Imagining an alternative economy, in which one's work does not sabotage one's bodily or psychic well-being, is the task Melville sets for himself. Thus, chapter upon chapter rehearses the making of the world of Mardi and the writing of *Mardi*. Whether the narrator is describing the tobacco containers which have been "work[ed] into bowls" or the idols made "with wonderful industry" in Hevaneva's factory, everything announces itself in Mardi as made.⁴ The following passage, for example, painstakingly charts the labor involved in producing the gourds used by the Mardian royalty for drinking wine: "[The gourds] are plucked from the tree; and emptied of their pulp, are scratched over with minute marks, like those of a line engraving. The ground prepared, the various figures are carefully etched. And the outlines filled up with delicate punctures, certain vegetable oils are poured over them, for coloring" (180). The artisans making these gourds have much in common with Melville, whose own "minute marks" fill in blank pages and whose "figures are carefully etched." Furthermore, these self-reflexive images of Melville's own literary labors allude to what we might call a strategy of visible labor which pervades *Mardi* and helps explain its dismal reception.

This textual emphasis on work finds its mirror image in the critical responses to *Mardi*, which often voiced their dissatisfaction of the text in the language of work. The consensus was either that Melville had worked too hard at writing *Mardi* and/or that readers had to work too hard at reading it. *The Southern Literary Messenger*, for example, laments the fact that "the labor of production must have been great, since every page fairly reeks with 'the smoke of the lamp.'" *The Albion* notes, "In Mr. Melville's style we notice a too habitual inversion, an overstraining after anti-thesis and Carlyleisms, with the not unfrequent sacrifice of the natural to the quaint." Reminiscent of Greene's review of *White-Jacket*, George Ripley of the *New York Daily Tribune* blasts Melville for "leaving his sphere, which is that of graphic, poetical narration, and launching out into the dim, shadowy, spectral, Mardian region of mystic speculation and wizard fancies." Melville's "labor of production," "his overstraining," and his departure from the "proper" sphere of work produced enormous strains on the reader (and still do), making the reading experience of *Mardi* uncomfortably similar to hard work.[5]

The discourse of literary criticism suggests that general debates about the meaning(s) of one's labor were crucial to aesthetic evaluations of literature. A heightened anxiety about labor in general, due to foundational changes in the structure and meaning of work, helped to construct an aesthetic paradigm that demanded the invisibility of literary labor and of the laborer as well. Indeed, one cannot talk about the profound changes brought about by industrialization and specialization in the antebellum North without first addressing the iconic status of the work ethic in its various discursive manifestations. Although *The Voice of Industry*, a mid-nineteenth-century radical newspaper, often found fault with developments in the workplace, it consistently advocated the redemptive value of work, as evidenced in the following article, simply entitled "Labor": "We believe that man is by nature, an industrious being, fond of life and activity, of mind and body, that if he follows the dictates of his natural unperverted impulses and inclinations, he will produce a superabundance of all that can add to his happiness and make him truly great, physically and intellectually."[6] The various articulations of the work ethic, whether they appeared in radical newspapers, religious sermons, or middle-class conduct books, promised individuals economic, corporeal, and spiritual benefits. Such idealizations of work, however, became increasingly difficult to maintain as new structures of work seriously compromised the promises of the work ethic and work itself seemed no longer capable of delivering the economic and psychic goods. According to many factory workers, economic mobility was fast becoming an illusion, mental elevation was no longer the result of a new regime of work that lasted from dawn until dusk, and the spiritual rewards that should come from a job well done were things of the past.

Melville's *Mardi* powerfully delineates the deleterious effect of factory labor on workers and exposes the fictions upon which the work ethic is based. In the chapter "Mohi Tells of One Ravoo, and They Land to Visit Hevaneva, a Flourishing Artisan," Hevaneva narrates the assembly-line production of idols which eventuates in their commodification: "When I cut down the tree[s] for my idols . . . they are nothing but logs; when upon those logs, I chalk out the figures of my images, they yet remain logs; when the chisel is applied, logs they are still; and when all complete, I at last stand them up in my studio, even though then they are logs. Nevertheless when I handle the pay, they are as prime gods" (354). The "artisan's" appropriation of the factory workers' labor, as well as their profits, is evident in the use of the first person. More interesting, perhaps, is Hevaneva's description of the magical change that occurs when he handles the pay. Like Marx's description of the transformation that occurs when a product "steps forth as a commodity . . . [and] is changed into something transcendent," here the idol loses its relation to its maker and is changed at the instant of exchange from log to "prime god."[7] The transcendence of the commodity, for Marx's analysis as well as Melville's, depends upon the erasure of the producer. Thus, we learn a great deal more about the idols "of every variety of pattern; and of every size; from that of a giant, to the little images worn in the ears of the ultra devout" (353) than we do about the workers who make them. Represented solely in terms of their function on the assembly line, the bodies of the workers disappear and the body of the product is foregrounded. Instead of describing the eyes and ears of the journeymen, Hevaneva explains how the workers repair damaged idols by "touching up the eyes and ears [and] resetting their noses" (354). It is as though the specialization and invisibility of the journeymen serve as the precondition for the variety and presence of the commodity.

Melville's representation of workers damaged (and here erased) by their work was not unique. These anxieties were most acutely expressed in working-class publications and speeches to working-class audiences. But it is important to remember that these same worries were being articulated by the middle class as well, though in a slightly different way. Augustus Woodbury, in a series of lectures delivered in the Westminster Church of Providence, Rhode Island, sings the praises of hard work but nevertheless acknowledges the necessity of "out of door recreations . . . to rest the body and the mind." Similarly, in his 1849 conduct manual, Daniel C. Eddy reminded an audience that "the body was not made for constant toil, the mind was not formed for constant study . . . [God] has fitted man for enjoyment, as well as labor, and made him susceptible of pleasurable emotions." Whereas working-class analyses of work focused primarily on improving conditions of labor, debates within the middle class seemed to stress the construction and maintenance of a new temporal and geographical space called "recreation" or "leisure." Literature became a particularly important arena for the preservation of the work ethic through the construction of what we might call an "ethic of rest." Reading should be an exercise (not a taxing one) in nostalgia, which leads the reader to a sense of recaptured simplicity and youth. Eddy, for example, claims that "reading is a recreation which combines pleasure with utility, amusement with profit. It does not weary the body, it does not exhaust the mind, it does not corrupt the heart. It brings vigor to each, and gives relaxation and change, and fits us for the more laborious and irksome duties of life."[8] Here reading equips one for the more strenuous duties in the world of work but nevertheless insinuates the values of work, that is, utility and profit, within the reading experience itself.

The opening chapters of *Mardi* stage Melville's problematic relation to separating the spheres of literature and work, and the rest of the novel can be read as his attempt to arrive at a more satisfactory understanding and application of that relation. The first chapter promises to follow the rules set down by literary critics, inviting us to accompany the narrator on a journey similar to the pleasant and entertaining ones of *Typee* and *Omoo*. "We are off!" (3), he energetically declares, and we expect be be amused on the trip with the anticipation of adventures (the narrator is a sailor on a whaling ship) and the promise of new sights (the setting is the exotic Pacific). As a consequence of having jumped ship because of what he calls the Captain's "tacit contravention of the agreement between [them]" (6), the narrator finds himself in the enviable position of seeking excitement in the islands to the west that are "invested with all the charms of dreamland" (7). Similarly, nineteenth-century readers began *Mardi* with the hope of leaving behind the everyday world of work and entering the exciting world of leisure where they could escape certain people (like the Captain) who might back out of their agreements. Instead *Mardi* itself seems to jump ship, and in the process leaves the reader stranded and, in the words of a *Saroni's Musical Times* reviewer, "gasping for breath."[9]

Although its opening promises "vistas [which] seemed leading to worlds beyond" (8), *Mardi* almost immediately retracts this promise and announces its challenge to the reader in the second chapter, "A Calm." Meditating on the physical and spiritual experience of being in a calm, the narrator tells us that his entire belief system starts to unravel as "doubts overtake him as to the captain's competency to navigate his ship" (10) and describes this discomfort in terms of reading: "If a reader of books, Priestley on Necessity occurs to him; and he believes in that old Sir Anthony Absolute to the very last chapter. His faith . . . however begins to fail; for the geography, which from boyhood he had implicitly confided in, always assured him, that though expatiating all over the globe, the sea was at least margined by land. That over against America, for example, was Asia. But it is a calm, and he grows madly skeptical" (9–10). The calm demarcates that interstitial moment in which the narrator will choose either the sweetness of leisure or the path of industry. Unable to move forward in typically American fashion, what will the narrator do? According to jeremiads against idleness, the worst thing the narrator could do would be to relax and enjoy the calm, which is precisely what he does when he falls in love with Yillah, a native of Mardi. As their love affair unfolds, his initial discomfort with idleness turns into a dangerous enjoyment of it: "With Yillah seated at last in [his] arbor, [he] looked round, and wanted for naught" (189). He has the distinctly un-American "desire [not] to roam" (161). Until Yillah disappears.

Whereas a delicate balance between Ahab's and Ishmael's narrative impulses is sustained in *Moby-Dick*, the conflict in *Mardi* between the narrator's Ishmael-like journey toward knowledge, and his Ahab-like pursuit of Yillah overwhelms him and the narrative. The remainder of *Mardi*, or the next 193 chapters, requires us to endure the calm that the narrator experiences in Chapter 2. For the narrator, that experience forces him to question the meaning of "idleness." Although one might look idle while going through a calm or while reading, a great deal of work might be going on: "He may sleep if he can, or purposely delude himself into a crazy fancy, that he is merely at leisure . . . but he may not lounge; for to lounge is to be idle; to be idle implies an absence of any thing to do; whereas there is a calm to be endured" (10). Readers who might imagine that reading is a leisurely activity apart from work soon learn, like the narrator, that reading *Mardi* requires a great deal of labor. By forcing the reader to endure the calm that is *Mardi*, the text not only challenges its audience to examine its aesthetic expectations but transgresses the proper relations between leisure and labor time.

If idleness in the opening chapters metamorphoses so as to become a kind of work, we have seen that work in the chapters describing Heva-neva's idol factory becomes a kind of idleness. By unraveling the dichotomy which aligns literature with idleness, Melville's text works toward a re-definition of literature as work and, more specifically, literature as mean-ingful and rewarding work. Thus, at the same time that *Mardi* presents and critiques a number of unacceptable versions of production (and non-production), Melville is attempting to come up with a satisfying version of labor that has as its most significant component the visibility of his (and other workers' in *Mardi*) literary labors. The most visible example of this visibility is Melville's inclusion of an allegory about the making of *Mardi* in the chapter about Lombardo's Koztanza, a text much like *Mardi* by an author much like Melville. Babbalanja, one of the main characters, quotes Lombardo as saying: "Who will read me? Say one thousand pages – twenty-five lines each – every line ten words – every word ten letters. That's two million five hundred thousand a's, and i's, and o's to read" (601). If the reader had any doubt that she should read this discussion about Koz-tanza in terms of Melville's *Mardi*, the reference to the a's, i's, and o's makes the connection perfectly clear, since one of *Mardi*'s chapters is en-titled "A, I and O." Just as significant, though, is the way in which tex-tuality is reduced to its most fundamental terms – the letters of the alphabet. In an 1862 essay titled "Reading," Henry Ward Beecher asserts, "the ready reader never thinks of *letters*. It is only the *word* that he sees. And even the word seems to lose individuality, and is but a member of something else, – a sentence. But even the sentence seems not to be seen, but to be seen through."[10] Melville, of course, allows no such distancing between the major participants in the reading experience, which would include reader, author, and text. He refuses to let his text (and himself) become part of an economy that requires an erasure of his labor.

Mardi appropriately ends with its main characters reaching the island of Serenia and discovering there the possibility of fulfilling labor where "men strive to live together in gentle bonds of peace and charity" (623). Although our travelers initially dismiss this experimental utopia as being "based upon the idlest of theories" (623), they come to see the wisdom of its religious and economic ways. In contrast to what obtains on Hevaneva's island, the religion of Serenia requires neither temples nor idols, because "this isle is all one temple to his praise [and] every leaf is consecrated his" (628). Its religion is based on a true understanding of Christian principles, which significantly include the fair distribution of labor: let "no man toil too hard, that thou may'st idle be" (637). What first looks like idleness is, in fact, the calm that one attains through fair and rewarding labor.

As with *Mardi*, reviewers of *Moby-Dick* charged Melville with having "toil[ed] too hard," leaving them with little more than a sense of its author's colossal hubris. Critics emphasized Melville's refusal to participate in the required aesthetic of self-denial, though they attributed his unusual style to unrestrained egotism and literary ineptitude as opposed to any ideological and aesthetic differences of opinion. The *United States Magazine and Democratic Review*, for instance, claimed: "Mr. Melville never writes naturally. His sentiment is forced, his wit is forced, and his enthusiasm is forced. And in his attempts to display to the utmost extent his powers of 'fine writing,' he has succeeded, we think, beyond his most sanguine expectations." Although *Moby-Dick* garnered some favorable responses for its originality and occasional displays of charm, most reviewers had a field day indicting it for manifold artistic, moral, and metaphysical transgressions. The *Literary Gazette* was representative in its assessement that "this is an odd book, professing to be a novel; wantonly eccentric; outrageously bombastic. . . . The author has read up laboriously to make a show of cetalogical learning." In the same vein, the *London Atlas* attacked *Moby-Dick* for "a certain besetting sin of extravagance" and then attacked Melville by imagining the following scene of literary labor: "This unbridled extravagance in writing, this listless and profitless dreaming, and maundering with the pen in the hand, is as it were supported and backed by the wildness of conception and semi-supernatural tone of the whole story." Although Melville had assured his father-in-law that "economy is my mottoe," reviewers found his economy to be an inflationary one.[11] His labors had been mighty, but the result was failure.

With the reviews of *Mardi*, Melville had experienced firsthand the pain inflicted by reviewers trying to force him back into the writing style of *Typee* and *Omoo*. *Moby-Dick* is preoccupied with articulating and accounting for the pain and mournfulness that are involved in such transformations of labor, as Melville is committed to reconfiguring his own status as literary laborer so as to avoid such pain. Arguably, with respect to his reading public, he finds himself in a position not unlike that of workers who, in the 1840s and 1850s, were denied worker's compensation from their employers. Melville's father-in-law, Chief Justice Lemuel Shaw, in fact handed down two key decisions in the cases of *Farwell* v. *Boston and Worcester Railroad* and *Albro* v. *Agawam Canal Company*, which stated that employers could not be held "accountable," to use his word, for accidents incurred by workers on the job.[12] Like these workers, Melville is accountable to employers (readers and reviewers), who in turn are not accountable to him. Because he has entered into a contract with them having "full knowledge of the risks," Melville can, de jure, hold no one but himself responsible, though he vacillates between blaming himself and his reviewers. This is somewhat akin to the situation in which Ahab finds himself. If what Ahab seeks is a figure of accountability, whom else except himself (and the whale) can he hold responsible for his dismemberment? Surely not Captain Peleg or Captain Bildad, who describe themselves as "part owners and agents" of the *Pequod*; their accountability as agents is protected by their status as part owners. Rather than seeing Melville and Ahab engaged in what Wai-chee Dimock calls a "battle for sovereignty," I would suggest that both are pursuing a solution to the problem of accountability. If Ahab's pursuit ends in death, it is not because Melville wishes "to command absolutely" but because he finds in Ishmael a less self-destructive means of existing in a world where accountability is the burden of individual agents who, de facto, function neither as individuals nor as agents.[13]

Besides Ahab, to whom we shall return, Perth, the Blacksmith, is one of the starkest illustrations of how workers' psychic and corporeal agency was being reconfigured in the antebellum period. He is a casualty of the new economic order, like many aboard the *Pequod*, who has "toiled away, as if toil were life itself, and the heavy beating of his hammer the heavy beating of his heart."[14] The fabric of the work ethic is severely mangled when a complete adherence to work leads not to spiritual and economic reward but to intense suffering and personal damage, particularly bodily. Perth's wounded body is the topic of conversation as Ahab, who understandably takes great interest in Perth's pain and his response to it, observes the seabirds that follow the *Pequod* and remarks, "Thou liv'st among them without a scorch" (487). Perth responds: "I am scorched all over, Captain Ahab . . . I am past scorching; not easily can'st thou scorch a scar" (487). Like the forge at which he works, the Blacksmith's body must become scorched all over in order to accomplish its necessary tasks. Only when he is "past scorching" can he be the perfect worker who toils "as if toil were life itself" (484). No longer different from the machine that he operates, "this old man's was a patient hammer wielded by a patient arm" (484). The attributes of his body parts, whether they be his heavy heart or his patient arm, are now an effect not of Perth's agency but of his hammer.

Both Perth and Ahab have suffered the loss of part of their bodies ("the extremities of both feet" [485] in Perth's case), but whereas Perth's response to this loss is "sanely woful" (487), Ahab accepts neither the diminution of his body nor the fact that he can hold no human being accountable as the source of his suffering. "Impatient of all misery in others that is not mad" (487), Ahab protests against the lack of agency that Perth has accepted, though all the while depriving every crew member aboard the *Pequod* of agency: "All of the individualities of the crew, this man's valor, that man's fear; guilt and guiltiness, all varieties were welded into oneness, and were all directed to that fatal goal which Ahab their one lord and keel did point to" (557). The words "Ahab their one lord and keel" hint at Ahab's own mechanization, which is fully developed in his man order to the Carpenter: "Imprimis, fifty feet high in his socks; then, chest modelled after the Thames tunnel; then, legs with roots to 'em, to stay in one place; then arms, three feet through the wrist; no heart at all, brass forehead, and about a quarter of an acre of fine brains" (470). Although Ahab hates the fact that technology (in the form of his prosthetic leg) has become necessary to his body, the man order reveals his avid desire for a total mechanization of a body that would empower him.

Ahab's inorganic leg provides the occasion for Melville's inquiry into the psychic stakes of individual agency because it is the artificial limb that destroys the categories of the human and the nonhuman, the organic and machine, by which Ahab had understood the world and himself. This suture in Ahab's body effects a hermeneutic of bodily indeterminacy which leads to a potentially endless reconfiguration of all experience such that the "veriest trifles capriciously carry meanings" (237). Just as Ahab can no longer understand his hybrid body, he can neither contain nor comprehend the "capriciously" and fundamentally unstable world of signs surrounding him. In the chapter titled "The Sphinx," Ahab movingly pleads with the decapitated head of the whale, "Speak, thou vast and venerable head . . . speak, mighty head, and tell us the secret thing that is in thee" (311). As this scene suggests, Ahab remains convinced that there is meaning in "all visible objects" (164), and he is determined to get at it. By trying to locate the point from which all meaning originates, he hopes to discover and destroy what has compromised his individual agency. However, Ahab's belief that Moby Dick constitutes that point not only diminishes but enslaves him from the start.

Unlike Ahab, who is dedicated to the project of finding and maintaining origins, including the origin of individual agency, Ishmael is determined not only to undermine such notions but to reveal their invidiousness. The "capriciousness" of meaning, which drives Ahab to distraction, delights Ishmael because of his dedication to disseminating and parodying the notion that an individual determines meaning. Ishmael avoids Ahab's demise not simply by reascribing accountability to the market economy but rather by challenging the very foundation upon which accountability rests – individual agency. Whereas Ahab's dedication to the significance of his own labor means the erasure of others' labors and the assumption of individual accountability, Ishmael's adherence to the principle of visible labor means the foregrounding of *all* labor and laborers and the (utopian) dissemination of accountability. In this respect, Ishmael's strategy involves a reconfiguring of *literary* labor (for above all, Ishmael is a writer) in the ways in which he defines writing as simultaneously an individual and a collective, a centered and dispersed, enterprise.

To the extent that Ishmael takes upon himself the literary burden of authoring a "systematization of cetology" (136), for example, it makes sense to read his way of going about such a project as an allegory of Melville's own literary labors in constructing *Moby-Dick*. In contrast to Oh-Oh, the book collector of *Mardi*, who fails to mention the authors whose books fill his antiquarian library, the "Extracts" section of *Moby-Dick* is a moving homage to authorial labor in the tradition of the Homeric catalogue of ships. Quotation after quotation, all having to do with whale sights or whale lore, records not only the continued interest in whales through the ages but also the vast number of literary laborers who devoted their energies to compiling and constructing such records. The presence of this community is foregrounded throughout the text and most visibly in "Cetology," where Ishmael acknowledges that his own cetological taxonomy will have "to be filled in all its departments by subsequent laborers" (136).

Although Ishmael ceaselessly calls attention to himself as a writer, in "The Affadavit" he characterizes himself as a somewhat curious, almost careless one: "I care not to perform this part of my task methodically" (203); "I do not know where I can find a better plan than just here, to make mention of one or two other things, which to me seem important" (205). This self-consciousness reaches its pinnacle in his remarks about the uses to which a certain layer of dead whale skin can be put: "I have several such dried bits, which I use for marks in my whale-books. It is transparent, as I said before; and being laid upon the printed page, I have sometimes pleased myself with fancying it exerted a magnifying influence. At any rate, it is pleasant to read about whales through their own spectacles, as you may say" (305–6). This passage is especially interesting, for as in some of the negative reviews of Melville, which focused on the issue of literary labor, here Melville includes a scene of the labor of reading and, more particularly, a tableau of reading a whale-book not unlike *Moby-Dick*. The scene of reading is here imagined not in terms of the words on the page but rather in terms of the object (or former subject) used, in this case whale skin, to magnify the words on the page. Ishmael is not being a good reader in the conventional sense because he gets caught up in a reading of the whale skin – the mechanism that is supposed to make the task of reading

whale-books all the easier. Although the whale skin is transparent, its transparency tells a very powerful story if readers are willing and able to read
it. For Ishmael's reading leads to a confrontation with an entire economy
that has turned the whale into a magnifying glass. This story of the whale's
disembodiment, moreover, is difficult, even painful to read – as is *Moby-
Dick* and as is the very passage describing the scene of reading: "That same
infinitely thin, isinglass substance, which, I admit, invests the entire body
of the whale, is not so much to be regarded as the skin of the creature, as
the skin of the skin, so to speak; for it were simply ridiculous to say, that
the proper skin of the tremendous whale is thinner and more tender than
the skin of a new-born child. But no more of this" (306). Perhaps the
magnifying glass will make the reader's labor less onerous. More important, however, is the difficulty of the passage itself. The work the reader
must do in making her way through the self-referentiality, the repetitive
diction, and the halting prose suggests both the laborer who writes such
prose and the laborer who reads it. Ishmael's writing makes visible not
only the economy that has turned the whale into a transparent magnifying
glass but also the economy that tries to turn Melville into a transparent,
invisible author.

When critics came to *Pierre* (1852) only a year after *Moby-Dick*, their
outrage at Melville was equal only to what they perceived as Melville's
outrages against them. Indeed, Melville had launched a campaign of his
own against literary critics in the infamous chapter "Young America in
Literature," perhaps in response to some of the cruel ad hominem attacks
leveled at Melville himself in reviews of *Moby-Dick*. *The Literary Gazette*,
for instance, noted that after reading *Moby-Dick*, readers would wish Melville "and his whales at the bottom of an unfathomable sea." In another
review, Ahab's character is not only deemed "a monstrous bore," but "his
ravings, and the ravings of some of the tributary characters, and the ravings
of Mr. Melville himself, meant for eloquent declamation, are such as would
justify a writ *de lunatico* against all the parties." In "Young America in
Literature," Melville depicts the arbiters of literary taste as vapid, pompous,
and superficial. Their response was cutting and personal. The *American
Whig Review* wrote of *Pierre*, "Mr. Melville is a man wholly unfitted for
the task of writing wholesome fictions . . . his fancy is diseased." The *Boston Post* agreed: "To save it [*Pierre*] from almost utter worthlessness, it
must be called a prose poem, and even then, it might be supposed to emanate from a lunatic hospital rather than from the quiet retreats of Berkshire." Critics urged Melville to return to his seagoing adventure tales and
scorned his interest in "the subtleties of psychological phenomena." Moreover, their reviews challenged Melville's psychological competence, col-

lapsing the distinctions between Melville, narrator, and Pierre (not a difficult thing to do), turning Melville's psychic interior into a subject and object of public debate. How to protect interior spaces, whether bodily or psychic ones, would be one of Melville's large subjects in many of his subsequent texts.[15]

The exterior and interior spaces in Melville's short works of the 1850s shrink considerably. Instead of the expansiveness of *Moby-Dick*, we occupy the cramped quarters of "Benito Cereno," the law offices of "Bartleby," and the factory of "The Paradise of Bachelors and the Tartarus of Maids." In much of the short fiction, Melville is interested in interrogating the relations between his own scenes of literary production and other scenes of production. "The Paradise of Bachelors and the Tartarus of Maids" considers many of the same issues as *Moby-Dick*, though the figure of the writer, lacking Ishmael's sense of parody or curiosity, is inescapably complicitous in the exploitation taking place in the paper factory. In the "Tartarus of Maids" we witness the production of whiteness, bereft of the multiple significations it carried in "The Whiteness of the Whale," as the paper machine drains the rosiness of the girls' cheeks until the product, "rose-hued note paper," takes on their rosiness, leaving "rows of blank-looking girls, with blank, white folders in their blank hands, all blankly folding blank paper."[16] Melville's construction of fictional character here seems to recapitulate the machine's relation to the "blank-looking girls." Yet it is crucial to note that the paper is *not* blank. Although the narrator somewhat mystically describes the paper and the women as "destined to be scribbled on" (333), the paper already has a story, which is the story of exploitation (the same story that Ishmael reads on the magnifying glass made of whale skin). The rose, moreover, signifies the aestheticizing of this clearly unaesthetic story. Melville wants no part of this aesthetic. It is the mark of alienating, disfiguring, and divided labor.

If "The Paradise of Bachelors and the Tartarus of Maids" is Melville's most direct response to the problematic effects of divisions of labor as they manifest themselves in terms of gender, class, and narrative structure (after all, the story is a diptych), "Bartleby" (1853) is his most enigmatic reply to such divisions as they specifically apply to the labor of writing. The distinctions between the tartarian factory, where working-class women produce paper, and the legal office "at No. _____ Wall Street," where middle-class men use that paper, evaporate.[17] Both are engaged in the act of copying, and that is all they can do. The presumably intellectual, promisingly original activity of writing – that which is meant to be distinguished from working-class manual labor – takes on the structure of mechanical repro-

duction ruinous to the minds and bodies of workers. Writing, as it is practiced in the law office, turns out to be the most manual labor imaginable.

Everyone in the narrator's chambers writes or at least starts out writing,
as in the case of Bartleby. But the shared activity of writing produces powerful divisions which radiate throughout the tale, whether they be physical
ones, such as the partitions separating labor and management, tempera-
mental ones, such as the characterological fluctuations between Turkey and
Nippers, or textual ones, such as the inflexible distinctions between original
manuscripts and copies. It is Bartleby's "unaccountable" (35) originality,
which takes the form of a refusal to occupy the position of copier, that so
undoes the narrator and the foundations of his power. Yet Bartleby's originality lies not so much in the fact that he undermines the divisions of labor
upon which the narrator's authority depends, but rather in that this undermining itself is so unaccountable in its systematic (or is it unsystematic?)
operations.

By "preferring not to," Bartleby undoes the delicate balance of efficiency
and inefficiency that the narrator has managed to turn into "a good natural
arrangement, under the circumstances" (10). Unlike Turkey and Nippers,
whose occasional assaults against the workplace can be incorporated because they emanate from selves that can be understood or at least rationalized, Bartleby's assaults are unaccountable, hovering between the
"involuntary" (17) and the "strange[ly] willful" (17). Bartleby in effect goes
on strike without ever asserting that he has done so, and thus withholds
from his employer the right to discipline and punish.[18] His preferences are
denials of self ("I am not particular" [40]) that paradoxically meta-
morphose into intractable statements of individual agency, leaving the narrator "burning to be rebelled against" (18). Moreover, in preferring not to
copy, Bartleby takes back from the narrator what is rightfully the scrivener's – the status of the original and an originality that cannot be copied.
The fact that Bartleby resists copying, both in his job as scrivener and in
his very personhood, means for the narrator "an irreparable loss to literature" (3). Loss and unaccountability constitute the terms of the narrator's
economy, which is based on profitability and certitude. Clearly, though,
economy, whether gastronomic, verbal, or corporeal, is also Bartleby's
motto, but it is one which radically undermines the commercial and psychic
epistemologies of the narrator's economy.

The narrator in "Bartleby" spends a great deal of time trying to get inside
Bartleby's head. What motivates him to act (or not to act) the way he does?
How are his (Bartleby's) preferences at odds with my (the narrator's) assumptions? In crucial ways, the narrator responds to Bartleby as reviewers
responded to Melville, whose texts prompted critics to tell him how to write

and to comment upon his psychological health. Bartleby's decision to refuse the narrator entry into his interior psychic space, and his preference not to copy, reflect at once Melville's decision not to capitulate to his critics and to find for himself a narrative position which protects him from personal violation. As his critics noted, this made for strange, difficult, almost unreadable texts. Reviews of *The Confidence-Man*, for example, were less caustic than confused: "we frankly acknowledge our inability to understand it. . . . You might, without sensible inconvenience, read it backwards." The character(s) of the confidence man also bewildered Melville's contemporaries, as it still does. In maintaining that Melville had an obligation to create "fictitious creatures such as Nature might herself have made," the *Literary Gazette* objected to the impenetrable characters aboard the *Fidèle* and the narrator's unnatural relation to them.[19]

There is a strategic deployment of surfaces in Melville's later works, which makes impossible the violent intrusions into corporeal and psychic interiorities that define the operations on the *Pequod*, the paper factory, the law office where Bartleby "works," and many of the reviews of Melville's texts. In Bartleby-like fashion, the narrator of *Billy Budd* finds a way to spare his characters from similar violation by refusing to let the reader into his characters' interiorities, especially Billy's. Although Melville wrote *Billy Budd* in his final years, he never completed the text. This task was taken up in 1924 by Raymond Weaver, who three years before had published *Herman Melville: Mariner and Mystic*. Weaver's text helped to inaugurate what has been called "the Melville revival" in America – a revival, it should be noted, that was initiated by a handful of British enthusiasts of Melville – and which also saw the publication of Lewis Mumford's 1929 critical biography, *Herman Melville*. Melville, of course, was not alive to see the resuscitation of his works and reputation, and the writing of *Billy Budd* discloses his unresolved concerns about critical invasions into his psychic world. In fact, *Billy Budd* reveals that it is the very positing of individual agency at an interior core that permits Vere via Claggart to exercise his discipline and to mete out his subsequent punishments. By refusing to get inside his characters – *Billy Budd* is ironically subtitled "An Inside Narrative" – Melville points to the logic of interiority that ultimately destroys Billy.

Melville's strategy in the novella is one of superficial observation – superficial not in the sense of fleeting or vapid, but rather in the sense of attention to surfaces. This attention to surfaces is apparent early in the text as the narrator remarks upon Billy's complexion that "thanks to his seagoing, the lily was quite suppressed and the rose had some ado visibly to flush through the tan."[20] Elsewhere, the narrator invokes the language of interiority while refusing to enter into Billy's consciousness: "The moral nature was seldom out of keeping with the physical make. Indeed, except as toned by the former, the comeliness and power, always attractive in masculine conjunction, hardly could have drawn the sort of honest homage the Handsome Sailor in some examples received from his less gifted associates" (44). How the interior workings of Billy's body are to be represented, whether from the inside or the outside, is a crucial narrative problem. Getting inside Billy yokes an act of negative homoeroticism with the construction of interiority, as we shall see in the case of Claggart. The narrator avoids this dangerous conjunction by situating his own homoerotic depiction of Billy at the borders of his body. Throughout the text the narrator insists upon remaining at the surfaces of Billy's body while nevertheless claiming that his story is "restricted . . . to the inner life of one particular ship and the career of an individual sailor" (54).

Claggart, on the other hand, is committed both to the military strategy of impressment and to the notion of interiority. He warns Vere that Billy conceals "a mantrap . . . under the ruddy-tipped daisies [of his cheeks]," that he is "a deep one." Claggart's words suggest that Billy *must* have an inside potentially at odds with the surfaces of his body. The idea of depth, which posits an interiority in contrast to Billy's "youth and good looks" (94), fuels the legal machinery that is used to convict Billy of mutiny when necessary. Presumably, by countering depth with superficiality, interiority with exteriority, Billy could effectively challenge Claggart's position. But by making Billy and his world completely exteriorized and by narrating that world at its surfaces, Melville's text reveals that Claggart's appeal to Billy's interiority is merely a fiction that provides him the necessary excuse to get the disiplinary machine going, a machine that Vere himself is only too happy to keep running. It is not the case that the narrator denies Billy interiority; he just won't try to represent it, for to represent it would be to reproduce the kinds of violations committed by Claggart and Vere. In stark contrast to labor reformers and management spokespersons, who were united in their commitment to the logic of interiority and the "natural," *Billy Budd* is committed to its opposite. Only when read in the context of the contemporary debate about workers' bodies can one see how radical was Melville's delineation of characters who completely lacked interiority.

Labor reformers advocated an antagonistic stance to industrialization based on the belief that machinery prohibits workers from gaining the potential rewards of the work ethic, as well as developing into anything other than mindless addenda to their machines. Thus, William Demarest Lloyd, in *Men, The Workers*, positions the worker's "natural" body against the machine's "artificial" constitution: "through the body only can they [workers] approach the higher realms of truth; they therefore believe the body to be as sacred as the soul, and that if one is to be holy the other must be whole."[21] Labor Commissioner Carroll Wright assumed the opposite position by invoking the ideology of the work ethic, with its promises of spiritual and intellectual reward. Unlike those who worried about the anesthetizing effects of machinery on workers, he claimed that "machinery [was] constantly lifting men out of low into high grades of employment [and] constantly surrounding them with an intellectual atmosphere." Wright further argued that "factories are . . . the legitimate outgrowth of the universal tendency of association which is inherent in our nature, and by the development of which every advance in human improvement and human happiness has been gained."[22] Of course Lloyd and his supporters would have seen themselves in opposition to Wright and his supporters. Both sides, however, shared an important rhetorical technique: the use of "nature" as a strategy for bolstering their positions.

By dispensing with any pretense of the workers' naturalness, Melville's text undercuts arguments of those who rely on the immutability of the worker's nature in their attempts to reconstruct that nature through mechanization. Even Billy, who has been described as "one of Nature's innocents" or "the vital urge incarnate," seems as much a product of art as of nature.[23] The narrator describes the completely unnatural world of the crew members aboard *The Bellipotent*: "every sailor is accustomed to obey orders without debating them; his life afloat is externally ruled for him; he is not brought into that promiscuous commerce with mankind where unobstructed free agency on equal terms – equal superficially at least – soon teaches one that unless upon occasion he exercise a distrust keen in proportion to the fairness of the appearance, some foul turn may be served him" (87). In this description, reminiscent of naval life in *White-Jacket*, the sailors aboard the *Bellipotent* are portrayed as, by necessity, constructed by codes. Such codes are essential because without them people might naively assume that "unobstructed free agency" is something good and true, something about which one does not have to be profoundly distrustful. The laborers aboard the *Bellipotent* mechanically obey their masters. As a unit, they function so efficiently aboard the *Bellipotent* that the narrator finds it "unnecessary to particularize [any] other crew members" (63) besides Claggart. Nevertheless, the text's crisis centers on the supposedly mutinous intention of the sailors.

Characterization in *Billy Budd* is thus contingent upon a fundamental unnaturalness that ultimately exposes the category of nature as an enabling myth with which Vere permits himself the opportunity to execute his power. (It is worth recalling, in this respect, that claims about Melville's nature, as well as demands for natural characters, had featured prominently in critics' negative responses to his novels.) The term "nature" is used so often in *Billy Budd* that its meaning is quickly seen to be wholly arbitrary. This is precisely Melville's point. Vere effectively deploys the category of nature when he reminds the members of the drumhead court that they have "ceased to be natural free agents" because "martial law [is] now operating through" them. The categories of nature and interiority here converge as Vere presents a model of interiority that can be manipulated, depending upon whether or not a particular situation requires an "allegiance to Nature" or "to the King" (110). The notion that this allegiance to Nature is somehow more valid, more "natural" than the allegiance to the King is shown to be a fiction because the term "nature" itself undergoes so many permutations. When, for example, Vere speaks to the illegally formed jury, he assures them that, "did [Billy] know our hearts, I take him to be of that generous nature that he would feel even for us on whom in this military necessity so heavy a compulsion is laid" (113). The deployment of Billy's "generous nature" is tactical and effective. It comes precisely at the moment when Vere is about to leave the jurors so that they can make their decision. Vere gets the desired verdict. The fear that the worker's "nature" will arise and protest its mechanized condition allows those in power to anticipate the mutiny which then permits the exercise of authority. Both Vere and Claggart fear "what sailors are" (112), that is, what their nature is.

But their nature is, of course, constructed by those "Benthamites of War" (57) who have erected a prisonlike structure on the *Bellipotent* and will not "tolerat[e] an infraction of discipline" (60). Even though Vere has no reason to believe Claggart's accusation against Billy and claims that he will not "permit himself to be unduly disturbed by the general tenor of his subordinate's report" (93), once the charge is articulated, the martial machinery begins to move – all because of "what sailors are." Whether or not Billy committed the crime makes no difference. A "real" mutiny and a "fictional" mutiny become the same thing. Vere makes this point while admonishing the judges: "Your clement sentence they would account pusillanimous. They would think that we flinch, that we are afraid of them – afraid of practicing a lawful rigor singularly demanded at this juncture, lest it should provoke new troubles. What shame to us such a conjecture on their part, and how deadly to discipline" (113). Those in power must respond to an alleged mutiny the same way they would react to an actual one. And the historical fact of an actual one, in this case the Nore Mutiny, adds one more piece of evidence proving that a sailor's nature is mutinous.

By relying on Billy's supposedly instinctual or natural anger about his impressment (after all, he is a deep one), Claggart easily raises the specter of mutiny, which then permits Vere to exercise his beloved "forms" (128).

Billy's final words, "God bless Captain Vere" (123), both affirm and ironically subvert Vere's official code, his "forms." Billy, the worker, who "made no demur" (45) when impressed into naval service, blesses his executioner. More interesting, perhaps, is the issue of Billy's body, which remains just the least bit untamed, even though it has been domesticated through the interventions of Vere, the Purser, and the Surgeon. The "lack of spasmodic movement" (125), as the narrator calls it, ends up producing an excess of meaning. His body remains untamed enough to evoke a "murmur" (126) among the crew, which makes Vere realize "the necessity for unusual action" (128). What calls for such unusual action on Vere's part is the unusual inaction of Billy's body – the fact that he doesn't ejaculate. What is inside never gets outside and what is "natural" remains invisible. Billy's body remains consistently impenetrable or, more precisely, unpenetrated by the narrator.

The insides of Billy's body do not circulate, but externalized representations of that body do in the several conclusions of the text. After the execution, for example, an article in a naval chronicle, like the deposition in "Benito Cereno," reports that "the criminal paid the penalty of his crime. The promptitude of the punishment has proved salutary. Nothing amiss is now apprehended aboard H.M.S. *Bellipotent*" (131). Exteriorizing Billy, as we have seen, allows the narrator to remain outside of the cultural logic that destroys him by imputing interiority to him. By quoting "History . . . without comment" (114) and citing newspaper articles (also without comment) that depict Claggart as "vindictively stabbed to the heart by the suddenly drawn sheath knife of Budd" (130), the narrator at the conclusion of *Billy Budd* remains consistent in his own refusal to impute interiority or agency to the logic that informs this version of the story, thereby undermining the "official" account completely.

By the time Melville wrote *Billy Budd*, he was acutely aware of the possibility of reproducing in his relation to his characters the problematics of the marketplace which he had so trenchantly analyzed throughout his career. His work as a writer, in other words, confronted the same problematics as any other kind of work in nineteenth-century America. Finding a way out of this analogical bind became his task. He adopted a variety of strategies ranging from a rather explicit confrontation in *Mardi*, *Moby-Dick*, and "The Paradise of Bachelors and the Tartarus of Maids" with the aesthetic of invisible labor as defined by literary criticism of the period, to a more opaque undermining of individual agency in "Bartleby" and *Billy*

Budd. When Melville writes to Shaw that "economy is my mottoe," it is no doubt partially true. He realized the need to be efficient and economical, especially when writing to his father-in-law, the person who was heavily subsidizing him. But it is also true that if economy, as understood by Shaw, were Melville's motto, he would not have written so many of the texts that got him into economic trouble. Clearly, as his career unfolded, his notion of economy shifted and expanded so as to force complex reconsiderations of the market economy and his literary labors in it. These reconsiderations, in turn, forced Melville to create within his fictions alternative economies with quite different mottoes ("I prefer not to" being the most memorable), which enabled him to avoid inflicting upon his characters and himself the psychic and bodily violations he had found to be the consequences of a market economy.

NOTES

1. Quoted in *Melville: The Critical Heritage*, ed. Watson G. Branch (London: Routledge & Kegan Paul, 1974), 234.
2. Quoted in Jay Leyda, *The Melville Log: A Documentary Life of Herman Melville, 1819–1891* (New York: Gordian Press, 1969), vol. 1, 316.
3. Labor historian Stuart Blumin claims that in the period between 1820 and 1860, there was a "divergence of economic circumstances between men who 'worked with their heads' and men who 'worked with their hands' which suggests a hardening of class boundaries along the manual–nonmanual fault line" (*The Emergence of the Middle Class: Social Experience in the American City, 1760–1900* [Cambridge: Cambridge Univ. Press, 1989], 121). An excellent account of the ideological significance of work can be found in Daniel Rodgers, *The Work Ethic in Industrial America, 1850–1920* (Chicago: Univ. of Chicago Press, 1985). For a fine reading of the discourse of work in the antebellum period, see Nicholas Bromell, *By the Sweat of the Brow: Literature and Labor in Antebellum America* (Chicago: Univ. of Chicago Press, 1993).
4. Herman Melville, *Mardi: And a Voyage Thither* (1849), ed. Harrison Hayford, Hershel Parker, and G. Thomas Tanselle (Evanston and Chicago: Northwestern Univ. and the Newberry Library, 1970), 373, 353. All further quotations from *Mardi* are noted in the text.
5. These reviews can be found in *The Melville Log*, vol. 1: "Letters from New York" in the *Southern Literary Messenger* 1849; *New York Daily Tribune* 1849.
6. *The Voice of Industry*, August 21, 1845.
7. Karl Marx, *Capital*, ed. Frederick Engels (New York: International Publishers, 1967), vol. 1, 71.
8. Augustus Woodbury, *Plain Words to Young Men* (Concord, N.H.: Edson C. Eastman, 1858), 147, 80; Daniel C. Eddy, *The Young Man's Friend: Containing Admonitions for the Erring; Counsel for the Tempted; Encouragement for the Desponding; Hope for the Fallen* (Lowell: Nathaniel Dayton, 1851;

orig. 1849), 84, 94. For a more in-depth account of the strategic deployment of the work ethic, see my book, *The Literature of Labor and the Labors of Literature: Allegory in Nineteenth-Century American Fiction* (Cambridge: Cambridge Univ. Press, 1995).

9. Quoted in Hugh W. Hetherington, *Melville's Reviewers: British and American, 1846–1891* (Chapel Hill: Univ. of North Carolina Press, 1961), 125.

10. Henry Ward Beecher, "Reading," in *Eyes and Ears* (Boston: Ticknor, 1862), 188.

11. These reviews can be found in *Melville: The Critical Heritage*: United States Magazine and Democratic Review, January 1852; Literary Gazette, December 6, 1851; *Moby-Dick as Doubloon: Essays and Extracts (1851–1970)*, ed. Hershel Parker and Harrison Hayford (New York: Norton, 1970); and the London *Atlas*, November 1851. The Melville citation appears in an October 6, 1849, letter to his father-in-law, Lemuel Shaw, which is quoted in *The Melville Log*, vol. 1, 340.

12. Leonard Levy, *The Law of the Commonwealth and Chief Justice Shaw* (Cambridge: Harvard Univ. Press, 1957), 176; see also pp. 169–75.

13. Wai-chee Dimock, *Empire for Liberty: Melville and the Poetics of Individualism* (Princeton: Princeton Univ. Press, 1989), 114.

14. Herman Melville, *Moby-Dick; or, The Whale* (1851), ed. Harrison Hayford, Hershel Parker, and G. Thomas Tanselle (Evanston and Chicago: Northwestern Univ. and the Newberry Library, 1988), 487. All further quotations from *Moby-Dick* are from this edition and are noted in the text.

15. These reviews can be found in *Melville: The Critical Heritage*: Literary Gazette, December 6, 1851; Southern Quarterly Review, January 1852; American Whig Review, November 1852; Boston Post, August 4, 1852; National Era, August 19, 1852.

16. Herman Melville, "The Paradise of Bachelors and the Tartarus of Maids," in *The Writings of Herman Melville: The Piazza Tales and Other Prose Pieces, 1839–1860*, ed. Harrison Hayford et al. (Evanston and Chicago: Northwestern Univ. and the Newberry Library, 1987), 328. All quotations from this short story are from this edition and are noted in the text.

17. Herman Melville, "Bartleby," in *Billy Budd and Other Stories* (New York: Penguin, 1986), 4. All quotations from this short story are from this edition and are noted in the text.

18. Read in the context of antebellum labor disputes, Bartleby's actions (or preferences) can be seen as exemplifying one temporarily effective though ultimately self-destructive way of halting the machinery of production. For other readings of Bartleby and work, see Michael Rogin, *Subversive Genealogy: The Politics and Art of Herman Melville* (New York: Knopf, 1983); Brook Thomas, *Cross-examinations of Law and Literature: Cooper, Hawthorne, Stowe, and Melville* (Cambridge: Cambridge Univ. Press, 1987); and Gillian Brown, *Domestic Individualism: Imagining Self in Nineteenth-Century America* (Berkeley: Univ. of California Press, 1990).

19. These reviews can be found in *Melville: The Critical Heritage*: Mrs. Stephen's New Monthly Magazine, June 1857; Literary Gazette 1857.

20. Herman Melville, *Billy Budd, Sailor (An Inside Narrative)*, ed. Harrison Hayford and Merton M. Sealts, Jr. (Chicago: Univ. of Chicago Press, 1962), 50.

All further quotations from *Billy Budd* are from this edition and are noted in the text.

21. William Demarest Lloyd, *Men, The Workers* (New York: Doubleday, 1909), 30.

22. Carroll Wright, *Some Ethical Phases of the Labor Question* (Boston: American Unitarian, 1902), 151, 93.

23. Lewis Mumford, *Herman Melville* (New York: Literary Guild, 1929), 354; John Seelye, *Melville: The Ironic Diagram* (Evanston: Northwestern Univ. Press, 1970), 163.

PAUL GILES

"Bewildering Intertanglement": Melville's Engagement with British Culture

In her Introduction to a 1994 collection of critical essays, Myra Jehlen writes of how in America "Melville has remained canonical through the whole period of canon-busting." According to Jehlen, new styles of literary evaluation may have found different things to admire in Melville, but they have not sought to devalue his central "importance or brilliance."[1] Melville has not, however, enjoyed a similar prominence within the British critical domain as it has developed professionally since the Second World War. Whereas Hawthorne and, to an even greater extent, Henry James have evoked a great deal of admiration and explication within British circles, engagement with Melville's more bulbous and erratic texts has remained spasmodic. My purpose in this essay is to suggest reasons for this comparative neglect, and to suggest how some of this discomfort may arise not so much from any simple antagonism on Melville's part toward the British tradition, but from the way he interacts with it in a perverse and parodic manner, turning its apparently legitimating structures inside out.

Melville's relative invisibility within the field of later-twentieth-century British culture is all the more telling given his cult status among various maverick thinkers in Britain around the end of the Victorian era. Hershel Parker, in fact, has suggested that the initial "revival of Melville's reputation was almost exclusively a British phenomenon," arising out of a general interest in the American author among various groups of artistic and political rebels, notably the Pre-Raphaelites and, later, the Fabian Socialists.[2] In the 1860s and 1870s, poets like Dante Gabriel Rossetti and James Thomson were attracted to Melville because of the way his broad cultural iconoclasm seemed to be linked, at some vital level, with an ambience of sexual freedom, an issue that greatly concerned British radicals of this era. A few years later, Thomson's influence helped indirectly to generate an admiring circle of Melville acolytes in the provincial town of Leicester, guided by James Billson, a political and religious iconoclast who worked in the legal profession. In 1884, Billson wrote to the American author of how "here in Leicester your books are in great request . . . as soon as one is discovered (for that is what it really is with us) it is eagerly read and passed round a rapidly increasing knot of 'Melville readers.' " Another of this Leicester set, J. W. Barrs, was friendly with Henry S. Salt, who has been described by Parker as the first "Melville scholar" since he published two diligently researched essays on the American writer in the *Scottish Art Review* of November 1889 and the *Gentleman's Magazine* in 1892.[3]

In cultural terms, Salt might be seen in many ways as the typical British champion of Melville's writing around the turn of the twentieth century. After a traditional upbringing, he returned to spend nine years as a master at his old school, Eton, before creating such a stir by his interest in rebellious figures like Shelley, Swinburne, and Thoreau that he was obliged to leave this bastion of educational conservatism. He then forged links with the Fabian Society and the newly emerging Labour Party, and became a proselytizer for causes such as vegetarianism and the Humanitarian League. He continued to publish widely on British authors whom he could cast as outsiders – William Godwin, Thomas De Quincey – as well as vigorously promoting American authors like Emerson, Hawthorne, Poe, and Whitman, in addition to Melville. He also developed friendships with other intellectuals who shared his recalcitrant tendencies: William Morris, George Bernard Shaw, Edward Carpenter, Havelock Ellis. Ellis himself corresponded briefly with Melville in 1890, when the pioneering psychologist was, as he put it, "making some investigations into the ancestry of distinguished English & American poets and imaginative writers, with reference to the question of race."[4]

All of these bohemian characters looked to Melville as an emblem of authentic nature, as an untrammeled spirit who seemed to offer an exuberant alternative to the stuffy principles of British society. A similar pattern was repeated, on a less intellectually self-conscious level, by maritime authors like W. Clark Russell and John Masefield – Masefield spoke in 1912 about Melville's "picturesqueness and directness" – as well as by fantasists like J. M. Barrie, who cherished *Typee* and *Omoo* as an escape back into the adventure world of boyhood.[5] These British enthusiasts were impressed by the way Melville's fictional heroes fail to accommodate themselves to the landlocked preoccupations of an insular society, and their nonconformist sympathies anticipate the line taken by the most famous British advocate of Melville in the early twentieth century, D. H. Lawrence. *Studies in Classic American Literature* (1923) evokes the spirit of the New World as a welcome escape from the repressive confines of British culture, specifically celebrating Melville's "slithery" and "uncanny magic" and going on to describe him as "a futurist long before futurism found paint."[6]

Lawrence's whole style of articulation involves something new, of course, but it is worth emphasizing that the provincial, antiestablishment milieu from which Lawrence himself emerged had been remarking upon the qualities of Melville for some forty years.

A new edition of *Moby-Dick* in 1921, edited by Viola Meynell for the "World Classics" series, helped to direct attention more generally toward the kind of American primitivism which was often seen at this time as a welcome antidote to nineteenth-century bourgeois values. J. W. N. Sullivan, writing in the *Times Literary Supplement* of 1923, specifically differentiates Melville's "profundities" and "mystical" dimensions from the "perfectly clear-cut and comprehensible affair" that comprised the "world of the Victorians."[7] In *Aspects of the Novel* (1927), E. M. Forster similarly acclaims Melville's prophetic capacity to break through the "tiresome little receptacle" of social morality and to encompass larger, metaphysical forces of evil. Forster equates this confounding of materialism with Melville's modernist skills of elusiveness and indirectness: "The essential in *Moby Dick*, its prophetic song, flows athwart the action and the surface morality like an undercurrent. It lies outside words." It is noticeable, though, how Forster's private commonplace book is considerably less vague on the sources of this obliquity, commenting specifically upon "H.M.'s suppressed homosex."[8] A generation later, another sexual rebel, W. H. Auden, was to proffer an existential interpretation of Melville's sea novels: in *The Enchafèd Flood* (1951), Auden writes of how the departure from land in *Moby-Dick* signifies "a commitment to a necessity which, however unpleasant, is at least preferable to . . . the meaningless freedom on shore." This psychological "necessity" involves a rupture of domestic conventions, and Auden's discussion of *Billy Budd* is one of the first to insist directly on how the motive underlying Claggart's hostility to Melville's cherubic hero is "homosexual desire."[9] In the same year, another self-consciously gay artist, Benjamin Britten, produced his operatic version of *Billy Budd* for the 1951 Festival of Britain.

In general, though, it is noticeable how British critics in the first half of the twentieth century tended to focus upon Melville's earlier narratives – *Typee, Omoo, Redburn, Moby-Dick* – and to emphasize their romantic, atavistic energies. There was relatively little conception of how Melville's fiction might be intricately interwoven with issues of hierarchical authority and control, and it could be that his texts were considered acceptable to British readers as long as they could be said simply to embody "the stark forces of nature," as E. L. Grant Watson suggests in a 1920 issue of the London *Mercury*.[10] When, however, a later generation of scholars began unpacking more assiduously the cultural implications and undercurrents of

Melville's work, British readers who were quite at home with the reflective ironies and social ambiguities of James or Hawthorne found themselves less comfortable with the more profane implications of Melville's aggressive irreverence.

This growing transatlantic divide in the reception of Melville's work during the middle years of the twentieth century was not helped by the propensity of many American critics at this time to underline links between the author and the "Young America" movement, to which he was introduced by Evert Duyckinck in 1846. Certainly Duyckinck's brand of cultural nationalism provided a framework and impetus for what was to prove the most productive period of Melville's literary career, the early years which saw the appearance of the celebrated sea romances, as well as the satirical allegory, *Mardi*. "Hawthorne and His Mosses," published by Duyckinck's *Literary World* in August 1850, is the critical essay by Melville that provides a manifesto for this patriotic spirit: he critiques Washington Irving, among others, for his "self-acknowledged imitation of a foreign model" and urges American writers to abandon their "leaven of literary flunkyism towards England."[11] Melville's piece echoes the critical assumptions in Duyckinck's own review of *White-Jacket* in the same journal a few months earlier, where Duyckinck praises Melville for the way he "tests all his characters by their manhood," a process considered to be "thoroughly American and democratic" since it involves "no patronage" in its representation of ordinary sailors.[12] However, the more complex style of *Moby-Dick* elicited a negative review from an uncomprehending Duyckinck in November 1851, leading Melville to cancel his subscription to the *Literary World* three months later. That effectively concluded Melville's interest in the politics of cultural separatism. In this light, it is one of the ironies of literary history that Melville's reputation as a figurehead of nationalism should have been reinvigorated some hundred years later by the critical readings characteristic of the Cold War era, readings that pitted the individualistic energies of Melville's all-American heroes against the restrictive shackles of more traditional societies. In the wake of F. O. Matthiessen's *American Renaissance* (1941), Melville became canonized as a romancer dedicated to exploring the possibilities of liberty, a writer prepared heroically to confront estrangement from the material circumstances of his corrupt world in order to aspire toward an imaginative and putatively spiritual freedom.

More recent work on Melville has, of course, moved away from this dualistic paradigm. The antitheses pitting frontier spirit against the restrictive shackles of the Old World, individualism against totalitarianism, have been undermined by questions about the extent to which such binary oppositions work simply to define each other. More generally, theoretical interrogations of the status of agency in Melville's writing have suggested how his fictional characters tend to find themselves pushing up against inherited social structures rather than being in a position to objectify or transcend them. This question about agency quickly becomes a metaphysical one involving imponderable ontological issues about the meaning of origins; but, in a less abstract sense, a greater willingness to examine the ways Melville's fiction negotiates intertextually with the circumscribed genius of English literature has focused more attention on the extent to which the author's chosen field of inquiry involves not simply the narrower terrain of the United States but the more expansive circuits of North Atlantic culture in general. Lawrence Buell theorizes these interactive movements as a form of postcolonial anxiety: Melville's art, Buell suggests, should be seen as embroiled within a "much more complicated transnational historical matrix" than the master narratives of nationalism or slavery that have become almost synonymous with American Renaissance texts over the past fifty years.[13] Yet, in the light of ways in which his writing reflects various complications of an international scene, Melville might appear not so much a postcolonial writer as a post-postcolonial, a Janus-faced figure who finds uncomfortable parallels between markedly divergent cultures.

As with most American writers of his era, Melville's professional career was heavily involved with English literary models and professional paradigms. He himself undertook three expeditions to Britain during the first half of his life, each of which offered a different perspective on English culture. In June 1839, he sailed from New York to Liverpool on board the *St. Lawrence*, a trip that was to form the basis of his transatlantic comparisons in *Redburn*. On his second visit, though, the focus was more upon London as a center of literary trade and commerce. It had been another London publishing company, John Murray, that had first brought the author into print after Melville's brother, Gansevoort, then Secretary of the American Legation in London, had taken the manuscript of *Typee* to England with him in 1845. Four years later, in October 1849, Melville decided to act as his own agent and left New York for London with a view to placing *White-Jacket* with English publishers. He succeeded in selling the novel to Richard Bentley and then spent several weeks touring London and Paris before leaving Portsmouth to return to the United States on Christmas Day. On this trip, Melville also acquired a huge number of English books to take home with him: works by Ben Jonson, Beaumont and Fletcher, Samuel Butler, James Boswell, Sir Thomas Browne, Horace Walpole, Charles Lamb, Shakespeare, Marlowe, De Quincey, William Godwin, and others. He also took an opportunity to dine in Elm Court, Temple, describing in his journal how he "had a glorious time" in this "Paradise of

Batchelors" (sic).[14] The story deriving from this experience, "The Paradise of Bachelors and the Tartarus of Maids," was to appear in *Harper's* in April 1855.

Finally, in October 1856, Melville sailed from New York to Glasgow on the first leg of his voyage to the Middle East, a pilgrimage that he was to re-create imaginatively some twenty years later in *Clarel*. It was on the outward leg of this journey that he renewed his acquaintance with Hawthorne, then American Consul in Liverpool, an encounter that Hawthorne chronicled famously in his notebooks by remarking how Melville appeared to be suffering from "a morbid state of mind" and could "neither believe, nor be comfortable in his unbelief."[15] On his return trip, Melville passed through England again in April and May 1857, spending time admiring the Turner collection at the National Gallery in London before traveling north to sail home from Liverpool. On this final expedition, Melville's mood appears generally pensive and philosophical, and he ruminates in his journal on the Old World as a site of tradition and determinism. The tone is set on the initial voyage over to Glasgow, when Melville engages a passenger, one George Rankin, in a series of discussions about "fixed fate." It continues as the author wanders through Europe: he appears discomfited by the monuments of Italy ("Started for Appian Way. Narrow, – not like Milton's Way – not suitable to dignity &c.") but is more at ease among the collegial landscapes of Oxford, where he feels impelled to confess "with gratitude my mother land" and to acknowledge that he knows "nothing more fitted by mild & beautiful rebuke to chastise the sophomorean pride of Am[erica] as a new & prosperous country."[16]

Without seeking to delineate excessively causal relationships between life and art, my suggestion would be that all of Melville's texts comprise, in some fashion, travel narratives. Obviously enough, the early books which describe voyages to the South Seas involve clashes between different cultures, and it is not difficult to relate this to a cross-cultural comparativeness, predicated upon a "politics of nonidentity," in which nationalist teleologies and traditions become problematized by theoretical confrontations between different cultures.[17] This, of course, is the classic site of postcolonial criticism, with its focus upon the "join" or border that reconfigures essentialist identity as unstable hybridity: "Where, once, the transmission of national traditions was the major theme of a world literature," writes Homi Bhabha, "perhaps we can now suggest that transnational histories of migrants, the colonized, or political refugees – these border and frontier conditions – may be the terrains of world literature."[18] While this may be relatively clear in relation to Melville's earlier texts, the more difficult question concerns the ways these "dialogical or transferential" structures work their way into his later fiction. In what ways does a continuing postcolonial encounter with the British empire come to frame, indeed in some ways define, the range of Melville's artistic ambitions?

Redburn, published in 1849, constitutes in many ways the most straightforward example of cross-cultural critique. Like Melville in 1839, Wellingborough Redburn crosses the Atlantic and lands at Liverpool, where he is confronted by "a confused uproar of ballad-singers, bawling women, babies, and drunken sailors":

> But where are the old abbeys, and the York Minsters, and the lord mayors, and coronations, and the May-poles, and Fox-hunters, and Derby races, and the dukes and duchesses, and the Count d'Orsays, which, from all my reading, I had been in the habit of associating with England? Not the most distant glimpse of them was to be seen.[19]

Stereotypes are dismantled, and Liverpool comes to seem more like New York than Redburn has supposed. The same process of demystification also works in reverse: on his whirlwind visit to London, Redburn assures the anxious Englishman, Harry Bolton, that not all "Yankees lived in wigwams, and wore bear-skins." On the contrary, declares Redburn:

> New York was a civilized and enlightened town; with a large population, fine streets, fine houses, nay, plenty of omnibuses; and . . . for the most part, he would almost think himself in England; so similar to England, in essentials, was this outlandish America that haunted him.   (280)

This notion of America being "so similar to England, in essentials" is a theme that runs throughout *Redburn*. The trajectory of the narrative is not so much the linear quest as the disillusioning circle, where the protagonist ends up where he began, in the knowledge that the promised land turns out in the end to be only a chimera.

Relinquishing his fantasies of a pastoral England, Redburn is confronted instead with a statue of "four naked figures in chains . . . seated in various attitudes of humiliation and despair" at the base of a pedestal depicting Lord Nelson expiring in the arms of the goddess Victory (135). In a strategy characteristic of Melville's hybridized idiom, his narrator here begins to construct figurative analogies between different types of slavery, juxtaposing the racial discrimination familiar to him from nineteenth-century America with the social and economic slavery he sees around him in England:

> These woe-begone figures of captives are emblematic of Nelson's principal victories; but I never could look at their swarthy limbs and manacles, without being involuntarily reminded of four African slaves in the market-place.

And my thoughts would revert to Virginia and Carolina; and also to the historical fact, that the African slave-trade once constituted the principal commerce of Liverpool; and that the prosperity of the town was once supposed to have been indissolubly linked to its prosecution.   (135)

One of the tendencies Melville takes from Emerson (and later from Thomas Carlyle, whose work he reads in 1850) is an intellectual proclivity to run different objects or ideas into one another. This is the transcendental style of embracing disparate entities within one all-encompassing circle; in Melville's case, though, these mirrors of similitude lack the metaphysical idealism with which they are endowed by Emerson, and are in fact more likely to betoken the *mise-en-abîme* of fate, in which every object inescapably foreshadows the next. Thus in *Redburn*, the dominating posture of Nelson evokes the power relations of racial slavery, and this in turn is conflated in the narrator's mind with the oppressions of the class system as it manifests itself in Liverpool, whose "masses of squalid men, women, and children" (201) are bound under the yoke of British dominion. By affiliating American slavery of race with British slavery of class, Melville appears to project both of these power systems beyond the order of worldly empiricism into a realm where they become imbued with some shadowy, quasi-Calvinistic sense of fate.

Associated with this pessimism is a profound skepticism about the ways in which such power struggles become rationalized and naturalized within particular social contexts. *Mardi*, published earlier in the same year as *Redburn*, is a satirical allegory that once again uses the form of a voyage to subvert local pieties which have become reified and institutionalized through established custom. Like Swift in *Gulliver's Travels*, Melville deploys the travel narrative to diminish and ridicule the rulers who equate their own small domain with the size of the universe: "to the people of the Archipelago the map of Mardi was the map of the world."[20] Melville's extravagant tone here evokes a world of ironic pastoral, where mock paradises are no sooner glimpsed than exposed. In his quest for Yillah, the narrator keeps coming across "sweet forms of maidens like Eves in Edens ere the Fall" (549), though he recognizes that their prelapsarian status is no more valid than his own amiable inclination toward divinity: "I now perceived that I might be a god as much as I pleased" (176).

Though hard going at times, *Mardi* is a comic narrative whose effectiveness has been generally underestimated, and its burlesque possibilities are seen to good purpose in the sections specifically reflecting the political antagonisms in Europe and America. "King Bello" appears as monarch of "Dominora," England, a land dedicated to acquiring more territories;

meanwhile, at the entrance to "Vivenza," the United States, is an arch bearing the inscription: "In this republican land all men are born free and equal. . . . Except the tribe of Hamo" (512–13). Through its continually desublimating process, Melville's style works to denaturalize these established authorities, which consequently find themselves travestied and traversed by unstable zones of comic parody. Richard H. Brodhead describes *Mardi* as something like a "first draft of all [Melville's] subsequent works," and certainly it is not difficult to see how the author reworks these kinds of metaphysical conceits and figurative analogies in a more controlled way in *Moby-Dick*.[21] Here, once more, the idiom of the travel narrative trains a mobile, ironic light upon the obsessive nature of primitive beliefs. Captain Bildad's Quaker infatuation with the Scriptures, which he has been studying for thirty years, is placed alongside Queequeg's devotion to Yojo, "his black little god" (68), whose apparently infallible predictions elicit an unflattering comparison on Ishmael's part with "ants worshipping a toadstool" (81). Such chains of analogy again decenter and demystify the internal structures of belief within this fictional narrative, so that religious emblems become reduced merely to forms of crazed fetishism, akin to Ahab's futile passion for running down the white whale.

In biographical terms, the influence of English literature on the composition of *Moby-Dick* is well known. Six months after beginning to write the novel, Melville started to reconceive its shape in the light of his recent readings in Shakespeare and Thomas Carlyle. He greatly admired Shakespeare – though not, he insisted, the vacuous elitism that went along with the Bard's reputation, as indicated by "the number of the *snobs* who burn their tuns of rancid fat at his shrine."[22] Indeed, in the essay extolling the "power of blackness" in the "hither side of Hawthorne's soul," the very essay that campaigns fiercely against "literary flunkyism towards England," we find Melville seeking to reinvent Shakespeare as another exponent of "deep far-away things," with a putatively Calvinistic feeling for "dark characters" who find themselves "[t]ormented into desperation."[23] Whatever the merits of this as a critique of the English dramatist, it is not difficult to see how *Moby-Dick* appropriates Shakespeare in an attempt self-consciously to grapple with what the author takes to be universal themes. The multilayered dramatic interludes and Shakespearian soliloquies, as well as the metaphysical speculations with which the text is larded, testify to Melville's desire to overcome a cultural "anxiety of influence" by projecting his novel beyond American provincialism into the "unshored, harborless immensities" of world literature.[24]

Carlyle's *Sartor Resartus*, which first appeared in 1833–4, but which Melville borrowed from Duyckinck's library in July 1850, more specifically furnished Melville with a prototype for his playful, iconoclastic style in *Moby-Dick*. Carlyle's work, like that of Melville, establishes an inner structural dialectic between transcendence and irony, spirit and matter. Through this dialectic, philosophical inquiries into the "azure of Eternity" and the symbolic truths underlying "blind Custom" find themselves framed, if not circumscribed, by Professor Teufesldröckh's fussy discussions of clothes, editorial apparatuses, and other aspects of the familiar human world.[25] Yet Melville, like Carlyle, also takes on board the paradoxes of German Romantic irony, self-consciously manipulating his narrative stance to subvert the premises of empiricism so as to create space for an infusion of spirit into the fractured world of "the terraqueous Globe" (114). Carlyle's chapter entitled "Symbols," with its proposition that "the Universe is but one vast Symbol of God" (166), clearly prefigures Emerson's "Nature," published two years later. Of course, the thematic associations between Carlyle and Melville are less obvious than those between Carlyle and his good friend, Emerson; typically enough, Melville was unsuccessful in his attempts to meet Carlyle in England in 1849. Yet it might be argued that the style and tone of *Moby-Dick* in many ways more closely approximate Carlyle's rhetorical manner than anything that Emerson wrote. For whereas Emerson's aphoristic and ecstatic language aspires mimetically to imitate his transcendental doctrines, Carlyle and Melville both choose playfully to balance their neoplatonic idealism against the voices of imperfect narrators, narrators who can act for the reader as conduits between familiar everyday circumstances and the more abstract regions of metaphysics. Ishmael, like Teufesldröckh, helps to maintain a comic tone that Emerson's writing generally lacks.

Melville's language, then, moves chameleonically between epic and mock epic, the idealistic and the aggressively deflationary. Part of his "slithery" quality, as Lawrence describes it, consists in traducing established conventions from English literature and culture by sliding them rhetorically into new, parodic forms. Through wordplay and metaphorical analogy, Melville demystifies the cherished icons of British civilization and reconfigures them within burlesque modes. In Chapter 25 of *Moby-Dick*, for instance, the narrator talks about how the whale's sperm oil, "in its unmanufactured, unpolluted state," is used at royal coronations: "Think of that, ye loyal Britons! we whalemen supply your kings and queens with coronation stuff" (114). Again, the author uses the metamorphosing force of similitude for subversive purposes, introducing analogies which deprive petrified British customs of an authority that rests necessarily upon a suppression of their more arbitrary attributes. It is, perhaps, hardly surprising that the whole of Chapter 25, dealing with this coronation oil, was omitted by Richard

Bentley when he published the first English edition of the novel. (Melville always enjoyed tweaking the pretensions of British royalty: "long live the 'prince of whales,' " he jokes in his journal after visiting Windsor Castle on 22 November 1849.)[26] Later in *Moby-Dick*, Ishmael implicitly mocks the whole idea of the English Victorian novel through the way the mariners "humorously discourse of parlors, sofas, carpets, and fine cambrics" as they scrub the decks. This cleaning takes place after "an affair of oil," and the decks are rendered so "immaculate" that the sailors would "object not to taking tea by moonlight on the piazza of the forecastle" (428), as though they might be in a novel by Trollope or George Eliot. *Moby-Dick*, like the *Pequod* itself, is "pitched about by the most riotously perverse and cross-running seas" (221), intertextually arguing with traditional English manners but gaining much of its satirical energy and philosophical depth from a rebarbative relationship with British models. In Chapter 69, the narrator argues openly with Samuel Johnson's staunch empiricism: "Are you a believer in ghosts, my friend? There are other ghosts than the Cock-Lane one, and far deeper men than Doctor Johnson who believe in them" (309). The "ghosts" here are not just spiritual specters, but also the shades of British history and tradition by which Melville, as a Young American author, finds himself spooked.

As John Carlos Rowe notes, one of the characteristic styles in texts of the "American Renaissance" is a strategy of defamiliarization whereby "the very formlessness of American prose . . . evolves into a form in its own right." Classic American writings of this time self-consciously position themselves in a rebarbative and sometimes parodic relation to more established European genres. In this sense, there is always some circuit of commerce between "tradition and originality," Europe and America, involving a series of negotiations to which only the critical method of "comparatism" can do justice.[27] At the same time, however, Melville's peculiar capacity to hollow out the assumptions of institutionalized culture leads him to create in *Moby-Dick* a work of fiction in which the sense of interiority is, as Leo Bersani notes, almost entirely abolished. For instance, as Bersani says, the philosophical idea of homoeroticism is introduced so easily into *Moby-Dick* precisely because, in psychological terms, so little is at stake; Melville's characters, unlike those of Gide or Proust, never engage subjectively with affairs of this kind, and this is why the experience of *Moby-Dick* for the reader is often one of puzzlement and alienation.[28] Although every kind of interpretive mode is made available within the novel, they all seem to manifest themselves in a belated and inconsequential fashion: even the idea of Providence becomes a jokey, aesthetic idea, orchestrated by "those stage managers, the Fates" (7).

Bersani understands this as a paradoxical attempt on the author's part to annul the "unrelenting analogical habit" upon which *Moby-Dick*'s rhetorical manner is predicated. According to Bersani, Melville appears to suspend or frustrate every hermeneutic impulse, so that his text might aspire to a style of utopian negation in which any similarity with English prototypes becomes undermined and the novel is, quite literally, "incomparable."[29] But it is possible to look at these maneuvers in another way and to suggest that these radically demystifying analogies work self-consciously to promulgate an American cultural identity by disenfranchising the English heritage, rendering the assumptions of that tradition transparent and aesthetically visible. It is, finally, impossible in this novel to transcend the boundaries of linguistic association: every stab at originality turns out to involve reduplication; every character who would be "free as air" finds himself "down in the whole world's books" (472). Yet it is the way these famous books are renegotiated, their well-worn assumptions opened up to revisionist scrutiny, that constitutes Melville's great challenge to the canonical imperatives of British culture.

One example of how these intertextual analogies operate can be seen through Melville's relation to Milton. After analyzing Melville's annotations in his copy of Milton's poetry, Robin Sandra Grey concludes that the American author "ascribes to Milton calculated, highly self-conscious interrogations of the divine scheme that Milton cleverly and often ironically camouflages by ascribing to the character of Satan." Melville did not follow Blake in believing Milton was of the devil's party without knowing it; on the contrary, Melville reads Satan in Book 9 of *Paradise Lost* as Milton's mouthpiece, as the snake quizzes the divinity on why he keeps his worshippers "low and ignorant." "This is one of the many profound atheistical hits of Milton," concludes Melville: "A greater than Lucretius since he teaches under a masque, and makes the Devil himself a Teacher & Messiah."[30] Whatever the merits of this as literary criticism, it is highly illuminating in relation to the representation of Ahab, whose desire for revenge on the white whale is as anguished as Satan's quest in Milton's poem for vengeance against God. In this sense, *Moby-Dick* might be understood as a blasphemous reworking of *Paradise Lost*, a scenario in which the drive for revenge overwhelms any theological framework or moral restraint, connoting instead a philosophical demurral from the paths of Christian order and a transgressive flirtation with the darker powers of anarchy.

Besides censoring the section on how the ceremonial oil for royal coronations derives from the profane practices of whaling, the editor at the publishing house of Richard Bentley made a sizable number of other excisions when Melville's novel was first published in England as *The Whale* on 18 October 1851. (Melville had changed his mind about the title in September 1851, too late for Bentley, though not for Harper and Brothers in New York, which brought it out as *Moby-Dick* on 14 November.) The English edition omitted most of the supposedly indecorous references to the Bible: thus, farcically enough, "that's Christianity" became "that's the right sort," while "Providence" is recast as "those three mysterious ladies." Likewise, the "crucifixion on Ahab's face" was toned down, becoming the blander "eternal anguish in his face." Other alleged obscenities were simply omitted, including references to Nature "painting like the harlot," the "back parts, or tail" of the whale, and so on.³¹

Such editorial caution, however, failed to prevent *The Whale* from being harangued by English reviewers for its blasphemy and indecency. The anonymous contributor to *John Bull*, for instance, complained of "some heathenish, and worse than heathenish talk" in the novel, which was, he said, "calculated to give . . . serious offence." This writer was appalled that Melville "should have defaced his pages by occasional twists against revealed religion which add nothing to the interest of his story, and cannot but shock readers accustomed to a reverent treatment of whatever is associated with sacred subjects." Other English reviewers equated these moral transgressions with Melville's apparently wild and lawless rhetoric, a literary style of "eccentricity" (*Britannia*), "purposeless extravagance" (*Illustrated London News*), or "rhapsody run mad" (*Spectator*). The London *Morning Chronicle* of 20 December 1851 epitomizes this early English reception of *The Whale*, with the reviewer associating the "strange contents" of Melville's epic with its willful rejection of Anglo-Saxon empiricism. The profligate author is said to display his "old extravagance, running a perfect muck throughout the three volumes, raving and rhapsodizing in chapter after chapter – unchecked, as it would appear, by the very slightest remembrance of judgment or common sense."³²

Accusations of an aversion to judgment and common sense were also much in evidence in relation to *Pierre*, which appeared one year later. The arguments began even before the novel was published, with Richard Bentley, stung by the commercial failure of *The Whale* in Britain, offering the author a substantially lower rate for his new work and also insisting upon certain "alterations" (made either by Melville or by "a judicious literary friend") to ensure that the book would be more acceptable to English audiences.³³ Melville refused these terms, and in fact *Pierre* never found an English publisher; its pages were shipped across the Atlantic by the Harpers, and then bound and distributed within Britain by Sampson, Low, Son and Company. This circuitous approach would not have helped sales, but it is unlikely that *Pierre* would have done well in Britain anyway, since it almost entirely forgoes that "comfortable, good-humoured feeling" of roomy interiority, with its illusion of aesthetic transparency, which Henry James later associated with the theoretical *"naïveté"* of English Victorian fiction.[34] By contrast, the strategy of Melville's textual excursion involves appropriating the conventional apparatus of the English domestic novel while twisting its assumptions inside out, so that all the affective sympathy usually associated with this genre is lost. This, of course, is why readers have found it so difficult to engage with the narrative of *Pierre*; it is a cerebral performance rather than an imitation of what F. R. Leavis liked to call "felt life."

Pierre starts by parodying the ancient British convention of dedicating literary works to royalty. Just as in "old times authors were proud of the privilege of dedicating their works to Majesty," the author explains, so his own volume is proffered to "Greylock's Excellent Majesty," Greylock being "the majestic mountain . . . my own more immediate lord and king – [which] hath now, for innumerable ages, been the one grand dedicatee of the earliest rays of all the Berkshire mornings" (vii). Hershel Parker suggests some kind of link here with "Wordsworthian attitudes," and it is certainly true that oblique references to Wordsworth are to be found scattered throughout Melville's works: in the story "Cock-A-Doodle-Doo," which specifically parodies Wordsworth's "Resolution and Independence," and in *White-Jacket*, where the narrator comments sardonically on how "the business of writing verse is a very different thing on the gun-deck of a frigate, from what the gentle and sequestered Wordsworth found it at placid Rydal Mount in Westmoreland."[35] Throughout Melville's writing, we see an impulse iconoclastically to refract these inchoate aspects of American life by playing native idioms off against more seasoned models of English vintage; Melville engages with Wordsworth only to traduce ironically the English poet's paradigms of emotional attachment and empathy.

Yet Melville's intertextual dialogue with British culture is more complex than this series of oppositions might suggest. As *Pierre* demonstrates, the thematic direction involves not just antagonism but also equivalence. Only a few pages into the novel, the narrator briskly disposes of the binary opposition between "monarchical" Britain and "demagoguical" America (8) by describing how the aristocratic genealogies of England are no less circuitous and arbitrary than those of America:

In England the Peerage is kept alive by incessant restorations and creations. One man, George III, manufactured five hundred and twenty-two peers. An earldom, in abeyance for five centuries, has suddenly been assumed by some commoner, to whom it had not so much descended, as through the art of the lawyers been made flexibly to bend in that direction. For not Thames is so sinuous in his national course, not the Bridgewater Canal more artificially conducted, than blood in the veins of that winding or manufactured nobility. (10)

Through Melville's favorite trope of reversal, the nouveaux riches in Old England are contrasted with "the hundreds of unobtrusive families in New England who, nevertheless, might easily trace their uninterrupted English lineage to a time before Charles the Blade" (10). This leads the narrator to conclude with a paradoxical and sardonic flourish: "our America will make out a good general case with England in this short little matter of large estates, and long pedigrees – pedigrees I mean, wherein is no flaw" (11). *Pierre*'s narrator thus unravels the popular stereotype pitting English authenticity against American fakery, thereby constructing a heavily ironic framework for this American example of the family romance. In Victorian England, this literary genre was predicated upon recognizable forms of social stability in terms of family situations, class positions, and so on. Melville's novel, though, throws a scathing light upon these cultural and fictional conventions through its radical self-reflexivity, its skeptical consciousness of the fabricated nature of its artistic prototype. Of Lucy Tartan, for example, the narrator admits: "It is needless to say that she was a beauty; because chestnut-haired, bright-cheeked youths like Pierre Glendinning, seldom fall in love with any but a beauty" (23). In this context, it is interesting that English writer John Fowles should have nominated *Pierre* as a model for his postmodernist novel *The French Lieutenant's Woman* (1977), another highly self-conscious metafiction which both imitates and parodically critiques the premises of the Victorian novel.[36]

Yet *Pierre*, like its hero, maintains an incestuous relationship with the tradition from which it would depart. Though *Pierre* is written against the "countless tribes of common novels" (141), it still appears doomed at some level to imitate them, just as Ahab in *Moby-Dick* finds he cannot escape various forms of analogical similitude with the despotic kings of old England. One of the structural paradoxes of Melville's literary career is that his sense of originality can construct itself only through various forms of deviance whereby the author's styles of idiosyncratic transgression are pushed against the institutional constraints of cultural stability and the continuities of canonical expression. Melville's most overt treatment of American experience as intertextual process occurs in his three diptychs, linked pairs of short stories, which directly compare particular scenes in Britain and the United States. "Poor Man's Pudding and Rich Man's Crumbs" juxtaposes the conditions of the "native American poor" (296) with a description of how peasants fare under the system of aristocratic patronage in England, while "The Two Temples" compares Grace Church in New York City with the more worldly rituals of a London theater. In the best known of these diptychs, "The Paradise of Bachelors and the Tartarus of Maids," Melville constructs elaborate parallels between the Inns of Court in London, where bachelors in the legal profession enjoy rich feasts, and a snowy hamlet in New England, where "blank-looking girls" work at the paper mills.[37] The comparative method here works through contrast, of course, but this contrast depends upon prior analogies, as the narrator himself acknowledges: "Though the two objects did by no means completely correspond, yet this partial inadequacy but served to tinge the similitude not less with the vividness than the disorder of a dream" (326). Hence this juxtaposition becomes almost surreal, a mode of "inverted similitude" (327), in which conceptual matrices of heaven and hell are superimposed upon two quite different sets of circumstances, linked only by the accident of gender exclusivity. Furthermore, the image of these girls "all blankly folding blank paper" (328) seems to hint, in Melville's typically enigmatic fashion, at some kind of vacancy underlying these analogical designs of reduplication. While cognizant of the arbitrary nature of this "folding" or comparative method, the author nevertheless foregrounds such metaphorical construction of syntactic parallels as the condition of all knowledge.

All of these diptychs, turning upon an axis of similitude and difference, represent five-finger exercises for Melville's major theme of the analogical interaction between British and American cultures. But the most elaborate consideration of how national identities become "snarled" occurs in *Israel Potter*, where Melville takes a young American sailor imprisoned by the British during the War of Independence and shows how the calamities that befall him not only confuse his personal identity but also undermine the very notion of a sovereign state. After his capture, Israel is taken to England, where he finds himself so "metamorphosed . . . in all outward things, that few suspected him of being any other than an Englishman."[38] Subsequently, he meets up in Paris with Benjamin Franklin, who talks of employing Israel on a spying mission, but then doublecrosses and abandons his compatriot. As a cosmopolitan figure from the skeptical world of the Enlightenment, Franklin is portrayed as acting coolly toward Israel's more naive and romantic involvement with his native land. Israel then establishes himself as quartermaster aboard Captain

John Paul Jones's American warship, which engages in confused conflict with an English vessel, the *Serapis*:

> Never was there a fight so snarled. The intricacy of those incidents which defy the narrator's extrication, is not ill figured in that bewildering intertanglement of all the yards and anchors of the two ships, which confounded them for the time in one chaos of devastation. (120)

As these two ships find themselves "manoeuvering and chasseing to each other like partners in a cotillon" (124), Israel makes "a rush for the stranger's deck" (132), thinking he will be followed by others from the American vessel. In the melee, however, the American *Ariel* departs, leaving Israel stranded once more among the English and forced to resume his role as an impostor.

According to F. O. Matthiessen, Melville set out in *Israel Potter* "to portray the tragedy of exile," with the novel implying "how much Melville had reflected on the American character."[39] But the tragedy here, if there is one, consists in the flimsiness of this abstract idea of "American character" that Israel clings to. In this narrative, the inchoate nature of the naval battle, in which "Israel is Sailor under Two Flags, and in Three Ships, and All in One Night" (85), reflects the muddled and arbitrary status of national identity and of patriotic allegiance more generally. Though the hero remains nostalgic for his homeland, Melville's novel also implies how much Israel's mental images are generated by simple sentimentality as he becomes "bewitched by the mirage of vapors" (165) accumulating around his dreams of America. In this light, all imagined associations with particular places or countries come to seem like romantic illusions. Working in his later years as a brickmaker in London, Israel yearns for the "agile mists" climbing the "purple peaks" (165) of his old New England home, and he paints to himself "scenes of nestling happiness and plenty, in which the lowliest shared" (166). But he also unmasks his own pastoral fantasies by coming to reflect upon how slavery, considered in the term's broadest sense, should be considered as a universal rather than a merely local or political phenomenon:

> Sometimes, lading out his dough, Israel could not but bethink him of what seemed enigmatic in his fate. He whom love of country made a hater of her foes – the foreigners among whom he was now thrown – he who, a soldier and sailor, had joined to kill, burn and destroy both them and theirs – here he was at last, serving that very people as a slave, better succeeding in making their bricks than firing their ships. . . . Poor Israel! well-named – bondsman in the English Egypt. But he drowned the thought by still more recklessly spattering with his ladle: "What signifies who we be, or where we are, or

what we do?" Slap-dash! "Kings as clowns are codgers – who ain't a nobody?" Splash! "All is vanity and clay."   (157)

Israel's plaintive "who ain't a nobody?" echoes Ishmael's famous "who
aint a slave?" three years earlier. According to Carolyn L. Karcher, *Israel
Potter* signifies how "questions of national identity and patriotism that
loomed so large at the outset appear utterly irrelevant in the face of the
desperate plight Israel shares with the English working class."[40] Wherever
he goes and whichever country he affiliates himself with, Israel cannot seem
to escape the condition of thralldom. Israel's predicament is given metaphorical expression by an incident at Falmouth, on the south coast of England, when he is recognized by an American, Sergeant Singles, who
threatens to expose him as a traitor to both the English and the American
causes. At this moment, the hapless exile finds himself "doubly hunted by
the thought, that whether as an Englishman, or whether as an American,
he would, if caught, be now equally subject to enslavement" (152). Again,
this perplexing situation functions as a microcosm of the novel's wider
pattern, in which the whole idea of loyalty to a particular nation becomes
hopelessly "snarled," lost in "bewildering intertanglement" (120).

One notion that becomes increasingly significant in Melville's later writing
is that of imposture or masquerade. It provides a subtitle for *The Confidence-Man: His Masquerade*, in which the protagonist assumes a chame-
leonic series of disguises designed to ensnare gullible passengers on a
Mississippi steamboat. It forms the basis also for the "shadowy tableau"
of "Benito Cereno," in which the representation of slavery in terms of self-
conscious acting, role playing, and disguise works to defamiliarize that cultural institution, making it appear a caricature of itself and therefore
reversible.[41] On the side of Captain Delano's ship in "Benito Cereno" hangs
a "shield-like stern-piece" comprising "a dark satyr in a mask, holding his
foot on the prostrate neck of a writhing figure, likewise masked" (49). Such
masks may connote the more impersonal aspects of power struggles within
the ubiquitous interchanges of slavery, but they also imply the ways in
which power seeks to mask or efface itself, a notion that becomes particularly obvious toward the end of this narrative. The idea of masking has
been associated by Louise J. Kaplan with modes of psychological perversion, where a series of false façades problematizes the boundaries between
external demeanor and internal consciousness, ensuring that "nothing is
ever as it first seems to be."[42] Thus the maneuvers of masquerade involve
a dislocation of fixed reference, with the more customary teleologies of
moral meaning being held in suspension. In this light, part of Melville's

challenge to Victorian cultural institutions involves a transformation of established social assumptions into elaborate masquerades. Within these shadowy realms, authority is constituted through fetishistic paraphernalia or some inward, self-gratifying perversion rather than according to any coherent ethical imperative or metaphysical sanction. By shifting attention from the signified to the signifier, Melville extends his image of the masquerade into a disconcertingly political realm, reconstituting American culture, in the broadest sense of that term, within an aesthetic framework.

Jonathan Arac emphasizes how Melville, like Hawthorne, was developing at this time a theory of art and literature as qualitatively different from the more mechanistic routines of the social realm. Within this new romantic idiom, says Arac, the ability of the imagination to reconfigure and reorder material contexts was considered paramount.[43] Yet I would argue that this aesthetic capacity in Melville never degenerates into rarefied transcendence or escapism because the author's textual personae are continually involved in intertextual engagements that open up the prospect of differences, radical alterity, between American and British cultures. In Melville's eyes, the genius of American literature lies in its belatedness, its lack of originality or authenticity, its swerving away from the traditions of English literature. Consequently, the subversive qualities of the American idiom involve the ways it parodies or intertextually revises those cultural expectations associated with the British heritage. American literature, in other words, aestheticizes British literature, works to disenfranchise its moral underpinnings, while turning its conventions into forms of elaborate masquerade; consequently, British literature is made different by the advent of American culture, which opens up an alternative agenda, a world elsewhere. Similarly, by a reciprocal movement, this intertextual relationship with the Old World serves to aestheticize American culture itself, to reconceive social and political institutions in the United States as fluid and even chimerical phenomena, informed by the romantic lights of the imagination rather than by any kind of empirical or scientific knowledge. In this way, Melville's comparative style works to justify his aesthetic expenditures; it is these processes of cross-cultural mirroring that most revealingly backlight the strange and artificial masks endemic to any given set of social customs.

The culmination of these cross-cultural perspectives manifests itself in *Billy Budd*, Melville's last work, a narrative whose specific engagement with British culture has not sufficiently been recognized. All the main characters in this story are English, and, as the long historical prologue makes clear, the context for this tale is the revolutionary climate of the late eighteenth century. Billy Budd finds himself transferred symbolically from America to Britain, from a ship called the *Rights-of-Man* to one by the name of *Bellipotent*, whose martial echo recalls "King Bello," the allegorical King of England in Melville's *Mardi* some forty years earlier. Captain Vere's own name, meanwhile, is appropriated from Andrew Marvell's poem "Upon Appleton House," a panegyric to the English country house:

> Within this sober frame expect
> Work of no foreign architect . . .
> But all things are composed here
> Like Nature, orderly and near . . .
> This 'tis to have been from the first
> In a domestic heaven nursed,
> Under the discipline severe
> Of Fairfax, and the starry Vere.[44]

In keeping with this xenophobic outlook ("no foreign architect"), Melville's Captain Vere is said to be deeply perturbed about "the disruption of forms going on across the Channel," and he sees in the Nore Mutiny which threatened the British Navy in 1797 a disturbing memento of the French Revolution, akin to "the distempering irruption of contagious fever in a frame constitutionally sound."[45]

Several critics have taken the fictional narrative that unfolds within this framework to indicate the growing conservatism of Melville's later years, his discomfort with the violence that accompanies insurrection, his preference for the stable society advocated by Edmund Burke rather than the doctrine of individual rights put forward by Thomas Paine. Many of the earlier critical essays on *Billy Budd*, in fact, address themselves to the imponderable question of whether or not Vere was right to hang Billy, whether the tale should be seen as a reactionary endorsement of legal formalism or a liberal critique of its authoritarian assumptions. As Brook Thomas observes, however, this question has been framed in the wrong way. Rather than seeing Vere as tragic hero or nefarious hypocrite, it makes more sense to consider the internal logic through which different systems of government operate and the ways in which the structural indeterminacy of Melville's narrative exposes law as an ambiguous and historically contingent process.[46] Justice in *Billy Budd* is acted out according to ideological directives; it does not reflect abstract or divine truths. This is why the story is subtitled *An Inside Narrative*: it deliberately plays with discrepancies between outward appearance and inward psychology, between the façade of authority Captain Vere must maintain and the subterranean tensions that comprise "the inner life of one particular ship" (54). Hence, of course, the motif of secrecy and concealment that runs throughout this narrative. Claggart's "ferreting genius," obviously enough, involves an ability to manipulate "wires of underground influence" (67); but the "secret currency" (65) circulating around Claggart is mirrored and validated by a sequence of images that envisions the ship's world as a multilayered and opaque phenomenon: the narrator talks of the ship's "levels" as "so like the tiered galleries in a coal mine" (122), where what happens on one level is not necessarily evident to those on another plane. "War looks but to the frontage, the appearance," remarks Vere a little earlier (112), thereby implying those events behind the scenes to which he turns a British naval commander's highly trained blind eye.

There are several levels on which these tensions between blindness and insight in *Billy Budd* operate. The most obvious of these latent discourses involves repressed sexuality. Sexual attraction here becomes fictionally refracted into forms of disciplinary authority, with Billy perfectly cast in the role of masochistic innocent, not only unable to fathom Claggart's motives but even incapable of responding vocally to his charges; instead, Billy can only stand helpless, "like one impaled and gagged" (98).[47] Taking up these disjunctions between "frontage" and rear sight, Eve Kosofsky Sedgwick's reading of *Billy Budd* projects this "queer" interpretation into the domain of Captain Vere's own relationship with the young hero, pointing out how "Vere's supposedly impartial motivations toward Billy Budd are also founded on a Claggart-like partiality as against which, however, they as well are imperiously counterpoised."[48] Upon his first sight of Billy, for instance, the Captain "had congratulated Lieutenant Ratcliffe upon his good fortune in lighting on such a fine specimen of the genus homo, who in the nude might have posed for a statue of young Adam before the Fall" (94); and he subsequently recommends to the executive officer that Billy be promoted "to a place that would more frequently bring him under his own observation, namely, the captaincy of the mizzentop, replacing there in the starboard watch a man not so young whom partly for that reason he deemed less fitted for the post" (95). The rhetorical tone here strategically reflects the duplicitous cast of Melville's narrative in which eminently respectable façades cover, but can never quite conceal, more compulsive motivations.

This is why the court martial and eventual execution of Billy are appropriately cast as elaborate theatrical performances. Vere takes care at the trial to position himself visibly above the other officers, and he skillfully suppresses his own affective involvement as Billy is publicly hanged, a moment at which the Captain's "phallogocentric" authority is consummated: he "stood erectly rigid as a musket in the ship-armorer's rack" (124). Vere's admitted rationale – to others and perhaps to himself – is that he represents no more than an agent of that "martial law operating through us" (110), the impersonal system of justice through which good order is maintained in the British Navy. Yet Melville's text involves a reappraisal of this legal framework according to what is described in Chapter 11 as a kind of negative Calvinist theology, negative in the sense that it involves a Calvinist cultural urge to rip the protective veil off established social hierarchies, even if the specifically religious justifications for such iconoclasm are no longer seen as tenable:

> In a list of definitions included in the authentic translation of Plato, a list attributed to him, occurs this: "Natural Depravity: a depravity according to nature," a definition which, though savoring of Calvinism, by no means involves Calvin's dogma as to total mankind. Evidently its intent makes it applicable but to individuals. . . . Civilization, especially if of the austerer sort, is auspicious to it. It folds itself in the mantle of respectability. It has certain negative virtues serving as silent auxiliaries. (75–6)

Throughout this story, various kinds of "depravity" fold themselves "in the mantle of respectability," creating a narrative structure that oscillates uneasily between a familiar logic of social discourse and the more impenetrable conditions of absence and silence.

This negative Calvinism, along with the sexual subtexts, has the effect of defamiliarizing and radically undermining the fictions of British justice which *Billy Budd* recounts. Writing under the austere influence of Schopenhauer, his favorite philosopher during the last decade of his life, Melville in this story represents British justice as a kind of masquerade, an affective charade which manages to invest itself with an idea of impersonal truth. In a tone more fatalistic than oppositional, he implies how the visible emblems and external rituals of this culture depend upon a suppression of libidinal investments and psychopathological forms of deviance, as well as upon a positivistic rejection of the more obscure enigmas of metaphysical inquiry. *Billy Budd*, in fact, takes British culture and demystifies its assumptions in the light of American cultural perspectives. As such, it makes a fitting conclusion to a literary career in which Melville was continually reconfiguring British models within an American idiom. The multiple reports that conclude *Billy Budd* – the newspaper account in *News from the Mediterranean*, the elegiac poem from the foretopman – once again operate to dislocate the central narrative, to reposition it within the ironic framework of what Barbara Johnson calls the text's "snowballing of tale-telling."[49] It is noticeable how *News from the Mediterranean*, a British publication, circulates the fiction that Billy Budd was a foreigner: "though mustered into the service under an English name the assassin was no Englishman, but one of those aliens adopting English cognomens." Claggart, by contrast, is represented as a loyal servant of His Majesty, thereby re-futing, "if refutation were needed, that peevish saying attributed to the late Dr. Johnson, that patriotism is the last refuge of a scoundrel" (130). In this conventional kind of reportage, insurrection becomes associated automat-ically with what is foreign or alien. Melville's skill, though, lies in framing the plot of this novel within a matrix of estrangement, holding up the customs of English authority to the dark glass of comparative conscious-ness.

This is not to suggest that such comparative consciousness locates issues of "imperial" authority simply within an English context, any more than it associates the idea of America exclusively with aspects of "private con-science" (111). Indeed, Chapter 21 of *Billy Budd* mentions the similar case of "the U.S. brig-of-war *Somers*," where the American Captain Mackenzie put down a prankish rebellion led by Philip Spencer, son of the U.S. Sec-retary of War. Spencer was hanged in accordance with what is described here as "the so-called Articles of War, Articles modeled upon the English Mutiny Act" (113). There is a longer discussion of this affair in *White-Jacket*, but Melville's comparative method is designed not just to contrast reified notions of different national situations but also to demonstrate how they complicate and interpenetrate each other's local autonomy and iden-tity. In this instance, the author indicates how draconian methods of mar-tial law found their way into the American Navy through the influence of English models. Hence the projection of *Billy Budd* into a British milieu fulfills one of the traditional responsibilities of comparative literary per-spectives: to shed light back on the text's culture of origin. By reconstruct-ing an imaginary version of British authority, Melville creates a virtual space to reflect upon the growth and development of American culture.

From a British perspective, similarly, Melville's "riotously perverse and cross-running seas" effectively fragment established conventions into a du-plicitous world of reflection where they come to appear disconcertingly bizarre while at the same time oddly familiar, as in some crazy-mirror hall. Melville's imaginative genius lies in his capacity radically to estrange re-ceived ideas, to re-create ethical and political categories within a danger-ously unstable aesthetic mode. Just as *Pierre* involves an unbalanced parody of the English genre of feudal property and familial propriety, *Billy Budd* reimagines British justice as a self-gratifying phenomenon, an objectification of imaginative desires rather than a statement of more substantial truths. It is hardly surprising that Joseph Conrad, a typically conservative convert to English values, should have criticized *Moby-Dick* for having "not a sin-gle sincere line in the 3 vols of it"; indeed, a general reluctance within twentieth-century British culture to engage with the more disorienting aspects of modernism in general is one of the pressures that has worked to marginalize Melville's influence within this sphere.[50] The author's ultimate achievement, however, was to reject separatisms and homologies of all kinds, and to forge a style of comparative cosmopolitanism in which different cultures interact analogically with each other without ever being collapsed into the objects of some synthesized or monocular vision. In *Moby-Dick*, Ishmael records how the two eyes of the whale are so far apart that it "must see one distinct picture on this side, and another distinct picture on that side" (330), and he goes on to record his admiration for the "comprehensive, combining, and subtle" brain of the whale, which enables it to "examine two distinct prospects" simultaneously (331). It is an image which epitomizes Melville's traversal of cultural space across the North Atlantic divide, space intersected by the "snarled" and intertwined cables of similarity and difference.

NOTES

1. Myra Jehlen, Introduction, *Herman Melville: A Collection of Critical Essays*, ed. Myra Jehlen (Englewood Cliffs, N.J.: Prentice-Hall, 1994), p. 3.
2. Hershel Parker, "Historical Note," in *Moby-Dick; or, The Whale*, by Herman Melville, ed. Harrison Hayford et al. (Evanston and Chicago: Northwestern University Press and Newberry Library, 1988), p. 732. Subsequent page references to this edition appear in the text.
3. Herman Melville, *Correspondence*, ed. Lynn Horth (Evanston and Chicago: Northwestern University Press and Newberry Library, 1993), p. 724; Parker, "Historical Note," p. 739.
4. Melville, *Correspondence*, p. 764.
5. For Masefield's response, see Hershel Parker and Harrison Hayford, eds., *Moby-Dick as Doubloon: Essays and Extracts (1851–1970)* (New York: Norton, 1970), p. 124. Barrie recommends *Typee* and *Omoo* in a letter to the Dutch novelist Maarten Maartens on 20 November 1893. *Letters of J. M. Barrie*, ed. Viola Meynell (London: Peter Davies, 1942), p. 28.
6. D. H. Lawrence, *Studies in Classic American Literature* (1923; rpt. Harmondsworth: Penguin, 1971), pp. 139, 154.
7. Parker and Hayford, eds., *Moby-Dick as Doubloon*, pp. 159–60.
8. E. M. Forster, *Aspects of the Novel*, ed. Oliver Stallybrass (Harmondsworth: Penguin, 1962), pp. 130, 126, 171.
9. W. H. Auden, *The Enchafèd Flood; or, The Romantic Iconography of the Sea* (London: Faber, 1951), pp. 67, 122.
10. Parker and Hayford, eds., *Moby-Dick as Doubloon*, p. 136.
11. Herman Melville, "Hawthorne and His Mosses," in *The Piazza Tales and Other Prose Pieces, 1839–1860*, ed. Harrison Hayford et al. (Evanston and Chicago: Northwestern University Press and Newberry Library, 1987), pp. 247–8.

12. Watson G. Branch, ed., *Melville: The Critical Heritage* (London: Routledge and Kegan Paul, 1987), p. 228.

13. Lawrence Buell, "Melville and the Question of American Decolonization," *American Literature* 64 (1992): 233.

14. Herman Melville, *Journal of a Visit to London and the Continent, 1849–1850*, ed. Eleanor Melville Metcalf (London: Cohen and West, 1949), p. 68.

15. Nathaniel Hawthorne, *The English Notebooks*, ed. Randall Stewart (New York: Modern Language Association of America, 1941), p. 433.

16. Herman Melville, *Journal of a Visit to Europe and the Levant*, ed. Howard C. Horsford (Princeton: Princeton University Press, 1955), pp. 56, 209, 267.

17. Ross Posnock, "The Politics of Nonidentity: A Genealogy," *boundary 2* 19, No. 1 (Spring 1992): 37.

18. Homi K. Bhabha, *The Location of Culture* (London: Routledge, 1994), p. 12.

19. Herman Melville, *Redburn: His First Voyage*, ed. Harrison Hayford et al. (Evanston and Chicago: Northwestern University Press and Newberry Library, 1969), p. 133. Subsequent page references to this edition appear in the text.

20. Herman Melville, *Mardi, and A Voyage Thither*, ed. Harrison Hayford et al. (Evanston and Chicago: Northwestern University Press and Newberry Library, 1970), p. 176. Subsequent page references to this edition appear in the text.

21. Richard H. Brodhead, "Mardi: Creating the Creative," in Jehlen, ed., *Herman Melville*, p. 39.

22. Merrell R. Davis and William H. Gilman, eds., *The Letters of Herman Melville* (New Haven: Yale University Press, 1960), p. 79.

23. Melville, "Hawthorne and His Mosses," p. 244.

24. Jonathan Arac, *Commissioned Spirits: The Shaping of Social Motion in Dickens, Carlyle, Melville, and Hawthorne* (New Brunswick: Rutgers University Press, 1985), p. 156.

25. Thomas Carlyle, *Sartor Resartus*, ed. Kerry McSweeney and Peter Sabor (Oxford: Oxford University Press, 1987), pp. 146, 196. Subsequent page references to this edition appear in the text.

26. Melville, *Journal of a Visit to London*, p. 39.

27. John Carlos Rowe, *Through the Custom-House: Nineteenth-Century American Fiction and Modern Theory* (Baltimore: Johns Hopkins University Press, 1982), pp. 24, 193.

28. Leo Bersani, *The Culture of Redemption* (Cambridge: Harvard University Press, 1990), p. 146.

29. Ibid., p. 153.

30. Robin Sandra Grey, "Surmising the Infidel: Interpreting Melville's Annotations on Milton's Poetry," *Milton Quarterly* 26 (1992): 108.

31. William S. Ament, "Bowdler and the Whale: Some Notes on the First English and American Editions of *Moby-Dick*," *American Literature* 4 (1932): 39–46.

32. Branch, ed., *Melville: The Critical Heritage*, pp. 255, 260, 257, 288.

33. Leon Howard, "Historical Note," in *Pierre; or, The Ambiguities*, by Herman Melville, ed. Harrison Hayford et al. (Evanston and Chicago: Northwestern University Press and Newberry Library, 1971), p. 379. Subsequent references to Melville's narrative appear in the text.

34. Henry James, "The Art of Fiction" (1884), in *The House of Fiction*, ed. Leon Edel (London: Rupert Hart-Davis, 1957), p. 24.

35. Hershel Parker, "Melville and the Berkshires: Emotion-Laden Terrain, 'Reckless Sky-Assaulting Mood,' and Encroaching Wordsworthianism," in *American Literature: The New England Heritage*, ed. James Nagel and Richard Astro (New York: Garland Press, 1981), p. 65; Herman Melville, *White-Jacket; or, The World in a Man-of-War*, ed. Harrison Hayford et al. (Evanston and Chicago: Northwestern University Press and Newberry Library, 1970), p. 40.

36. Ruth Christiani Brown, "*The French Lieutenant's Woman* and *Pierre*: Echo and Answer," *Modern Fiction Studies* 31 (1985): 115–32.

37. Melville, *The Piazza Tales and Other Prose Pieces*, p. 328. Subsequent page references to these diptychs are taken from this edition and appear in the text.

38. Herman Melville, *Israel Potter: His Fifty Years of Exile*, ed. Harrison Hayford et al. (Evanston and Chicago: Northwestern University Press and Newberry Library, 1982), p. 27. Subsequent page references to this edition appear in the text.

39. F. O. Matthiessen, *American Renaissance: Art and Expression in the Age of Emerson and Whitman* (New York: Oxford University Press, 1941), pp. 491, 493.

40. Carolyn L. Karcher, *Slavery Over the Promised Land: Slavery, Race, and Violence in Melville's America* (Baton Rouge: Louisiana State University Press, 1980), p. 104.

41. Melville, *The Piazza Tales*, p. 50. Subsequent page references to Melville's narrative are taken from this edition and appear in the text.

42. Louise J. Kaplan, *Female Perversions: The Temptations of Emma Bovary* (New York: Doubleday, 1991), p. 43.

43. Jonathan Arac, "Narrative Forms," in *The Cambridge History of American Literature, Volume Two: Prose Writing, 1820–65*, ed. Sacvan Bercovitch (Cambridge: Cambridge University Press, 1995), p. 607.

44. Andrew Marvell, *The Complete Poems*, ed. Elizabeth Story Donno (Harmondsworth: Penguin, 1972), pp. 75, 98.

45. Herman Melville, *Billy Budd, Sailor (An Inside Narrative)*, ed. Harrison Hayford and Merton M. Sealts, Jr. (Chicago: University of Chicago Press, 1962), pp. 128, 55. Subsequent page references to this edition appear in the text.

46. Brook Thomas, *Cross-Examinations of Law and Literature: Cooper, Hawthorne, Stowe, and Melville* (Cambridge: Cambridge University Press, 1987), p. 212.

47. Robert K. Martin describes Billy Budd as "a sado-masochistic drama" concerned with "the sexual attraction between power and powerlessness" in *Hero, Captain, and Stranger: Male Friendship, Social Critique, and Literary Form in the Sea Novels of Herman Melville* (Chapel Hill: University of North Carolina Press, 1986), pp. 107–8.

48. Eve Kosofsky Sedgwick, *Epistemology of the Closet* (Berkeley: University of California Press, 1990), p. 109.

49. Barbara Johnson, "Melville's Fist: The Execution of Billy Budd," *Studies in Romanticism* 18 (1979): 585.

50. Frederick R. Karl, *Joseph Conrad: The Three Lives* (London: Faber, 1979), p. 615.

II

ROBERT MILDER

Melville and the Avenging Dream

It was something, I guessed, in the primal plan; something like a complex
figure in a Persian carpet. He highly approved of this image when I used it,
and he used another himself. "It's the very string," he said, "that my pearls
are strung on."

Henry James, "The Figure in the Carpet"[1]

Weary with the invariable earth, the restless sailor breaks from every
enfolding arm, and puts to sea in height of tempest that blows off shore.
But in long night-watches at the antipodes, how heavily that ocean gloom
lies in vast bales upon the deck; thinking that that very moment in his
deserted hamlet-home the household sun is high, and many a sun-eyed
maiden meridian as the sun. He curses Fate; himself he curses; his senseless
madness, which is himself. For whoso once has known this sweet
knowledge, and then fled it; in absence, to him the avenging dream will
come.

Melville, *Pierre*[2]

"He" in James's parable of authors and readers is novelist Hugh Vereker,
"I" an unnamed young critic who gives himself to deciphering what Vereker calls "the organ of life" in his work (James 234). "A triumph of
patience, of ingenuity" (James 231), Vereker's "figure in the carpet" is dis-
coverably present in his novels, and among James's objects in the story is
the professed one of rebuking a criticism that "is apt to stand off from the
intended sense of things, from such finely-attested matters, on the artist's
part, as a spirit and a form, a bias and a logic, of his own."[3] Like any
writer, James would have the critic see the text as he himself saw it, with
deference to the pressure of meaning objectified through structure and technique and with tactful reticence toward the private springs of art. Yet beneath or beyond the conscious authorial purpose that James, like Vereker,
may have inscribed in his writing are the controlling mental structures that
inscribed James himself and of which he could have been only partially

conscious. It is no secret that authors repeat themselves, tell versions of the same stories, ring changes on a constellation of themes, reenact dramatic postures, and rehearse core fantasies. In this they are instruments as much as creators of their recurring myths, and it would be problematic in some cases to decide whether the author is constructing his characteristic fable or the fable constructing the author.

There is no single unequivocal figure in any literary carpet (all reading being a matter of contextualization), yet some authorial patterns do obtrude themselves with particular force. "Melville never wrote anything but the same book, which he began again and again,"[4] Albert Camus remarked, thinking of the "unappeasable" quest announced in *Mardi*, consummated dramatically in *Moby-Dick*, subverted in *Pierre*, and laid ironically, if only temporarily, to rest in *The Confidence-Man* (Camus seems not to have known *Clarel*). A quest, certainly, but a quest for what, undertaken from what private urgencies, and repeated with what inflections of theme and tone across nearly thirty years of a career, forty-five if one counts the late poetry and *Billy Budd*?

My point of entry into Melville is the soliloquy of his seeker and some-time alter ego, Rolfe, in Part 3 of *Clarel* as he contemplates a lone palm tree (symbol of paradise) at the monastery Mar Saba deep in the Judean mountains. Like Melville, Rolfe is a physical and metaphysical adventurer, but nowhere is he closer to his creator than in the palm tree meditation that retraces Melville's experience in the Marquesas as presented in *Typee*: "the dangerous descent into the valley, the being taken as a god . . . , the bathing girls, the peaceful life, the effort to prevent escape, the escape."[5] " 'Abide, for here is peace,' " the islanders beg Rolfe, who nonetheless feels impelled to abjure "the simple joy, / And hurr[y] over the briny world away." "Renouncer!" he chides himself years later beneath Mar Saba's mystical palm:

> is it Adam's flight
> Without compulsion or the sin?
> And shall the vale avenge the slight
> By haunting thee in hours thou yet shalt win?[6]

The theme of Rolfe's soliloquy is the Fall – a lapse from innocence not through transgression but from an instinct that innocence, however appealing, is insufficient. Polynesia is nature, community, physical delight, and "simple joy," but with an emphasis upon the adjective ("simple") that fatally devalues the noun. Symbolically, Polynesia is the outward representation of what William Ellery Sedgwick called "an inward and universal phase of human experience, obtaining in individuals and peoples alike; – the phase in which life lies along the easy slopes of spontaneous, instinctive being, in which human consciousness is a simple and happy undertaking of rudimentary sensations and simple sensuous impressions." And yet, Sedgwick adds, "it is forced upon us to know that Typee is not the human thing itself."[7] If Polynesia will not do, however, Rolfe's chronic restlessness suggests that mature intellectuality also will not do. What, then, is "the human thing," and how is it to compensate us for the loss of paradise, the self-dispossessing allegiance to mind?

In framing such a question in *Typee* and later writings, Melville was offering his own version of the common Romantic reformulation of the Fall – the belief, in M. H. Abrams's words, "that man, who was once well, is now ill, and that at the core of the modern malaise lies his fragmentation, dissociation, estrangement, or (in the most highly charged of these parallel terms) 'alienation.' "[8] By the time of *Moby-Dick*, of course, Melville was saturated in Romantic myth; he had talked post-Kantian metaphysics with German-American scholar George J. Adler, read Goethe, Schiller, and Jean Paul, sampled broadly in the English Romantics (especially Coleridge and Carlyle), and listened to and read Emerson. He inhabited a transatlantic community of discourse modified in unique ways by New World possibility yet sharing as well in the philosophical tendencies that marked the transition from Enlightenment to Romantic ideas of nature, the self, and the direction of history and from Romantic to mid-Victorian ones. Melville's particular fate was to have experienced a paradise that most Romantics could only theorize about; to have fronted nature not at Walden Pond or even in the rugged Lake country of Wordsworth but on the vast Pacific; to have absorbed from his travels a free and unillusioned sense of life only later assimilated to his reading; and to have come of intellectual age at the midcentury moment when Romantic confidence in the individual and the race was shading into Victorian doubt. Add to this the special imperatives of Melville's temperament, never purged or outgrown, and one has the elements for a distinctive recasting of nineteenth-century myth.

Rolfe's soliloquy at Mar Saba ends, significantly, with a question, not a statement: "And shall the vale avenge the slight / By haunting thee in hours thou yet shall win?" A perpetual seeker himself, Melville could neither resolve this question nor dismiss it as experience and an inward deepening gave a new aspect to the journey he first elected, then found himself compelled to take. To Camus' remark that "Melville never wrote anything but the same book," one might thus append John Bryant's, "Melville never wrote the same book twice,"[9] which is as true of Melville's works rhetorically and in the peculiar turn they give his recurrent myth as Camus' is true of the myth itself. Each of his four most inclusive books (*Mardi, Moby-Dick, Pierre*, and *Clarel*) traces the figure in full, yet each adjusts its relative proportions and tonal coloring as the myth is refracted through Melville's intellectual and emotional being at the time. To address the contours of Melville's myth is thus to deal synchronically with the basic structure of his imagination and diachronically with its successive "seasons," or unfolding across biographical and historical time.

CASTING OFF

Having inaugurated his career with two fictionalized South Sea travelogues, *Typee* and *Omoo*, Melville began his third book, *Mardi*, as a "narrative of *facts*," only to feel "irked, cramped & fettered by plodding along with dull common places."[10] *Mardi* would transform itself twice before Melville was done with it, becoming first a " 'Romance of Polynesian Adventure' " (*Corr* 106), then, in response to Melville's initial soundings in "the world of mind,"[11] a philosophical anatomy surveying the range of human thought and activity but focused with mounting urgency on the problems of knowledge, good and evil, faith and doubt, and immortality that would occupy Melville throughout his career. The protagonist of the romance is the shadowy first-person narrator, Taji, who wins, then loses, a maiden named Yillah and searches for her unavailingly through the Mardian archipelago, Melville's symbol for the world. The protagonist of the anatomy is the philosopher Babbalanja, a quester of a more inward sort whose object is truth and the ideal way of life, and whose dialogues and soliloquies soon become the book's center of gravity.

Together, the narratives of Taji and Babbalanja are the symbolic and intellectual representations of a myth of severance from the source whose Christian analog is the lapse from Eden. For Taji, Yillah is less a woman than "the earthly semblance of that sweet vision, that haunted my earliest thoughts" (*M* 158). In Freudian terms Melville is invoking the "oceanic principle," or the sense of cosmic belongingness enjoyed by the ego before it "separates off an external world from itself."[12] Anomalous in Freud, who confessed to never having experienced it, this feeling is prominent in Jung, who saw "the individual psyche" as beginning "in a state of complete undifferentiated unconsciousness, a primordial wholeness that exists prior to and encompasses all opposites," and from which it necessarily detaches itself during the process of individuation. The loss of Yillah is a symbolic fall from this early paradisaical state, and the quest to recover her, projected forward in time and space, is essentially the retrograde search for a happiness located at the origins of individual and cultural life.

Though drawn from experience and imagination more than from reading in his near-contemporaries, Melville's narrative in *Mardi* recalls the archetypal Romantic myth of "the ascending circle, or spiral" (Abrams 188), which recast Christian and neo-Platonic ideas of paradise, paradise lost, and paradise regained in an account of secular history that applied both ontogenetically to the development of the self and phylogenetically to the progress of the race. In writers like Schelling and Hegel, Abrams observes, "the Christian history of the creation, fall, and redemption was translated to the realm of human consciousness as stages, or 'moments,' in its evolving knowledge," beginning with an "initial act" of severance through reflection and leading finally to a "unifying and integrative" consciousness higher than the lost innocence (Abrams 188–9). In short, the remedy for the pain of knowing was more knowing. Comparing ancient and modern poetry, Schiller called the original mode of consciousness "naive" and the contemporary one "sentimental." The naive (or natural) individual, he argued, could be "perfect" within the capacities of his "finite" being and the demands of his situation, the modern (or civilized) one only imperfect within *his*. The modern's *striving* was "infinitely preferable" for Schiller to the natural man's *attainment*, yet immersed in his transition state and feeling himself "at a disadvantage compared with one in whom nature functions in her absolute perfection," the modern could never be certain of his superiority, much less find happiness in his turbulent condition.[13] The genre of literary idyll (which would include Rolfe's sojourn in Polynesia and Taji's with Yillah) seemed to Schiller an escapist revolt designed to "lead us backwards into our childhood in order to secure to us . . . a peace which cannot last longer than the slumber of our spiritual faculties." At the same time, Schiller's notion of "greatness" as a matter of "degrees" measured against the "infinite" fullness of a distant future left the time-bound self dispossessed of paradise, bereft of God, and embarked on an arduous journey with little prospect of "that higher harmony which rewards the combatant and gratifies the conqueror."[14] Where Bunyan's pilgrim had fortified himself with Scripture and an abiding faith in God, Romantic pilgrims had only a driving but not inexhaustible energy and a dim acanonical belief that historically and cosmologically all went well. Victorian pilgrims half a century later would not even have that. They would need to live in and for the process of growth without the confidence that growth would make them happier, adjust them to the world, or earn them a heavenly reward.

Like Arnold's "Empedocles on Etna" or Tennyson's "In Memoriam," *Mardi* dramatizes the transition from the Romantic quest for knowledge and self-integration to the Victorian experience of doubt and fragmentation. In shifting his book from Taji (a naive hero of action) to Babbalanja (a modern hero of thought), Melville signals that he, too, has "cast off" innocence and can only press forward in search of some new relationship between mind and world. If the prospect exhilarated him, it also kept returning him to the same philosophical dead ends. The chapter aptly titled "Babbalanja Discourses in the Dark" is a miniature of *Mardi*'s quest, opening with a bold assertion of man's will to know, continuing through a long and futile monologue on God, fate, good and evil, and related questions of identity and moral responsibility, and ending with the wisdom that it is best to live virtuously and avoid metaphysical speculation, a wisdom Babbalanja himself is too intense to follow. Unable to resolve Babbalanja's quest intellectually or dramatically, Melville converted his character to the Christian humanism of Serenia, his Mardian paradise, in what amounted to an undisguised accommodation. Conversion was Babbalanja's alternative to despair and psychic collapse, but it was not Melville's. Scarcely launched upon his own quest, Melville, like Schiller, could identify human worth with incessant striving, heedless for the moment of his destination and of the prodigal expenditure of energies. "So, if after all these fearful, fainting trances, the verdict be, the golden haven was not gained," he wrote in defense of *Mardi*'s "chartless voyage," "yet, in bold quest thereof, better to sink in boundless deeps, than float on vulgar shoals; and give me, ye gods, an utter wreck, if wreck I do" (*M* 557).

After the more circumscribed efforts of *Redburn* and *White-Jacket*, Melville returned to this note of brave adventuring in *Moby-Dick*. In place of paradise he set the comforts and securities of the land, and in place of the Mardian archipelago the "wonder-world"[15] of the ocean and the whale. Ishmael's eulogy for Bulkington in "The Lee Shore" (Ch. 23) is a displaced celebration of his own questing impulse and of Melville's: "But as in landlessness alone resides the highest truth, shoreless, indefinite as God – so, better is it to perish in that howling infinite, than be ingloriously dashed upon the lee, even if that were safety!" (*MD* 107). As early as "The Hyena" (Ch. 49), however, Ishmael begins to recoil from the quest as he discovers that the ocean, vast and indifferent, is no congenial home to man. "Brit" (Ch. 58) extends the theme and executes what will become a characteristically Melvillian "turn," or enforced reversal from the values of the sea to those of the land:

> Consider the subtleness of the sea; how its most dreaded creatures glide under water, unapparent for the most part, and treacherously hidden beneath the loveliest tints of azure. Consider also the devilish brilliance and beauty of many of its most remorseless tribes, as the dainty embellished shape of many species of sharks. Consider, once more, the universal cannibalism of the sea;

all whose creatures prey upon each other, carrying on eternal war since the world began.

Consider all this; and then turn to the green, gentle and most docile earth; consider them both, the sea and the land; and do you not find a strange analogy to something in yourself? For as this appalling ocean surrounds the verdant land, so in the soul of man there lies one insular Tahiti, full of peace and joy, but encompassed by all the horrors of the half known life. God keep thee! Push not off from that isle, thou canst never return! (*MD* 274)

Beset like Rolfe by the avenging dream, Ishmael urges us to cling to that core of Polynesian innocence deep within us, yet he himself, in taking to sea, has let go of it forever. The quest, having begun, can only press forward in search of some as yet unimaginable harmony of self and world.

Dramatically, the quest involves sailor Ishmael's encounters with the wonders and terrors of the ocean; philosophically, it comes to center on narrator Ishmael's retrospective effort to know the whale, at once a "portentous and mysterious monster" (*MD* 7), a representative piece of nature, and a symbol for Creation and the powers that govern it. This latter action begins in "Cetology" (Ch. 32) with a seriocomic echo of Job ("What am I that I should essay to hook the nose of this leviathan?" [*MD* 136]) that allies Ishmael's hunt with Ahab's. To comprehend the whale is to subject nature to human dominion through knowledge as Ahab would subject it to human dominion through force. Yet the living whale, like the living God, will not be known. It cannot be adequately painted or sculpted; its hieroglyphic markings are undecipherable; its face (or want of face) defies physiognomical reading; and the seemingly intelligent gestures of its tail "remain wholly inexplicable" (*MD* 378). "Dissect him how I may, then, I go but skin deep," Ishmael concludes with mock exasperation: "I know him not, and never will" (*MD* 379). The world, Ishmael discovers, cannot be repossessed through the "power of organized knowing" (Abrams 189), nor can individuals heal themselves through such an effort.

Can the Fall be repaired alternatively through holistic vision? In "The Grand Armada" (Ch. 87) Ishmael penetrates the chaotic outer circles of a whale herd under attack and enters the region of "enchanted calm which they say lurks at the heart of every commotion" (*MD* 387). He has reached the generative core of Creation, nurturing and ostensibly benign. Melville himself enjoyed such moments of harmony; the " 'all' feeling," he called the sensation in a letter to Hawthorne: "You must often have felt it, lying on the grass on a warm summer's day. Your legs seem to send out shoots into the earth. Your hair feels like leaves upon your head. But what plays the mischief with the truth," he quickly added, "is that men will insist upon the universal application of a temporary feeling or opinion" (*Corr* 194).

Nowhere perhaps does Melville differ more from the Transcendentalists than in his skepticism that a fleeting sense of oneness with nature could be ground for metaphysical belief. The vision of serenity in "The Grand Armada" is not, significantly, a cosmic affirmation but a trope for the "eternal mildness of joy" (*MD* 389) located at the center of the self. This inner peace is not the "insular Tahiti" Ishmael sacrificed in going to sea, nor is it the self-completion Romantics envisioned as the culmination of the quest. Far from reunifying the world through knowledge or vision, Ishmael has learned to thrive upon limited knowledge, fitfully glimmering vision, and chronic disunity. The epistemological wall that maddens Ahab is acknowledged by Ishmael with a quizzical agnostic shrug that transforms the quest from a drive toward certitude into a picaresque intellectual travelogue – an *activity* rather than a *teleology*, and one whose indeterminacies allow for an endlessly creative play of mind upon fact.

Philosophically, Ishmael owes his tenor of being to an Absurdist acceptance of his and humanity's position as cosmic outcasts. His phrase "genial, desperado philosophy" (*MD* 226) encapsulates both his working metaphysics and his affective response to them, a despair that is giddily liberating and that joins him to the human community in shared defense against nature's indifference. By the time of "A Squeeze of the Hand" (Ch. 94), Ishmael has come around to a brotherhood of man asserted not under the fatherhood of God but in its very absence. Queequeg is a main contributor to this new secular religion, a figure of unfallen self-integration and fraternity "entirely at his ease; preserving the utmost serenity; content with own companionship; always equal to himself" (*MD* 50). Preintellectual, indeed largely prelinguistic, Queequeg is no pattern for Ishmael, but as D. H. Lawrence long ago observed he embodies a mode of being – instinctive, sensuous, affectionate – that the self-estranged Westerner needs to recover to become whole. "We can't go back to the savages: not a stride," Lawrence wrote, but "we can take a great curve in their direction, onward."[16] Ishmael's "marriage" to Queequeg is a symbolic incorporation of Polynesia – not a "return" to paradise (lost forever) but a cultivation of the inwardly paradisaical that eases the journey of the self through a broken world and nourishes the communal activity of building a future.

"HM had a mind rare of men, and . . . capable of founding a new humanitas," Charles Olson remarked.[17] Melville's response to the modern fall into knowledge propounded by Romantic theorists was not an appeal to the meliorism of history, still less a Transcendentalist summons to vision, but a conviction that the alienness of Creation must be recognized as such and that human beings, in Ishmael's words, must "eventually lower, or at least shift, [their] conceit of attainable felicity; not placing it anywhere in the intellect or the fancy; but in the wife, the heart, the bed, the table, the saddle, the fire-side, the country" (*MD* 416). This return movement from sea to land did not mean renouncing the quest so much as abating its self-destructive intensity – in a sense coopting the avenging dream by relocating the quester within the human community. The difference between Melville's "new humanitas" and Whitman's is that instead of joyously aligning itself with Creation, it was evoked by Creation's harsh indifference. What Whitman called life's "simple, compact, well-join'd scheme"[18] was for Melville "the visable [sic] truth" or "absolute condition of present things as they strike the eye of the man who fears them not" – "present things" because ultimates were unknowable and "absolute condition" because honesty allowed no prudent dissembling of the facts (*Corr* 186). Fraternalism in Melville is not only democratic *and* tragic; it is democratic *because* tragic, our common vulnerability to "the universal thump" instructing us to "rub each other's shoulder-blades, and be content" (*MD* 6).

In its jaunty, unillusioned naturalism, Ishmael's wisdom is Melville's, but it is scarcely the whole of Melville's, nor was "wisdom" always the determinant of his sensibility. So far as the quest pointed toward a salutary accommodation to life, Ishmael was its comic hero and avatar of a new consciousness, even of a redeemed social order. Melville's intellect, ethical nature, and capacity for delight all converged in Ishmael. It was the buried, nonrational part of his being that "rock[ed him] with a prouder, if a darker faith" (*MD* 497) and countered the Ishmaelean pull with an impulse toward apocalyptic confrontation ("converse") he exulted in, if perhaps only half-understood.

MAKING CONVERSE

Just before his climactic three-day encounter with Moby Dick, Ahab utters his own version of the avenging dream as he unburdens himself to Starbuck in "The Symphony":

> [W]hat a forty year's fool – fool – old fool, has old Ahab been! Why this strife of the chase? . . . Close! stand close to me, Starbuck; let me look into a human eye; it is better than to gaze into sea or sky; better than to gaze upon God. (*MD* 544)

Appealing to fatality, Ahab ends by turning away from Starbuck or so dispiriting Starbuck that the mate turns away from him; yet while Ahab seems one of those individuals destined to break himself upon the universe, he visibly glories in his defiance and feels himself transfigured by it. In his more lucid moments Ahab knows that he has crystallized the vision of a

258

mood and that a deeper fidelity to experience would mean submitting to the whole revolving cycle of moods, none of which has final authority. " 'There is no steady unretracing progress in this life,' " he soliloquizes in "The Gilder" (Ch. 114):

> we do not advance through fixed gradations, and at the last one pause: – through infancy's unconscious spell, boyhood's thoughtless faith, adolescence' doubt (the common doom), then scepticism, then disbelief, resting at last in manhood's pondering repose of If. But once gone through, we trace the round again; and are infants, boys, and men, and Ifs eternally. Where lies the final harbor, whence we unmoor no more? In what rapt ether sails the world, of which the weariest will never weary? Where is the foundling's father hidden? Our souls are like those orphans whose unwedded mothers die in bearing them: the secret of their paternity lies in their grave, and we must there to learn it. (*MD* 492)[19]

Ishmael, too, is subject to the round of ontological moods, and the progressive education that seems to culminate in the landed wisdom of "A Squeeze of the Hand" is qualified by hints that the older Ishmael returns to the sea, presumably to learn the same lessons over again.[20] The ideal community imagined aboard ship can never be actualized in historical America, nor can the lure of God and Truth be wholly exorcised. The strongest counterargument to Ishmael's "new humanitas" is that he himself is only partially and temporarily satisfied by it. The practical difference between Ishmael and Ahab is that Ahab, trapped in the warring cycle of faith and doubt, chooses to force the question by challenging the gods and making them declare themselves, if only by condescending to kill him.

In "Moby Dick" (Ch. 41), Ishmael makes Ahab's hunt a surrogate action that draws upon "the sum of all the general rage and hate felt by his whole race from Adam down" (*MD* 184). Just as Ishmael goes to sea as a stand-in for all water-gazing landsmen, Ahab plays out the cosmic resentments most humans feel but dare not express and are too sane or too prudent – too bound by the reality principle or the moral sense – to enact. Resurrected from the delirium that followed the loss of his leg, Ahab is a *post*tragic hero – a Lear returned to strength but not to serenity or a Job unreconciled by the whirlwind – and his pursuit of "an audacious, immitigable, and supernatural revenge" (*MD* 186) is an answer to the hitherto unthinkable question "What next?" Whatever process of moral disintegration Ahab may undergo during the course of *Moby-Dick*, it is crucial to remember that Melville's first allusions associate him with heroes and redeemers (Christ, Prometheus, Perseus) and that Moby Dick, as Job's whale, is identified with a principle of chaos which presides over Creation and which the

Lord himself (or his agent the Messiah) is destined to punish "with his sore, and great, and strong sword" (*MD* xviii).[21] The mythic plot of *Moby-Dick* is thus a reenactment of the "dragon-killing theme" Northrop Frye describes as the "central form of quest romance,"[22] and Ahab, who sets sail on Christmas Day, is a would-be messiah whose hunt for Moby Dick is an effort to deliver humanity from the conditions of the fallen world. Ahab's "quenchless feud" (*MD* 179) seems Ishmael's, as it seems the crew's and is meant to seem the reader's, because it taps grievances rooted deeply in the race's collective unconscious or in the universally perceived disparity between the world human beings desire and the world they inhabit.

This is the overtly metaphysical layer of Ahab's hunt; having established Ahab's representativeness, however, Ishmael proceeds to hint at a "larger, darker, deeper" (*MD* 198), and more unconscious part of his character, a "root of grandeur" buried "far beneath the fantastic towers of man's upper earth" and owing its tragic nobility to a divine disinheritance:

> So with a broken throne, the great gods mock that captive king; so like a Caryatid, he patient sits, upholding on his frozen-brow the piled entablature of the ages. Wind ye down there, ye prouder, sadder souls! question that proud, sad king! A family likeness! aye, he did beget ye, ye young exiled royalties; and from your grim sire only will the old State-secret come.
>
> (*MD* 185–6)

Ishmael's "exiled royalties" are all those who feel a lurking divinity in themselves and whose impelling motive is to answer Ahab's question "Where is the foundling's father hidden?" (*MD* 492) and discover the "State-secret" of their lineage. There is a way to disclose paternity," Charles Olson wrote of *Moby-Dick*: "declare yourself the rival of earth, air, fire, and water."[23]

"Disclosing paternity" is a theme that links several of the most cryptic passages in *Moby-Dick* and that appears in the notations Melville inscribed on the end pages of a volume of Shakespeare sometime before July 1851:

> Ego non baptizo te in nominee Patris et Filii et
> Spiritus Sancti – sed in nomine
> Diaboli. – Madness is undefinable –
> It & right reasons extremes of one.
> – Not the [*inserted later above line with caret below* (black
>   art)] Goetic but Theurgic magic –
> seeks converse with the Intelligence, Power, the
> Angel. (*MD* 970)[24]

"Ego non baptizo" are Ahab's words in "The Forge" (Ch. 113) and Melville's own in a June 1851 letter to Hawthorne describing *Moby-Dick*'s "motto (the secret one)" (*Corr* 196). Diabolism in both instances seems metaphoric and intended not so much to connote evil (black art) as to suggest a principle of opposition to the Father, the aim of which, as in theurgic magic generally, is to "open for itself a converse with the world of spirits, and win as its prerogative the power of miracle."[25] In Melville the traditional means and end of theurgic magic are reversed, as power (sourced in madness) becomes a vehicle for achieving converse itself, or compelling genealogical recognition from a Father who has absented himself from Creation and severed kinship with his children.

The overt and covert levels of Ahab's hunt interweave themselves in the tangled rhetoric of "The Candles" (Ch. 119), a chapter at once so emotionally intense and allusively opaque that Melville seems to have written it from and for himself. Sailing toward Moby Dick in the midst of a violent thunderstorm, Ahab takes hold of the lightning chains descending from the mainmast and puts himself in vital touch with the Divine:

> 'Oh! thou clear spirit of clear fire, whom on these seas I as Persian once did worship, till in the sacramental act so burned by thee, that to this hour I bear the scar; I now know thee, thou clear spirit, and I now know that thy right worship is defiance. To neither love nor reverence wilt thou be kind; and e'en for hate thou canst but kill; and all are killed. . . . Come in thy lowest form of love, and I will kneel and kiss thee; but at thy highest, come as mere supernal power, and though thou launchest navies of full-freighted worlds, there's that in here that remains indifferent. Oh, thou clear spirit, of thy fire thou madest me, and like a true child of fire, I breathe it back to thee.'
>
> (*MD* 507)

"I as Persian" is an allusion to Zoroastrianism, a dualistic religion that posited a god of goodness (Ormuzd, associated with fire) and an independent god of evil (Ahriman); "so burned by thee" recalls Ahab's "slender rod-like" white scar, compared earlier to the mark lightning makes when it sears a "great tree" (*MD* 123). Literally, Ahab is saying that he used to worship a god of putative goodness until he was struck by lightning during an act of prayer; figuratively, he is suggesting a more cumulative process in which experience gathered to confute his belief in a beneficent Creator. Zoroastrianism is Melville's means of displacing an indictment of Christian metaphysics for an audience sensitive to the slightest hint of blasphemy. In substance, Ahab is measuring the ascribed character of the biblical God against the Divinity inferable from the nature of experience. He is holding

God to the traditional religious promise and, finding Him wanting, is protesting against a "supernal power" unsanctified by justice or love. From one point of view, Ahab is Satanic; from another, he represents the last and fullest flowering of the Christian tradition, which now in its Victorian twilight turns against itself and, in the name of Christian values, calls God to account for not governing like God and destroys itself in a climactic gesture of immolation.

But if Ahab is a rebel against fallen Creation, he is also, more profoundly, an outcast son "agonized over paternity," as Olson said of Melville himself.[26] Responding to the flashes of lightning he interprets as a divine answer, Ahab continues:

'Oh, thou magnanimous! now do I glory in my genealogy. But thou art but my fiery father; my sweet mother, I know not. . . . There lies my puzzle; but thine is greater. Thou knowest not how came ye, hence callest thyself unbegotten; certainly knowest not thy beginning, hence callest thyself unbegun. I know that of me, which thou knowest not of thyself, oh, thou omnipotent. There is some unsuffusing thing beyond thee, thou clear spirit, to whom all thy eternity is but time, all thy creativeness mechanical. Through thee, thy flaming self, my scorched eyes do dimly see it. Oh, thou foundling fire, thou hermit immemorial, thou too hast thy incommunicable riddle, thy unparticipated grief. Here again with haughty agony, I read my sire. Leap! leap up, and lick the sky! I leap with thee; I burn with thee; would fain be welded with thee; defyingly I worship thee!'   (MD 508)

Ahab's new and still more arcane context is Gnosticism, which Melville knew from Pierre Bayle's *Historical and Critical Dictionary* and perhaps from Andrews Norton's *Evidences of the Genuinesss of the Gospels* (1844), and in which he found a dualism consonant figuratively with his own. "The scheme of the Gnostics," Norton observed, was in part "a crude attempt to solve the existence of evil in the world." What separated the Gnostics from other heretical sects was their determined opposition to the Old Testament, whose God they found morally repugnant and at odds with the spirit of the four Gospels. Rejecting the orthodox Christian account of evil, the Gnostics distinguished between the spiritual principle in the universe, or Supreme Being, and the Creator of the material world, who governed nature "in the belief that he [was] himself the Supreme God." Although the Creator was less a malignant power than a blind, mechanical one, he tyrannized over the spiritual life of humanity with an oppressiveness that prompted the hope of a redeemer. The Leviathan of Job, who ruled as "a king over the children of pride" (Job 41: 34), was an agent of the

Gnostic Creator; the Old Testament Jehovah was the Creator himself; and Jesus was an emissary from the Supreme Being sent not only to slay Leviathan but to announce the dethronement of the mechanical God by the spiritual one.[27]

Gnosticism's appeal for Melville as an organizing cosmological metaphor and a lodestone for feelings of protest lay in its recognition of a radically fallen world whose "imperfections and evils," in Norton's words, ". . . could not be the work of a good and omnipotent Being, but bore evident marks of an imperfect maker."[28] In *Clarel* Melville's pilgrims debate the dualistic character of experience with reference to both Zoroastrianism and Gnosticism, associating the wicked God Ahriman with Jehovah and setting the New Testament God against the Old ("Jehovah was construed to be / Author of evil, yea, its god; / And Christ divine his contrary" [C 3,5: 41–3]).

The god Ahab addresses in "The Candles" is a version of the Gnostic Creator, a "mechanical" power (MD 508) ignorant of his origin and allied to two other representations of mindless divinity in *Moby-Dick* – the great whale itself, "dumbly lowering with the doom of boats, and ships, and men" (MD 346), and the *Pequod*'s carpenter, whose "impersonal stolidity . . . so shaded off into the surrounding infinite of things, that it seemed one with the general stolidity discernible in the whole visible world" (MD 467). Glimpsing, but only "dimly," some power beyond the spirit of the fire, Ahab is a would-be believer who shares the Gnostics' sense of a fallen world but is denied access to their transcendent vision. For Ahab the only manifest God is the Creator, a Father who, however imperfect, made him from his divine fire and is the source of the exiled royalty he feels in himself. What Ahab craves at bottom is not vengeance so much as recognition or union, and his means are like those of a child ignored by a remote parent who goads and provokes until the parent is exasperated into an act of intimate violence.

A despair at ever winning such recognition underlies Ahab's expression of the avenging dream in "The Symphony"; denied converse with the divine, Ahab is powerfully drawn toward the compensatory satisfactions of the human. The chapter illustrates a special form of the tragic *anagnorisis* – not the "adequate moral recognition"[29] that F. O. Matthiessen found wanting in the unrepentant Ahab, but the hero's understanding of "the determined shape of the life he has created for himself, with an implicit comparison with the uncreated potential life he has forsaken."[30] In showing us Ahab's torment, Melville is not simply heightening the pathos of his story in preparation for the final catastrophe; he is contrasting two kinds of lives, the unremittingly spiritual (Ahab's) and the domestically moral

(Starbuck's), and underscoring the emotional costs of Ahab's choice. For a time, it appears as if Ahab has indeed been "a forty years' fool," but the vindication withheld by the Father's silence is earned by Ahab himself through the transfiguring medium of grief. "Dragged into Stubb's boat with blood-shot, blinded eyes" after the first day's chase (*MD* 551), Ahab, an image of defeat, is metamorphosed by the very intensity of his woe into an image of human godlikeness. "In an instant's compass," Melville writes in a visible endorsement of Ahab's exaltation,

> great hearts sometimes condense to one deep pang, the sum total of those shallow pains kindly diffused through feebler men's whole lives. And so, such hearts, though summary in each one suffering; still, if the gods decree it, in their life-time aggregate a whole age of woe, wholly made up of instantaneous intensities; for even in their pointless centres, those noble natures contain the entire circumferences of inferior souls. (*MD* 552)

The relationship of Ishmael to Ahab, and of both to Melville himself, is perhaps best revealed by a passage from the "visable truth" letter Melville wrote Hawthorne in the spring of 1851 in response to *The House of the Seven Gables*:

> We think that into no recorded mind has the intense feeling of the visable [*sic*] truth ever entered more deeply than into this man's. By visable [*sic*] truth, we mean the apprehension of the absolute condition of present things as they strike the eye of the man who fears them not, though they do their worst to him, – the man who, like Russia or the British Empire, declares himself a sovereign nature (in himself) amid the powers of heaven, hell, and earth. He may perish; but so long as he exists he insists on treating with all Powers upon an equal basis. If any of those Powers choose to withhold certain secrets, let them; that does not impair my sovereignty in myself; that does not make me tributary. And perhaps, after all, there *is* no secret. We incline to think that the Problem of the Universe is like the Freemason's mighty secret, so terrible to all children. It turns out, at last, to consist in a triangle, a mallet, and an apron, – nothing more! We incline to think that God himself cannot explain His own secrets, and that He would like a little information upon certain points Himself. We mortals astonish Him as much as He us. But it is this *Being* of the matter; there lies the knot with which we choke ourselves. As soon as you say *Me*, a *God*, a *Nature*, so soon you jump off from your stool and hang from the beam. Yes, that word is the hangman. Take God out of the dictionary, and you would have Him in the street. (*Corr* 186)

Writing nominally of Hawthorne, Melville is eulogizing himself, and his reference quickly slips from "Hawthorne" to the "sovereign nature" to "myself" and "me." Equally important, the ontological world of the passage undergoes a concurrent change. Through some logic of emotional escalation, the "visable truth" (a condition) is transformed first into a set of "present things" possessed of agency (they may "do their worst" to the man of courage), then into the quasi-objective "powers of heaven, hell, and earth" amid which the "sovereign nature" stands, and finally into an array of haughty, personified "Powers" with whom (not which) the "sovereign nature" treats "upon an equal basis." Phrase by phrase, the naturalistic world of the "visable truth" is transformed into a refractory, deified one that allows Melville to register his own godlikeness through opposition to it. As the urgencies of his nature vent themselves in rhetoric, however, his mind tips back toward sanity (the Ishmaelean pole) and the world again seems an empty collection of objects, governed (if governed at all) by a divinity as phlegmatic as the Gnostic Creator. Yet "God" is a problem that cannot be waived by a temperament shaped and held by the old religious vocabulary. The words "*Me, a God, a Nature*" may be linguistic traps, but they are traps Melville cannot long avoid because the *need* for God, if not the belief in him, is inscribed deeply and permanently in his being.

The oscillations of the "visable truth" letter will be a constant in Melville's work to the very end. On some level the hunger for "converse" with the absent Father is almost certainly a transposition of the young Melville's feeling of abandonment by his actual father – Allan Melvill having died when Herman was twelve. "An unresolved experience of bereavement"[31] seems a likely source for the pathos that belongs to Melville's vision of cosmic orphanhood, but "bereavement" must be broadened to include desolateness, frustration, anger, and a driving compulsion to justify oneself before the only arbiter that matters. To "make converse" is not finally to protest against or symbolically avenge the conditions of life, though this is the cognitive idiom it assumes; it is to assert one's filial godlikeness in the doubt-ridden modern world, in which, as Schiller said, "the relative worth of a man" is "never determinable."

THE AVENGING DREAM

Pierre recasts the Melvillean myth of "converse" in its hero's dream of the Titan Enceladus, the incestuous product of Heaven and Earth who assaults the sky to reclaim his divine patrimony. Fashioned from Pierre's remembrance of a mountain scene – an enormous half-buried rock that seemed to "writh[e] from out the imprisoning earth," an armless trunk, as if it would storm the "majestic mount" about it (*P* 345) – the dream combines Ishmael's image of the "captive king" with the tableau of Ahab challenging the heavens in "The Candles." Dismemberment (implicitly sexual), impotence, exile, and paternal disinheritance are the motifs in both books, whose heroes are justified not by success but by ceaseless and outwardly futile aspiration. "For it is according to eternal fitness," Melville writes in *Pierre*, "that the precipitated Titan should still seek to regain his paternal birthright even by fierce escalade. Wherefore whoso storms the sky gives best proof he came from thither! But whatso crawls in the moat before that crystal fort, shows it was born within that slime, and there forever will abide" (*P* 347).

If *Pierre* reaffirms the heroic temper, it does so only after a relentless questioning in which Melville lays bare not only his hero's pretensions to greatness but his own. In *Mardi* and *Moby-Dick* the avenging dream had chided the folly of sacrificing happiness to truth; in *Pierre* Melville interrogates the very truthfulness of "truth" and the purity of the motives for seeking it. The book is Melville's deconstruction of the Ahabian element in himself, performed with a self-lacerating irony born, it would seem, from a psychospiritual shock even deeper than Melville's possible discovery that his father may have sired an illegitimate child.[32]

Sexuality, specifically incest, is Melville's vehicle for exposing the psychic clay that taints even the most apparently selfless actions, but it would be a mistake to see Melville's unmasking of the heroic as stemming from a narrowly sexual view of human character. What attracts Pierre to his half-sister Isabel is the aura of melancholy that seems to spiritualize her beauty and hint of a larger, deeper, more mysterious, and infinitely more alluring world than the daylight one associated with his aptly named fiancée, Lucy. Isabel is an anima figure, an externalization of Pierre's own undeveloped self beckoning him to explore the spiritual world and, through the "selectest chamberlains to knowledge," "Gloom and Grief" (*P* 169), to realize his nature. Orphaned by the discovery of his father's adultery and his mother's heartless conventionalism, Pierre casts off from the known world to live (so he imagines) for God – the perfect heavenly Father replacing the now-fallen earthly one. The irony is that beneath the endless layers of casuistry and rationalization that gild his behavior Pierre is essentially pursuing a glorified image of himself.

Melville leads Pierre step by step to the same frustrations his earlier questers had met, but as Pierre is younger and more quixotically high-minded and the narrative voice more distant and coolly analytic, the process has the painfulness of spiritual exposé, as if Melville were looking at the hero, and through him at his recently outgrown self, from underneath. Pierre is no match for the epistemological ambiguities that assail him, let alone for the psychic revelation that acquaints him with his hidden sexual motives. As the quest becomes increasingly problematic for Pierre, so does its opposite, everyday happiness, embodied in a Lucy who reenters the narrative and shows a surprising strength and wisdom. Is truth to be found, after all, in the cheerful and healthy – the despised "ordinary" – rather than in the alluringly sad, the quasi-transcendent? The question cuts to the heart of Melville's own commitments since *Mardi*, so that in dissecting Pierre's grand enthusiastic resolution to champion Isabel (and thereby God) against the world, it is with a terrible sense that the avenging dream may not be the obligatory price one pays for intellectual maturation but a self-inflicted punishment that overtakes the spiritual poseur impatient with common life:

> There is a dark, mad mystery in some human hearts, which, sometimes, during the tyranny of a usurper mood, leads them to be all eagerness to cast off the most intense beloved bond, as a hindrance to the attainment of whatever transcendental object that usurper mood so tyrannically suggests. . . .
>
> Weary with the invariable earth, the restless sailor breaks from every enfolding arm, and puts to sea in height of tempest that blows off shore. But in long night-watches at the antipodes, how heavily that ocean gloom lies in vast bales upon the deck; thinking that that very moment in his deserted hamlet-home the household sun is high, and many a sun-eyed maiden meridian as the sun. He curses Fate; himself he curses; his senseless madness, which is himself. For whoso once has known this sweet knowledge, and then fled it; in absence, to him the avenging dream will come.   (P 180–1)

Twelve books later, when Pierre himself arrives at this point, he confronts what Melville calls the "hardest" lesson: that the quester who has renounced happiness for truth finds himself not only exiled from the social world (the mother) but "likewise despise[d]" by the gods (the father), who "own him not of their clan" (P 296). At work on his book – a *Bildungsroman* that replicates Melville's own intellectual journey – Pierre begins to feel himself an orphaned "toddler . . . toddling entirely alone" (P 296). Though unacknowledged by the gods, Ahab is never "despised" by them or patronized by the author. The note of diminishment in *Pierre* is a function not of divine remoteness or of the futility of the quest (continuing themes in Melville's work) but of a sudden corrosive skepticism toward the nature and value of aspiration.

Whatever the inciting source in Melville's life or thought, the theme of the gods' contempt – essentially, of the quester's own self-contempt – was disturbing enough for him to return to it thirty-odd years later in his poem "Timoleon," an adaptation of Plutarch's story of the Corinthian soldier and statesman who kills his tyrant-brother Timophanes, ruler of the city, and discovers himself "Estranged through one transcendent deed"[33] from the citizenry at large and from his proud, strong-willed mother, Timophanes's champion. Where Plutarch dwelt on Timoleon's return from voluntary exile to deliver Corinth from the Carthaginians, Melville focuses on the inner drama of one who believes he hears a "mandate" to action "peremptory from the skies" (ll. 96–7). In the climactic stanza, having sacrificed temporal happiness to duty, Timoleon feels himself abandoned by the spiritual father-world on which he has staked his life, and like Pierre he carries his quarrel to the "Arch Principals" of the universe (1. 151). In his bitter reaction to divine silence, Pierre comes to suspect that "Virtue and Vice" are but "two shadows cast from one nothing" (P 274); so does Timoleon, who, in a desperate thrust toward converse, pleads with the gods to signal their existence and thereby to justify his:

> O, tell at last,
> Are earnest natures staggering here
> But fatherless shadows from no substance cast?
> Yea, *are* ye gods? Then ye, 'tis ye
> Should show what touch of tie ye may,
> Since ye, too, if not wrung are wronged
> By grievous misconception of your sway.
> But deign, some little sign be given –
> Low thunder in your tranquil skies;
> Me reassure, nor let me be
> Like a lone dog that for a master cries. (ll. 163–73)

Receiving no answer, Timoleon eventually earns the praise of his countrymen as Corinth's savior, but the question goes unresolved whether glory belatedly won shows the vindication of "high Providence" or merely the workings of "Chance" (1. 19). The poem is a loose allegory of Melville's life and career and seems particularly applicable to the sense of betrayal he may have felt during the winter of 1851–2 as the reviews of *Moby-Dick* (largely mixed and underappreciative) began to appear. It has been suggested that Melville recast *Pierre* at this time, using his book to vent his exasperations as a writer.[34] This may be true so far as his digressions on authorship are concerned; but the obtuseness or hostility of a middlebrow audience was virtually to be expected, and it could be defiantly borne so long as Melville, like Pierre, was able to feel "a higher support" (P 296) – to imagine himself, along with Hawthorne "and some others, forming a chain of God's posts" around the world and enduring the large and small trials of their position with the consciousness of belonging to an elect fraternity (*Corr* 195).

It was the loss of this internal prop more than the philistinism of his readership that was responsible for the sardonic tone that controls even the earliest books of *Pierre*. Indeed, rather than a primary cause of Melville's subversion of the heroic, the hostility of his audience served ultimately as a counter to it, rekindling Melville's sense of embattlement and inaugurating what amounted to a new phase of his myth. Viv-à-vis the gods and his own truth-telling earnestness, Pierre (retracing Melville's journey) enters ever more ambiguous and ego-dissolving regions: "For the more and the more that he wrote, and the deeper and the deeper that he dived, Pierre saw the everlasting elusiveness of Truth; the universal lurking insincerity of even the greatest and purest written thoughts. Like knavish cards, the leaves of all great books were covertly packed. He was but packing one set the more; and that a very poor jaded set and pack indeed. So that there was nothing he more spurned, than his own aspirations; nothing he more abhorred than the loftiest part of himself" (P 339). At this very nadir, however – the point at which Melville seems to have begun his book and to which he apparently meant to lead its hero – the paths of character and author unexpectedly crisscross. The "universal Blearedness and Besottedness" (P 339) that demoralizes Pierre rouses Melville himself to an emphatic reassertion of self-worth evidenced in the emerging rhetoric of Titanism. The meaning of Pierre's Enceladus dream, opaque to Pierre but not to his creator, is that heaven storming is itself deifying, however foredoomed to failure and however flawed the quester. The mark of Melvillean greatness is no longer converse with the gods (an exploded fantasy) but an aspiration whose vaulting point is resistance to the mediocrity of earth. The avenging dream has thus itself been avenged through a purely internal measure of divinity that can accommodate both the jeers of society and the indifference of the gods, the repudiation by the mother *and* the silence of the father. By the end of *Pierre*, even as his hero stumbles bewilderedly to his death, Melville has exorcised a heroism that sought the transcendent; he has begun to understand that the more authentic greatness is that of the "soul-toddler," whose challenge is to be mother and father, earth and heaven, to himself.

LIVING AS A GOD

By the time of *Clarel*, Melville's soul-toddler had grown into a god. Depth, earnestness, candor, generosity, and genial humor were the marks of this figure likened by Melville to the Indian hero-god Rama, whose trial was never to recognize and exult in his divinity but to suffer it as a peculiar psychic birthmark and live "vainly puzzled at the wrong / Misplacing him in human lot" (C 1, 32: 3–4). Rolfe is the Rama of *Clarel*, a descendant of Babbalanja and Ishmael but differenced from them by a ripe maturity and, reflecting the breadth of Melville's thinking after his trip to Europe and the Near East in 1856–7, by a historical understanding that contextualized the Romantic quest within two thousand years of Western history.

It is hard to overestimate the importance of Melville's travels in initiating what would become a second growth. "Forego the state / Of local minds inveterate" (C 1, 1: 96–7), Clarel is advised by an American in Palestine. So Melville did in regarding Palestine, Egypt, classical Greece, and Renaissance Italy, judging first for himself, then later through the lens of writers like Matthew Arnold, who set the Christian hope of immortality within the larger framework of European thought, with pagan naturalism at one end and scientific naturalism at the other. The world of *Clarel* is the harshly beautiful world of *Moby-Dick* (desert replacing ocean) infused with a historicism like that of "Stanzas From the Grande Chartreuse" or (especially) "Obermann Once More," Arnold's verse outline of a civilization borne up, then abandoned by "That gracious Child, that thorn-crown'd Man."[35] The dialogues in *Clarel* echo Arnold's feeling of God-bereftness, but where Arnold hoped to save Christianity, even if he could not literally believe in it, Melville, like Henry Adams or Yeats, looks grimly ahead to a brutish materialism symbolized by some "shapeless birth" that will command society's devotional energies (C 3: 5, 81). To live as a god in such a world is neither to confront the traditional gods, as Ahab sought to do, nor to oppose the gods of the earth, as Melville did at the end of *Pierre*; it is to immerse oneself in history and labor to shape a viable creed for a post-Christian age.

The titular hero of *Clarel*, a young American divinity student in the Holy Land, is not a dedicated quester like Melville's earlier protagonists but a virginal idealist who would happily be delivered from the need to quest. In the early cantos Clarel is flanked by two beckoning figures: an apostate Catholic (Celio) who challenges him to follow his own example and "brave / All questions on that primal ground / Laid bare by faith's retreating wave" (C 1, 19: 27–9) and a young Jewish girl (Ruth) who promises to silence all questions through love and domestic content. Ruth is the Yillah of *Clarel*, a seeming "legate to insure / That Paradise is possible / Now as hereafter," and yet, "deeper viewed," a being with something "amiss" in her hinting of the fragility of paradise (C 1, 16: 161–3, 171). Clarel intuits this but would submerge his perplexities in "solacement of mate" (C 1, 2: 8), the beloved functioning as an ontological bulwark, much as Arnold's female auditor does in "Dover Beach." Clarel is not permitted the consolation of love, however; Ruth's father is murdered, the house is temporarily closed according to Jewish custom, and Clarel is drawn by circumstance to join a group of pilgrims journeying through the Judean wilderness.

To enter the desert is equivalent to going to sea ("Sands immense / Impart the oceanic sense" [C 2, 11: 37–8]) but with a heightened feeling of proximity to the divine, for this is the ground of sacred history, the very home of the Old Testament God, "direful yet holy – blest tho' banned" (C 2, 11: 89). "Is the desolation of the land the result of the fatal embrace of the Deity?" Melville asked in his journal.[36] Or does the scorched, blasted terrain argue the absence of a Deity? And which, after all, is more appalling – a God "visaged in significance / Of settled anger terrible" (C 2, 11: 70 –1) or no God at all? Part 2 of *Clarel* reenacts the mythic phase of discovery in *Mardi* and *Moby-Dick* as it explores the face of nature and God and conducts the pilgrims through the desert to the Tartarean Dead Sea, the geographical and spiritual low point of the journey. In *Moby-Dick* the occasional rainbow hinted at the possible harmonization of light and color, the divine and the earthly; Part 2 of *Clarel* closes aptly with a "fog-bow" appearing in "silence . . . from behind the veil" – "colorless," wispy, "half-spent," and ephemeral – "A thing of heaven, and yet how frail," hovering for a time, paling away, then vanishing altogether (v. C 2, 39: 149–61).

The pilgrims who wonder at the fog-bow comprise "an Anacharis Clootz deputation," if not from "all the ends of the earth," as in *Moby-Dick* (MD 121), then surely from all points of the philosophical and psychological spectrum. If a grim, tormented character like Mortmain recalls Ahab and Arnold's Empedocles – his very name suggesting the "dead hand" of the past – others look prophetically ahead to the range of late-nineteenth- and twentieth-century spiritual types: the Hawthornesque Vine to Pater and the darker aesthetics, the liberal cleric Derwent to diluted, benevolist Protestantism, the embittered Southern reactionary Ungar to Henry James's Basil Ransom (and Agrarian poet-critic John Crowe Ransom), and Clarel himself to Thomas Mann's young quester in *The Magic Mountain*, Hans Castorp. The vitality of the characters is remarkable given the terse, stylized poetic idiom they are made to speak, which is more pliant in revealing the movement of thought and feeling and the tensions between characters than all but the very best of Melville's prose.

The psychologism of *Clarel* is more than a technical advance; it belongs to the poem's effort to explore not merely the substance of belief but its origins in temperament and experience, its moods and waverings, and its consequences for behavior. Melville writes with distance as a connoisseur of life philosophies yet also with deep commitment, measuring his characters by a standard of earnestness and intent on justifying a quest that can have no end, receive no adequate recognition from society, and bring little satisfaction to the quester himself. The opening lines of Part 3 ("Mar Saba") raise the matter directly when they ask what supernal reward may accrue to "tried and ransomed natures" (C 3, 1: 3). Mortmain calls religion " 'man's appeal from fellow-clay' " and cites the " 'Tibetan faith' " in which " 'death emancipates the good, / Absorbs them into deity, / Dropping the wicked into bestialhood' " (C 3, 3: 55, 57–9). But heavenly reward in *Clarel* is as problematic as heavenly converse in *Moby-Dick*; the post-Christian pilgrim must find his vindication in human time or do without.

In *Mardi*, *Moby-Dick*, and *Pierre* the avenging dream called up an earlier happiness the quester had forgone; in *Clarel* (besides Rolfe's nostalgia for the South Seas) it presents itself as a standing temptation the quester must continually resist. The special form the dream took at this point in Melville's career was a heightened responsiveness to sensuous pleasure, prompted in large part by his travels in the more relaxed, non-Protestant cultures of the Mediterranean. In his journal of 1856–7 Melville set the starkness of the desert against the fleshpots of Cairo: "The booths & cafes. Leapers, tumblers, jugglers, smokers, dancers, horses, swings, (with bells) sherbert, &c. Lovely at evening. In morning, golden sun through foliage. Soft luxurious splendor of mornings. Dewy. Paridise [sic] melted & poured into the air" (J 77). In *Clarel* this languorous hedonism is associated chiefly with latter-day Greeks, who inherit the joyous paganism of classical times without the philosophical severity or the elevating discipline of form. The Greeks of Syra struck Melville in precisely this way even before he came upon the distinction between Hebraism and Hellenism developed in Germany by Schiller and the Schlegels and popularized for an Anglo-American audience by Arnold in *Culture and Anarchy*. Arnold's Hellenism is a valuable aesthetic counterweight to a civilization blindly devoted to moral and mechanical ends; Melville's, rather differently and more in keeping with its Germanic sources, is an open sensualism alluring in the young but shallow and apt to turn coarse in later life as the moral nature fails to develop. The rose is Melville's symbol for secular hedonism, the cross for aspiring spirituality. The rosy young Cypriote singing of the pleasures of " 'care-killing wine' " in " 'funeral Siddim' " (C 3, 4: 3, 23) is a figure of such prepossessingly good nature and animal health that the pilgrims can only wish him prosperity in his creed and exemption from the sobering trials of maturity. Far less attractive is the merchant from Lesbos who presides over the revels at Mar Saba and typifies "the older Hellenes" who (in Shirley M. Dettlaff's words) "have deliberately and thus reprehensibly prolonged their moral childhood" by turning their gaze from evil, suffering, sin, and death, and from all Judea represents.[37]

Positioned between the Hebraic and the Hellenic, the overly strenuous and the dissipated, Clarel can only wonder at "such counter natures in mankind" and question whether "in frames of thought / And feeling, there

be right and wrong" (C 3, 21: 39, 33–4). Schiller saw these "counter natures" as incomplete and needing "to be synthesized to produce the fully
human person," as they could be and occasionally were " 'in a few rare
individuals who . . . always existed and always will.' "[38] Melville is more
critical of Hellenism, largely because the question of how to live did not,
for him, mean accommodating himself to the natural so much as striving
to be divine, whatever *that* might mean in a world without visible divinity.
Although balance is a requirement of the Rama figure, the litmus tests of
character in *Clarel* are earnestness and integrity, even to the point of a
tolerant but firm dismissal of trifling indulgence. Rolfe's own geniality, unlike the Lesbian merchant's, *comports with* his earnestness; it is not, at its
highest, a relief from thought so much as a fraternalization of it reminiscent
of Melville's nights of brandy and cigars with Hawthorne and later celebrated in his poem "The Age of the Antonines," where revelers "reasoned
of fate at the flowing feast, / Nor stifled the fluent thought."

If Rolfe is more driven than the Antonine philosophers, it is because he
lives after, not before, an age of faith and is burdened with a hunger for
the divine they could not have known. "Earnest" is the word used pre-
eminently for Rolfe, often by himself in irony or mock disgust, as if conscious that his intensity bordered on the ridiculous or uncompanionable in
a world that most took easily enough. Like Melville himself, as Hawthorne
described him, Rolfe "can neither believe nor be comfortable in his unbelief; and he is too honest and courageous not to try to do one or the other.
If he were a religious man, he would be one of the most truly religious and
reverential; he has a very high and noble nature, and [is] better worth
immortality than most of us."[39] The achievement of Rolfe is not simply to
strike a balance between earnestness and amiability but to sustain a kind
of fideistic agnosticism that burns with the will to know while resisting
appeals to closure that would slight the facts of suffering and evil (liberal
meliorism), demean human nature (scientific materialism), or abridge one's
intellectual independence (Catholic orthodoxy). Rolfe's godlikeness has
nothing immediately to do with finding or worshipping God, still less with
defying Him; it represents the deification of the human personality that
comes from living searchingly and without illusion under the extraordinary
pressures of spiritual life, among them the proscription that keeps the
seeker from ever knowing his divinity.

Clarel's fate, if he can rise to it, is to mature into Rolfe. He would not
do so willingly. Rolfe unsettles him with the incisiveness of his questionings
and the frankness of his manner. Clarel would prefer to submit to Derwent
or Vine – to the former for philosophical reassurance, to the latter for an
intimacy that dissolves matters of doubt in personal union. But Vine rebuffs

him, and Derwent's decorous optimism seems increasingly shallow and eva-
sive. In the end Clarel looks to Ruth for deliverance, but Ruth and the
paradise she represents are dead, just as Yillah was dead for Taji, and
Clarel's destiny – humanity's, Melville implies – is to travel the Via Crucis
as best he can, shouldering his doubt and perhaps, like Rolfe, maturing
under its burden.

Although *Clarel* takes the form of a search for God, its deepest concern
is with the nature and destiny of man. Melville has not given over the divine
so much as he has accepted its unknowability and turned his mind to be-
haviors that are deifying or degrading. The old opposition between "ape
and angel" has been severely "aggravate[d]" in what he calls "Darwin's
year" (C 4, 35: 12, 14, 1), but its enduring significance is as a metaphor
for competing earthly and heavenly orientations. "The running battle of
the star and clod / Shall run forever – if there be no God" (C 4, 35: 16–
17) – that is to say, if doubt proves to be a permanent condition and
humans are left to define themselves by choice in a silent world. In *Moby-
Dick* and *Pierre* the hero sought his apotheosis through fealty (however
inverted) to the Divine. The triumph of *Clarel* is to reassert man's godlikeness in the practical absence of the divine, and to do so with a quiet,
unassuming dignity at once humble in aspect and regally proud.

More, perhaps, than any corpus in English except Shakespeare's, Melville's
writing traces the four seasonal phases of myth Northrop Frye ascribes to
the organizing structure of Western literature: the mythos of Summer (romance), of Autumn (tragedy), of Winter (irony), and of Spring (comedy).[40]
Mardi is Melville's romance, *Moby-Dick* his high tragedy, *Pierre* his ironic
tragedy, and *Clarel* his month-of-March comedy. "Comedy" may seem the
last word to use for an exhaustive meditation on declining faith set in the
Judean desert, yet so far as *Clarel* dramatizes the shedding of an old cultural
skin and the painful but prophetic birth of the modern, it looks ahead, as
comedy does, to the advent of a new order.

This is not to say that *Clarel* represents a final word or that the avenging
dream has been laid to rest. In "The Bench of Boors" from *Timoleon* (1891;
the composition of the poem cannot be precisely dated) Melville asks
whether the drowsy, beer-soaked peasants in Tenier's painting are not better adjusted to life than his sleepless, thought-burdened speaker. Yet the
poem is immediately followed by another, "The Enthusiast," whose epigraph is borrowed from a line Melville checked in Job ("THOUGH HE
SLAY ME YET WILL I TRUST IN HIM"), and whose concluding words
reaffirm the aspiring spirit: "Though light forsake thee, never fall / From
fealty to light." "The running battle of the star and clod" never ceased to

run for Melville, but neither was his allegiance ever in serious doubt. "Keep true to the dreams of thy youth," he wrote on a scrap of paper pasted beside his writing desk in his last years.[41] The triumph of *"the spirit above the dust"* (C 4, 35: 11) did not depend for Melville wholly on an afterlife; it was a condition of being he savored inwardly during life itself, obscure as he was in his old age and uncertain, like Rolfe, whether he was a god or an over-earnest pretender. Polynesia – the avenging dream at its most seductive – never faded from his imagination, but neither did it control his assignments of value. Heavenly aspiration and creaturely content were rival centers generating the mythic shape of his work, but with a bias always toward the heavenly. The figure in his carpet is thus surprisingly constant – virtually foreordained – in its essential shape. What changes across the forty-five years of his literary career are the relative proportions of the figure, its lights and colors, its affective tone, and its philosophical depth of field. Above all, it is a *living* figure, caged, it is true, in the permanent confines of his imagination yet struggling within them, in some sense against them, resolved never to yield to the clod, however much at times Melville might doubt the luminousness of the star.

NOTES

1. Henry James, "The Figure in the Carpet," *The Novels and Tales of Henry James* (New York: Scribner's, 1909), XV, pp. 240–1.
2. Herman Melville, *Pierre*, ed. Harrison Hayford et al. (Evanston and Chicago: Northwestern Univ. Press and The Newberry Library, 1971), pp. 180–1. Subsequent references to *Pierre* are included in the text and abbreviated P.
3. James, Preface, *Novels and Tales*, XV, p. xvi.
4. Albert Camus, "Herman Melville," *Lyrical and Critical*, trans. Philip Thody (London: Hamish Hamilton, 1967), p. 206.
5. Walter E. Bezanson, "Discussions," in Melville, *Clarel: A Poem and Pilgrimage in the Holy Land*, ed. Harrison Hayford et al. (Evanston and Chicago: Northwestern Univ. Press and The Newberry Library, 1991), p. 817.
6. *Clarel* (Northwestern–Newberry Edition), Part 3, canto 29: 11. 68, 74–9. Subsequent references to *Clarel* are included in the text, abbreviated C, and identified by part, canto, and lines.
7. William Ellery Sedgwick, *Herman Melville: The Tragedy of Mind* (Cambridge, Mass.: Harvard Univ. Press, 1944), pp. 27–8, 30.
8. M. H. Abrams, *Natural Supernaturalism* (New York: Norton, 1971), p. 145. Subsequent references to *Natural Supernaturalism* are included in the text. I cite Abrams's account of Romanticism not for its authoritativeness, which has been questioned, but for its pertinence as a gloss on Melville, whose imagination was deeply tinged with what Jerome McGann calls "the Romantic ideology." See McGann, *The Romantic Ideology* (Chicago: Univ. of Chicago Press, 1983).

9. John Bryant, "Herman Melville: A Prospective," *Melville Society Extracts*, No. 88 (1992), 11.

10. Melville, *Correspondence*, ed. Lynn Horth (Evanston and Chicago: Northwestern Univ. Press and The Newberry Library, 1993), p. 106. Subsequent references to this volume are included in the text and abbreviated *Corr*.

11. Melville, *Mardi and A Voyage Thither*, ed. Harrison Hayford et al. (Evanston and Chicago: Northwestern Univ. Press and The Newberry Library, 1970), p. 557. Subsequent references to this volume are included in the text and abbreviated *M*.

12. Freud, *Civilization and Its Discontents*, trans. James Strachey (New York: Norton, 1962), pp. 15, 12; Martin Bickman, *The Unsounded Centre: Jungian Studies in American Romanticism* (Chapel Hill: Univ. of North Carolina Press, 1980), p. 39.

13. Friedrich von Schiller, *"Naive and Sentimental Poetry" and "On the Sublime,"* trans. Julius A. Elias (New York: Ungar, 1966), p. 113.

14. Ibid., p. 163.

15. Melville, *Moby-Dick, or The Whale*, ed. Harrison Hayford et al. (Evanston and Chicago: Northwestern Univ. Press and The Newberry Library, 1988), p. 7. Subsequent references to this volume are included in the text and abbreviated *MD*.

16. D. H. Lawrence, *Studies in Classic American Literature* (1923; rpt. New York: Viking, 1961), p. 137.

17. Charles Olson to Merton M. Sealts, Jr., quoted in Sealts, *Pursuing Melville* (Madison: Univ. of Wisconsin Press, 1982), p. 104.

18. Walt Whitman, "Crossing Brooklyn Ferry," *Leaves of Grass*, ed. Sculley Bradley and Harold W. Blodgett (New York: Norton, 1973), l. 7.

19. Until recently, editions of *Moby-Dick* mistakenly ascribed Ahab's words to Ishmael. The error arose from the absence of quotation marks surrounding the passage in the 1851 American and English editions of *Moby-Dick*, and it was repeated in all subsequent printings until the Northwestern–Newberry edition of 1988.

20. For example, the will Ishmael draws up in "The Hyena" after realizing the precariousness of his life in nature is the "fourth" will of his "nautical life" (*MD* 227); others may have followed. Paul Brodtkorb, Jr., suggestively explores Ishmael's oscillation between land and sea in *Ishmael's White World* (New Haven: Yale Univ. Press, 1965).

21. Isaiah, 27:1. Melville establishes the Scriptural context for Ahab's quest by including the verse from Isaiah as the last of the five biblical quotations at the beginning of his prefatory "Extracts" (*MD* xviii). The Oxford Annotated Bible identifies the Leviathan of Job as "not an ordinary crocodile, but the sea-monster ... which was associated with chaos" (Revised Standard Edition [New York: Oxford Univ. Press, 1962], p. 653). Derived from the ancient myths and scriptures that preceded the Old Testament, Leviathan has analogues in most of the important mythologies of the world; it is a variant of those primeval dragons or sea monsters which preside over Creation – sometimes with the sanction of God, as in Job; sometimes in opposition to God, as in *Beowulf* – and which the hero sets out to slay as champion of captive humanity. On Leviathan, see James Hastings, ed., "Demons and Spirits," *En-*

cyclopaedia of Religion and Ethics (New York: Scribners, 1908–26), IV, p. 598.

22. Frye, Anatomy of Criticism (Princeton: Princeton Univ. Press, 1957), p. 189. This paragraph draws upon material from my essay "Nemo Contra Deum. . . . : Melville and Goethe's Demonic," in Ruined Eden of the Present, ed. G. R. Thompson and Virgil L. Lokke (West Lafayette, Ind.: Purdue Univ. Press, 1981), pp. 219–20.

23. Charles Olson, Call Me Ishmael: A Study of Melville (San Francisco: City Lights Books, 1947), p. 85.

24. The Northwestern–Newberry Edition of Moby-Dick accurately transcribes Melville's entries and provides a helpful scholarly gloss (MD 955–70).

25. R. A. Vaughan, Hours with the Mystics (London: Strahan, 1880), p. 46.

26. Olson, Call Me Ishmael, p. 82.

27. Andrews Norton, The Evidences of the Genuineness of the Gospels (Cambridge, Mass., 1844), II, p. 57; Hastings, Encyclopaedia of Religion and Ethics, VI, p. 236. Thomas Vargish explores Melville's knowledge and use of Gnosticism in "Gnostic Mythos in Moby-Dick," PMLA, 81 (1966), 272–7.

28. Norton, Evidences, III, pp. 46–7.

29. F. O. Matthiessen, American Renaissance (New York: Oxford Univ. Press, 1941), p. 456.

30. This definition of anagnorisis is Northrop Frye's. Frye, Anatomy of Criticism, p. 212.

31. Neal L. Tolchin, Mourning, Gender, and Creativity in the Art of Herman Melville (New Haven: Yale Univ. Press, 1988), p. 5.

32. See Amy Puett Emmers, "Melville's Closet Skeleton: A New Letter About the Illegitimacy Incident in Pierre," in Studies in the American Renaissance, 1977 (Boston: Twayne, 1978), pp. 339–42; and Henry A. Murray, Harvey Myerson, and Eugene Taylor, "Allan Melvill's By-Blow," Melville Society Extracts, 61 (1985), 1–6. Reviewing the evidence, Hershel Parker concludes that "there is, as of now, no way of knowing" whether Allan Melvill "father[ed] this particular child" (Herman Melville, Vol. I, 1819–1851 [Baltimore: Johns Hopkins Univ. Press, 1996]), p. 65.

33. "Timoleon," Collected Poems, ed. Howard P. Vincent (Chicago: Packard/ Hendricks House, 1949), 1, 142. All subsequent references to the poems cite the texts in this edition.

34. See Hershel Parker, "Why Pierre Went Wrong," Studies in the Novel, 8 (1976), 7–23; and Brian Higgins and Parker, "The Flawed Grandeur of Melville's Pierre," New Perspectives on Melville, ed. Faith Pullin (Edinburgh: Univ. of Edinburgh Press, 1978), pp. 162–96.

35. Matthew Arnold, "Obermann Once More," Poetry and Criticism of Matthew Arnold, ed. A. Dwight Culler (Boston: Houghton Mifflin, 1961), l. 167. For Melville's debt to Arnold, recorded in marginalia and reflected in Clarel, see Walter E. Bezanson, "Melville's Reading of Arnold's Poetry," PMLA, 69 (1954), 365–91.

36. Melville, Journals, ed. Howard C. Horsford with Lynn Horth (Northwestern Univ. Press and The Newberry Library, 1989), p. 91. Subsequent references to this volume are included in the text and abbreviated J.

37. See Shirley M. Dettlaff, " 'Counter-Natures in Mankind': Hebraism and Hel-

lenism in *Clarel*," *Melville's Evermoving Dawn: Centennial Essays*, ed. John Bryant and Robert Milder (Kent, Ohio: Kent State Univ. Press, 1997), p. 199. My discussion in these pages is indebted to Dettlaff's admirable essay.

38. Dettlaff, " 'Counter-Natures,' " p. 195.
39. Nathaniel Hawthorne, *English Notebooks*, quoted in Jay Leyda, *The Melville Log: A Documentary Life of Herman Melville, 1819–1891* (1951), 2 vols. (New York: Gordian Press, 1969), II, p. 429.
40. See Frye, *Anatomy of Criticism*, pp. 131–239.
41. Eleanor Melville Metcalf, *Herman Melville: Cycle and Epicycle* (Cambridge: Harvard Univ. Press, 1953), p. 284.

ANDREW DELBANCO

AFTERWORD

We have arrived at a contemplative moment in our relation with the least containable or, to use Melville's own image, most Vesuvian of classic American writers. One sign of this reflective mood is that each contributor to this book takes seriously the word "companion" in its title – a word at odds with the sort of performative criticism in which the literary text becomes a stage upon which the critic feels entitled, even required, to mount a show.

The Cambridge Companion to Herman Melville, by contrast, is conceived and written in a spirit of deference to, though hardly uncritical reverence for, its subject. We hope the result is a book worth consulting, disputing, and – if it does its job – soon supplanting. One reason a work of this sort may be useful at the present time is that the conditions for thinking about Melville have changed substantially from what they were even a decade ago. Seven years past the centenary of his death, virtually all his writings, including his letters and journals, have now reached print (or are soon to be published) in the Newberry Library–Northwestern University Press edition, which is justly recognized as one of the monuments of modern textual scholarship. At the same time, virtually everything known or knowable about Melville's thinly documented life has been assembled in large new biographies by Laurie Robertson-Lorant and Hershel Parker; and whatever details have not made it into these books will soon appear in raw form in the expanded *Melville Log*. Barring the discovery of another cache of papers such as the family correspondence that came to light in 1983 (now in the New York Public Library), it seems unlikely that we shall learn much more than we already know about his habits and experiences. And given the scarcity of surviving manuscripts, it seems equally unlikely that future editors will make more than minor adjustments in the texts in which he transformed these experiences into art.

These conditions call for a stock-taking moment, and the contributors to this volume have tried to comply. As befits an end-of-a-century work, there are notes of prophecy in this book – in Lawrence Buell's suggestion, for instance, that Melville's long, forbidding poem, *Clarel*, may yet strike the ear of some strong poet who, by acknowledging it as a forebear, could carry it out of obscurity into the living canon. There are also retrospective refinements of established critical opinion – as in Paul Giles's remark that, for Melville, the "mirrors of similitude," which the romantics found throughout nature, "lack the metaphysical idealism with which they are endowed by Emerson, and are in fact more likely to betoken the *mise-en-abîme* of fate, where every object inescapably foreshadows the next."

Although they range widely in topic and theme, all the essays in this book dissent from prevailing dogmas – from such mutually exclusive claims as that Melville was a champion of democracy or an enemy of egalitarianism, that he was an abolitionist at heart or a reluctant Unionist, that his turn from prose to poetry marks a falling off or an artistic fulfillment. The Melville we meet here is a roving pilgrim for whom, as Jenny Franchot puts it, there is "no endpoint of spiritual conviction or final disillusionment." In his hopeful moods, he can be a bracing version of Emerson's "man thinking." But in his dark moments, he is Enceladus – the figure whom he calls, in *Pierre*, "the most potent of all the giants, writhing from out the imprisoning earth."

Given the sad fact that at the end of our century racial strife remains a pressing and ominous American problem, it is no surprise that it is in those essays that take up the theme of race that this questing figure emerges most vividly – notably in Sterling Stuckey's demonstration of how deeply Melville's work was marked by his awareness of African American music and dance, which he may have witnessed as a boy wandering out onto Broadway or as a young man prowling Manhattan. Performing the rare feat of reading the much-read *Moby-Dick* in a way both fresh and persuasive, Stuckey shows how, in such chapters as "Midnight, Forecastle," Melville captured *"in the process of their formation,* music and dance that are now emblematic of American culture." And Stuckey goes on to show how the great novella "Benito Cereno" becomes a coded celebration of the genius of the mutinous slaves even as it registers Melville's revulsion at their vengeance.

Melville used the word "race" (as in the famous apostrophe to America's manifest destiny in *White-Jacket*, where he proclaims that "God has predestinated, mankind expects, great things from our race") without any implication that nature has divided the human species into superior and inferior variants. He seems to have thought of race as a synonym for what we would call culture – a set of historically evolved, and still evolving, instincts, habits, and manners that function as norms by which a group designates its membership and transmits, with inevitable loss, its collective memory from generation to generation. On the question of whether this evolution is teleological in the Hegelian sense (there are moments, as in the patriotic paean in *White-Jacket*, when Melville seems to think so) or an unsupervised process of chance (as Darwin was to describe it in nature soon after Melville's major works appeared), he seems to have been more or less agnostic. What he was sure of was that the outward marks by which human beings organize themselves into ranks and cadres have an arbitrary significance, that they are cultural inscriptions rather than expressions of some inner essence of the self. But he also knew that without such markers, most human beings would find themselves lost in an illegible world. And so, "rather than dismiss contemporary beliefs about race, nation, and self," as Samuel Otter puts it in his essay on the early fiction, Melville "acknowledges his attraction to these beliefs and probes their sources and power."

This was a writer, in other words, who found his own culture both indefensible and indispensable – a paradox that explains why his rage against established doctrines rarely overwhelms his prudence. "Conservative" is much too blunt a word for describing him, but there is a part of him (smaller than the corresponding part in his friend Nathaniel Hawthorne) that withholds the last measure of contempt from his own culture, no matter how contemptible he may find it. He has sometimes been mistaken for a radical despiser of culture or as a writer culpably friendly toward established power. One of the virtues of *The Cambridge Companion* is that it declines to traffic in such caricatures. It gives us, instead, a writer whose mood is better described – to use Melville's own exquisite phrase – as "the pondering repose of If."

If Melville's inward struggle between acquiescence and revolt is revealed with particular clarity in the essays on race, it stands as well at the center of Robert K. Martin's chapter on the similarly charged theme of sexuality. Writing about Tommo's desertion of a whaling ship in *Typee*, Martin remarks that "stepping out of the culture, abandoning ship, means opening the possibility of discovering a new sexual freedom and a new taxonomy of desire, but it also means losing the landmarks that guide our 'natural' responses." Melville took this leap in his fiction and probably in his life, and he wrote about "stepping out" with an excitement that both shocked and titillated the readers of his time. But it should not be forgotten that his most fearless seekers – Bulkington, Ahab – are swallowed by the sea upon which they dare to venture.

Melville was, in short, an artist of what he called, in the subtitle of *Pierre*, "the ambiguities." He knew, as Wyn Kelley suggests in her essay on *Pierre*, that the institution of family, by which the instinctual life is contained and channeled, can be both a sanctuary from and an incubator of the worst human passions. This is the Melville who punctures the smugness of all reformers by asking, "with what quill did the Secretary of the Society for the Suppression of Cruelty to Ganders formerly indite his circulars," but who is also outraged by the condition of the poor and likens all who live unchastened by their misery – without exempting himself – to "people sitting up with a corpse, and making merry in the house of the dead." It is impertinent, if not impossible, to read the Liverpool chapters of *Redburn* or the great story "Bartleby, the Scrivener" without feeling ashamed of our collective insouciance.

But if *The Cambridge Companion* is to claim and hold more than a few specialist readers, it must be more than just another sampler of critical opinion about a self-contradictory writer. It must disclose to us a Melville of contemporary salience and urgency. And so, I think, it does. Poised between rage at the ways of the world and caution at the prospect of revising it, he died in obscurity near the end of a century when American intellectuals were just beginning to acknowledge the frightful symmetry between the savagery and creativity of their civilization. Today he commands many more readers than he attracted during his lifetime. He seems remarkably prescient of our time – when the Enlightenment promise of progress, in some respects impressively fulfilled, has been answered by equally powerful evidence that the human capacity for cruelty always exceeds its previous attainments, especially when pressed into the service of perfectionist ideals. Melville knew these dualities. He dramatized them in such masterworks as *Moby-Dick* and "Benito Cereno," where men reveal themselves as both bestial and heroic under conditions in which the distinction between vengeance and justice is lost in the passion of rage.

These works, among many others, furnish reasons that anyone even faintly alert to history will recognize in Melville's art a prophetic mirror of our waning century. Is there in our literature a study of demagoguery more profound than *Moby-Dick*? Is there a meditation more searching than "Bartleby, the Scrivener" on how a corporate society diffuses responsibility, turning it from an obligation felt by the accountable self into an elusive abstraction we evade or disclaim? To readers of his own time, Melville seemed excessively "metaphysical" in his treatment of such moral questions. Apparently, he wrote too rudely for prevailing taste. But to readers of our time, for many of whom the pieties with which he clashed have become vacant or quaint, he strikes us as a contemporary – because if we imagine him transported into our own murderous century, he seems equipped to witness it without surprise.

To sum up the distinctive quality highlighted in this book, let me propose as the occasion for a brief coda a famous remark by Melville's contemporary Ralph Waldo Emerson. By force of contrast, it is a remark that tells us something about what made Melville unwelcome in his own time and something about what draws us to him now. "The invariable mark of wisdom," Emerson wrote in *Nature* (1836), "is to see the miraculous in the common." Despite his impatience with Emerson's sometimes relentless geniality, Melville shared Emerson's conviction that most of us walk through the days and years of our lives with clogged senses, unmoved by the manifold miracle of creation. In some moods, Melville is an Emersonian preacher of sensory and spiritual awakening. But this hortatory writer is not the one who stands at the common core of the essays that make up this *Companion*.

The Melville we meet here, if I may tamper with Emerson's phrase, is one who believes that a mark of wisdom is to see the *ridiculous* in the common. He is the Melville who invites us, in the opening chapters of *Moby-Dick*, to watch the education of a nervous boy as he goes to bed with a cannibal, and finds himself uncertain the next morning about whether it is better to wash one's face or chest, or put one's boots on first or last, or pray to the Christian God rather than to a wooden idol set up between the andirons of their shared fireplace. This is the seriously mischievous Melville who points out that gentlemen and ladies who shudder at the vulgarities of whaling are glad to light their lamps with whale oil and to stretch their skirts over whalebone hoops. He is the writer who points out that the most haughty kings have their heads anointed, "even as a head of salad," with sperm oil.

He is, in other words, a writer alive not just to the hypocrisies that attach themselves to gentility and prudishness and pomp, but to the incongruities with which any and every civilization is stitched together. For postmodern readers alert to this patchwork quality of experience, Melville's fascination derives from his unflinching recognition that every culture is contingent, transient, and, in its inevitable claim to divine sanction, absurd – a theme broached in Elizabeth Renker's essay on the book in which he presents these themes most starkly, *The Confidence-Man*. His career can be understood as a progression from an amused encounter (in *Typee* and *Omoo*) with this theme of discordance between truth and presumption, through an increasingly ironic scrutiny of the pretensions of his own swaggering country (beginning in *Mardi* and sustained through *The Confidence-Man*), to a chastened meditation (in *Clarel* and *Billy Budd*) on what resources are left to a mind that has divested itself of the illusion that there is some transcendent basis for any particular set of human arrangements.

Among those who first grasped the relation between wit and anxiety in Melville's temperament was another of his contemporaries, Nathaniel Hawthorne, who recognized how violently his friend recoiled from the pretension of those who appoint themselves guardians of truth, but who also remarked of him that "we seldom see men of less criticizable manners than he." In this simultaneous irony and respect for "manners" – a word in which Hawthorne invested much more than the notion of etiquette or politeness usually conveys – there is a clue to Melville's modernity. He writes, on the one hand, with an irreverent humor that spares no dignitaries, platitudes, prejudices, or idols – including himself when he becomes overearnest or grave. But there is in his work also the contrapuntal theme of the extreme fragility of culture as something that should not be lightly discarded. His works fall naturally into a form that John Bryant, borrowing a musical term, describes as a "two-part invention."

One hears the dual theme at high volume in "Benito Cereno," when the insufferably smug New England sea captain, Amasa Delano, finds that his unexamined ideas about the docility and servility of blacks are coming apart under the pressure of what he actually sees, and that his effort to hold on to his once serviceable ideas is failing. As the mutinous slave Babo demolishes Delano's fabricated world of white masters and black valets, Melville writes about the breakdown with satisfaction. But he also conveys the poignancy of Delano's panic. Here is the great scene where, trying to comprehend why slaves aboard the Spanish slave ship seem menacing and uncowed, Delano leans over the water in a spell of what would be described in our own century as existential nausea. Gazing toward the boat that will carry him back to the comfort of his own ship,

> he leaned against the carved balustrade, again looking off toward his boat; but found his eye falling upon the ribbon grass, trailing along the ship's water-line, straight as a border of green box; and parterres of sea-weed, broad ovals and crescents, floating nigh and far, with what seemed long formal alleys between, crossing the terraces of swells, and sweeping round as if leading to the grottoes below. And overhanging all was the balustrade by his arm, which, partly stained with pitch and partly embossed with moss, seemed the charred ruin of some summer-house in a grand garden long running to waste.
>
> Trying to break one charm, he was but becharmed anew. Though upon the wide sea, he seemed in some far inland country; prisoner in some deserted chateau, left to stare at empty grounds, and peer out at vague roads, where never wagon or wayfarer passed.

This flash of radical doubt that the world as Delano knows it makes any metaphysical sense has many analogues in Melville's writing. He had written a version of it in "Bartleby," the story of a scrivener who, in Cindy Wein-stein's phrase, "goes on strike without ever asserting that he has done so." Narrated by an unnamed lawyer who hires Bartleby and eventually aban-dons him, it is the story of an employee who forces his employer to confront rules of obligation he has hitherto taken for granted until he "begins to stag-ger in his own plainest faith . . . [and] begins, as it were, vaguely to surmise" that in the dispute between them "all the justice and all the reason is on the other side." What could be more ridiculous, this lawyer starts to wonder, than men entombing themselves in a Wall Street office and scratching away at papers that document the extent of other men's property? But if Bartleby's rebellion should prove a contagion (as it threatens to become), and other conscripts to the organized office madness should copy him and cease their work, how would the world be reconceived? On what basis, if the present structure should tumble down, will it be revised and rebuilt?

Seen in this way, as simultaneous exposures of the deformity and fragility of culture, Melville's books refuse to distinguish clearly between victims and villains – between Babo and Delano, or the idle scrivener and his of-ficious boss, or, in the most personal of his writings, between Billy Budd and Captain Vere. All these works are meditations on what Robert Milder calls, in a deeply felt essay that describes Melville's life as an arduous pil-grimage, the "cosmic orphanhood" of man. This sense of abandonment is most memorably personified in the tormented figure of Ahab, whose genius (on fullest display in "The Quarter Deck" chapter of *Moby-Dick*) is to convince his crew that they should share his pain and his dream of ven-geance. Melville shares Ahab's suspicion that there may be "nought be-yond" the surfaces in which men try to read transcendent meanings which they might construe as commandments. He writes with immense conviction of Ahab's anguish at this thought – that the mutilation he has suffered might not be the result of any discernible intent; and he sympathizes with Ahab's scorn for those who will not squarely face the blankness or "white-ness" on which they scribble their invented patterns of meaning.

To be saved from Ahab's soul-curdling bitterness is Ishmael's blessing. "No more my splintered heart and maddened hand were turned against the wolfish world," he says with devotional gratitude toward Queequeg, the "soothing savage" who redeems him with love. It is a redemption, as Milder suggests, that Melville may never have experienced fully himself. One hears in Ishmael's words the keynote of a writer unembarrassed by the grandeur of his theme: the universal human problem of reconciling ourselves to our aloneness and our mortality.

SELECTED BIBLIOGRAPHY

Critical studies of Melville's works are numerous. This bibliography emphasizes book-length studies published in the last twenty years, though seminal early works and a sampling of provocative recent articles are also included. Readers should not regard the categories as impermeable; in practice, biography, bibliography, and criticism are not so easily separable.

MELVILLE'S WRITINGS

The Northwestern–Newberry Edition of *The Writings of Herman Melville* (1968–), edited by Harrison Hayford, Hershel Parker, and G. Thomas Tanselle, is standard and nearly complete. For critical discussions of the Northwestern–Newberry Edition, prompted by the 1988 publication of its volume of *Moby-Dick*, see Peter Shillingsburg, "The Three *Moby-Dicks*," *American Literary History* 2 (1990): 119–30; John Bryant, "Text and Discourse: The New *Moby-Dick*," *Resources for American Literary Study* 18 (1992): 179–93; and Julian Markels, "The *Moby-Dick* White Elephant," *American Literature* 66 (1994): 105–22. For an annotated edition that has had an important influence on Melville studies, see also the sporadically published volumes in the Hendricks House series, *The Complete Works of Herman Melville*. In the following list of standard texts, the first publication date is provided parenthetically. Also noted parenthetically, where appropriate, are titles of the first British publications.

Billy Budd, Sailor (An Inside Narrative). Ed. Harrison Hayford and Merton M. Sealts, Jr. Chicago: University of Chicago Press, 1962.
Clarel: A Poem and Pilgrimage in the Holy Land (1876). Ed. Harrison Hayford, Hershel Parker, and G. Thomas Tanselle. Evanston and Chicago: Northwestern University Press and The Newberry Library, 1991.
Collected Poems of Herman Melville. Ed. Howard P. Vincent. Chicago: Hendricks House, 1947. [Includes *Battle-Pieces* (1866), *Timoleon* (1881), and *John Marr and Other Sailors* (1888)]
The Confidence-Man: His Masquerade (1857). Ed. Harrison Hayford, Hershel Par-

ker, and G. Thomas Tanselle. Evanston and Chicago: Northwestern University Press and The Newberry Library, 1984.

Correspondence. Ed. Lynn Horth. Evanston and Chicago: Northwestern University Press and The Newberry Library, 1993.

Israel Potter: His Fifty Years of Exile (1855). Ed. Harrison Hayford, Hershel Parker, and G. Thomas Tanselle. Evanston and Chicago: Northwestern University Press and The Newberry Library, 1982.

Journals. Ed. Howard C. Horsford and Lynn Horth. Evanston and Chicago: Northwestern University Press and The Newberry Library, 1989.

Mardi: and a Voyage Thither (1849). Ed. Harrison Hayford, Hershel Parker, and G. Thomas Tanselle. Evanston and Chicago: Northwestern University Press and The Newberry Library, 1970.

Melville's Marginalia. Ed. Walker Cowan. 2 volumes. New York: Garland, 1987.

Moby-Dick; or, The Whale (1851; *The Whale*). Ed. Harrison Hayford, Hershel Parker, and G. Thomas Tanselle. Evanston and Chicago: Northwestern University Press and The Newberry Library, 1988.

Omoo: A Narrative of Adventures in the South Seas (1847). Ed. Harrison Hayford, Hershel Parker, and G. Thomas Tanselle. Evanston and Chicago: Northwestern University Press and The Newberry Library, 1968.

The Piazza Tales and Other Prose Pieces, 1839–1860 [Includes *The Piazza Tales* (1856)]. Ed. Harrison Hayford, Alma A. MacDougall, and G. Thomas Tanselle. Evanston and Chicago: Northwestern University Press and The Newberry Library, 1987.

Pierre; or, The Ambiguities (1852). Ed. Harrison Hayford, Hershel Parker, and G. Thomas Tanselle. Evanston and Chicago: Northwestern University Press and the Newberry Library, 1971.

Redburn: His First Voyage, Being the Sailor-boy Confessions and Reminiscences of the Son-of-a-Gentleman, in the Merchant Service (1849). Ed. Harrison Hayford, Hershel Parker, and G. Thomas Tanselle. Evanston and Chicago: Northwestern University Press and The Newberry Library, 1969.

Typee: A Peep at Polynesian Life. (1846; *Narrative of a Four-Months' Residence among the Natives of a Valley of the Marquesas Islands.*) Ed. Harrison Hayford, Hershel Parker, and G. Thomas Tanselle. Evanston and Chicago: Northwestern University Press and The Newberry Library, 1968.

Weeds and Wildings Chiefly: with a Rose or Two, by Herman Melville. Ed. Robert Charles Ryan. Evanston: Northwestern University Press, 1967.

White-Jacket: or, The World in a Man-of-War (1850). Ed. Harrison Hayford, Hershel Parker, and G. Thomas Tanselle. Evanston and Chicago: Northwestern University Press and The Newberry Library, 1970.

BIBLIOGRAPHIES AND GUIDES

In addition to the following texts, useful bibliographic information can be found in the Melville chapter in *American Literary Scholarship: An Annual* (Durham: Duke University Press, 1963–), the quarterly *Melville Society Extracts*, the annual MLA Bibliography, and the bibliographic discussions in the Northwestern–Newberry Edition.

Boswell, Jeanetta. *Herman Melville and the Critics: A Checklist of Criticism*. Metuchen, N.J.: Scarecrow Press, 1981.

Bryant, John, ed. *A Companion to Melville Studies*. Westport, Conn.: Greenwood Press, 1986.

Bryant, John. *Melville Dissertations, 1924–1980: An Annotated Bibliography and Subject Index*. Westport, Conn.: Greenwood Press, 1983.

Delbanco, Andrew. "Melville in the '80s." *American Literary History* 4 (1992): 709–25.

Higgins, Brian. *Herman Melville: An Annotated Bibliography, 1846–1930*. Boston: G. K. Hall, 1979.

Herman Melville: A Reference Guide, 1931–1960. Boston: G. K. Hall, 1987.

Kier, Kathleen E. *A Melville Encyclopedia: The Novels*. Troy, N.Y.: Whitson, 1994.

Phelps, Leland. *Herman Melville's Foreign Reputation: A Research Guide*. Boston: G. K. Hall, 1983.

Wright, Nathalia. "Herman Melville." In *Eight American Authors: A Review of Research and Criticism*. Ed. James Woodress. New York: W. W. Norton, 1971, pp. 173–224.

BIOGRAPHICAL STUDIES AND RESOURCES

Important archival material may be found in the Melville Family Papers, Gansevoort–Lansing Collection, The New York Public Library, New York City; and at The Houghton Library of Harvard University. Other important Melville repositories include The Newberry Library, The Berkshire Athenaeum, and the Clifton Waller Barrett Library at the University of Virginia. Howard's biography had been regarded as standard; it has been superseded by those of Parker and Robertson-Lorant. Parker's voluminous biography has the facts and more. Robertson-Lorant's relatively compact biography, though a bit presentist in its portrayal of Melville as champion of social justice, may be the best life for the general reader. Rogin's provocative recontextualization must also be reckoned with. A crucial resource for Melville studies has been Leyda's *The Melville Log*, which is in the process of being revised and supplemented by Parker.

Anderson, Charles R. *Melville in the South Seas*. New York: Columbia University Press, 1939.

Arvin, Newton. *Herman Melville*. New York: William Sloane, 1950.

Cohen, Hennig, and Donald Yannella. *Herman Melville's Malcolm Letter: "Man's Final Lore."* New York: Fordham University Press and The New York Public Library, 1992.

Dillingham, William B. *Melville and His Circle: The Last Years*. Athens: University of Georgia Press, 1997.

Garner, Stanton. *The Civil War World of Herman Melville*. Lawrence: University Press of Kansas, 1993.

Gilman, William H. *Melville's Early Life and Redburn*. New York: New York University Press, 1951.

Howard, Leon. *Herman Melville: A Biography*. Berkeley: University of California Press, 1951.

Leyda, Jay, ed. *The Melville Log: A Documentary Life of Herman Melville, 1819–1891.* 1951. 2 vols. Reprint with supplement. New York: Gordian Press, 1969.

Metcalf, Eleanor. *Herman Melville: Cycle and Epicycle.* Cambridge: Harvard University Press, 1953.

Miller, Edwin Haviland. *Herman Melville: A Biography.* New York: Braziller, 1975.

Mumford, Lewis. *Herman Melville.* New York: Harcourt, Brace, and Company, 1929.

Parker, Hershel, *Herman Melville: A Biography. Volume I, 1819–1851.* Baltimore: Johns Hopkins University Press, 1996.

Robertson-Lorant, Laurie. *Melville: A Biography.* New York: Clarkson Potter, 1996.

Rogin, Michael Paul. *Subversive Genealogy: The Politics and Art of Herman Melville.* New York: Alfred A. Knopf, 1983.

Sealts, Merton M., Jr. *The Early Lives of Melville: Nineteenth-Century Biographical Sketches and Their Authors.* Madison: University of Wisconsin Press, 1974.

Melville as Lecturer. Cambridge: Harvard University Press, 1957.

Weaver, Raymond M. *Herman Melville.* New York: Doran, 1921.

Yannella, Donald, and Hershel Parker, ed. *The Endless Winding Way in Melville: New Charts by Kring and Carey.* Glassboro, N.J.: Melville Society, 1981.

Young, Philip. *The Private Melville.* University Park: Pennsylvania State University Press, 1993.

CRITICAL RECEPTION

Branch, Watson G., ed. *Melville: The Critical Heritage.* London: Routledge and Kegan Paul, 1974.

Hayes, Kevin J., ed. *The Critical Response to Herman Melville's Moby-Dick.* Westport, Conn.: Greenwood Press, 1994.

Hayes, Kevin J., and Hershel Parker, ed. *Checklist of Melville Reviews.* Evanston, Ill.: Northwestern University Press, 1991.

Hetherington, Hugh W., ed. *Melville's Reviewers, British and American, 1846–1891.* Chapel Hill: University of North Carolina Press, 1961.

Higgins, Brian, and Hershel Parker, ed. *Herman Melville: The Contemporary Reviews.* New York: Cambridge University Press, 1995.

Parker, Hershel, ed. *The Recognition of Herman Melville: Selected Criticism since 1846.* Ann Arbor: University of Michigan Press, 1967.

SOURCE STUDIES

Bercaw, Mary K. *Melville's Sources.* Evanston: Northwestern University Press, 1987.

Coffler, Gail H. *Melville's Classical Allusions: A Comprehensive Index and Glossary.* Westport, Conn.: Greenwood Press, 1985.

Newman, Lea Bertani Vozar. "Melville's Copy of Dante: Evidence of New Connections between the *Commedia* and *Mardi.*" *Studies in the American Renais-sance,* 1994, pp. 305–36.

Pommer, Henry F. *Milton and Melville.* Pittsburgh: University of Pittsburgh Press, 1950.

Sealts, Merton M., Jr. *Melville's Reading.* Revised and enlarged edition. Columbia: University of South Carolina Press, 1988.

Wright, Nathalia. *Melville's Use of the Bible.* Durham: Duke University Press, 1949.

COLLECTIONS OF CRITICAL ESSAYS

These volumes provide excellent introductions to the range of critical responses to Melville. Collections such as Parker and Hayford's *Moby-Dick as Doubloon* are particularly good sources for seminal pre-1976 essays.

Bloom, Harold, ed. *Ahab.* New York: Chelsea House, 1991.

Brodhead, Richard. *New Essays on Moby-Dick.* Cambridge: Cambridge University Press, 1986.

Bryant, John, and Robert Milder, ed. *The Evermoving Dawn: Essays in Celebration of the Melville Centennial.* Kent, Ohio: Kent State University Press, 1997.

Budd, Louis J., and Edwin H. Cady. *On Melville: The Best from American Liter-ature.* Durham: Duke University Press, 1988.

Burkholder, Robert, ed. *Critical Essays on Herman Melville's "Benito Cereno."* New York: G. K. Hall, 1992.

DeMott, Robert J., and Sanford E. Marovitz, ed. *Artful Thunder: Versions of the Romantic Tradition in American Literature, in Honor of Howard P. Vincent.* Kent, Ohio: Kent State University Press, 1975.

Duban, James, ed. *Melville and His Narrators* (special issue of *Texas Studies in Literature and Language* 31 [1989]).

Higgins, Brian, and Hershel Parker, ed. *Critical Essays on Herman Melville's Moby-Dick.* New York: G. K. Hall, 1992.

Higgins, Brian, and Hershel Parker, ed. *Critical Essays on Pierre.* Boston: G. K. Hall, 1983.

Hillway, Tyrus, and Luther S. Mansfield, ed. *Moby-Dick: Centennial Essays.* Dal-las: Southern Methodist University Press, 1953.

Inge, M. Thomas, ed. *Bartleby the Inscrutable: A Collection of Commentary on Herman Melville's Tale "Bartleby the Scrivener."* Hamden, Conn.: Archon Books, 1979.

Jehlen, Myra, ed. *Herman Melville: A Collection of Critical Essays.* Englewood Cliffs, N.J.: Prentice-Hall, Inc., 1994.

Lee, A. Robert, ed. *Herman Melville: Reassessments.* London: Barnes and Noble, 1984.

Milder, Robert, ed. *Critical Essays on Melville's Billy Budd, Sailor.* Boston: G. K. Hall, 1989.

Parker, Hershel, and Harrison Hayford, ed. *Moby-Dick as Doubloon: Essays and Extracts (1851–1970).* New York: Norton, 1970.

Pullin, Faith, ed. *New Perspectives on Melville*. Kent, Ohio: Kent State University Press, 1978.

Sachs, Viola. *L'Imaginaire Melville: A French Point of View*. Paris: Press Universitaires de Vincennes, 1992.

Sten, Christopher, ed. *Savage Eye: Melville and the Visual Arts*. Kent, Ohio: Kent State University Press, 1991.

Stern, Milton R., ed. *Critical Essays on Herman Melville's Typee*. Boston: G. K. Hall, 1982.

Thompson, G. R., and Virgil L. Lokke, ed. *Ruined Eden of the Present: Hawthorne, Melville, and Poe: Critical Essays in Honor of Darrel Abel*. West Lafayette, Ind.: Purdue University Press, 1981.

STUDIES OF MELVILLE

Adler, Joyce. *War in Melville's Imagination*. New York: New York University Press, 1981.

Arac, Jonathan. " 'A Romantic Book': *Moby-Dick* and Novel Agency." *boundary 2*, 17 (1990): 40–59.

Baird, James. *Ishmael: A Study of the Symbolic Mode in Primitivism*. Baltimore: Johns Hopkins University Press, 1956.

Barbour, James. " 'All My Books Are Botches': Melville's Struggle with *The Whale*." In *Writing the American Classics*. Ed. James Barbour and Tom Quirk. Chapel Hill: University of North Carolina Press, 1990, 25–52.

Baym, Nina. "Melville's Quarrel with Fiction." *PMLA* 94 (1979): 903–23.

Bellis, Peter. *No Mysteries Out of Ourselves: Identity and Textual Form in the Novels of Herman Melville*. Philadelphia: University of Pennsylvania Press, 1990.

Berthoff, Warner. *The Example of Melville*. Princeton: Princeton University Press, 1962.

Bickley, R. Bruce, Jr. *The Method of Melville's Short Fiction*. Durham: Duke University Press, 1975.

Bowen, Merlin. *The Long Encounter: Self and Experience in the Writings of Herman Melville*. Chicago: University of Chicago, 1960.

Braswell, William. *Melville's Religious Thought: An Essay in Interpretation*. Durham: Duke University Press, 1943.

Breitweiser, Mitchell. "False Sympathy in Melville's *Typee*." *American Quarterly* 34 (1982): 396–417.

Brodtkorb, Paul, Jr. *Ishmael's White World: A Phenomenological Reading of Moby-Dick*. New Haven: Yale University Press, 1965.

Bryant, John. *Melville and Repose: The Rhetoric of Humor in the American Renaissance*. New York: Oxford University Press, 1993.

"Melville's L-Word: First Intentions and Final Readings in *Typee*." *New England Quarterly* 63 (1990): 120–31.

Buell, Lawrence. "Melville and the Question of American Decolonization." *American Literature* 64 (1992): 215–37.

Chase, Richard. *Herman Melville, A Critical Study*. New York: Macmillan, 1949.

Cowan, Bainard. *Exiled Waters: Moby-Dick and the Crisis of Allegory*. Baton Rouge: Louisiana State University Press, 1981.

Crain, Caleb. "Lovers of Human Flesh: Homosexuality and Cannibalism in Melville's Novels." *American Literature* 66 (1994): 25–53.

Creech, James. *Closet Writing/Gay Reading: The Case of Melville's Pierre*. Chicago: University of Chicago Press, 1993.

Davis, Merrell R. *Melville's Mardi: A Chartless Voyage*. New Haven: Yale University Press, 1952.

Delbanco, Andrew. "Melville's Sacramental Style." *Raritan* 12 (1993): 69–91.

Dillingham, William B. *An Artist in the Rigging: The Early Work of Herman Melville*. Athens: University of Georgia Press, 1972.

Melville's Later Novels. Athens: University of Georgia Press, 1986.

Melville's Short Fiction, 1853–1856. Athens: University of Georgia Press, 1977.

Dimock, Wai-chee. *Empire for Liberty: Melville and the Poetics of Individualism*. Princeton: Princeton University Press, 1989.

Dryden, Edgar A. *Melville's Thematics of Form: The Great Art of Telling the Truth*. Baltimore: Johns Hopkins University Press, 1968.

Duban, James. *Melville's Major Fiction: Politics, Theology, and Imagination*. DeKalb: University of Illinois Press, 1983.

Finkelstein, Dorothy Metlitsky. *Melville's Orienda*. New Haven: Yale University Press, 1961.

Fisher, Marvin. *Going Under: Melville's Short Fiction and the American 1850s*. Baton Rouge: Louisiana State University Press, 1977.

Franklin, H. Bruce. *The Wake of the Gods: Melville's Mythology*. Stanford: Stanford University Press, 1963.

Goldman, Stan. *Melville's Protest Theism: The Hidden and Silent God in Clarel*. DeKalb: Northern Illinois University Press, 1993.

Heimert, Alan. "*Moby-Dick* and American Political Symbolism." *American Quarterly* 15 (1963): 498–534.

Herbert, T. Walter. *Marquesan Encounters: Melville and the Meaning of Civilization*. Cambridge: Harvard University Press, 1980.

Moby-Dick and Calvinism: A World Dismantled. New Brunswick, N.J.: Rutgers University Press, 1977.

James, C. L. R. *Mariners, Renegades, and Castaways: The Story of Herman Melville and the World We Live in*. 1953. London: Allison and Busby, 1985.

Karcher, Carolyn. *Shadow over the Promised Land: Slavery, Race, and Violence in Melville's America*. Baton Rouge: Louisiana State University Press, 1980.

Kelley, Wyn. *Melville's City: Urban and Literary Form in Nineteenth-Century New York*. New York: Cambridge University Press, 1996.

Kenny, Vincent. *Herman Melville's Clarel: A Spiritual Autobiography*. Hamden, Conn.: Shoe String Press, 1973.

Markels, Julian. *Melville and the Politics of Identity: From King Lear to Moby-Dick*. Urbana: University of Illinois Press, 1993.

Martin, Robert K. *Heroes, Captains, and Strangers: Male Friendship, Social Critique, and Literary Form in the Sea Novels of Herman Melville*. Chapel Hill: University of North Carolina Press, 1986.

Matterson, Stephen. "Indian-Hating in *The Confidence Man*." *Arizona Quarterly* 52 (1996): 21–36.

McCall, Dan. *The Silence of Bartleby*. Ithaca: Cornell University Press, 1989.

Milder, Robert. "The Composition of *Moby-Dick*: A Review and a Prospect." *Emerson Society Quarterly* 23 (1977): 203–16.

——. "The Rhetoric of Melville's *Battle-Pieces*." *Nineteenth-Century Literature* 44 (1989): 173–200.

Miller, James E., Jr. *A Reader's Guide to Herman Melville*. New York: Farrar, Straus, & Cudahy, 1962.

Olson, Charles. *Call Me Ishmael: A Study of Melville*. San Francisco: City Lights Books, 1947.

Otter, Samuel. *Melville's Anatomies: Bodies, Discourse, and Ideology in Antebellum America*. Berkeley: University of California Press, 1998.

Parker, Hershel. *Reading Billy Budd*. Evanston: Northwestern University Press, 1990.

Pease, Donald E. "*Moby Dick* and the Cold War." In *The American Renaissance Reconsidered*. Ed. Walter Benn Michaels and Donald E. Pease. Baltimore: Johns Hopkins University Press, 1985, 113–55.

Person, Leland S., Jr. "Melville's Cassock: Putting on Masculinity in *Moby-Dick*." *ESQ* 40 (1994): 1–26.

Post-Lauria, Sheila. *Correspondent Colorings: Melville in the Marketplace*. Amherst: University of Massachusetts Press, 1996.

Quirk, Tom. *Melville's Confidence Man: From Knave to Knight*. Columbia: University of Missouri Press, 1982.

Rampersad, Arnold. *Melville's Israel Potter: A Pilgrimage and a Progress*. Bowling Green, Ohio: Bowling Green University Popular Press, 1969.

Renker, Elizabeth. *Strike through the Mask: Herman Melville and the Scene of Writing*. Baltimore: Johns Hopkins University Press, 1996.

Rosenberry, Edward H. *Melville and the Comic Spirit*. Cambridge: Harvard University Press, 1955.

Rowe, John Carlos. "Melville's Typee: U.S. Imperialism at Home and Abroad." In *National Identities and Post-Americanist Narratives*. Ed. Donald E. Pease. Durham: Duke University Press, 1994, 255–78.

Samson, John. *White Lies: Melville's Narrative of Facts*. Ithaca: Cornell University Press, 1989.

Schultz, Elizabeth. *Unpainted to the Last: Moby-Dick and Twentieth-Century American Art*. Lawrence: University Press of Kansas, 1995.

Sealts, Merton M., Jr. *Pursuing Melville, 1940–1980*. Madison: University of Wisconsin Press, 1982.

Sedgwick, William Ellery. *Melville and the Tragedy of the Mind*. Cambridge: Harvard University Press, 1944.

Seelye, John. *Melville: The Ironic Diagram*. Evanston: Northwestern University Press, 1971.

Sherrill, Rowland A. *The Prophetic Melville: Experience, Transcendence, and Tragedy*. Athens: University of Georgia Press, 1979.

Short, Bryan C. *Cast by Means of Figures: Herman Melville's Rhetorical Development*. Amherst: University of Massachusetts Press, 1992.

Shurr, William H. *The Mystery of Iniquity: Melville as Poet, 1857–1891*. Lexington: University Press of Kentucky, 1972.

Spanos, William V. *The Errant Art of Moby-Dick: The Canon, the Cold War, and the Struggle for American Studies*. Durham: Duke University Press, 1995.

Stein, William Bysshe. *The Poetry of Melville's Late Years: Time, History, Myth, and Religion.* Albany: State University of New York Press, 1970.

Sten, Christopher. *The Weaver-God, He Weaves: Melville and the Poetics of the Novel.* Kent, Ohio: Kent State University Press, 1996.

Stern, Milton R. *The Fine Hammered Steel of Herman Melville.* Urbana: University of Illinois Press, 1957.

Thompson, Lawrance R. *Melville's Quarrel with God.* Princeton: Princeton University Press, 1952.

Tolchin, Neal L. *Mourning, Gender, and Creativity in the Art of Herman Melville.* New Haven: Yale University Press, 1988.

Trimpi, Helen P. *Melville's Confidence Men and American Politics in the 1850s.* Hamden, Conn.: Archon Books, 1987.

Vincent, Howard P. *The Tailoring of White-Jacket.* Evanston: Northwestern University Press, 1970.

The Trying out of Moby-Dick. Kent, Ohio: Kent State University Press, 1980.

Wallace, Robert K. *Melville and Turner: Spheres of Love and Fright.* Athens: University of Georgia Press, 1992.

Warren, Robert Penn. "Melville the Poet." *Kenyon Review* 8 (1946): 208–23.

Wenke, John. *Melville's Muse: Literary Creation and the Forms of Philosophical Fiction.* Kent, Ohio: Kent State University Press, 1995.

Wiegman, Robyn. "Melville's Geography of Gender." *American Literary History* 1 (1989): 735–53.

Zoellner, Robert. *The Salt-Sea Mastodon: A Reading of Moby-Dick.* Berkeley: University of California Press, 1973.

LITERARY AND HISTORICAL STUDIES WITH SECTIONS ON MELVILLE

Some of the most influential work on Melville has appeared in contextual and theoretical studies that address a range of authors. The Melville texts that provide the focus of discussion, when limited to one or two, are indicated parenthetically.

Aaron, Daniel. *The Unwritten War: American Writers and the Civil War.* New York: Oxford University Press, 1973. [*Battle-Pieces*]

Arac, Jonathan. *Commissioned Spirits: The Shaping of Social Motion in Dickens, Carlyle, Melville, and Hawthorne.* New Brunswick: Rutgers University Press, 1979. [*Moby-Dick*]

Bell, Michael Davitt. *The Development of American Romance: The Sacrifice of Relation.* Chicago: University of Chicago Press, 1980.

Bercovitch, Sacvan. *The Rites of Assent: Transformations in the Symbolic Construction of America.* New York: Routledge, 1993. [*Pierre*]

Bercovitch, Sacvan, and Myra Jehlen, ed. *Ideology and Classic American Literature.* New York: Cambridge University Press, 1986.

Bergmann, Hans. *God in the Street: New York Writing from the Penny Press to Melville.* Philadelphia: Temple University Press, 1995. ["Bartleby," *The Confidence-Man*]

Brodhead, Richard H. *Hawthorne, Melville, and the Novel*. Chicago: University of Chicago Press, 1976.

Bromell, Nicholas K. *By the Sweat of the Brow: Literature and Labor in Antebellum America*. Chicago: University of Chicago Press, 1993. [*Redburn*]

Brown, Gillian. *Domestic Individualism: Imagining Self in Nineteenth-Century America*. Berkeley: University of California Press, 1990. [*Pierre*, "Bartleby"]

Cameron, Sharon. *The Corporeal Self: Allegories of the Body in Melville and Hawthorne*. Baltimore: Johns Hopkins University Press, 1981.

Caserio, Robert L. *Plot, Story, and the Novel: From Dickens and Poe to the Modern Period*. Princeton: Princeton University Press, 1979. [*White-Jacket, Moby-Dick*]

Cassuto, Leonard. *The Inhuman Race: The Racial Grotesque in American Literature and Culture*. New York: Columbia University Press, 1997. [*Typee*, "Benito Cereno"]

Castronovo, Russ. *Fathering the Nation: American Genealogies of Slavery and Freedom*. Berkeley: University of California Press, 1995. [*Moby-Dick, Israel Potter*]

Charvat, William. *The Profession of Authorship in America, 1800–1870: The Papers of William Charvat*. Ed. Matthew J. Bruccoli. Columbus: Ohio State University Press, 1978.

Dekker, George *The American Historical Romance*. New York: Cambridge University Press, 1987.

Douglass, Ann. *The Feminization of American Culture*. New York: Alfred A. Knopf, 1977.

Eigner, Edwin M. *The Metaphysical Novel in England and America: Dickens, Bulwer, Melville, and Hawthorne*. Berkeley: University of California Press, 1978.

Fiedelson, Charles. *Symbolism and American Literature*. Chicago: University of Chicago Press, 1953.

Fiedler, Leslie. *Love and Death in the American Novel*. New York: Criterion Books, 1960.

Franchot, Jenny. *Roads to Rome: The Antebellum Protestant Encounter with Catholicism*. Berkeley: University of California Press, 1994. ["The Two Temples," "Benito Cereno"]

Franklin, H. Bruce. *Prison Literature in America: The Victim as Criminal and Artist*. New York: Oxford University Press, 1989.

Fussell, Edwin S. *Frontier: American Literature and the American West*. Princeton: Princeton University Press, 1965. [*Moby-Dick, The Confidence-Man*]

Gilmore, Michael T. *American Romanticism and the Marketplace*. Chicago: University of Chicago Press, 1985. [*Moby-Dick*, "Bartleby"]

The Middle Way: Puritanism and Ideology in American Romantic Fiction. New Brunswick: Rutgers University Press, 1977.

Grey, Robin. *The Complicity of Imagination: The American Renaissance, Contests of Authority, and Seventeenth-Century English Culture*. New York: Cambridge University Press, 1997. [*Mardi, Moby-Dick*]

Hoffman, Daniel. *Form and Fable in American Fiction*. New York: Oxford University Press, 1961. [*Moby-Dick, The Confidence-Man*]

Irwin, John T. *American Hieroglyphics: The Symbol of the Egyptian Hieroglyphics in the American Renaissance*. Baltimore: Johns Hopkins University Press, 1980. [*Moby-Dick, The Confidence-Man*]

Jehlen, Myra. *American Incarnation: The Individual, the Nation, and the Continent.* Cambridge: Harvard University Press, 1986. [*Pierre*]

Johnson, Barbara. *The Critical Difference: Essays in the Contemporary Rhetoric of Reading.* Baltimore: Johns Hopkins University Press, 1980. [*Billy Budd*]

Lawrence, D. H. *Studies in Classic American Literature.* 1923. New York: Penguin Books, 1977. [*Typee, Moby-Dick*]

Leverenz, David. *Manhood and the American Renaissance.* Ithaca: Cornell University Press, 1989. [*Moby-Dick*]

Levin, Harry. *The Power of Blackness: Poe, Hawthorne, Melville.* New York: Alfred A. Knopf, 1958.

Levine, Robert S. *Conspiracy and Romance: Studies in Brockden Brown, Cooper, Hawthorne, and Melville.* New York: Cambridge University Press, 1989. ["Benito Cereno"]

Lewis, R. W. B. *The American Adam: Innocence, Tragedy, and Tradition in the Nineteenth Century.* Chicago: University of Chicago Press, 1955. [*Billy Budd*]

Lindberg, Gary. *The Confidence Man in American Literature.* New York: Oxford University Press, 1982. [*The Confidence-Man*]

Mailloux, Steven. *Interpretive Conventions: The Reader in the Study of American Fiction.* Ithaca: Cornell University Press, 1982. [*Moby-Dick*]

Marx, Leo. *The Machine in the Garden: Technology and the Pastoral Ideal in America.* New York: Oxford University Press, 1964. [*Moby-Dick*]

Matthiessen, F. O. *American Renaissance: Art and Expression in the Age of Emerson and Whitman.* New York: Oxford University Press, 1941.

McWilliams, John P., Jr. *The American Epic: Transforming a Genre, 1770–1860.* New York: Cambridge University Press, 1989. [*Moby-Dick*]

    Hawthorne, Melville, and the American Character: A Looking-Glass Business. New York: Cambridge University Press, 1984.

Miller, Perry. *The Raven and the Whale: The War of Words and Wits in the Era of Poe and Melville.* New York: Harcourt Brace & World, 1956.

Morrison, Toni. "Unspeakable Things Unspoken: The Afro-American Presence in American Literature." *Michigan Quarterly Review* 28 (1989): 1–34. [*Moby-Dick*]

Mumford, Lewis. *The Golden Day: A Study in American Experience and Culture.* New York: Boni and Liveright, 1926.

Nelson, Dana D. *The Word in Black and White: Reading "Race" in American Literature, 1638–1867.* New York: Oxford University Press, 1992. ["Benito Cereno"]

Paglia, Camille. *Sexual Personae: Art and Decadence from Nefertiti to Emily Dickinson.* New Haven: Yale University Press, 1990. [*Moby-Dick*]

Pease, Donald E. *Visionary Compacts: American Renaissance Writings in Cultural Context.* Madison: University of Wisconsin Press, 1987.

Porte, Joel. *In Respect to Egotism: Studies in American Romantic Writing.* New York: Cambridge University Press, 1991. [*Moby-Dick*]

Railton, Stephen. *Authorship and Audience: Literary Performance in the American Renaissance.* Princeton: Princeton University Press, 1991. [*Moby-Dick*]

Reising, Russell T. *Loose Ends: Closure and Crisis in the American Social Text.* Durham: Duke University Press, 1996. [*Israel Potter*]

Reynolds, David S. *Beneath the American Renaissance: The Subversive Imagination in the Age of Emerson and Melville.* New York: Alfred A. Knopf, 1988.

Reynolds, Larry J. *European Revolutions and the American Literary Renaissance.* New Haven: Yale University Press, 1988. [*Moby-Dick*]

Richardson, Robert D., Jr. *Myth and Literature in the American Renaissance.* Bloomington: Indiana University Press, 1978.

Rowe, John Carlos. *Through the Custom-House: Nineteenth-Century American Fiction and Modern Theory.* Baltimore: Johns Hopkins University Press, 1982. ["Bartleby"]

Sedgwick, Eve Kosofsky. *Epistemology of the Closet.* Berkeley: University of California Press, 1990. [*Billy Budd*]

Simpson, David. *Fetishism and Imagination: Dickens, Melville, Conrad.* Baltimore: Johns Hopkins University Press, 1982. [*Moby-Dick*]

Slotkin, Richard. *Regeneration through Violence: The Mythology of the American Frontier, 1600–1860.* Middletown, Conn.: Wesleyan University Press, 1973. [*Moby-Dick*]

Smith, Henry Nash. *Democracy and the Novel: Popular Resistance to Classic American Writers.* New York: Oxford University Press, 1978. [*Moby-Dick*]

Stuckey, Sterling. *Going through the Storm: The Influence of African-American Art in History.* New York: Oxford University Press, 1994. ["Benito Cereno"]

Suchoff, David. *Critical Theory and the Novel: Mass Society and Cultural Criticism in Dickens, Melville, and Kafka.* Madison: University of Wisconsin Press, 1994. [*White-Jacket, Moby-Dick*]

Sundquist, Eric J. *Home as Found: Authority and Genealogy in Nineteenth-Century American Literature.* Baltimore: Johns Hopkins University Press, 1979. [*Pierre*]

    To Wake the Nations: Race in the Making of American Literature. Cambridge: Harvard University Press, 1993. ["Benito Cereno"]

Sweet, Timothy. *Traces of War: Poetry, Photography, and the Crisis of the Union.* Baltimore: Johns Hopkins University Press, 1990. [*Battle-Pieces*]

Thomas, Brook. *Cross-Examinations of Law and Literature: Cooper, Hawthorne, Stowe, and Melville.* New York: Cambridge University Press, 1987.

Wadlington, Warwick. *The Confidence Game in American Literature.* Princeton: Princeton University Press, 1975.

Wald, Priscilla. *Constituting Americans: Cultural Anxiety and Narrative Form.* Durham: Duke University Press, 1995. [*Pierre*]

Weinstein, Cindy. *The Literature of Labor and the Labors of Literature: Allegory in Nineteenth-Century American Fiction.* New York: Cambridge University Press, 1995.

Weisbuch, Robert. *Atlantic Double-Cross: American Literature and British Influence in the Age of Emerson.* Chicago: University of Chicago Press, 1986. ["Bartleby"]

Weisburg, Richard H. *The Failure of the Word: The Protagonist as Lawyer in Modern Fiction.* New Haven: Yale University Press, 1984. [*Billy Budd*]

Williams, Susan S. *Confounding Images: Photography and Portraiture in Antebellum America.* Philadelphia: University of Pennsylvania Press, 1997. [*Pierre*]

Yellin, Jean Fagan. *The Intricate Knot: Black Figures in American Literature, 1776–1863.* New York: New York University Press, 1972. ["Benito Cereno"]

Ziff, Larzer. *Literary Democracy: The Declaration of Cultural Independence in America.* New York: Viking, 1981.

INDEX

Printed in the United Kingdom
by Lightning Source UK Ltd.
134357UK00002B/217-225/A